D0519745

Public Sector Performanc

...tre & Librar...

ASPA Classics

Conceived and sponsored by the American Society for Public Administration (ASPA), the ASPA Classics series will publish volumes on topics that have been, and continue to be, central to the contemporary development of public administration. The ASPA Classics are intended for classroom use and may be quite suitable for libraries and general reference collections. Drawing from the *Public Administration Review* and other journals related to the ASPA sections, each volume in the series is edited by a scholar who is charged with presenting a thorough and balanced perspective on an enduring issue. These journals now represent some six decades of collective wisdom. Yet, many of the writings collected in the ASPA Classics might not otherwise easily come to the attention of future public managers. Given the explosion in research and writing on all aspects of public administration in recent decades, these ASPA Classics anthologies should point readers to definitive or groundbreaking authors whose voices should not be lost in the cacophony of the newest administrative technique or invention.

Public servants carry out their responsibilities in a complex, multidimensional environment. The mission of ASPA Classics is to provide the reader with a historical and firsthand view of the development of the topic being considered. As such, each ASPA Classics volume presents the most enduring scholarship, often in complete, or nearly complete, original form on the given topic. Each volume will be devoted to a specific continuing concern to administrators of all public sector programs. Early volumes in the series address public sector performance, public service as commitment, and diversity and affirmative action in public service. Future volumes will include equally important dialogues on classic ideas as enduring ideas, reinventing government, public budgeting, and public service ethics.

The volume editors are to be commended for volunteering for the substantial task of compiling and editing these unique collections of articles, which might not otherwise be readily available to scholars, teachers, and students.

ASPA Classics Editorial Board

Marc Holzer, Editor-in-Chief
Rutgers, State University of New Jersey, Campus at Newark

Walter Broadnax, University of Maryland
Beverly Cigler, Pennsylvania State University
Patricia Ingraham, Syracuse University
Richard C. Kearney, East Carolina University
Don Kettl, University of Wisconsin
Camilla Stivers, Cleveland State University

Public Sector Performance

Management, Motivation, and Measurement

edited by

Richard C. Kearney
East Carolina University

Evan M. Berman
University of Central Florida

Westview Press
A Member of the Perseus Books Group

ASPA Classics

All rights reserved. Printed in the United States of America. No part of this publication may be reproduced or transmitted in any form or by any means, electronic or mechanical, including photocopy, recording, or any information storage and retrieval system, without permission in writing from the publisher.

Copyright © 1999 by Westview Press, A Member of the Perseus Books Group

Published in 1999 in the United States of America by Westview Press, 5500 Central Avenue, Boulder, Colorado 80301-2877, and in the United Kingdom by Westview Press, 12 Hid's Copse Road, Cumnor Hill, Oxford OX2 9JJ

Library of Congress Cataloging-in-Publication Data
Public sector performance : management, motivation, and measurement /
edited by Richard C. Kearney, Evan M. Berman.
p. cm.
Includes bibliographical references and index.
ISBN 0-8133-6827-8 (hc). — ISBN 0-8133-6828-6 (pb)
1. Government productivity. 2. Organizational change.
3. Organizational effectiveness. 4. Public administration.
I. Kearney, Richard C. II. Berman, Evan M.
JF1525.P67P87 1999
352.3—dc21 99-10751
CIP

The paper used in this publication meets the requirements of the American National Standard for Permanence of Paper for Printed Library Materials Z39.48-1984.

10 9 8 7 6 5 4

Contents

Part 2
Performance Strategies 119

Part 3
Performance Measurement 263

Tables and Figures

Tables

Figures

INTRODUCTION

Richard C. Kearney and Evan M. Berman

This book, *Public Sector Performance*, brings together articles whose ideas continue to drive and shape public management today.

Government performance is important to citizens and public managers alike. Citizens expect the law to be enforced, the environment protected, labor health and safety laws obeyed, and a plethora of goals to be accomplished. Against the background of growing citizen expectations, and the widespread belief that a performance deficit exists at all levels of government, public managers have continued to develop new ways to meet public objectives. Each period in U.S. public administration has seen the development of new strategies to improve productivity, largely in response to challenges of the times. Examples include new ways of organizing work, managing quality, and motivating employees. Many of these efforts are currently placed within the realms of New Public Management and Reinvention. People who work in government organizations are seeking to improve their capabilities, approaches, and results and to transform their enterprises into high-performance organizations.

Although the approaches are "new," most performance strategies are grounded in enduring beliefs and core principles. These include the possibility of determining outcomes, the practicality of scientific analysis applied to management, and the pressing need for increased responsiveness and accountability. Such principles link past and present performance management efforts and provide, quite simply, a compass for managers today—even as they address the unique challenges of our times. Perhaps it is so that each generation rediscovers essential truths. This volume presents certain performance-related verities in ready-to-use format, encompassing enduring, time-tested beliefs that are now rightly regarded as a cornerstone of professional public management. Their application promises to help reconstruct the public trust in and support for government that is so needed today.

In sum, these articles are essential reading for any public manager who is interested in improving public organizations by "getting the job done."

What Is Performance?

Performance in this context is defined as managing public programs for outcomes. Managers use public resources and mandates to ensure that their programs meet public objectives and expectations. The meaning of the term *performance* is similar to that of the term *productivity* as, for example, the effective and efficient use of resources to achieve outcomes. However, performance is broader than some narrow meanings of productivity (efficiency, for example). Many private sector applications emphasize only efficiency, but a distinguishing feature of public performance is that it is guided and assessed by multiple, equally important standards of effectiveness, efficiency, and equity.

In recent years, there has been a renewed emphasis on measuring public program performance. Public programs are open to criticism when those in charge cannot show what has resulted from the expenditure of public resources. Measurement helps increase accountability and, thereby, trust between public organizations and citizens. It is a key component of organizational performance. Thus, the articles in this reader reflect enduring concerns of performance measurement and management.

Pathways to Performance

The development of performance management in public organizations has occurred along the following pathways, shaped by the tensions and themes discussed below.

Organizing Work. Driven by changing priorities or technology, each administrative period has witnessed efforts to organize and reorganize work. Pre–World War II efforts frequently focused on defining the optimal shape and size of organizations in order to respond to increased demands for services as well as to the perceived need for greater control over employees involved in specialized tasks and assignments. In recent years, information technology and the prevalence of complex, multifaceted problems have led toward more fluid, networked organizations that are flatter and feature greater responsibility for employees. Frederick Taylor-like efforts to control and specialize work processes (Charlie Chaplin's movie *Modern Times* comes to mind) were eventually superseded by "reinventing" and "reengineering" efforts aimed at increasing the timeliness, efficiency, and responsiveness of work while reducing mistakes. Thus, over time, work and work processes continue to be rationalized in the face of new priorities and possibilities.

Managing Employees. The job of managing people continues to be essential to performance in public organizations. Managers have long acknowledged the conflict between the need for employees to conform to organizational goals and the need for employee autonomy and self-expression. The former increases predictability at the expense of creativity (and often motivation) and, hence, productivity, too. The latter has the opposite effect. Even Frederick Taylor recognized the importance of employee self-determination, although his scientific management principles severely limited it. Today, as clients and citizens expect greater customization of services, employees are being cross-trained and given greater latitude to respond to citizen needs. They are now being held accountable for outcomes as well as for following correct procedures and not violating any laws. However, the tensions between conformity and creativity remain.

Measuring Performance. Measurement helps determine how well organizations and employees are performing, and it is also used by managers to provide public accountability. The trend since World War II has been to make measurement ever more precise, encompassing, and timely so that it can be used for fine-tuning and continuous improvement. Measurement is increasingly used to provide on-going information about public sector performance. Although significant gains have been made, especially in performance-based budgeting, measurement continues to be imperfect, in large part because many goals of public organizations are complex, multidimensional, and longterm. Further improvements in measurement are needed.

Overcoming Resistance. Managers have long been baffled and befuddled by the tendency of organizations to resist even minor changes. Some managers have likened resistance to organizational change to punching an airbag: It just keeps coming back in new shapes or forms. Employees and managers have a plethora of ways to resist change. It has been argued that knowing *how* to change organizations is just as important, and quite possibly more practical, than knowing *what* to change. Efforts to improve performance include a long-standing search for lessons, tips, and rules that assist managers to overcome employee fear, uncertainty, and resistance.

Foundations: Beliefs and Principles

Many readers of this volume will not be able to escape the thought that performance management should be based on some common beliefs and principles. Although the field does not have a consensus about such core beliefs and principles, the following are offered for consideration.

Optimism. Performance management is based on the stubborn belief that improvement is possible and, indeed, important to the betterment of human and organizational conditions. Performance management requires this act of faith. Such optimism stands in contrast to the detached skepticism of many observers, including some of the writers whose work is included in this volume; they take a dim view about the possibility of performance improvement. Is optimism or pessimism warranted? In the final analysis, both points of view reflect attitudes about an uncertain future. These different perspectives also color the assessment of past efforts. Whereas skeptics, for example, consider Total Quality Management (TQM) a failure (afterall, it has been largely abandoned by managers and consultants in recent years), optimists point to the TQM legacy of significant increases in public agencies' attention to customer needs. Optimists also believe that TQM represents an evolutionary learning experience that is being continued under different names, such as reengineering. It seems that performance management is by necessity optimistic; otherwise, why bother with change if it cannot lead to something positive?

A Realistic View. Performance management is optimistic but not blind. Performance management acknowledges the importance of getting an accurate read on the possibilities for improvement while recognizing sources of organizational resistance and other barriers to success. Improvement begins with diagnosis and continues through relevant performance-enhancement techniques. The musings of skeptics inform performance management about the need to address various threats, but they do not kill improvement efforts. Professional managers often welcome criticism and concerns that help reveal real problems and limitations of performance improvement.

Balancing Analysis with Politics. It is widely recognized that technical analysis and analytical strategies must be combined with organizational decision-making processes that result in consensus-building and support for performance management. This is politics with a small *p* which deals with bureaucratic in-fighting and resistance to change while, for example, speaking truth to power. Integrative decision-making processes offer an opportunity for improvement by utilizing the input of those with relevant experiences and insights. If politics is disjointed from efforts to implement performance improvement, success is extremely unlikely.

Use of Science for Analysis. Performance management welcomes suggestions and new strategies for improvement from whatever source they arise, including suggestions advanced by employees, clients and citizens, and elected officials as well as from the best practices of other organizations. Other sources include innovations in science and technology. Although the limitations of science are acknowledged, careful scientific analysis of public management and public programs can provide a wellspring of new ideas for improvement. New technology, especially information technology, offers a wide range of improvement opportunities. Performance management takes an optimistic view that science and technology will continue to yield dividends in the future.

Inspired Leadership. Performance management builds on a foundation of technical and ethical knowledge. Leaders determine which values their organizations promote and also how these values are reflected through strategies and program goals. Such determinations require the courage of convictions and solid professional skills. Employees and citizens expect public efforts to be consistent with their needs and to reflect ethical and legal principles. Thus, performance management is guided by ethical principles. Professional knowledge is also needed, however. Managers require detailed knowledge when exercising judgment in performance management or ensuring that changes are, for example, consistent with legal requirements that affect their programs or jurisdictions.

Selection of Articles

The articles in this volume have been selected on the basis of several criteria. First, all have been published in journals sponsored by the American Society for Public Administration (ASPA). Second, they are interesting, thought provoking, and instructive, which makes them appropriate for classroom use. Third, they are classics, in the sense of having enduring value and having been cited frequently in the literature. We have also included excerpts from selected articles as boxes, which, although less well-known, add to these classics. Finally, selection takes into consideration the topical areas of other volumes planned for the ASPA Classics series so that redundancy is minimized. For example, this volume does not include articles that might more appropriately be placed in volumes on human resource management or budgeting.

The articles in this volume are organized into three sections. The first section provides the foundation and background of performance management. The articles in Part 1 discuss the process of organizational improvement and impediments to its success. Part 2 examines specific performance management strategies, including those dealing with quality, employee motivation, and privatization. It also includes an overview of strategies-in-use. Part 3 addresses issues of performance measurement. The articles in the third section include those that urge managers to improve measurement of program performance as well as those that provide detailed advice on this issue.

We hope that readers of this volume gain an appreciation for these classics of performance management and apply these time-tested insights to improve the performance of their own organizations.

Part One

Performance Foundations

Performance management builds on a foundation of insight and knowledge about how organizations work and what common barriers to improvement they confront. It also requires definition and demarcation. In the following articles, Quinn (1978) shows how productivity is intertwined with many different concepts, thereby resulting in considerable confusion. However, he provides a measure of clarity to the field by focusing on the manager's view of productivity, emphasizing an action orientation and developing measures of organizational performance. He further provides an overview of strategies for organizational improvement, many of which are discussed by other authors in this volume. The box by Ayres and Kettinger (1983) identifies the five fundamental pathways to efficiency improvement.

Honadle (1981) provides a framework of "capacity-building." She defines capacity as the ability of public organizations to govern and make decisions. This approach suggests numerous targets for performance management, including better planning, policy-making, ability to attract resources, and program management. The accompanying box by Rosenblum and McGillis (1979) discusses how consultants can help increase the capacity and performance of organizations. However, improvement may also result from eliminating processes or activities that cause poor performance. In this vein, Drucker (1980) identifies six "sins of public administration." These include setting unrealistic goals, doing too much at once, overstaffing, inadequate experimentation, insufficient learning from feedback, and the failure to abandon. Caiden's box (1991) lists 175 additional "malpractices" that also impair performance.

Managing people is critical to performance. According to Platt (1947), managers must act according to the specific, situational facts: "To be sure, there are some generalizations (about human behavior), but these only guide the manager as he grapples with the particular conditions of his organization ... The first major problem of the manager is to know what the present (human) relationships are and what they mean." Well-intended generalizations and "magic bullets" seldom work. Platt discusses factors that increase or detract from human productivity, such as individual incentives, environmental conditions, inter-personal relations in the workplace, policies, and work processes. The box by Brown (1983) notes the fundamental importance of wanting to do better as a prerequisite for improvement. Argyris (1994) explains how performance improvement efforts are stymied when individuals draw up their defenses against unwelcome feedback. By contrast, they are advanced when individuals are able to recognize how existing practices, procedures, and policies adversely affect their goals. This suggests that managers need to apply a theory of human learning, while paying attention to bureaucratic and other practices that reinforce poor results.

Stephens (1988) describes a model, applied in a case setting, for changing the culture and work processes of organizations. These strategies are typical of large-scale change processes, and are readily adapted in other settings. He stresses that top managers must define the values of organizations. They must review policies and develop people-centered strategies to get lower managers and supervisors "on board" and committed to change.

Ammons (1985) identifies thirty-seven political, bureaucratic, resource and other barriers to performance management in government. The implication is that managers are likely to encounter "a good many" of these in their endeavors and that they do well to anticipate them in the planning and implementation of performance management. In this regard, Balk (1984) highlights the importance of working with the legislature. Gabris (1986) also examines barriers, especially those that arise during improvement efforts. He identifies five problems caused by performance management strategies as well as strategies for dealing with them. Taken together, these articles round out a rich understanding of the scope, substance, and context of performance management.

1

Productivity and the Process of Organizational Improvement

Why We Cannot Talk to Each Other

Robert E. Quinn

The week before I sat down to write this paper, I was involved in running an intensive three-day productivity workshop for 33 public-sector executives. At the end of the three days, the participants were asked to make a collective list of the major things they learned about productivity. Three themes emerged from the exercise. The first had to do with the meaning of terms. The participants were impressed by the many different views and definitions of productivity and by the fact that productivity, in many ways, is simply a buzz word or catchall for a number of basic concepts that they had long understood. The second theme had to do with their feelings of frustration and relief. They were frustrated by the many barriers to productivity improvement and measurement in government and by the fact that there are no simple answers. They were relieved, however, to know that others were experiencing the same difficulties in their improvement efforts and that no one agency was much worse off then any other. The final theme had to do with guidelines for success, and the participants proposed a number of principles for implementing change.

The above themes reflect two very different concerns. The first theme reflects a concern for meaning, while the second and third themes reflect a

"Productivity and the Process of Organizational Improvement: Why We Cannot Talk To Each Other," *Public Administration Review* 38 (January/February, 1978): 41–45.

concern for action. This paper will focus both on meaning and on action. First we will consider why the meaning of productivity is not clear. Second, a recently developed model of the improvement or action process will be presented.

A Problem With Meaning

While the concern for productivity in the public sector is not new, the intensity of concern has increased steadily during the past ten years. In fact, one observer states that productivity has become "the very hottest new word" among many of the nation's public administrators.[1] The enthusiasm for the concept is facilitated by the fact that at the abstract level everyone is for productivity. It seems to be a simple and uncomplicated concept. It is not.

One of the biggest problems facing the public productivity movement is the assumption that everyone shares a common definition of the term productivity. The assumption is false. The authors who write about productivity discuss it from perspectives rooted in such diverse subject areas as measurement, labor relations, training and development, management, budget, and finance. Academicians and practitioners specializing in each of these areas tend to have different interests, views and opinions from counterparts in each of the other areas. Consequently, they define productivity in different ways. There simply is no commonly shared definition. Productivity tends to be intertwined with the concepts of efficiency, savings, cutbacks, measurement, effectiveness, and performance. The result is considerable confusion.

It is helpful to consider three of the more dominant orientations in the productivity field. These include the perspectives of the economist, the industrial engineer, and the practicing manager. An ideal type, or typical description, of each perspective appears in Table 1.1.

The general orientation of economists with a macro-viewpoint is societal. They tend to deal with such macro-issues as national growth, competitiveness on the world market, rising wages, and deteriorating gains in real income. Economists usually emphasize the need for getting more from present resources in the society, and define productivity precisely as the ratio of outputs to inputs with some consideration for output quality assumed or stated.

Industrial engineers usually focus on the organizational throughput, and have a high concern for workflow, equipment, measurement, and control. Usually the expressed need is for increased efficiency through the manipulation, measurement, and control of the throughput process. Their definition is usually the same precise statement of output over input, with some assumed or stated consideration for quality level.

Administrators have a managerial orientation. They live in a fast-paced, environment. They do not lie awake at night worrying about the nation's competitive edge in the world market nor do they exclusively focus upon workflow, equipment, control, and measurement. Rather, they feel the need to improve the over-all performance of the organization, and give their attention to the specific problems at hand. These may range from the current budget to motivating an unenthusiastic subordinate. The most important difference, however—at least as far as productivity is concerned—is that administrators do not use a precise, input/output, definition of productivity. For them productivity is usually an ambiguous, shifting concept centered on the over-all performance or functioning of the organization. Administrators may use it one way at one time and another way at another time.

Manager's View of Productivity

Support for the above analysis of differences in definitions comes from a recent study by Katzell and Yankelovich.[2] Basing their conclusions on a large survey of managers and union leaders in the private sector, the researchers showed that most managers do not employ a precise definition. Instead, they see productivity in terms of their own organizational context, and they see the concept in a broader, more qualitative way than the economist: By productivity managers mean (1) the efficiency and effectiveness of the operation (88%); (2) intangibles such as disruptions, "shrinkage," sabotage, and other indicators of trouble in the organization (73%); (3) rates of absenteeism and turnover, as well as measures of output (70%); (4) measures of customer or client satisfactions (64%); and (5) intangibles such as employee loyalty, morale, and job satisfaction (55%).

Katzell and Yankelovich argue that their findings about managerial perceptions and productivity are important because they help to explain the limited support that economists have given to managerial views on the value of such changes as job restructuring, personnel manipulation, and the incentive systems. They point out that the situation "can now be viewed more as a failure of communication than as a difference of substance."

Some may argue that the managerial definition of productivity is really the concept of organizational effectiveness, a term that Barnard generated in order to differentiate between accomplishment of organizational objectives and the idea of efficiency.[3] Unfortunately, the meaning of effectiveness has become as unclear as the meaning of productivity.

Definitions of effectiveness range from the inclusion of very specific concepts such as output quality, client satisfaction, and goal attainment to the inclusion of very broad concepts such as systems maintenance or the ability of the organization to survive.[4] An excellent illustration of the confusion is provided by Steers, who reviewed the criteria used in 17 multi-variate models of organizational effectiveness.[5] After demonstrating the considerable variation in the criteria used to measure effectiveness, Steers questioned the very existence of the construct: "From the findings to date, it appears that either the effectiveness construct is invalid or that there may indeed be such a valid construct for which the relevant observable criteria have not yet been discovered." Therefore, to call the managerial definition of productivity "organizational effectiveness" does not appear to be an immediate solution to our definition and communication problems.

Three points help summarize the discussion to this point. First, much of the current interest in productivity is based on the economic argument that more yield must be obtained from our present resources. The administrator, however, is much more concerned with immediate pressures for organizational performance than with the state of society. Such pressures may or may not be in the direction of efficient resource use. Second, much of the concern for measurement comes from the industrial engineer. Such concerns, however, may be irrelevant or antithetical to the concern of the administrator, Public services are not easy to measure, and measurement may have negative rather than positive consequences. For example, weighing the amount of garbage collected may lead to the watering down of the load before it arrives at the weighing station. Finally, while economists and industrial engineers have a precise definition of productivity, the administrator has an ambiguous definition that has to do with over-all performance. These differences help to explain why the word productivity is used in so many different ways and why it has become so unclear. We will return to this issue after considering the improvement process as it usually takes place.

An Action Model

In a recent study of managerial work, Mintzberg argued that administrators thrive on action. They live in a stimulus-response world that puts a premium on verbal information and quick decisions. Administrators have little time for philosphical reflection or academic analysis. In his study, Mintzberg describes a number of roles that are commonly played by the administrator. One of these he calls the role of entrepreneur:

> In the entrepreneur role the manager acts as initiator and designer of much of the controlled change in his organization. The word "controlled" implies that this role encompasses all activities where the manager makes changes of his own free will—exploiting opportunities, solving nonpressing problems. Thus, although the term entrepreneur is borrowed from the economists, we view the entrepreneurial function in a significantly broader content. The economists have tended to focus on all managerial work associated with systematic change in ongoing (as well as new) organizations.
>
> Entrepreneurial work begins with scanning activity. As part of his monitor role, the manager spends much of his time scanning his organization, looking for opportunities and for situations that may be considered problems . . .

> Having discovered a problem or opportunity, the manager may decide that it is necessary for his organization to take action to improve an existing situation. At this point the design phase of decision-making begins. What is most interesting about the "decision" to improve a situation is that it is not really just that—rather, it emerges as a series of smaller decisions and other activities sequenced over a period of time.[6]

It is in the entrepreneurial decision sequence—the decision on what action to take in order to improve a given situation—that we can best understand the managerial view of productivity. The action sequence is situation-specific and oriented toward problem-solving. Typically, administrators ask "How do I get the organization from where it is today to where I want it to be tomorrow?" In selecting the various alternatives, they consider the potential costs of each. For example, an action that would greatly improve the input/output ratio may mean considerable loss in flexibility. In assessing the trade-off they may or may not conclude that such a change would be an improvement in the over-all system.

The idea of over-all improvement or organizational performance is a complex concept that is broader than efficiency, in the input/output sense, or effectiveness, in the goal-attainment sense. The question then arises: Is it

TABLE 1.1 An Ideal Type of Three Dominant Orientations in the Area of Productivity

	Economist	*Industrial Engineer*	*Administrator*
General orientation	Societal focus: e.g., national growth, world market, real income	Technical focus: workflow, measurement, equipment and control	Administrative focus: e.g., pressures for action, budgets, coordination, motivation
The need identified	More yield from the present workforce and equipment in society	Better measurement and control; more efficient throughput	Better overall performance of the organization
Definition of productivity	Precise: Output over input with quality considered	Precise: Output over input with quality considered	Ambiguous: Better performance, with specific meaning varying from situation to situation

possible to describe the dimensions of organizational performance and the process of organizational improvement? The answer is *yes.*

In the private sector there have been some attempts to specify the ends that managers most often seek. The ends identified in those studies include maximizing profits, maintaining efficiency, promoting high morale, producing effective subordinates, high production, organizational growth, industrial leadership, organizational stability, social welfare, and innovation.[7] While some of these criteria of performance apply to the public sector, many do not.

In the first phase of a recent public-sector study, 120 public administrators were interviewed by the author and asked to identify an incident that they would consider their most outstanding improvement action.[8] Once a particular change was isolated, the respondents were then asked to list the specific results of the change. Thus the results reflected, in a very concrete sense, how they defined improvement. In the second phase of the study, a list of 33 criteria was compiled from the first-phase data. Then a questionnaire was prepared and mailed to top administrators in state government organizations across the United States. By use of a mathematical technique called factor analysis, it was possible to identify empirically six objectives that administrators commonly pursue in trying to improve their organizations:

Objectives of Administrators

(1) *Output process* or *effectiveness* reflects an improvement in the quantity, quality, and timeliness of outputs or services, and also a resulting increase in the satisfaction of output recipients. (2) *Coordination* means an improvement in decision-making, communication, planning, the integration of subunits, and relationships with other units. (3) *Motivational climate* has to do with the orientation of unit members; it is reflected by an improvement in initiative, involvement, satisfaction, identification with the unit, cooperation, creativity, and interpersonal relations. (4) *Stability-equilibrium* is improved as strain and pressure are reduced, as stability or balance is increased, and as workforce retention improves. (5) *Savings* simply means economizing. Savings increase as money and other resources are conserved. (6) *Resource acquisition* is reflected by increasing revenues or profits, growth in size of the unit and a generally increased ability to acquire resources.

The list above provides six empirical dimensions of organizational performance as perceived by operating public administrators. Notice that the first objective, which involves an improved output process and increased client satisfaction, has been labeled "output process or effectiveness." The use of effectiveness is consistent with the above-mentioned original differentiation made by Barnard in that it reflects goal attainment rather than systems maintenance.[9] However, administrators are also very concerned with the other five dimensions listed above. In a given situation, an improvement on one dimension may mean difficulties in terms of another. Also, while managers must be concerned with all six dimensions of performance, a particular manager may put a high priority on one or more specific outcomes at one point in time and then switch priorities at a later point. Predictably, different types of organizations and situations may generate a need for improvement on different dimensions. Indeed, a manager might even find disincentives for working on particular dimensions. Saving money, for example, is a behavior that often generates more personal costs than benefits for a manager in the public sector.

How Do We Get There From Here?

In this study described above, not only the outcomes of improvement actions were investigated but also the means. Means are the type of changes employed in order to improve dimensions of performance. The eight means or types of change are identified below.

1. *Modification of perceptions and attitudes* is an attempt to change emotions, beliefs, values, and attitudes by increasing the information flow to people, a task accomplished by explaining policies, instituting staff meetings, keeping an open office door, and other such communications mechanisms.
2. *Modification of the authority system* is aimed at increasing the responsiveness of management, and at improving authority relations, decision processes, and communication systems. Attempts to modify the formal chain of command, clarification of authority relations, delegation, the development of policy teams, reassignment of supervisory responsibility, are examples.
3. *Structural reorganization* is simply a reorganization of the system. It means changing such things as size of the unit, staffing procedures, physical arrangements, or budgeting processes.
4. *The process of measurement and evaluation* involves setting goals and objectives, measuring progress, and evaluating results. It is reflected by the implementation of management by objectives, management information systems, and program planning and budgeting.
5. *Modification of work methods through technology* entails changes in equipment, work methods, control systems, forms and tracking devices, and work processes. It is most often reflected by attempts at automation and might include

computerizing placement procedures, receipt posting, case tracking, and reporting processes.

6. *Retraining and replacement* are people changes. Personnel may be taught new skills as a result of redefined duties, responsibilities, and job qualifications. Replacement activities include hiring, firing, and other forms of personnel replacement.
7. *Modification of the workflow* usually involves rearrangement of units or jobs so that the path or sequence of workflow is altered. Examples include separating unlike units or jobs, putting similar units or jobs together, and delegating routine parts of a job to new paraprofessionals. Such changes often modify intergroup relationships.
8. The final means or type of change is *introducing a new program.* Such innovation usually involves new products or services.

The above changes describe levers that administrators often manipulate to change their organizations. Naturally, they are not mutually exclusive. More than one type of modification may be involved in a given change effort. In addition, there may be other types of changes. The present list, however, emerged empirically from the improvements most often mentioned by administrators.

These findings help us to understand a great deal about the process of improving organizational performance. Naturally, such an initial description leads to many additional questions about the change process, and our ongoing research efforts hopefully will provide answers. For example, what are the relationships between the means and ends? Are there certain types of changes that tend to result in certain kinds of outcomes? If certain relationships do occur regularly in given situations, a knowledge of such patterns would be most helpful in planning the change process. For example, in our initial efforts we found the set of relationships that appear in Table 1.2. Because of the exploratory nature of the study, and because there were no controls (for specific types of work, unit size, etc.), the relationships in Table 1.2 must be seen as very tentative. However, they are provocative and illustrate the potential for continuing research. For example, considering just a few of the relationships in Table 1.2, suppose the following hypothetical statements proved to be consistently recurring phenomena:

- The primary means for improving effectiveness of outputs is to modify work methods.
- Modifications in work methods negatively affect motivational climate.

- Use of information-sharing mechanisms leads to improved motivational climate.
- Reorganizations negatively affect coordination and savings are not related to effectiveness.
- Retraining and replacement are not directly related to any positive outcomes.
- Sharing authority is positively related to motivational climate, coordination, and stability.

Such facts would have a powerful influence on our thinking and planning process. At this point they are simply provocative illustrations of the kind of information that might be generated. We are currently working on theories, measures, and designs that will allow us to discover if such patterns do exist.

While our future efforts should provide some exciting inputs into the planning process, the present data are important in and of themselves. They illustrate what ends public administrators pursue and what means they use in trying to improve their organizations. They also illustrate why the action-oriented administrator has difficulty communicating with academics who use terms that are both unclear and unsuited to administrative action.

TABLE 1.2 Pearson Correlations Between Means and Ends

Means	*Ends*					
	1 Output Process	2 Motivational Climate	3 Resource Acquisition	4 Coordination	5 Savings	6 Equitable Stability
1. Work methods	.13··	−.11···	.03	.05	.14··	−.10···
2. Information dissemination	−.08	.12···	.11···	.04	.05	.08
3. Structural reorganization	.05	−.05	.30·	−.06	−.12···	.04
4. Retraining-replacement	.07	.00	.10···	.00	−.04	.05
5. Authority system	.00	.13···	.09···	.33·	−.05	.12···
6. Objective setting	−.05	.11···	.21·	.09···	−.07	−.10···
7. Workflow	.08	.00	.00	−.07	.09···	.01
8. Programs	−.03	−.03	.13··	.01	−.06	.41··

n = 346

·p ≤ .001
··p ≤ .01
···p ≤ .05

BOX 1.1 Ayers and Kettinger Describe Five Pathways to Increased Efficiency

1. LOWER COSTS AND GREATER SERVICES

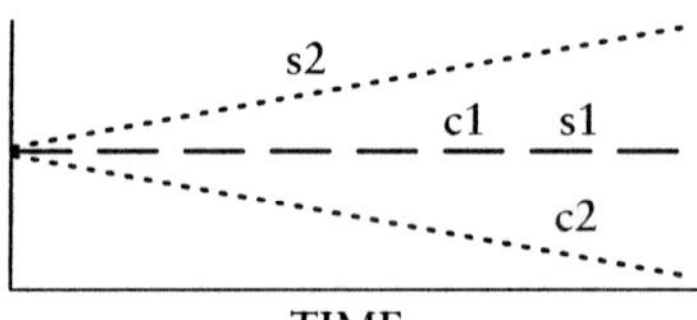

2. LOWER COSTS AND CONSTANT SERVICES

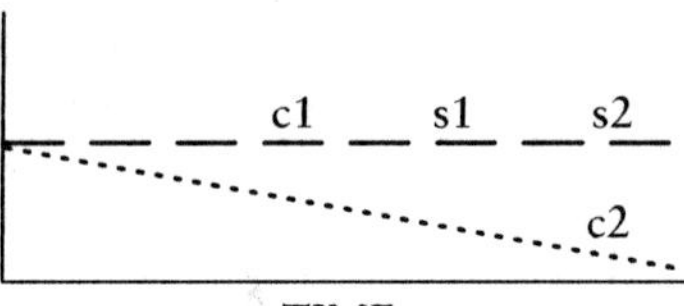

3. CONSTANT COSTS AND GREATER SERVICES

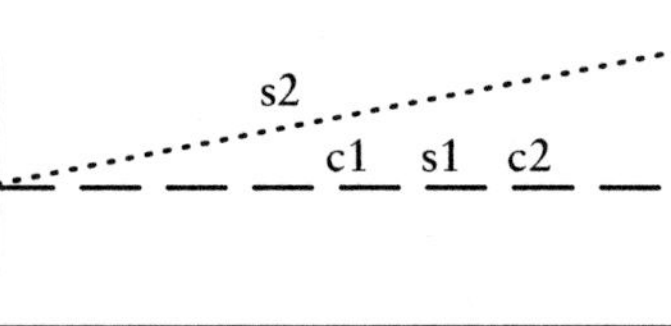

4. HIGHER COSTS AND GREATER INCREASE IN SERVICES

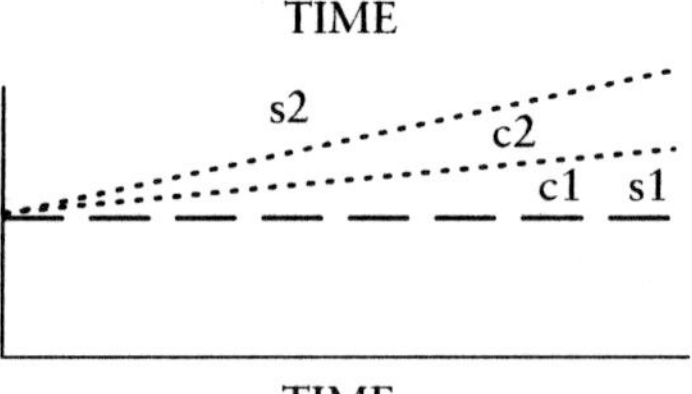

5. LOWER COSTS AND SMALLER DECREASE IN SERVICES

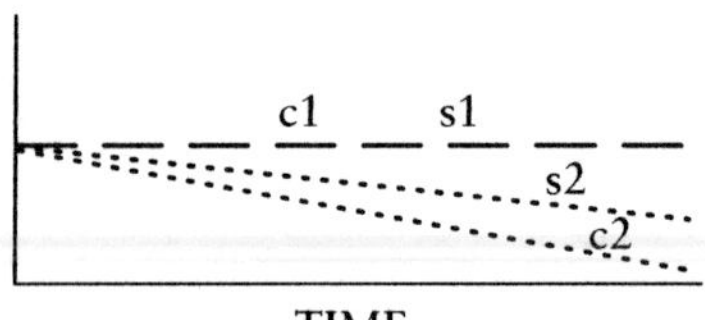

c1 = costs maintained at current levels in constant dollars
s2 = services maintained at current levels
c2 = costs in constant dollars in an alternative scenario
s2 = services in the alternative scenario

(Source: Q. Whitfield Ayres and William J. Kettinger, "Models of Increasing Productivity," in: "Information Technology and Models of Governmental Productivity," *Public Administration Review* 33 (November/December 1983): 561–566.)

Summary and Conclusions

Productivity has come to mean many things. For academicians with an analytical orientation, the term is usually equated with the input/output ratio or what is commonly termed efficiency. Administrators with an action orientation usually equate the meaning of the concept with the over-all performance of the system.

Because the word productivity is used in so many ways it is unlikely that problems in communication will disappear. Several suggestions, however, merit consideration. First, it may be useful to replace the term productivity with several other terms that are more precise. When we are concerned with the input/output ratio we should use the term efficiency. When we are concerned with goal attainment—meaning quality of outputs, client satisfaction, etc.—we should use the term effectiveness. When we are concerned with the over-all competence of the system, as reflected by the above dimensions of performance, we might use a new term such as organizational vitality. When we are concerned with action, or the process of improving organizational performance or vitality, then we would do well to consider the specific dimensions we are concerned about. These would include effectiveness, coordination, motivation, stability, savings, and resource acquisition.

By being aware of the different orientations that now exist, we can understand the current confusion. By adopting a new orientation we may be able to reduce confusion in the future.

Notes

1. John Thomas, "Government Accountability for What"?, *Public Productivity Review,* Vol. 1, No. 2 (1976).

2. George Guilder, "Public Sector Productivity," *Public Productivity Review,* Vol. 1, No. 1 (1976). Raymond Katzell and Daniel Yankelovich, *Work, Productivity, and Job Satisfaction* (New York: New York University, 1975).

3. Chester Barnard, *The Functions of the Executive* (Cambridge: Harvard University Press, 1938).

4. Jaisingh Ghorpade, *Assessment of Organizational Effectiveness: Issues, Analysis and Readings* (Pacific Palisades, California: Goodyear, 1971).

5. Richard Steers, "Problems in the Measurement of Organizational Effectiveness," *Administrative Science Quarterly,* 19 (1975).

6. Henry Mintzberg, *The Nature of Managerial Work* (New York: Harper and Row, 1973), pp. 78–79.

7. John P. Campbell, Marvin D. Dunnette, Edward E. Lawler, and Karl E. Weick Jr., *Managerial Behavior, Performance and Effectiveness* (New York: McGraw-Hill, 1970).

8. Robert E. Quinn, "Towards a Theory of Changing: A Means-Ends Model of the Organizational Improvement Process," presented at the TIMS International meeting. "Workshop on Organizational Design," July 25–27, 1977, in Athens, Greece.

9. Barnard, *The Functions of the Executive.*

2

A Capacity-Building Framework

A Search for Concept and Purpose

Beth Walter Honadle

Culture requires that we possess a complete concept of the world and of man; it is not for culture to stop, with science, at the point where the methods of absolute theoretic rigor happen to end. Life cannot wait until the sciences have explained the universe scientifically. We cannot put off living until we are ready.

—Jose Ortega y Gasset

When we engage in a pursuit, a clear and precise conception of what we are pursuing would seem to be the first thing we need, instead of the last we are to look forward to.

—John Stuart Mill

A growing number of persons (capacity builders) purport to be doing something they call "capacity building." They go about this activity in a variety of ways—demonstrations, grants, consulting, training and development, and circuit riding, to name a few. Capacity building tends to address specialized management issues—financial management, organization development, grantsmanship, and service integration, for instance—usually depending upon the purview and interests of the capacity builders.

These characteristics of capacity building are not necessarily bad. Attempts to address the broad gamut of management issues may be overly ambitious and do the client a disservice. Bolstering management practices

"A Capacity-Building Framework: A Search for Concept and Purpose," *Public Administration Review* 41 (September/October, 1981): 575–580.

in specific areas can build support for extending administrative improvements to others. Further, by making changes incrementally, useful knowledge is gained for application to future innovations. Hence, it may be wise to focus attention on selected management problems.

In too many cases, however, capacity building is conceived of as the application of a particular approach to every management problem in any context. Or it is considered as the improvement of a facet of management which is equated with organizational capacity.

An urgent need exists for a concept and purpose in capacity building. This need is underscored by the recent budget-cutting climate, which means that governments will have to operate more efficiently and effectively with fewer resources. Further, with the Reagan administration's proposals to consolidate several categorical grant programs into block grants administered by the states, many of those affected—particularly mayors and interest groups that benefited from categoricals—have raised questions concerning the capacities of various states to take on new responsibilities. Since the administration's long-range plans also call for "revenue turnbacks," the states' fiscal and management capacities are both timely issues.

This article reviews some common conceptions of capacity. The objective of the following discussion is to propose an analytical framework for policy makers, researchers, and practitioners who must design, evaluate, and run programs.

The Conceptual Problem

A Council of State Community Affairs Agencies (COSCAA) report made the following observation about the need for a concept of "capacity":

> A necessary assumption which underlies programs aimed at building management capacity is that there is a definable, measurable phenomenon, "management capacity," which can be purposefully changed. There is a need to arrive at a consensus definition of this concept.[1]

It is unlikely that a consensus definition of "capacity" will ever be reached. Nevertheless, a reasonably integrated framework for pursuing this holy grail would help capacity builders map a sensible course.

Following are some prevailing conceptions about the meaning of "capacity." It is useful to review them because they have direct implications for the purposes of capacity-building programs.

Survival Versus Service

By some definitions, capacity measures the survival ability of organizations. R. T. Lenz defines strategic capability as "the capability of an enterprise to successfully undertake action that is intended to affect its long-term growth and development."[2]

This may be a proper view of "capacity" for business enterprises, but not for public organizations, because it ignores function. An organization may survive, but not perform a worthwhile function. Two decades ago, George A. Graham posed the question: "How Can Capacity to Govern Be Measured?" He began by rejecting survival as an index of capacity. He wrote:

> The simplest and oldest test of capacity to govern . . . survival . . . has limitations. Its chief definitive reading is negative, for it does not measure degrees of success or differences of capacity. Survival is an index which can be read only in retrospect. It is a clock which tells what time it was—never what time it is. The fact that a state has survived does not indicate that it will continue to.[3]

In contrast to the survival view of capacity, some writers stress the abilities of a public organization as service provider. A clear case of the latter type of definition is the following:

> There is a federal system with Congress at its center, and Older Americans (among other Americans) at its periphery.
>
> If any element of the system does anything that causes an element "farther out" in the system to become more competent in the use of its own powers and resources to accomplish social purposes, that's *capacity-building*.[4]

There are problems with this type of definition as well. Although it requires the organization to have a function, it is nonoperational. That is, for purposes of capacity building, it does not define what capable organizations do.

Politics Versus Rationality

Some views of capacity focus on such qualities of administration as politics, informal processes, and participation in contrast with others which stress rationality or the "perfection" of administration. Three writers—using the term "development"—infer that capacity building means "movement away from traditional structures based on custom and movement toward relationships based upon rules which achieve higher levels of rationality."[5]

A similar definition of capacity building is improving the ability of local government officials to make informed decisions "supported with analytical material and program information capable of describing objectives and priorities."[6] This conception of capacity building corresponds with rational views of capacity, such as "the ability to make decisions and allocate resources more 'rationally' by learning to use certain techniques and models developed for application to systems."[7]

The Tennessee Municipal League's (TML) definition also divorces capacity from politics. TML defines "true capacity" as: "'know how' that is built into the organizational structure on a continuing basis and which will be operating effectively regardless of changes in policy direction or political leadership."[8]

Robert Hawkins, on the other hand, has a markedly different perspective on capacity building—an explicit recognition of the political dimension of management:

> Capacity building is a concept that encompasses a broad range of activities that are aimed at increasing the ability of citizens and their governments to produce more responsive and efficient public goods and services. At its core capacity building is concerned with the selection and development of institutional arrangements; both political and administrative.[9]

Hawkins deliberately rejects the "notion of capacity building as the perfection of administrative systems," because it ignores politics.[10]

Likewise, COSCAA's working definition of capacity building encompasses ". . . political dynamics which usually limit the change options open to local officials."[11] If local politics constrain capacity-building efforts, proposed changes should incorporate the needs and desires of the political leadership in a community.

Inputs Versus the Total System

One of the most intriguing dichotomies in the realm of capacity-building definitions is that between capacity building as the ability to attract inputs and capacity as the effective functioning of a total system. According to one author, "obtaining adequate resources to meet the basic needs of its citizenry is, beyond doubt, the ultimate test of a government's viability."[12] Another study defined capacity-building "gaps" as "when resources are not available to meet community needs."[13] Two community development experts stated that, "The general intent [of capacity building] is to help the community build internal resources to carry on its developmental plans with a minimum of outside assistance."[14] By contrast, other writers shun this input-focused notion of capacity and argue that "capacity is better spent on local problem solving than on seeking Federal funds."[15] In other words, attracting inputs is vital to organizational capacity, but, alone, it is an insufficient concept of capacity.

A systemic view toward capacity building seeks to "build capacity of state and local governments to determine needs, seek solutions, process information, change priorities, programs, and procedures, provide feedback, and modify behavior on the basis of evaluation."[16] In a similar vein, Arnold Howitt calls the "management capacity" of a local government "its ability to identify problems, develop and evaluate policy alternatives for dealing with them, and operate government programs."[17] Howitt's definition does not require any kind of feedback mechanism.

Capacity Building for Whom?

Another question has been whether an organization's capacity should be built in order to make it more autonomous or to implement someone else's policies. Christopher Lindley believes that the function of capacity building is "to enhance the capability of local governments to perform intelligently and efficiently under their own direction."[18] This view is also expressed in an Office of Management and Budget (OMB) report on providing technical assistance (TA). The report defines TA as: "Aid provided by a source, upon request, to a recipient, which is oriented toward solving problems which are identified by the recipient but beyond its immediate capacity to resolve."[19]

This perspective is summarized by Anthony Brown, who writes:

> The primary goal of this approach [capacity building] is to develop the capacity of . . . jurisdictions . . . to manage their own affairs, and to more effectively protect and promote their interests and decrease their vulnerability to disruptive changes coming from without.[20]

There are others who would argue that capacity building is helping local communities meet external goals and criteria. A Tennessee Municipal League report states:

> When we use this term [capacity building] we are referring to any and all efforts directed toward helping municipal governments to plan and manage their affairs more effectively, and in accordance with national policy and recognized standards of professional competence.[21]

Another proponent of this kind of capacity building asserts: "Worries about the capability of local governments to produce . . . Nationally desirable outputs are legitimate, based on the record."[22] Such anxiety was fanned by the advent of general revenue sharing and other forms of fiscal decentralization in the 1970s. In the 1980s these concerns are renewed in face of budget cutbacks, block grants, and deregulation proposals.

Means Versus Results Improvement

"Capacity" has been defined in terms of both the activities an organization should be performing (means) and the results it should be achieving. The latter kind of definition is concerned less with *how* an organization does something as with *what* it does. An illustration of this type of definition is:

> Capacity-building simply implies the development of . . . government's potential for doing better the job that it is probably already in the process of accomplishing.[23]

Contrast this definition with one that stresses the *ways* in which public organizations fulfill their functions. For instance, one definition states:

> Administrative capability means the institutional capacity of a government . . . to formulate and carry out plans, policies, operations, or other measures to fulfill public purposes.[24]

There are also definitions that disregard the results an organization is to achieve. Hence, capacity is a measure of organizational potential. According to Lehan: ". . . to be capable is to be potentially effective in the environment."[25] Viewed this way, capacity is related to the "administrative stock" of an organization. Administrative stock has been defined as "a static inventory of resources (human, material, etc.) controlled by an organization."[26] These resources may or may not be activated and, consequently, represent only administrative potential. Administrative behavior, on the other hand, "is what organization members are doing that results in goods and services being delivered during a given period of time."[27] A related distinction is that made between the capacity to act and the will or resolve to act.[28]

In short, definitions of capacity vary in the extent to which they specify the activities that should be performed versus the results that are sought. One could argue, however, that a "capable" organization has the capacity to achieve all kinds of results. Hence, capacity building is only concerned with improving organizational means.

In light of the above, COSCAA's call for a consensus definition of management capacity is likely to go unanswered. It is probable, however, that some of the conceptual shortcomings of capacity building could be avoided if there were a general framework describing what capacity should involve.

A Capacity-Building Framework

Broadly speaking, capacity building has meant "increasing the ability of people and institutions to do what is required of them."[29] Such a broad definition is not very useful as a guide to developing and assessing programs because it can mean many things or almost nothing at all. It fails to specify what is to be built.

Most capacity-building efforts suffer from a lack of conceptual precision. The quite understandable reason for this shortcoming is that the pressure to do something has at times overridden the desirability of fully understanding what is being pursued.

As a means of clarifying the purposes and impacts of capacity building, following is a framework for conceptualizing future efforts of this type. Elements in the framework are: definitional characteristics, administrative practices, institutions, and organizational requirements.

Definitional Characteristics

"Capacity" is defined by the ability to:

- anticipate and influence change;
- make informed, intelligent decisions about policy;
- develop programs to implement policy;
- attract and absorb resources;
- manage resources; and
- evaluate current activities to guide future action.

Taken as a whole, these activities signify "capacity." Figure 2.1 is a diagram showing how the framework operates as a system. Without the ability to anticipate change, an organization is incapable of influencing the future except by default. Demographic changes, economic trends, and new legislation, for example, shape the future. Whether and how an organization responds to these signals determines its influence on changes that ultimately occur. Thus, capable bodies have the ability to make policy decisions based on organized, relevant information. They develop programs to implement those policies.

Organizations must be able to attract resources from the environment. Resources include such diverse inputs as community support and acceptance, citizen participation in decision making, tax revenues, intergovernmental aid, new technologies, private enterprise involvement, information, externally derived regulations, and others. These raw materials are grist for capable organizations to mill into usable form for themselves and for their clients.

The further ability to absorb resources is distinguished here from the capacity to attract resources since not every organization with the ability to secure resources has the ability to "spend" them. A community can obtain a grant to perform a planning function or build a facility but still lack the time, staff, skills, and instrumentalities to effectively use the funds. Similarly, a small community may not have the capacity to incorporate a given administrative technique into its operations because the data and other requirements of the procedure were devised for larger governments.

The ability to manage resources, moreover, is distinct from the ability to absorb resources. Management implies some "rational" application, allocation, and handling of the resources at one's disposal and not merely their disposal. A capable organization manages its physical, human, informational, and financial resources.

FIGURE 2.1 A Capacity-Building Framework

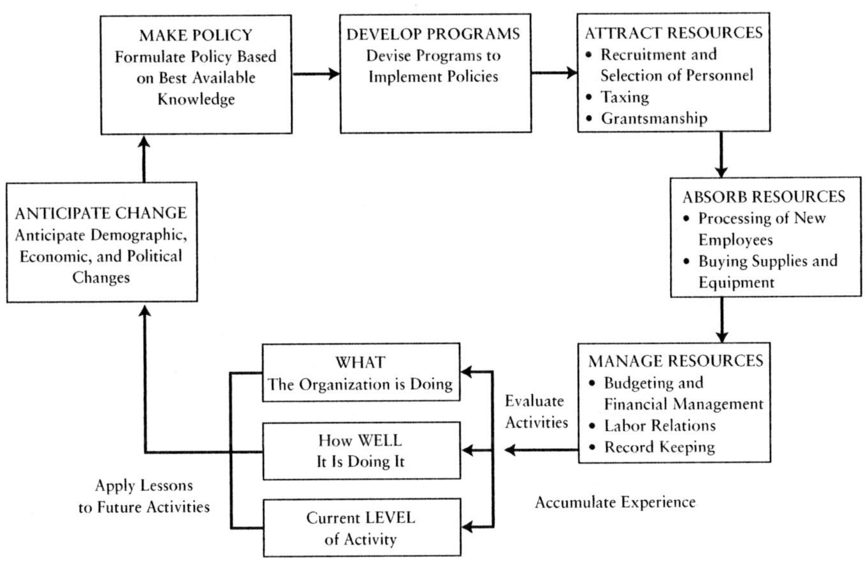

Finally, without evaluation of a community's experience with capacity building, such efforts are likely to be a one-shot undertaking. Thus, if capacity includes the ability to anticipate and influence change, there needs to be ongoing assessment of what the organization is doing. This should include: (a) monitoring what it is currently doing, (b) evaluating how well it appears to be doing it, and (c) assessing whether the current level of effort is appropriate over time. This information can be used to improve future organizational performance.

In sum, then, a conceptual framework for capacity building should include all of these components. Each alone is an insufficient definition of capacity. Although the ability to attract resources (sometimes dubbed grantsmanship) has often been equated with organizational capacity, for example, it is important from a grant giver's point of view to know if the recipients can absorb and manage funds effectively and apply what they learn from their experiences.

Administrative Practices

There are numerous administrative routines, programs, or procedures (the shorthand we have sometimes used for them is PODSCORB) necessary to implement the activities comprising "capacity." The ability to perform administrative practices "well" by reliance on modern, efficient techniques is usually what is meant by "good administration." Organizations not exhibiting "good" administrative techniques are said to lack "capacity." Examples of such administrative practices are internal resource allocation (e.g., budgeting, accounting), information management (e.g., record keeping), and periodic evaluation.

Institutions

Capacity is reflected in institutions. In fact, capacity building means institutionalizing or embodying strengths in an organization.

The established ways of doing things will necessarily vary according to particular communities' needs, legal mandates, and access to resources. They will also evolve over time to adapt to new situations that arise. Professional chief executive officers, area-wide planning bodies, grants-coordinators, and citizen participation processes are reflective of managerial, anticipatory, and attraction capabilities.

Organizational Requirements

Building management capacity implies that there must be either standards of adequacy or measures of demand for capacity. These are the benchmarks or indicators used to assess capacity or the lack thereof.[30]

The organizational requirements of capacity include but are not limited to the following:

- the ability to forge effective links with other organizations;
- processes for solving problems;
- coordination among disparate functions; and
- mechanisms for institutional learning.

One very important problem in capacity building is determining what should constitute minimal acceptable organizational standards or benchmarks. As Irwin Feller observed:

> It is one thing to say that Alabama's legislature should perform as well as, say, the average of the 50 states: it is another to say that all state legislatures should achieve some minimum level of performance . . . and yet another to say that California's . . . legislature should *fully* be the co-equal of the executive branch. . . .[31]

In short, there are numerous alternative ways of setting organizational requirements for capacity building to achieve. The point is that it makes a difference what standards are applied.

Policy Implications and Applications

This model has numerous ramifications for the practice of capacity building. It suggests that large infusions of money or administrative technology are not necessarily the appropriate answer to low levels of capacity. The capacity to attract and absorb resources is a necessary but not sufficient condition for good management. Smaller, less administratively sophisticated jurisdictions are incapable of absorbing the same level of resources as larger jurisdictions. The rate at which they absorb innovations also may differ. Even larger organizations may temporarily lack the authority to hire or the ability to process paperwork, making absorption impossible in the short run. Expending more resources on capacity building than a recipient can absorb in a given time frame is wasteful and counterproductive.

The framework presented here also advocates approaches to capacity building that favor the incorporation or institutionalization of "capacity" into the permanent structure of the target jurisdiction. This suggests less direct involvement of consultants, circuit riders, and similar external, transient actors in day-to-day administration and more emphasis on transferring their knowledge, skills, and insights to local managers. If there is one thing that capacity building does not mean it is creating dependency on outsiders for expertise.

It is useful to think at the outset about the ultimate objectives of capacity-building efforts. Admittedly, the goals of administrative development are hard to quantify. Nevertheless, measuring capacity-building effectiveness in such objective terms as dollars expended or communities served is a poor substitute for identifying the critical behaviors the program is intended to change. The framework proposed here is useful for analyzing the components of capable management.

One application is to analyze the capacities of block grant recipients to manage their programs. For example, it is relevant to ask whether they have enough of the right kinds of people—analysts, planners, financial experts, general managers—to identify needs, set priorities, allocate and manage the additional resources, and evaluate impacts. Further, ideally recipients should have institutions capable of supporting such an increase in responsibility.

Finally, the framework proposed here can serve as a checklist for diagnosing organizational weaknesses (and strengths). For instance, some communities in the South and West are experiencing renewed growth after decades of decline. The most capable communities would have management information systems to help them anticipate the sources and magnitudes of the growth. Having predictive capacity would enhance a community's chances of being able to influence outcomes so as to minimize the negative impacts of growth (e.g., pollution, crime) and maximize the benefits (e.g., jobs, better schools) associated with development. The most

BOX 2.1 Why Consultants Are Called In

Robert Rosenblum and Daniel McGillis

As the use of consultants has become more common, the need for their services has been taken more and more for granted. Thus, in planning for the performance of a particular task, many government agencies assume the need for consultant assistance and begin with the question of what should be asked of the consultant and which firm should be retained. The proliferation of consultants and consultant firms, and the broad acceptance of the government's need for their services, is due to several aspects of the political and bureaucratic structure. Among the several reasons why consultants may be called upon in lieu of using personnel already on the government payroll are the following.

A. Limitations on Hiring Civil Servants

The practice of restricting government hiring without consideration of what the actual staffing needs are to accomplish the legislatively-mandated activities is not unusual. In 1966, for example, with President Johnson's support.

> Congress enacted the Revenue Expenditure Control Act. It required the Executive Branch of Government to reduce itself in size to the level of employment in fact existing in 1964. The cosmetic public theory behind the Act was that the reduction of, and, stabilization of, a personnel ceiling for the Executive Branch would first cut, and then stabilize, Federal expenditures connected with personnel costs . . .

Whether there was a workload assessment which led to the enactment or whether it was more closely tied to anticipation of "big government" becoming a political issue is unclear. One of the results of that legislation and other restrictions on hiring government employees, however, may have been the increased utilization of consultants. When an agency is mandated to perform certain tasks and is accountable for the successful completion of those tasks but does not have the authority to hire the necessary staff its only recourse, short of failure, may be to award contracts or grants.

B. Needs for Special Skills

Even if bureaucratic agencies were not legally constrained in hiring enough staff to perform their legislatively-mandated tasks, there are significant practical constraints which necessitate their use of outside resources. The long battle for job security won by government employees through the establishment of elaborate civil service procedures has greatly improved the quality of life of thousands of such workers. An offshoot of such benefits as higher salaries and job security, however, is the reluctance by agencies to hire persons with

(continues)

BOX 2.1 (continued)

unique skills or whose training may limit their productivity to one project or type of project. Since government workers cannot easily be discharged, it may have become less cost-effective to hire a full-time person to perform a short term task and to have to keep that person on the payroll indefinitely, perhaps doing makeshift work, than it is to hire a consultant even though his or her costs include overhead and possible profit charges of a firm.

C. Evading Parkinson's Law

One of the very difficult things for the bureaucracy to do is to restrain itself. As stated by Katz and Kahn,

> One of the basic properties of social systems of the bureaucratic type is that they move toward maximization, toward growth and expansion. Parkinson (1957), in noting this tendency contends that increases in personnel and positions are not accompanied by increases in productivity.

Once the bureaucratic wheels are set in motion to accomplish a particular and discrete task, there tends to develop an organic-like momentum which drives the organization inevitably toward becoming institutionalized. Long after the completion of its reason for existence, its budget, staff, and workload continue to expand. It is this burgeoning quality of government agencies that seems to be at the heart of President Carter's recommendation for zero-based budgeting.

Consulting firms, on the other hand, are usually designed to enable rapid mobilization of interdisciplinary teams created specifically to perform relatively short term tasks, and then to have those teams dissolve or redefine their membership so as to qualify for another task, perhaps even for a different governmental agency. In a sense the flexibility of consultants to move from agency to agency on various tasks affords them the freedom from having to associate their livelihood with the longevity of any particular project.

One effect of calling in consultants, therefore, may be to frustrate the inevitability of Parkinson's Law. Because of the contractual nature of consulting, the tasks are agreed upon before work starts and generally are given relatively short life spans.

D. Rapid Project Turnaround

Tight, sometimes unrealistic, deadlines are endemic to the consulting profession. We do not know any staff member who at one time or another has not worked a 24-hour day in order to complete a project on schedule. Just as important, it is not unusual to find support personnel (typists, proof readers, administrative assistants) working through the night. Indeed most firms operate on a 24-hour basis when necessary and one need only schedule several hours

(continues)

BOX 2.1 (continued)

in advance for the appropriate typing, copying, graphics, or staff resources at virtually any given time. Thus, projects with particularly tight deadlines which would be simply impossible to complete on time if forced into a 9 to 5 schedule can reasonably be expected to be completed on time by many consulting firms. There was recently such a project completed by Abt Associates resulting in a report to Congress. Because of major delays in the procurement process, the time available to complete the research design, data collection, analysis, and final report was reduced from the anticipated sixteen months to four months. In the final hectic week of the project, production teams worked in shifts of 12 hours on and four hours off for six days in a row in order to have the report completed on time.

E. Assumed Objectivity

Government workers are imbedded in a political framework since the administrators of the federal agencies are typically political appointees. While many government employees could objectively assess issues in their area of expertise, the *appearance* of objectivity would still be likely to suffer because of the employees' ultimate supervision by politically appointed staff. Consultants are often called upon to perform studies due to their assumed objectivity with regard to the political issues in a given area. Consultants are viewed as disinterested third parties who can weigh the issues in an area on their merits rather than in the light of political considerations. The degree to which their actual objectivity is greater than that of government employees is, of course, debatable.

(Source: Robert Rosenblum and Daniel McGillis, "Why Consultants Are Called In," in: "Observations on the Role of Consultants in the Public Sector," *Public Administration Review* 39 (May/June 1979): 219–226.)

viable communities would develop policies drawing on reliable, pertinent data to assist them in mitigating adverse conditions and in encouraging desirable outcomes.

In other words, capable organizations are forward-thinking. This proactive stance behooves them when opportunities materialize. If a firm is looking for a place to locate it might well go to the community that planned for growth by enacting suitable policies in advance. Programs to modernize sewerage treatment facilities, revitalize downtown areas, or otherwise create an environment conductive to growth are necessary for carrying out policies. Having opted for certain programs, the community must attract resources to implement the programs. The community must assess its alternative sources of income, such as tax revenues, bonds, and intergovernmental aid in the form of grants and loans. It must also evaluate its other resources: personnel, information, capital facilities, and time! If the community has sufficient resources to operate a program it must manage the resources. Wise procurement, labor-management relations, financial administration, and day-to-day supervision of programs are essential to effectively meeting community objectives. At least as important are periodic reviews or evaluations. The communities should assess whether the programs are indeed doing what is needed to meet given objectives. Are they doing it effectively and efficiently? Could they be doing it better somehow? And, lastly, is the sheer amount of activity in an area appropriate? Could resources have been allocated more effectively?

To summarize, capable organizations do more than simply attract resources. In a period of fiscal retrenchment a way of assessing organizational capabilities is needed in order to get the most use from each taxpayer dollar.

Notes

1. Council of State Community Affairs Agencies. *The Delivery of Management Capacity Building Technical Assistance to Local Government: An Initial Inventory and Review of State DCA Strategies.* Funded by U.S. Civil Service Commission. Bureau of Intergovernmental Personnel Programs. Contract number 77DX09. Washington, D.C., January 1978, p. 2.

2. Definitions of "capacity" and "capacity building" are reviewed in Beth Walter Honadle, *Capacity-Building (Management Improvement) for Local Governments: An Annotated Bibliography,* U.S. Department of Agriculture, Economics and Statistics Service, Washington, D.C. March 1981. RDRR–28.

3. George A. Graham, *America's Capacity to Govern: Some Preliminary Thoughts for Prospective Administrators* (University: University of Alabama Press, 1960), p. 52.

4. E. H. White and Co., *Capacity-Building and Decentralization (Session E). AoA Staff Program Materials.* Prepared for U.S. Department of Health, Education and Welfare, Administration of Aging. SHR–0000620. Washington, D.C., October 1975. Emphasis in original.

5. William A. Giles, Gerald T. Gabris, and Dale A. Krane, "Dynamics in Rural Policy Development: The Uniqueness of County Government," *Public Administration Review,* Vol. 40, No. 1 (Jan./Feb. 1980), p. 24.

6. MATCH Institution, *Capacity Building for Medium Sized Cities: Petersburg, Virginia and Prichard, Alabama.* Vol. 1: *Petersburg Final Report and Appendix A.* Prepared for U.S. Department of Housing and Urban Development, Office of Policy Development and Research. Contract number H–2185R. Washington, D.C., Nov. 1976, pp. 1–2.

7. Charles F. Kettering Foundation, *Policy Development Pracuces to Assist Local Legislative Officials in Dayton and Cinctnnati.* Vol. 2: *Appendices A-Q, Background Data and Studies.* Prepared for U.S. Department of Housing and Urban

Development. Office of Policy Development and Research. Contract number H–2181R. Washington. D.C., Dec. 1975, p. 25.

8. Tennessee Municipal League, *Community Development Assistance for Tennessee Cities.* Vol. 1: *Final Report and Appendices A-E.* Prepared for U.S. Department of Housing and Urban Development. Office of Policy Development and Research. Contract number H–2184R. Washington. D.C., June 1976, p. 99.

9. Rober: B. Hawkins, Jr., *Extension Project: Capacity-Building for Small Units of Rural Government.* Prepared for U.S. Department of Agriculture, Extension Service, unpublished final draft. 1980. p. 2.

10. *Ibid.,* p. 4.

11. Council of State Community Affairs Agencies, p. 2.

12. John R. Coleman, "Local Government Viability—Do the Data Speak?" Paper presented at the American Society for Public Administration National Conference, Chicago, Ill., April 2, 1975, p. 14.

13. Anthony Andrew Hickey, "Decision-Making and Extra-Community Assistance to Rural Local Officials," Fairfax, Va.: George Mason University, Sept. 1979, p. 1.

14. Larry Gamm and Frederick Fisher, "The Technical Assistance Approach." *Community Development in America.* Ed. James A. Christenson and Jerry W. Robinson, Jr. (Ames: The Iowa State University Press. 1980), p. 55.

15. Alvin D. Sokolow, "Local Governments in Nonmetropolitan America: Capacity and Will," Paper prepared for the Future of Rural America Advisory Committee, Farmers Home Administration, U.S. Department of Agriculture, Washington, D.C., Oct. 1979, p. 37.

16. Judah Drob, "Targets of the Program," *Report of the OMB Study Committee on Policy Management Assistance.* Vol. III: *Background Papers and Resource Materials.* Washington, D.C.: National Science Foundation, June 1975, p. 1014.

17. Arnold M. Howitt, *Improving Public Management in Small Communities.* Policy Note P77–3. Cambridge. Mass.: Harvard University. Department of City and Regional Planning. March 1977, p. 1.

18. Christopher Lindley, "Changing Policy Management Responsibilities of Local Legislative Bodies." *Public Administration Review,* Vol. 35, Special Issue (Dec. 1975), p. 797.

19. Office of Management and Budget, "The New Federalism—Report on Technical Assistance," Internal document (written by Ann Macaluso), Nov. 1973, p. 1.

20. Anthony Brown, "Technical Assistance to Rural Communities: Stopgap or Capacity Building?" *Public Administration Review.* Vol. 40, No. 1 (Jan./Feb. 1980), p. 21.

21. Tennessee Municipal League, p. 11.

22. Edward Anthony Lehan, "The Capability of Local Governments: A Search for the Determinants of Effectiveness," *Connecticut Government,* Vol. 28, No. 3 (Spring, 1975), p. 2.

23. Guy D. Spiesman, Gary Dean Hulshoff, and Sam A. Mc-Connell, Jr., *Legislative Staff: The Equalizer in State Government.* Final Report of the Human Resources Services Staffing Demonstration of the Arizona State Legislature. R&D 12-p–55574/9. U.S. Department of Health, Education, and Welfare, Social and Rehabilitation Service, 1976, p. 4.

24. Donald C. Stone, "Proposed Strategy and Action to Increase the Administrative Capability of the Federal-State-Local System," *Report of the OMB Study Committee on Policy Management Assistance.* Vol. III: *Background Papers and Resource Materials.* Washington, D.C.: National Science Foundation, June 1975. p. 501.

25. Lehan, p. 3.

26. George Honadle, "Preliminary Report on Developing a System for Evaluating Institution-Building Components for the Provincial Development Program: Institution-Building in the PDP Context," in H. Amrah Muslimin, Mochtar Buchori, George H. Honadle, *Report on the Progress and Future of the Provincial Area Development Program.* Report compiled for the Ministry of Home Affairs, Republic of Indonesia, and for the U.S. Agency for International Development. Jakarta, Indonesia, April 1979, p. 12.

27. *Ibid.*

28. Sokolow, *op. cit.*

29. Chester A. Newland, "Local Government Capacity Building," *Urban Affairs Papers,* Vol. 3, No. 1 (Winter 1981), p. iv.

30. See, for example, Western Federal Regional Council. *Selected Elements and Indicators of Local Government Capacity.* Working paper prepared by the Capacity-Building Task Force of the Western Federal Regional Council. San Francisco, Calif., April 1975. See also, Edward A. Lehan, "The Capability of Local Governments: A Search for the Determinants of Effectiveness," *op. cit.,* pp. 3–4.

31. Irwin Feller, "Issues in the Design of Federal Programs to Improve the Policy Management Capabilities of State Legislatures," *Public Administration Review,* Vol. 35, Special Issue (Dec. 1975), p. 783.

3

THE DEADLY SINS IN PUBLIC ADMINISTRATION

Peter F. Drucker

I

No one can guarantee the performance of a public service program, but we know how to ensure non-performance with absolute certainty. Commit any two of the following common sins of public administration, and non-performance will inevitably follow. Indeed, to commit all six, as many public service agencies do, is quite unnecessary and an exercise in overkill.

(1) The first thing to do to make sure that a program will not have results is to have a lofty objective—"health care," for instance, or "to aid the disadvantaged." Such sentiments belong in the preamble. They explain why a specific program or agency is being initiated rather than what the program or agency is meant to accomplish. To use such statements as "objectives" thus makes sure that no effective work will be done. For work is always specific, always mundane, always focused. Yet without work there is non-performance.

To have a chance at performance, a program needs clear targets, the attainment of which can be measured, appraised, or at least judged. "Health care" is not even a pious intention. Indeed it is, at best, a vague slogan. Even "the best medical care for the sick," the objective of many hospitals in the British National Health Service, is not operational. Rather, it is meaningful to say: "It is our aim to make sure that no patient coming into emergency will go for more than three minutes without being seen by a qualified triage

---

"The Deadly Sins in Public Administration," *Public Administration Review* 40 (March/ April, 1980): 103–106.

nurse." It is a proper goal to say: "Within three years, our maternity ward is going to be run on a "zero defects" basis, which means that there will be no "surprises" in the delivery room and there will not be one case of post-partum puerperal fever on maternity." Similarly, "Promoting the welfare of the American farmer" is electioneering, while "Installing electricity in at least 25 percent of America's farms within the next three years"—the first goal of the New Deal's Rural Electrification Administration, which was, perhaps, the most successful public service agency in all our administrative history—was an objective that was specific, measurable, attainable—and attained. It immediately was converted into work, and very shortly thereafter, into performance.

(2) The second strategy guaranteed to produce non-performance is to try to do several things at once. It is to refuse to establish priorities and to stick to them. Splintering of efforts guarantees non-results. Yet without concentration on a priority, efforts will be splintered, and the more massive the program, the more the splintering effects will produce non-performance. By contrast, even poorly conceived programs might have results if priorities are set and efforts concentrated.

It is popular nowadays to blame the failure of so many of the programs of Lyndon Johnson's "War on Poverty" on shaky theoretical foundations. Whether poorly conceived or not, quite a few of the Headstart schools had significant results; every one of them, without exception, was a school that decided on one overriding priority—having the children learn to read letters and numbers—despite heavy criticism from Washington and from all kinds of dogmatists.

An even more impressive example is the Tennessee Valley Authority (TVA) in the thirties. Despite tremendous opposition, the bill establishing the TVA only passed Congress because its backers promised a dozen different and mutually antagonistic constituencies: cheap power, cheap fertilizer, flood control, irrigation, navigation, community development and whatnot. TVA's first administrator, Arthur Morgan, a great engineer, then attempted to live up to these promises and to satisfy every one of his constituencies. The only result was an uncontrollably growing bureaucracy, uncontrollably growing expenditures, and a total lack of any performance. Indeed, the TVA in its early years resembled nothing as much as one of those "messes" which we now attack in Washington. Then President Roosevelt removed Morgan and put in a totally unknown young Wisconsin utilities lawyer, David Lilienthal, who immediately—against all advice from all the "pros"—announced his priority: power production. Within a year. the TVA produced results. Lilienthal, by the way, met no opposition, but was universally acclaimed as a saviour.

(3) The third deadly sin of the public administrator is to believe that "fat is beautiful." despite the obvious fact that mass does not do work: brains

and muscles do. In fact, overweight inhibits work, and gross overweight totally immobilizes.

One hears a great deal today about the fallacy of "throwing money at problems," but this is not really what we have been doing. We have been throwing manpower at problems, with Vietnam, perhaps, being the worst example, and it is even worse to overstaff than to overfund. Today's administrators, whether civilian or military, tend to believe that the best way to tackle a problem is to deploy more and more people against it. The one certain result of having more bodies is greater difficulties in logistics, in personnel management, and in communications. Mass increases weight, but not necessarily competence. Competence requires direction, decision, and strategy rather than manpower.

Overstaffing is not only much harder to correct than understaffing, it makes non-performance practically certain. For overstaffing always focuses energies on the inside, on "administration" rather than on "results," on the machinery rather than its purpose. It always leads to meetings and memoranda becoming ends in themselves. It immobilizes behind a facade of furious busyness. Harold Ickes. FDR's Secretary of the Interior and one of the New Deal's most accomplished administrators, always asked: "What is the fewest number of people we need to accomplish this purpose?" It is a long time since anyone in Washington (or in the state governments) has asked that question.

(4) "Don't experiment, be dogmatic" is the next—and the next most common—of the administrator's deadly sins. "Whatever you do, do it on a grand scale at the first try. Otherwise, God forbid, you might learn how to do it differently." In technical or product innovation, we sometimes skip the pilot-plant stage, usually to our sorrow. But at least we build a model and put it through wind tunnel tests. In public service, increasingly we start out with a "position"—that is, with a totally untested theory—and go from it immediately to national, if not international, application. The most blatant example may have been the ultra-scholastic dogmatism with which we rushed into national programs in the "War on Poverty" that were based on totally speculative, totally untried social science theories, and backed by not one shred of empirical evidence.

However, even if the theories on which a program is based are themselves sound, successful application still demands adaptation, cutting, fitting, trying, balancing. It always demands testing against reality before there is final total commitment. Above all, any new program, no matter how well conceived, will run into the unexpected, whether unexpected "problems" or unexpected "successes." At that point, people are needed who have been through a similar program on a smaller scale, who know whether the unexpected problem is relevant or not, or whether the unexpected success is a fluke or genuine achievement.

Surely one of the main reasons for the success of so many of the New Deal programs was that there had been "small scale" experiments in states and cities earlier—in Wisconsin, for instance, in New York State or in New York City, or in one of the reform administrations in Chicago. The outstanding administrators of the New Deal programs—Frances Perkins at Labor, Harold Ickes at Interior, or Arthur Altmeyer at Social Security—were all alumnae of such earlier small-scale experiments. Similarly, the truly unsuccessful New Deal programs, the WPA for instance, were, without exception, programs that had not first been developed in small-scale experimentation in state or local governments but were initiated as comprehensive, national panaceas.

(5) "Make sure that you cannot learn from experience" is the next prescription for non-performance in public administration. "Do not think through in advance what you expect; do not then feed back from results to expectations so as to find out not only what you can do well, but also to find out what your weaknesses, your limitations, and your blind spots are."

Every organization, like every individual, does certain things well. They are the things that "come easy to one's hand." Nevertheless, every organization, like every individual, is also prone to typical mistakes, has typical limitations, and has its own blind spots. Unless the organization shapes its own expectations to reflect the accuracy of results, it will not find out what it does well and, thus, not learn to apply its strengths. Moreover, it will not find out what it does poorly and will, thus, have no opportunity to improve or to compensate for its weaknesses or its blind spots. Typically, for instance, certain institutions expect results much too fast and throw in the towel much too soon. A good many of the "War on Poverty" agencies did just that. Also, there are many organizations which wait much too long before they face up to the fact that a program or a policy is unsuccessful—our Vietnam policies, both civilian and military, probably belong here. One can only learn by feedback, and we know that feedback from results always improves performance capacity and effectiveness. Without it, however, the weaknesses, the limitations, the blind spots increasingly dominate. Without learning from results through feedback, any organization, like any individual, must inevitably deteriorate in its capacity to perform. Yet, in most public service institutions such feedback functions are either non-existent or viewed with casual skepticism. If the results do not conform to expectations, they are all too frequently dismissed as irrelevant, as indications of the obtuseness of clients, as the reactionary obscurantism of the public, or, worst of all, as evidence of the need to "make another study." Most public service institutions, governmental ones as well as non-governmental ones, are budget-focused, but the budgets measure efforts rather than results. For performance, the budget needs to be paralleled with a statement of expected results—and with systematic feedback from results—on expenditures and on efforts. Otherwise, the agency will, almost immediately, channel more and more of its efforts toward non-results and will become the prisoner of its own limitations, its weaknesses, and its blind spots rather than the beneficiary of its own strengths.

(6) The last of the administrator's deadly sins is the most damning and the most common: the inability to abandon. It alone guarantees non-performance, and within a fairly short time.

Traditional political theory, the theory inherited from Aristotle, holds that the tasks of government are grounded in the nature of civil society and, thus, are immutable: defense, justice, law and order. However, very few of the tasks of modern public administration, whether governmental or non-governmental public service institutions, such as the hospital, the Red Cross, the university, or the Boy Scouts, are of that nature. Almost all of them are manmade rather than grounded in the basic essentials of society, and most of them are of very recent origin to boot. They all, therefore, share a common fate: they must become pointless at some juncture in time. They may become pointless because the need to which they address themselves no longer exists or is no longer urgent. They may become pointless because the old need appears in such a new guise as to make obsolete present design, shape, concerns and policies. The great environmental problem of 1910, for instance—and it was a very real danger—was the horrendous pollution by the horse, with its stench and its liquid and solid wastes, which threatened to bury the cities of that time. If we had been as environmentally conscious then as we are now, we would have saddled ourselves with agencies which only ten years later would have become totally pointless and yet, predictably, ten years later they would have redoubled their efforts, since they would have totally lost sight of their objectives. Moreover, a program may become pointless when it fails to produce results despite all efforts, as do our present American welfare programs. Finally—and most dangerous of all—a program becomes pointless when it achieves its objectives. That we have a "welfare mess" today is, in large measure, a result of our having maintained the welfare programs of the New Deal after they had achieved their objectives around 1940 or 1941. These programs were designed to tackle the problems caused by the temporary unemployment of experienced (and almost entirely white) male heads of families—no wonder that they then malperformed when applied to the totally different problems caused in large measure by the mass movement of black females into the cities 10 or 15 years later.

The basic assumption of public service institutions, governmental or non-governmental ones alike, is immortality. It is a foolish assumption. It dooms the organization and its programs to non-performance and non-results. The only rational assumption is that every public service program will sooner or later—and usually sooner—outlive its usefulness, at least insofar as its present form, its present objectives, and its present policies are concerned. A public service program that does not conduct itself in contemplation of its own mortality will very soon become incapable of performance. In its original guise it cannot produce results any longer; the objectives have either ceased to matter, have proven unobtainable, or have been attained. Indeed, the more successful a public service agency is, the sooner will it work itself out of the job; then it can only become an impediment to performance, if not an embarrassment.

The public service administrator who wants results and performance will, thus, have to build into his own organization an organized process for abandonment. He will have to learn to ask every few years: "If we did not do this already, would we now, knowing what we know now, go into this?" And if the answer is "no," he better not say "let's make another study" or "let's ask for a bigger budget." He better ask: "How can we get out of this?" or at least: "How can we stop pouring more effort, more resources, more people into this?"

II

Avoidance of these six "deadly sins" does not, perhaps, guarantee performance and results in the public service organization, but avoiding these six deadly sins is the prerequisite for performance and results. To be sure, there is nothing very recondite about these "do's and don'ts." They are simple, elementary, indeed, obvious. Yet, as everyone in public administration knows, most administrators commit most of these "sins" all the time and, indeed, all of them most of the time.

One reason is plain cowardice. It is "risky" to spell out attainable, concrete, measurable goals—or so the popular wisdom goes. It is also mundane, pedestrian and likely to "turn off" backers or donors. "The world's best medical care" is so much more "sexy" than "every emergency patient will be seen by a qualified triage nurse within three minutes." Furthermore, to set priorities seems even more dangerous—one risks the wrath of the people who do not really care for electric power or fertilizer, but want to protect the little snail darter or the spotted lousewort. Finally, of course, you do not "rank" in the bureaucracy unless you spend a billion dollars and employ an army of clerks—"fat is beautiful."

Perhaps so, but experience does not bear out the common wisdom. The public service administrators who face up to goal-setting, to ordered priorities, and to concentrating their resources (the public service administrators who are willing to ask: "What is the smallest number of people we need to attain our objectives?") may not always be popular, but they are respected, and they rarely have any trouble at all. They may not get as far in their political careers as the ones who put popularity above performance, but, in the end, they are the ones we remember.

III

But perhaps even more important than cowardice as an explanation for the tendency of so much of public administration today to commit itself to policies that can only result in non-performance is the lack of concern with performance in public administration theory.

For a century from the Civil War to 1960 or so, the performance of public service institutions and programs was taken for granted in the United States. It could be taken for granted because earlier administrators somehow knew not to commit the "deadly sins" I have outlined here. As a result, the discipline of public administration—a peculiarly American discipline, by the way—saw no reason to concern itself with performance. It was not a problem. It focused instead on the political process, on how programs come into being. *Who Gets What, When, How?*, the title of Harold Lasswell's 1936 classic on politics, neatly sums up one specific focus of American public administration, with its challenge to traditional political theory. The other focus was procedural: "The orderly conduct of the business of government" an earlier generation called it. It was a necessary concern in an America that had little or no administrative tradition and experience and was suddenly projected into very large public service programs, first in World War I, then in the New Deal, and finally in World War II. We needed work on all phases of what we now call "management": personnel, budgeting, organization, and so on. But these are inside concerns. Now we need hard, systematic work on making public service institutions perform.

As I noted, for a century, from the Civil War until 1960 or so, performance of public service institutions was taken for granted. For the last 20 years, however, malperformance is increasingly being taken for granted. Great programs are still being proposed, are still being debated, and, in some instances, are even still being enacted, but few people expect them to produce results. All we really expect now, whether from a new Department of Education in Washington or from a reorganization of the state government by a new governor who preaches that "small is beautiful," is more expenditure, a bigger budget, and a more ineffectual bureaucracy.

The malperformance of public service institutions may well be a symptom only. The cause may be far more basic: a crisis in the very foundations and assumptions on which rests that proudest achievement of the Modern Age, national administrative government.

But surely the malperformance of the public service institution is in itself a contributing factor to the sickness of government, and a pretty big one. Avoiding the "deadly sins" of public administration may only give symptomatic relief for whatever ails modern government, but at least we know how to do it.

BOX 3.1 Bureaupathologies

Gerald E. Caiden

Vices, maladies, and sicknesses of bureaucracy constitute bureaupathologies. They are not the individual failings of individuals who compose organizations but the systematic shortcomings of organizations that cause individuals within them to be guilty of malpractices. They cannot be corrected by separating the guilty from the organization for the malpractices will continue irrespective of the organization's composition. They are not random, isolated incidents either. Although they may not be regular, they are not so rare either. When they occur, little action is taken to prevent their recurrence or can be taken as in the case of anorexia (debilitation) and *gattopardismo* (superficiality) (Dunsire and Hood, 1989). They are not just physical either; organizations also suffer definite mental illnesses or neuroses too—paranoid, compulsive, dramatic, depressive, and schizoid (deVries and Miller, 1985).

Altogether, some 175 or so common bureaupathologies are listed in alphabetical order for convenience (see Table).

Common Bureaupathologies

Abuse of authority/ power/position	Fear of change, innovation, risk	Lack of creativity/ experimentation	Reluctance to delegate
Account padding	Finagling	Lack of credibility	Reluctance to take decisions
Alienation	Footdragging	Lack of imagination	Reluctance to take responsibility
Anorexia	Framing	Lack of initiative	Remoteness
Arbitrariness	Fraud	Lack of performance indicators	Rigidity/brittleness
Arrogance	Fudging/fuzzing (issues)	Lack of vision	Rip-offs
Bias	Gamesmanship	Lawlessness	Ritualism
Blurring issues	Gattopardismo (superficiality)	Laxity	Rudeness
Boondoggles	Ghost employees	Leadership vacuums	Sabotage
Bribery	Gobbledygook/jargon	Malfeasance	Scams
Bureaucratese (unintelligibility)	Highhandedness	Malice	Secercy
Busywork	Ignorance	Malignity	Self-perpetuation
Carelessness	Illegality	Meaningless/make work	Self-serving
Chiseling	Impervious to criticism/ suggestion	Mediocrity	Slick bookkeeping
Coercion	Improper motivation	Mellownization	Sloppiness
Complacency	Inability to learn	Mindless job performance	Social astigmatism (failure to see problems)
Compulsiveness	Inaccessibility	Miscommunication	Soul-destroying work
Conflicts of interest/ objectives	Inaction	Miconduct	Spendthrift

(continues)

BOX 3.1 (continued)

Common Bureaupathologies (continued)

Confusion
Conspiracy
Corruption
Counter-productiveness
Cowardice
Criminality
Deadwood
Deceit and deception
Dedication to status quo
Defective goods
Delay
Deterioration
Discourtesy
Discrimination
Diseconomies of size
Displacement of goals/objectives
Dogmatism
Dramaturgy
Empire-building
Excessive social costs/complexity
Exploitation
Extortion
Extravagance
Failure to acknowledge/act/answer/respond
Favoritism

Inadequate rewards and incentives
Inadequate working conditions
Inappropriateness
Incompatible tasks
Incompetence
Inconvieience
Indecision (decidophobia)
Indifference
Indiscipline
Ineffectiveness
Ineptitude
Inertia
Inferior quality
Inflexibility
Inhumanity
Injustice
Insensitivity
Insolence
Intimidation
Iregularity
Irrelevance
Irresolution
Irresponsiblity
Kleptocracy
Lack of commitment
Lack of coordination

Misfeasance
Misinformation
Misplaced zeal
Negativism
Negligence/neglect
Nepotism
Neuroticism
Nonaccountability
Noncommunication
Nonfeasance
Nonproductivity
Obscurity
Obstruction
Officiousness
Oppression
Overkill
Oversight
Overspread
Overstaffing
Paperasserie
Paranoia
Patronage
Payoffs and kickbacks
Perversity
Phony contracts
Pointless activity
Procrastination
Punitive supervision
Red-tape

Spoils
Stagnation
Stalling
Stonewalling
Suboptimization
Sycophancy
Tail-chasing
Tampering
Territorial imperative
Theft
Tokenism
Tunnel vision
Unclear objectives
Unfairness
Unnecessary work
Unprofessional conduct
Unreasonableness
Unsafe conditions
Unsuitable premises and equipment
Usurpatory
Vanity
Vested interest
Vindictiveness
Waste
Whim
Xenophobia

(Source: Gerald E. Caiden, "Bureaupathologies," in: "What Really is Public Maladministration?," *Public Administration Review* 51 (November/December, 1991): 486–493.)

4

Humanizing Public Administration

C. Spencer Platt

In these times of transition toward consolidating the peace at home and abroad, public administrators are more than ever seeking ways to make the efforts of their organizations entirely productive. Much depends on the effectiveness with which the activity of people can be organized and managed for public purposes. Two aspects may be suggested: the organization of activity within public agencies, and the organization of relationships between the people comprising the agency and the public whom they serve. This discussion concerns internal agency organization and management.

To an unspecialized observer of systematized public agency management, a surprising amount of technical specialism has developed in such fields as position classification, salary administration, placement, organization structure, procedure analysis, and the like. A principal question is why in their efforts to achieve satisfactory working arrangements those responsible for the present condition of the "science, processes, and art of public administration" have paid so little attention to the systematic development of methods and skills of human relations. Public agencies are composed of people no less than business and industrial organizations, yet industry has taken the lead in finding ways to release and mobilize human energies in large organizations in order to achieve greater productivity and greater satisfaction for organization members. Can managers of government agencies meet this challenge of industrial management in developing better ways to make relationships among people on the job more productive?

"Humanizing Public Administration," *Public Administration Review* 7 (Summer, 1947): 193–199.

Many current discussions of industrial and labor relations reflect the advances made in the past few years in the understanding of relationships among people in many different circumstances, particularly among people at work.[1] Speculation as to why men work, what they want to get out of their daily work life, raises such questions as: What are the desires of the manager and the worker? Do they want merely the periodic pay envelope or check? Or is there something more that keeps groups of people functioning successfully together? Is there something more useful than the state of exhilaration—sometimes mistaken for morale—that follows "pep talk" methods? Why do some organization units work effectively and cooperatively over sustained periods, while others fall apart? Progressing from early pure speculation, consideration of these motivations and interrelationships has become systematic and experimental until today some reliable and useful understandings are being developed about the relationships among people at work.

Why Have Managers Become Interested?

Managers have become interested in relationships among people, and their needs, desires, and reactions, because they have seen that mechanical, technological, and procedural improvements in ways of doing business have often failed to produce desired results. The reasons have often been such matters as inability of people to function effectively as team members, failure of people to achieve adequate understanding among themselves, and failure of people to find personal satisfaction in their jobs. Managers have also become interested because these human problems have been highlighted by union-management negotiations. Seeking the real causes underlying grievances of various sorts, shop stewards and managers have found that complaints about such matters as pay rates, cafeteria facilities, lighting, noise, and fatiguing working conditions often must be regarded as overt symptoms only. Real causes are to be found in the reasons why a worker or a group of workers begin to feel uncertain, frustrated, insecure in their jobs; why they think management doesn't understand their problems.

To manage is to mobilize resources and utilize them for accomplishing a purpose. The human resources of an organization are potentially of great value. This potential can be realized when the energies, initiative, ideas, and vigilance of the organization members are fully released and continuously and spontaneously focused on accomplishing the organization's purpose. To mobilize and utilize resources the manager must get other people—subordinates, associates, even superiors—to take effective action. All managers have potential human relations problems. Many managers have experienced increased operating effectiveness when friction among people is prevented, or, failing prevention, eliminated.

Both public and private managers are concerned with the unresponsiveness of large aggregations of people.[2] Big organizations tend to become rigid and inflexible. Standard rules and procedures seem essential to assure orderly functioning, yet they often fail to meet the requirements of local differences. And local discretion can be entrusted only to understanding and "sensible" people, that is, people who will find good ways to adhere closely to general policy in meeting local requirements. Coordination of effort often fails between people who rarely, perhaps never, see each other, and maladjustments persist unless differing attitudes can be reconciled. It is difficult for a member of a large organization to feel confidence in an over-all purpose he does not really understand and to which his own work seems unrelated. Nor can he feel secure in leaders he rarely sees and whose influence comes to him diluted through many levels of hierarchy. Feeling little sense of accomplishment and success, he has no surge of self-confidence to carry him along. Thus it is easy for morale to be low in bureaucracies, public or private.

Yet large organizations can be made responsive. Members can achieve flexibility, coordinated effort, and high morale. Ways can be found to get members to assume responsibility, exercise initiative, and participate in formulating plans affecting their own future action. The rigidities of bigness can be relaxed to meet local conditions through people with proper attitudes and understandings.

How to achieve desired goals through the actions of other people is a main concern of both industrial and public managers. They are interested in better human relations management because they have seen that it can contribute to organization effectiveness.

Need for a Method and "Skill" of Human Relations

The "welfare" approach to good human relations is often excellent and fills a real need, but its limitations have been demonstrated. No quantity of off-the-job contacts among people—picnics, dances, athletics, and the like—can take the place of rewarding on-the-job contacts. Nor can they overcome the effects of unrewarding on-the-job contacts.

Habitual, day-by-day effectiveness in managing human relationships presupposes the development of some useful methods for sizing up a given group of people and for working out solutions to emerging problems. With some systematization, successful methods can be developed and passed on from one manager to another. Managers can approach operating problems with greater assurance that they can solve their human relations aspects. Personalities, like fingerprints. do not duplicate one another. But social researchers encourage us to believe there are general principles about human interaction patterns; indeed, very important ones have already been well tested.

The really penetrating insights brought to bear by managers on human relations problems rarely result from supervisory training in generalizations. Sometimes they are the result of astonishing intuitions. More often, they are the result of painstaking effort to understand why particular groups react as they do under given conditions. Ways need to be found for people of average competence to be trained in understanding human relations and given experience suitable for developing them as managers of human activity. Methods must be systematized and skills developed in which managers can become proficient. The results of the social research and developmental work thus far conducted in industry give promise that this is no idle hope, but is well started on the way to becoming a reality.

Some Well-Known Experiments

There have been many successful experiments in the development of better human relations in industry, and to single out a few is to ignore others less well known but nevertheless of great value. Those selected have been described in publications that are generally available.

The pioneer effort is well known (though not always understood)—the Western Electric Hawthorne Plant researches, a collaborative effort by that company and the Harvard Business School Industrial Research Staff, which were completed in the late thirties.[3] Here managers obtained results through systematic experimentation. Among other things, these experiments demonstrated that workers respond productively when they feel that management considers their welfare to be important. Although they did not show that financial rewards are unimportant, they did indicate that financial rewards must be supplemented. For the first time there was analyzed the spontaneous system of personal relationships which creates an informal unplanned organization, existing side by side with the formal organization structure planned by managers. These informal personal relationships in an organization can make or break the organization, depending on how well they are understood by management and how successfully management decisions take them into account. Here was evidence that human relationships are inevitable and can not be "gotten rid of." They are just as real a factor in operations as are machines and finances. The informal social organization of the factory should be understood, not fought.

Also in the late thirties, another important, though perhaps less well known research was carried on in another manufacturing concern, in collaboration with the Industrial Relations Section of the Massachusetts Institute of Technology.[4] An analysis was made of the frequency of contacts among the organization members. Study of the interactions taking place among the various members of the organization showed that breakdown in morale could be explained in terms of some crucial changes in interpersonal relationships which were not planned in the formal organization. When some unrecognized and undesirable relationships among the organization members were brought to light it was then possible to rearrange the formal relationships more realistically. In this experiment the interaction patterns previously studied mainly in the clinic were studied in the factory and used successfully to guide managerial action.

In more recent years, collaboration between the Committee on Human Relations in Industry of the University of Chicago and a number of neighboring business and industrial concerns has resulted in significant research findings relating to more effective management of human relations.[5] This research, too, has highlighted the importance of, and given new meaning to teamwork, communication, personal satisfaction, and the usefulness of information concerning the direction, frequency, etc., of the interactions among selected individuals and groups within the industrial organization.

More difficult to report are the innumerable individual company experiments and researches which seem to be going on all over the country conducted by factory human relations staffs, variously designated as industrial relations, personnel management, or other similar units. For example, the value of a democratic, participative form of management was demonstrated in a textile concern.[6]

An experience in a related field, having value to practical administrators, was the community management program of the U. S. War Relocation Authority. The results of the work done in the Poston, Arizona, Relocation Center have been systematically appraised both for their usefulness to the Relocation Center and in the light of requirements for administering occupied territory.[7] This appraisal of the actions of individuals and organizations under stress and the accompanying recommendations have relevance and ready adaptability to the needs of many public agency managers.

Ascertaining Local Human Relations Conditions

Successful efforts to improve the management of human activity and relationships have achieved effectiveness in large measure because they have emphasized that the manager must act according to the specific human facts of the local situation. This contrasts with some well-intentioned but often ineffective attempts to follow generalizations about good human relations management. To be sure, there are some tested generalizations, but these only guide the manager as he grapples with the particular conditions of his organization. Conflicts, frictions, stresses, tensions, do not arise in general; they develop out of concrete human conditions and must be dealt with in terms of those conditions. In seeking to improve the human relationships of his organization, the first major problem of the manager is to know what the present relationships are and what they mean.

How can the manager know and understand the facts about the concrete human relations situation in his own organization? How can he foresee emerging conflicts and remove the causes? How can he know the causes of present conflicts and dissatisfactions, in order to resolve them? Many approaches to understanding human relations at work have been worked out. A fourfold classification may be helpful at this point: (1) individual, (2) environmental, (3) cooperative, and (4) situational. Early in its development, personnel work concentrated exclusively on individual and environmental factors. Increasingly in the past few years, the cooperative and situational factors have been recognized.

Individual. Early efforts to increase the effectiveness of organized human activity centered on the individual worker—his abilities, wants, and reactions. Tests of skills and abilities, analyses of job requirements, transferability of skills, performance measures and analysis, attitude measures, fatigue factors—these have typified the individual approach. The conditions disclosed here led to such correctional measures as employee counseling, individual placement, skill training for employees, incentive pay plans, and supervisory training emphasizing "treating employees as individuals." The industrial psychologist, the industrial psychiatrist, and the industrial engineer have borne the main burden of the work done under this approach. It is an important and useful approach, but it needs to be supplemented.

Environmental. Environmental factors affecting people have also engaged the attention of those concerned with understanding the human situation. Lighting, posture chairs, modern washroom facilities, noise reduction, cafeteria and recreation facilities, accident prevention—these have all come in for their share of attention, with consequent improvement in many cases of work performance and satisfaction. The industrial psychologist, the industrial engineer, and the personnel worker have been mainly responsible for the advances made in the environmental field.

Cooperative. Beginning perhaps with the publication of the results of the Western Electric Hawthorne Plant experiments, the nature of interpersonal and group relationships have been regarded as important. More recently, numerous training efforts, the analysis of military morale, and the analysis of war production factory work teams, for example, have confirmed the Hawthorne findings and have revealed some specific factors building or breaking teamwork and cooperation. Emphasis is placed on factors influencing the cooperation of team members, among the most important of which is the group leadership which creates teamwork. Appraisal of interpersonal relationships in the work group is basic to this approach, which also includes understanding various types of leadership and leadership training methods. Current emphasis seems to be placed chiefly on democratic participative leadership methods. The social psychologist and the sociologist have been mainly responsible for the advances made in developing this cooperative approach to understanding problems of managing human activity.

Situational. Attempts to appraise and improve the management of human factors in operations along the three basic lines above noted are combined by those who find it essential to regard operations as a whole. This "total" approach can be called "situational." The situational view is dynamic and regards all factors as important, whether individual, environmental, or cooperative. It admits to consideration, in understanding the functioning of a work group, of any factor which may influence interpersonal relations. It is concerned with symptoms and basic causes of ineffective operations. It regards the work organization as a social system, with beliefs, symbols, habits, standards, rewards, punishments, etc. This view considers that such matters as organizational arrangements, procedures and methods, machine use, and layout all have important influence on human activity, along with such interpersonal matters as frequency and types of interactions among people. Those holding this view seek improvement of specific situations. The sociologist and the anthropologist have contributed greatly to the methodology of situational analysis. Managers and management analysts have helped to adapt these methods to workaday situations.

These four basic approaches have been used by managers and management advisers singly or in some combination to understand and improve the human relations conditions in their organizations. The Hawthorne experiments, for example, seem to have used all these approaches at one stage or another. It is perhaps too soon to single out some one viewpoint or system of appraisal as the "best." The real task is to develop fact-finding methods suitable to a variety of conditions and in any given situation to use the one best suited.

Illustrative Guides to Managing Human Activity

In organizing human activity, the purpose is to mobilize the resources of energy, initiative, and ideas lying latent within the people who compose the organization and to focus them on its problems and objectives. Whether the organization is successful depends in large measure on whether these potential human resources are made effective. Making human resources effective means getting people to act productively.

In the industrial and public management field we have many familiar precepts: responsibilities should be clear, reasons for changes should be thoroughly explained, misunderstandings should be cleared up promptly, jurisdictional disputes should be avoided and if they arise should be promptly settled, no favoritism should be shown, no person should be subject to the authority of more than one individual. There are many more, but these will illustrate. They are good general precepts. The manager must know, however, when and where responsibilities seem obscure to affected organization members. He may already have issued some piece of writing which he believes makes responsibilities clear cut in general. To know exactly where in his organization, as between just what two or more organization members, responsibilities are not clear, and to know how to proceed with clarifying action—these are facts of interpersonal relationships. Clarifying means securing better understanding between people. Coordination is not merely a matter of good planned structural relationships; it is chiefly the reality of effective day-to-day human activity.

What should managers do, once they understand the present relationships among the various members of the organization, to make sure that the energies of the members are expended productively both for the organization and for themselves? Of course, each organization, under the manager's leadership, must work out for itself the exact answers. That is administration, or at least a very large part of it. Yet there are some guides which have been experimentally evolved, and more are emerging as the development of human relations methodology goes on. The work is gaining new impetus as many social researchers turn back to problems of industrial human relations and away from such wartime matters as military morale, "psychological warfare," evaluation of enemy morale, and the post-hostilities administration of foreign peoples.

A few illustrative guides may be mentioned. New guides and new variations of old guides are being developed constantly. Guides toward solutions are not in themselves solutions for specific problems. Considered by themselves they are potentially useful and important theory. Utilized by managers to the extent and in the particular way required by the facts of a given situation, they can become significant for managerial action.

One set of guides is to be found in the beliefs and symbols by which most of our actions are strongly conditioned, perhaps even more than by logical reasoning. Whatever the manager himself may believe about his organization, he must remember that people generally act in accordance with their own understanding about the situations that affect them. They tend to understand in terms of beliefs and symbols, and their emotions and intuitions are at least as likely to guide them as logic and reason. Most people are strongly influenced in their relations with other people, in terms, for example, of relative status. People coming from different sorts of experience tend to have different beliefs and hence different understanding of the same situation. People in different positions in an organization tend to view the same situation differently. Managers who desire to secure the coordinated action of other people will be more successful if they first secure an understanding of how the other members of the organization view the current situation.

Another illustrative underlying concept is that people's relationships with each other in operating organizations are important, and when satisfactory tend to persist. If they are unsatisfactory, people tend to try to change them, seeking more satisfactory relationships. People tend to resist changes which appear to threaten the continuation of these satisfactory relationships. Most organizations must proceed through continuous change toward their objectives, else external influences tend to terminate the organization. Managers desiring to pilot their organizations through change toward objectives must understand how the internal "equilibrium" of interpersonal relationships in their organizations will be affected by proposed procedural, technological, or organizational change, and must work out some sort of compensations in order to maintain a "working balance" of satisfactory, stable, and efficient personal relationships.

Teamwork is important, too. People working together seem inevitably to form groups and build up feelings of group solidarity. It is not enough to treat people as individuals; they should also be treated as group members. The manager should understand that he is himself a group member, that his own behavior is a major factor in achieving teamwork. Realizing that groups tend to create informal relationships or structure, he can in his leadership decisions in the organization take these informal relationships into account, if he knows what they are, in such ways as to build effective team cooperation. "Real," as contrasted with "designated," leaders tend to emerge from work groups, and if the manager can get them to work toward the organization objectives, their spontaneous leadership role can be constructive.

Still another illustrative human relations guide relates to communication—not merely the issuance of memoranda by managers and their receipt by operating subordinates, but rather the achievement of effective two-way understanding. As has already been mentioned, this means chiefly understanding by organization members of the organization purposes as they are modified from day to day, and understanding by managers of the desires, complaints, and suggestions of the organization members. Two-way communication of this kind is of great value; it is most effective when it becomes habitual. Then all persons concerned tend toward free discussion of plans for the future, their problems, their uncertainties, and ideas for more effective operation. To achieve such a degree of free flow of communication, the manager must demonstrate not only that he knows it is necessary to handle complaints, to avoid favoritism, to keep confidences, to accept good suggestions, and to modify plans where necessary, but also that he can do these things well.

Another illustrative guide relates to participation by people in formulating policy that affects their own future actions. Even though it is often time

BOX 4.1 The Right Attitude

David S. Brown

For organizations, whether they be private companies, government agencies, factories, divisions, or groups, to do better, those in managerial positions must as individuals *want* to do better.

Managers—and, indeed, professional people at whatever level—must want to do more than to have mastered the skills their jobs require. They must want to do more than merely to satisfy the system, to satisfice. They must want to do more and better than their predecessors have done, and better than they themselves have previously done. *And they must want also to continue to improve.* Such "wants" must become needs.

There is a Spanish word which perhaps conveys this idea more effectively than any equivalent English word. It is *las ganas*—usually used in its plural form—and it means the urge to succeed, the "desire." It suggests determination, discipline, hard work. It is, in short, a quest for excellence. Managers, if they are to fulfill properly their responsibilities, must feel *las ganas.*

Whether one thinks of this as productivity improvement, as organizational development, as self-development, or by some other name, the effect is very much the same. The concern is with the improvement of performance, individual and group. This is the *managerial ethic* our times require.

(Source: David S. Brown. "The Right Attitude," in: The Managerial Ethics and Productivity Improvement," *Public Productivity Review* (September 1983): 223–250.)

consuming and sometimes seems impossible, it has been found that people usually work best when the future seems reasonably free from what might seem to them to be capricious change.

Managerial Sponsorship of Developmental Work

If managers of public agencies wish to meet this challenge of human relations management they can score soon by giving their attention to the experimental development of the methods and skills they require. There are practically no "ivory tower" laboratories where experimentation can be conducted. The spontaneous on-the-job relationships among the people who make up operating organizations must be the basis for this work. The researcher can work only where the manager will cooperate. The manager-researcher team is essential. The cost of such experiments in any single organization is small, and since the results can often be put to immediate practical use, the experiments can pay their own way. Industrial managers are already reaping the rewards of such cooperation.

A paramount need is for a few public agency managers to take the lead by collaborating in the conduct of "demonstration" projects. Through such projects these managers can gain benefits for their own agencies and show other managers how better human relations management can be attained. Better training methods can be developed for managers, operating deputies, administrative assistants, and other staff assistants. Provisions can be developed whereby continuous attention is given to creating better ways to assure teamwork, two-way communication, participation, etc. Experimental demonstrations are also helpful because they settle questions about utility.

Summary

1. Better management of human relations leads to greater organizational productivity and to greater satisfaction to organization members.
2. Much of the work on developing methods and skills for managing human relations is being done in private industry.
3. Public agency managers, too, can make their agencies more effective through the use of such methods and skills.
4. The methods and skills needed are simple tools of analysis and appraisal, plus reliable guides to effective action; they must be teachable to managers and their assistants of average competence.
5. Experimentation and demonstration are necessary; they must take place in actual work places, not in the laboratory. This requires collaboration between manager and human relations researcher.

Today's pressing public problems are in large measure concerned with better ways of organizing and managing human activity. Some contributions of first-rank significance are being made toward humanizing management. These methods and guides are available to public administrators who will learn how to apply them.

Notes

1. One meaningful popular discussion is a series of articles by Peter F. Drucker, "The Way to Industrial Peace." *Harper's Magazine,* November and December, 1946, and January, 1947. Schuyler Dean Hoslett, ed., *Human Factors in Management* (Park College Press, 1946), 322 pp., is a useful collection of recent articles of a less popular nature.

2. Marshall E. Dimock and Howard K. Hyde, *Bureaucracy and Trusteeship in Large Corporations,* TNEC Monograph No. 11 (Government Printing Office, 1940), 144 pp.

3. Several publications describe the Hawthorne researches. Some of the better known are: Elton Mayo, *The Human Problems of an Industrial Civilization* (Graduate School of Business Administration, Harvard University, 1933), 194 pp.; F. J. Roethlisberger and William J. Dickson, *Management and the Worker* (Harvard University Press, 1939), 615 pp.; T. N. Whitehead, *The Industrial Worker; A Statistical Study of Human Relations in a Group of Manual Workers* (Harvard University Press, 1938), 2 vols.

4. C. M. Arensberg and Douglas McGregor, "Determination of Morale in an Industrial Company," 1 *Applied Anthropology* 12–14 (1942).

5. The first in a series of publications is William F. Whyte, ed., *Industry and Society* (McGraw-Hill Book Co., 1946), 211 pp. Another to be published shortly is William F. Whyte, *Human Problems in the Restaurant Industry*. See also Burleigh B. Gardner and William Foote Whyte, "The Man in the Middle: Position and Problems of the Foreman," 4 *Applied Anthropology* 1–28 (1945); and Andrew H. Whiteford, William Foote Whyte, and Burleigh B. Gardner, "From Conflict to Cooperation," 5 *Applied Anthropology* 1–31 (1946).

6. John R. P. French. Jr., Arthur Kornhouser, and Alfred Marrow, "Conflict and Cooperation," 2 *Journal of Social Issues* 29–34 (1946).

7. Alexander H. Leighton. *The Governing of Men* (Princeton University Press, 1945), 404 pp.

5

Initiating Change that Perseveres

Chris Argyris

Types of Human Reasoning

Reasoning is the process that human beings use to move from what they know to what they do; that is, from thought to action. There are two primary types of reasoning: defensive and productive. Defensive reasoning is characterized by the following patterns:

- The premises that people develop for their causal explanations are tacit; they are not made explicit.
- The inference processes by which people move from premise to conclusion are also tacit.
- The data they use to generate their premises and conclusions are "soft"; that is, the data are not subjected to verification.
- The logic used to test conclusions is the same as that used to produce them.

Consequently, defensive reasoning is self-serving, anti-learning, and overprotective. It is used to maintain and reward existing patterns of behavior, or Model I theories-in-use[1] and organizational defensive routines.[2]

In contrast, productive reasoning is characterized by the following assumptions:

- Reasoning, or making inferences, is a key activity in designing and implementing action.

"Initiating Change that Perseveres," *Journal of Public Administration Research & Theory* 4 (July 1994): 343–355.

- Learning to make inferences explicit and to test their validity in practice is important to effective action.
- Designing activity to help self and others understand what is going on around them is central to initiating and sustaining action or change.

Productive reasoning is especially difficult for people in dynamic environments because it requires them to reexamine their basic assumptions and to test their judgments against changing conditions. It requires time, attention, and focus, scarce commodities in contemporary organizations where people operate under the stress of time constraints and multiple and conflicting demands on limited resources.

Concepts of causality underlie the basic processes of human reasoning and reflect the degree of certainty we hold that our actions will produce the intended consequences. There are two types of causal reasoning. Deterministic causality (if A, then B) reflects an ordered, static conception of the social world. We assume that if we take a given action, a known consequence will follow. Probabilistic causality (if A, then B, with an estimated probability of occurrence) reflects a more dynamic, uncertain conception of the world of action. That is, we calculate the probability that result B will occur if we take action A. We acknowledge the likelihood that B may not occur but take action A anyway, anticipating that action A may influence the occurrence of desired result B. In practice, people use both types of reasoning to design their worlds and seek to define the "efficient cause" for action.

In contrast to most current policy research and analysis, the process of reasoning from thought to action at the individual and organizational system levels needs to focus on action. If we are concerned with producing the results that we propose in our policy statements, we need to change our mode of reasoning. Since the world of action is dynamic and uncertain, probabilistic reasoning is more realistic and more accurate in assessing the likelihood of accomplishing our intended results. Yet, people feel more comfortable with the false certainty that is generated by deterministic reasoning, and they resist recognition of evidence that disconfirms this espoused theory (Argryis 1990 and 1993).

The discrepancy between the two types of causality leads to error in reasoning and consequently inhibits learning in organizational practice.

A Theory of Error

Discovering error constitutes the first step toward learning. An error is a mismatch between intentions and actual consequences. Learning occurs when you detect and correct errors in such a way that the correction perseveres.

Errors are produced by inconsistencies in governing values that underlie the strategies of action that human beings use to actualize their values. The key to understanding human action is through these designs or theories of action. If humans repeatedly act differently from their stated goals, it is important to reexamine the underlying values for a possible mismatch or error.

There are at least two ways to correct error (Argyris and Schon 1974 and 1978). The first way is to change the behavior (for example, reduce the back biting and bad mouthing among participants in an organization). This is single-loop learning. The second way is to change the governing values that lead to counterproductive behavior. This is double-loop learning.

Underlying the discovery of error is a set of assumptions about human behavior. These assumptions are:

- All human behavior is designed.
- Unawareness is behavior.
- Unawareness is designed, and humans keep themselves unaware of any mismatch between intentions and outcome.

If behavior is designed, what creates impairment? Impairment is faulty reasoning. Further, it is learned behavior. It is skilled unawareness. Skilled behavior becomes tacit; you produce it without becoming aware of it. Skilled behavior has three characteristics: it works, it suppresses negative feelings, and it seeks control.

We recognize social impairment as learned behavior when we observe people committing the same errors at different times and places and in different cultures. These errors persist even as people condemn them. Briefly, seven basic errors occur worldwide:[3]

- We act to create understanding and effectiveness, yet we create misunderstanding and ineffectiveness.
- People blame others or the system for poor decisions.
- The tried and proven way of doing things dominates organizational life, resulting in organizational inertia.
- Upward communication for difficult issues is often lacking.
- Games of deception such as budgetary politics and maneuvering are considered necessary evils.
- People do not behave reasonably even when it is in their interest, and usually the interest is defined by the person who says others are not behaving rationally.
- The myth of management team—most come apart, especially when they are experiencing problems that are embarrassing or threatening—for example, double-loop problems.

Each error represents a mismatch between what people publicly state as their intentions and what they actually are able to produce. Discovery of errors or mismatches between stated intentions and actions creates the basis for learning, which uses error as a point of departure from the status quo.

A Theory of Learning

Learning occurs when people produce what they say they know. This observation links learning to action in substantive ways. It also links learning inextricably to discovering the discrepancies between what they say and what they do. Two types of theories of action are observed in human behavior (Argyris and Schon 1974 and 1978). The first is what people say, or their espoused theory; the second is what people actually do, or their theory-in-use. In practice, there is often a discrepancy between the two, and people are unaware of this discrepancy. Surprisingly, inconsistency and unawareness are greatest when issues are potentially or actually embarrassing or threatening.

Although espoused theories vary widely, there is almost no variance in the theory-in-use. That is, the behavior of human beings varies widely, but not the theory they use to design and implement the behavior. For example, facesaving—the behavior varies widely, but the proposition that is followed to produce it appears the same. When encountering embarrassment or threat, bypass them and cover up the bypass. This observation has an important implication. If the theories-in-use are few in number, then understanding and facilitating learning should be more doable than one might have supposed.

These theories of action extend from individual behavior to organizational contexts. If most individuals seek unilateral control to protect their positions or power,[4] they create organizational behavioral worlds that are consistent with and protect the use of these same controlling patterns of thought and action. Consequently, they create organizational systems that limit rather than facilitate learning.

Organizational defensive routines are examples of limited learning systems. That is, an organizational defensive routine is any action, policy, or practice that prevents organizational members from experiencing embarrassment or threat. At the same time, it prevents members from discovering the causes of the embarrassment or threat, so that they could do something to change it. Organizational defensive routines are caused by a circular, self-reinforcing process that is composed of controlling theories-in-use and the resulting protective practices that reinforce the theories-in-use. They are individual *and* organizational. There is a very tight interlock between individual and organizational patterns of action, and there is little possibility of changing one without changing the other. Attempts to do so will likely lead to failure or, at best, temporary success.

These tightly linked routines of individual and organizational behavior pose demanding challenges for productive reasoning and learning. The senses of competence, self-confidence, and self-esteem of human beings are highly dependent upon their Model I theories-in-use and their protective organizational defensive routines. Consequently, individuals become skillfully incompetent. This message is likely to activate defensive routines, inhibiting the discovery of new sources of competence and skill. Defensive routines lock out the very information needed to overcome the sense of inadequacy that leads organizational members to develop such protective behavior in the first place.

In practice, theories-in-use are so internalized that they become tacit. Skilled behavior has three characteristics: it works, it appears effortless, and it is produced automatically. Individuals acting on the basis of skill do so without thinking. More confusing, human beings define social virtues such as caring, support, and integrity to be consistent with Model I. They are not likely to see the counterproductive features of these virtues.

If defensive routines limit learning and action, what kinds of organizational action foster learning? Organizations that can produce actionable knowledge create a supportive context for learning and improving performance. Actionable knowledge is information that actors can use to communicate the meanings that they intend. That is, knowledge that we produce has to be able to specify how to produce meanings but leave the actors free to select the specific words.

When controlling governing values are embedded in organizations, they constitute a near socially engineered impairment to learning. This impairment takes the form of organizational defensive routines that make the problem undiscussable and therefore perpetuate it. Organizational defensive routines are antilearning and overprotective, generating tacit, automatic behavior.

Power is critical to the functioning of organizational defensive routines, because organizational participants develop routines to legitimize their own protectedness and to increase their power. Consequently, those in power will tend to develop organizational defensive routines to legitimize and protect their own power. Ironically, in doing so they limit their learning capacity and, in a rapidly changing environment, are likely to undermine, through poor performance, the very power they are seeking to protect. The cases of David Stockman's downfall at OMB and NASA's Challenger accident illustrate vividly the adverse consequences of defensive routines.

Stimulating Learning for Action

If our preceding analysis is accurate, defensive reasoning persists because people use defensive reasoning to protect their existing positions. Consequently, they limit their opportunities for learning in order to reinforce their existing beliefs, which are familiar and allow some measure of certainty, even if false.

Initiating change requires breaking the self-sealing cycle of defensive beliefs and protective behavior. Two steps are critical to change. The first is to make previously undiscussable problems discussable. Learning behaviors, in contrast to controlling behaviors, are crafted in ways that encourage inquiry and testing.

Defensive, antilearning consequences are minimized as people genuinely discover that others also recognize the problem and are willing to offer suggestions for its resolution. The second, and very important, step is that embarrassment and threat are not bypassed. Rather, they are engaged and serve as the basis for productive reasoning and double-loop learning.

In this critical task of interrupting the closed cycle of defensive reasoning and behavior that limits learning, there are two potential assets available to managers or policy makers who seek change. The first is a genuine sense of stewardship that is observed repeatedly in human behavior. If you can engage people in the larger task of improving performance in their organization or community, most will respond favorably.[5]

Second, the management information system revolution has provided us with technology that allows the design of information practices to support individual and organizational learning. With the ready availability of computerized information programs and interactive telecommunications, tasks involved in organizational learning—monitoring individual and organizational performance, storing information in easily accessible form, retrieving relevant information, and measuring actual performance over time—are accomplished with relative ease and in a timely manner. Further, individuals can themselves read the record and discover discrepancies between stated goal and actual performance in a non-threatening setting. When such information is made available to the organization so that all members have access to the same information, the cloak of secrecy and control is lessened. By linking more accurate, more comprehensive, and more timely information to the observed sense of stewardship among organizational participants, practicing managers and policy makers can increase substantially the likelihood of learning in their respective organizations. As organizations begin to change their practices, individuals within them will feel less threatened and more willing to correct their mismatches between intent and action as part of an ongoing developmental process.

In practice, people will accept truth if it does not threaten the security of their position. When truth is threatening, they will massage it, cover it up, distort it; they will do anything except focus on truth. Consequently, they resort to even more defensive routines to protect their positions and cover up their inadequacies.

In the exquisite irony of defensive routines, people use information technology to play "gotcha" or to punish those who do reveal discrepancies between stated goals and actual performance, instead of using the technology to focus on learning. A major challenge for current organizational development and growth is to incorporate information technology into the developmental plans and daily practice of organizations in ways that genuinely facilitate productive learning.

Through my years of working with practicing organizations to assist them in the improvement of their performance, I have developed a standard exercise for the organizational participants. It is a simple exercise that can be done with any organization, but it leads the participants in a collective effort to discover and discuss a major problem confronting the organization.

First, we identify an actual problem that currently is troubling the organization. Second, I ask them, "How would you begin to solve this problem?" Not how would you solve this problem, but how would you begin?

Third, I ask them to take a sheet of paper, split the page, and, on the right hand side, write the actual conversation they would have with the person(s) with whom they are seeking a solution. On the left hand side, I have them write what they thought or felt during this conversation.

The exercise will yield a collage of cases from each participant. I collect the cases, maintain their anonymity, copy them, and give each participant a set of cases. Then they compare their left hand columns. The results are very similar; all the participants know what the problem is. By and large, people produced dysfunctional, counterproductive consequences to the very problems they spoke about.

From years of experience working with people in organizations, I conclude that people do not have strong egos. Rather, they are impaired in their judgments and actions. They are taught by society to cover up problems, and they are encouraged to do so by every control mechanism we know, beginning with accounting and ending with religion.

People do see that they are not very effective and that problems are discussable. But they do not believe that others will discuss these problems, therefore they do not. The process becomes self-sealing, and the opportunity for learning is lost. If, however, one can surface the problem for discussion, as through the simple exercise just described, people begin to learn that they all have the same impairment and can move toward learning.

Initiating Change in Performance

In summary, there are two major aspects involved in the process of initiating change. First, there is a set of interrelated action strategies that is useful in beginning change in organizational performance. Enacted in sequence, the following strategies support productive reasoning:

- Produce (relatively) directly observable data of participants' reasoning and actions.

- Encourage the participants to examine inconsistencies and gaps in the reasoning that underlies their actions.
- Surface and make explicit the rules that "must" be in their heads if they maintain that there is a connection between their designs for action and the actions that they produced.
- View any resistance, bewilderment, or frustration that results as further directly observable data that can be used to test the validity of what is being learned.
- Produce opportunities to practice Model II ways of crafting actions that will reduce the counterproductive consequences.

While following these strategies does not guarantee change, the probability of change occurring in organizations that use these strategies is increased.

Emotions or feelings play an important role in precipitating change. Productive reasoning is required to design and implement actions that encourage double-loop learning and lead to effective change. That process generates strong feelings. Progress toward change requires expressing those feelings as well as respecting them. It is important for organizational participants to explore the reasons for their feelings. Participants often see that their feelings were caused by defensive reasoning. Yet they need to test the validity of their view of the reasons for those feelings. This process can lead to new designs, new actions, new errors, and new learning. It is the basis for change.

Notes

1. For a full explanation of Model I theory-in-use, please see "Theories-in-Use Model I and Model II." In Chris Argyris. 1982. *Reasoning, Learning, and Action.* San Francisco: Jossey-Bass, 82–106.

2. Please see the discussion of organizational defensive routines in C. Argyris. 1990. *Overcoming Organizational Defenses.* Boston: Allyn and Bacon. See also "Defensive Routines that Limit Learning." In C. Argyris. 1993. *Knowledge for Action: A Guide to Overcoming Barriers to Organizational Change.* San Francisco: Jossey-Bass. 49–66.

3. These seven errors are discussed in detail in C. Argyris. 1990. *Overcoming Organizational Defenses.* Boston: Allyn and Bacon, 6–9.

4. See the full discussion of the theories of Model I and Model II behavior in C. Argyris and D. Schon. 1974. *Theory in Practice: Increasing Professional Effectiveness.* San Francisco: Jossey-Bass, and C. Argyris and D. Schon. 1978. *Organizational Learning: A Theory of Action Perspective.* Reading, Mass.: Addison-Wesley. See also C. Argyris. 1982. *Reasoning, Learning, and Action.* San Francisco: Jossey-Bass.

5. See, for example, the discussion of human beings as "intendedly moral" in C. Argyris. 1982. *Reasoning, Learning, and Action.* San Francisco: Jossey-Bass, 101–104.

6

Turnaround at the Alabama Rehabilitation Agency

James E. Stephens

Management of the change process has required constant attention to the routine, often mundane, daily activities of the organization.

This article describes the process used in an attempt to bring about a major organizational transformation in a medium-sized state human service agency, the Alabama Division of Rehabilitation and Crippled Children Service. In 1983, with nearly sixty years of history behind it, the division was characterized by unremarkable performance and an organizational environment geared toward maintenance rather than innovation and growth. In the summer of 1987, after three years of intensive involvement in an organizational development program designed to foster and sustain controlled change, the division is quickly gaining a national reputation among state rehabilitation agencies for its creative approaches to organizing and delivering rehabilitation services to persons with disabilities in Alabama.

The Division's Culture

The division provides restorative and rehabilitation services to Alabama's children and adults with disabilities, and its stated mission is to enable persons with disabilities to achieve social and economic independence. The

"Turnaround at the Alabama Rehabilitation Agency," *Public Productivity & Management Review* 11 (Spring 1988): 67–84.

division has a staff of 600, an annual budget of approximately $46 million, and responsibility for three major programs: children's medical services (crippled children), home-bound services, and vocational rehabilitation services. In FY 1986, the division served 65,912 persons with disabilities. In the vocational rehabilitation program, 36,867 adults were served, and 6,391 were returned to employment (Alabama Division . . . , 1986). The numbers of persons served and persons returned to gainful employment represent the traditional gross measures of effectiveness in state rehabilitation programs.

There is evidence in the state-federal program of rehabilitation that sixty-five years of compliance with rules and regulations has helped create an organizational environment that focuses primarily on the process of rehabilitation (how persons with disabilities are served) rather than the outcomes of rehabilitation (earnings at placement, functional gains in independence, and so on). Further complicating the state rehabilitation program environment is the tendency of most organizations to add internal controls on top of external controls. Also, many state rehabilitation agencies, once small, unnoticed organizations tucked away in state departments of education, have been relocated in large "umbrella" departments of state governments where they are much more subject to departmental oversight and control processes.

Through 1983 the division presented a classic, traditional profile among state rehabilitation agencies. The division was largely male dominated at the professional and managerial levels and paternalistic in its leadership style (Stephens and Latta, 1983). Policy decisions were typically made by a few at the top of the organization, and systems for quality assurance and budgeting were designed primarily for tight control and oversight activity by managerial staff. Promotion was most often based on tenure.

The division was organized along traditional hierarchical lines, with local supervisors having large spans of control while using policy and procedural systems and compliance checks to provide much of the task structure and focus for professional service-delivery personnel. The state was divided into six service areas, each with an area supervisor and one assistant. Three additional overlapping areas existed to provide special supervision for professionals serving persons with visual and auditory disabilities.

Supervision. In 1983 a survey of leadership behavior and job satisfaction was conducted in the division (Stephens and Latta, 1983). The *Leader Behavior Description Questionnaire* (Stodgill, 1962) and the *Job Descriptive Index* (Smith, Kendall, and Hulin, 1975) were used to develop individual and organizational profiles. Division supervisors were perceived by service delivery personnel as engaging in high levels of behavior associated with providing structure and emphasizing production. Behavior associated with allowing freedom in professional decision making and consideration for employees was significantly less prevalent.

Leadership. From the early 1950s through the end of 1983, only three men ran the division. For thirty years, the division was marked by paternalistic leadership at the top, which spread throughout the organization. Many line managers and supervisors in the division had been successful school principals, coaches, and teachers before coming to the division and subsequently brought with them paternalistic leadership styles learned in that environment.

In 1981 the former director of the division was indicted and convicted of fraud. The charges and conviction were related directly to activities engaged in while he was director. His successor, while a capable administrator, was more inclined to program maintenance than to innovation.

Control and Reward Systems. It is difficult in most human service delivery systems to establish a causal relationship between what professional service delivery personnel do and the outcomes achieved by recipients of the services. However, pressures to justify staff and budgets drive most human service organizations to initiate high levels of control, which are typically focused on elements of the service delivery process (how services are provided) rather than outcomes. State rehabilitation services organizations are no exception.

The division attempted to exercise tight control over its service delivery process, as evidenced by high demands for compliance to policy and procedure and consistent requirements for reporting activities. However, although systems were established and used to enhance high levels of control and compliance, the large spans of control of supervisors at the local level tended to negate mandated controls and allowed local practices to deviate. For example, a 1978 federal audit of the service delivery patterns in the division called into question the application of criterion being used to determine the eligibility of clients for the program.

The primary service delivery professional in a state rehabilitation organization, the rehabilitation counselor, closely fits the description of a street-level bureaucrat. Rehabilitation counselors exercise a wide range of discretion in decision making, especially those decisions made in making determinations of client eligibility, planning, provision of services, and case closure. Coupled with sometimes remote locations and substantial time spent out of the office, this discretionary decision-making power is difficult to control even with the most detailed process control system.

Given the supervision with large spans of control and highly detailed, report-heavy, control systems, the reward structure of the division was largely associated with and focused on the accurate completion and quantity of client case records. A 1982 survey (Stephens, 1982) in the division demonstrated that formal and informal reward systems primarily supported the achievement of process goals (numbers of persons determined eligible, numbers of client plans written, accurate maintenance of case records) rather than quality goals (accuracy of eligibility determinations, evidence of planned services resulting in greater client independence). Further evidence in the same survey supported the conclusion that supervisory practices and division policy and procedures also focused on the attainment of process goals.

Transition. In early 1984 the third of the three directors who had served the division for over thirty years announced his plans for retirement. Much speculation among staff centered on a likely successor. Most believed that a promotion would come from within the ranks, continuing a long tradition.

To the surprise of most and the dismay of some, the new director established two precedents for the division: the first "outsider" to be promoted to the directorship, and more startling to some, the first woman to head the division. The new director, Lamona Lucas, had been employed by the division but left in the early 1980s. Lucas was well grounded and experienced in rehabilitation and known to many staff. Few could have guessed the extent of changes to come.

Redefining the Organization (Slowly)

In June 1984 the division and the Georgia State University Rehabilitation Continuing Education Program for Administration and Management began a collaborative relationship that has now spanned three years. Through initial discussions with Lucas and executive team members, it became apparent that their desire for organizational change was broad in scope and would not likely be amenable to a quick fix. The initial intervention process began as a fundamental team-building process designed to cement relationships and enhance the productivity of what was to become a new executive team, and to help build a vision of what the organization would become over the next four to seven years. However, during initial meetings with the executive team, the primary objective for the intervention emerged: to develop a decision structure for the division that would allow decision making at all levels to occur within the context of a clearly defined mission, a common set of organizational values, and a set of long-range goals that were congruent with and driven by the organization's identified values.

Building a Decision Structure. Traditional attempts to bring about change in organizations typically begin with statements of current or predicted problems and move quickly to solutions or remedial steps to fix the identified discrepancy or move the problem state closer to a desired state. Often, statements of problems contain implied solutions that tend to narrowly define and limit the number of possible alternatives for addressing the problem. For example, the problem statement, "our employees need more training in job placement" is not really a statement of a problem but a solution to a problem as yet identified. If left untested, the statement could commit the organization to a course of action that may have little or no desired effect. In order to help the division overcome any tendency toward locking itself into courses of action before thorough analysis and planning could be conducted, an emphasis was placed on using an organizational intervention process that focused on defining what the organization wanted to become and then working backward to clarify and generate discrete change strategies.

Figure 6.1 depicts the intervention process used by the division to build the initial value-based decision structure, "Blueprint for the Future" (Figure 6.2). The first draft of the Blueprint was developed by the division's executive team. Within twelve months, all division staff, including service delivery, support, and clerical personnel, participated in the development, editing, and revision of the blueprint. Executive team development continued throughout this period and consisted of team functioning assessment, leadership assessment, and functional role assessment in relationship to identified values and goals.

Figure 6.3 illustrates how the intervention process works to drive values and goals from clusters of problems categorized according to broad organizational functions. It promotes intense discussion, debate, and dialogue that forces members of an organization to make choices among values and goals of sometimes near equal importance. It also allows the formal leaders of an organization to open the decision-making process to the scrutiny of all organizational members, increasing understanding of and commitment to values and goals.

Two major values, uncovered and put into words by the executive team and later revised and confirmed by all staff, appear to have sparked the energy required to sustain a long-term change effort. These values are: (1) We value the worth, dignity, and rights of persons with disabilities; (2) We value the contributions of all staff in achieving our mission. These two value statements, along with the rest of the value set (Figure 6.2), became the guideposts for descriptions of the future.

Goal statements for each value were derived by applying the "if" test: If we value the worth, dignity, and rights of persons with disabilities, then we will . . . Long before generating a laundry list of strategies and solutions, evidence of goal accomplishment was generated by asking the question: "How will we know if the goal is accomplished (what are we willing to accept as evidence)?" Delaying the laundry list of solutions also helped the division live up to one of its goals, that of "developing a leadership style that will promote staff participation in decision making." Describing ends

FIGURE 6.1 Generating a Value-Based Decision Structure

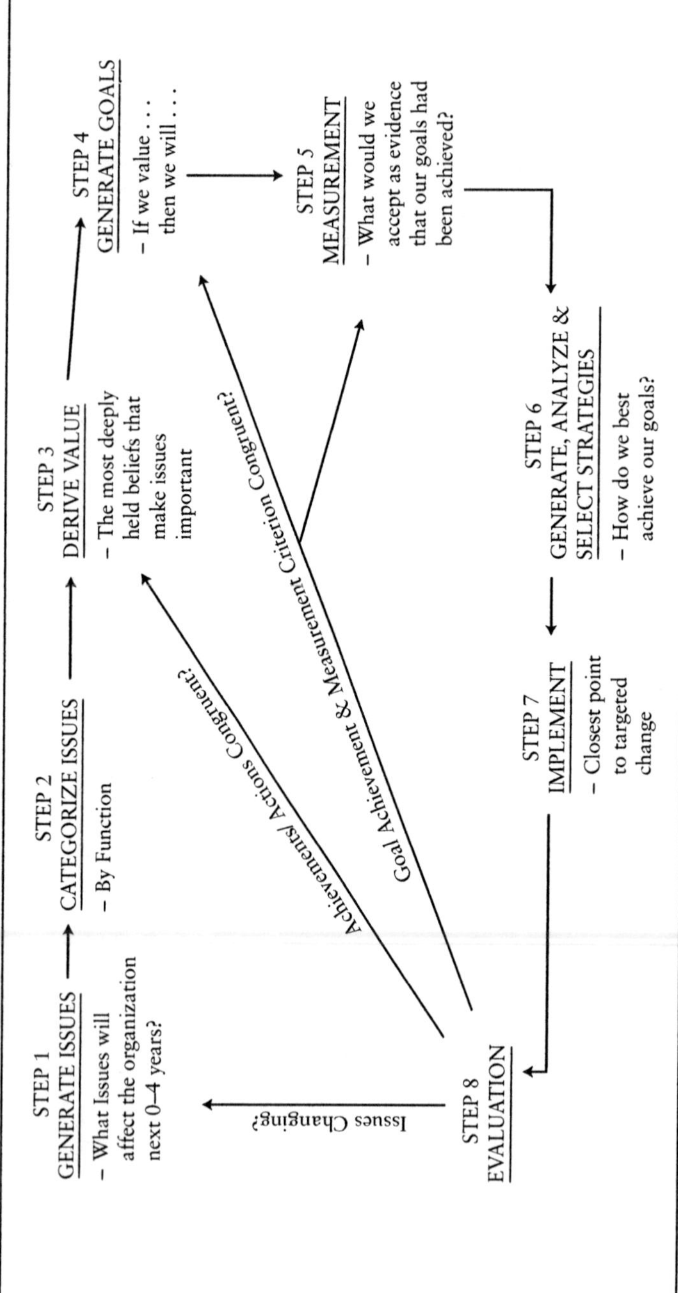

FIGURE 6.2 Blueprint for the Future

Value-Based Decision Structure

I. We value the worth, dignity and rights of persons with disabilities.

Goals:
1. Provide quality services which lead to quality outcomes, giving priority to persons with severe disabilities
2. Involve advocates and persons with disabilities in agency planning and policy development
3. Advocate for the rights of persons with disabilities

II. We value the contributions of all staff in achieving our mission.

Goals:
1. Recruit, employ, and promote qualified staff
2. Establish open and honest communication
3. Provide staff opportunities for personal and professional growth
4. Establish realistic performance and productivity standards
5. Reward exemplary job performance
6. Encourage staff creativity and innovation

III. We value an agency management style that provides opportunities for staff participation.

Goals:
1. Develop an agency management philosophy that promotes creativity and innovation
2. Provide management development opportunities for agency management staff
3. Promote an agency management style that encourages teamwork among all staff
4. Promote an agency management style that encourages greater staff participation in agency decision making

IV. We value maximum acquisition and the efficient and effective management of resources.

Goals:
1. Acquire maximum financial and other resources
2. Increase legislative support
3. Develop a management information system to measure the effective and efficient use or our resources
4. Develop and use appropriate technological advancements

V. We value public support.

Goals:
1. Inform the public of our mission and our goals
2. Develop partnerships with business and industry
3. Encourage greater staff commitment to and responsibility for development of community-based agency support

FIGURE 6.3 Illustration of Value-Based Decision Making

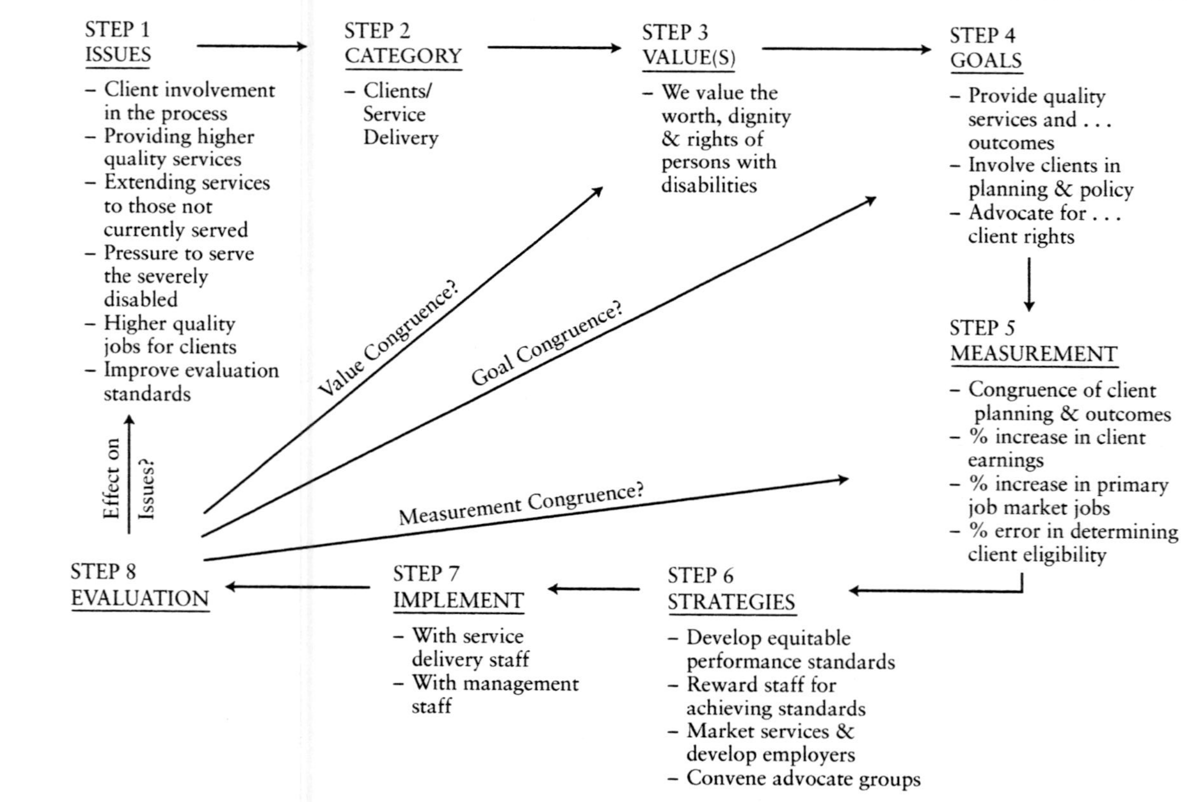

rather than means allows for strategies and solutions to be developed at the local level, closer to where implementation problems arise, and allows staff some flexibility depending on local needs and circumstances.

It should be noted that the intervention process is dynamic rather than static. As groups experience the process, a substantially different decision-making style is being experienced, a style that focuses on describing desired end states (goals) rather than describing problems (or symptoms of problems).

It is not likely that the values identified by the division will change over time. It is likely that the identified goals will change. Depending on progress toward meeting goals and changing demands in the organization's environment, some goals will become more or less important and new goals will emerge that will reflect current trends. Strategies for achieving goals should vary greatly in the long term, since they will be most affected by changes in legal mandates, regulations, and program thrust.

Significant Activities and Accomplishments

This section will reference the division's Blueprint for the Future (Figure 6.2) in order to illustrate how values, goals, and, ultimately, implementation are linked. Organizational changes and implementation of new programs and systems can be traced directly to goals and values (see Figure 6.3). Significant decisions made by the division's executive team and other organizational units are tested against the value-based decision structure.

The development of the Blueprint for the Future has been central to the change process in the division. That activity relates directly to values II and III and several of the goals contained in each value set. It is extremely risky to undertake such a massive and at times unpredictable step within any organization, especially considering the time and financial commitment required. Every staff member spent a minimum of two days involved in a workshop devoted to generating, editing, and revising basic organizational values and goals. The unspoken implication of the effort carried an attention-getting message to the staff: "We are serious about enlarging staff participation in decision making, and we are willing to take some risks in doing so!"

At stake in any such endeavor is the long-term credibility of the leader who initiates the effort. Often, organizations launch such programs only to shelve them when a crisis or a natural drift back to the routine occurs. Lucas and her immediate staff have been acutely aware of the necessity to maintain a constant focus on the expressed decision structure.

Systems Changes

The division's top goal (value I, goal 1), to "provide quality services that lead to quality outcomes," prompted staff to ask such questions as: "What are quality services?" "How are quality outcomes defined." "Do our current measurement systems adequately capture and reflect quality performance?" Called into question were the division's policy and procedures guidelines, management information system, quality assurance system, and performance standards for service delivery.

Policy Review and Revision. In developing policy and procedure, establishing performance standards, gathering program information, and defining quality, state rehabilitation programs have traditionally followed the lead established by the federal government. Much state program policy is taken verbatim from federal policy dictates. With the addition of state government-mandated policy and procedures along with procedures and processes added by the program, complicated guidelines become even more complex.

The division's basic policy and procedure manual, which had grown to 130 pages by 1984, was reviewed and revised by a team consisting of service delivery personnel (counselors), supervisors, and state office personnel. The policy revision team was surprised to find that the 130-page manual could be cut to a total of 27 pages and still do the job intended. What was needed was good policy, not necessarily more policy. The new manual meets the requirements of the law, provides substantive guidance to staff, and allows more freedom in decision making at the professional level. Also reinforced was the idea that greater freedom carries greater responsibility and that fewer rules would warrant stricter enforcement.

Using a project team to conduct the review and revision further reinforced value III, goal 4 and strengthened the implicit notion that those most affected by decisions should be involved in the decision-making process.

Evaluating Performance. Federal law governing the state-federal rehabilitation program is relatively straightforward in defining program eligibility, range and mix of services, financial requirements, and rationale for terminating services to individual clients. However, those persons labeled *clients* who enter the system seldom perfectly fit the system's need for order and predictability. Further complicating the situation is the difficulty of establishing and measuring causal relationships between services provided and outcomes achieved. As a result, measurement and evaluation of quantity tends to become the focus, with attempts to focus on quality receiving less attention.

Commitment to value I, goal 1 ("quality services . . . quality outcomes") established a clear need for the division to develop performance standards that could be related to quality. From among several sets of standards developed for rehabilitation programs, the division chose an existing set of process and quality standards developed by the Management Control Project (MCP) at the University of Georgia. MCP standards had been implemented and proven effective in thirteen state rehabilitation agencies, and MCP staff were experienced and competent in providing implementation assistance. The use of MCP standards also reinforced the expressed values and goals (value II, goal 4; value III, goal 4) associated with how professional staff should operate.

In the fall of 1986, extensive training of line management took place, with supervisors and managers involved in three full weeks of standards training. By May 1987 service delivery staff had been trained. The training was conducted by teams of line managers, and standards were fully implemented at the end of training.

Prior to training and implementation, a comprehensive review of casework was conducted by MCP staff using the new standards to evaluate service delivery patterns prior to implementation. Baselines were established, and a postimplementation review will be conducted to compare pre- and postresults. Reliability training has started for supervisors and will be conducted on a regular basis in order to ensure rater reliability and consistency in statewide application of the standards.

Quality Assurance. The overall quality assurance program for the division has been reassessed and brought into line with implications driven by the decision structure. In the past, the quality assurance function was highly centralized, and quality assessment and feedback was most often provided by central office staff or review teams comprised of supervisory staff. Service delivery staff often perceived the feedback as punitive rather than as a genuine attempt on the part of management to promote improved performance.

Current thinking in the division promotes the concept that the assurance of quality should be delegated to the lowest possible level. Although the technical responsibility for quality assurance for the total program will remain a centralized function, the actual assessment and feedback processes will occur between first-line supervisors and service delivery staff, with supervisors being held accountable for needed improvement in individual and unit performance. More important, the implementation of performance standards will provide service delivery staff the necessary tools to assess the quality of their work as it is being performed, thereby greatly reducing the element of surprise found in more traditional systems.

Aligning the Organization and Supervision with Values and Goals. Once the division developed and committed itself to a set of organizational values and concomitant goals, two questions immediately came into focus: "Are we organized in a way that reflects our values and will allow us to best achieve our goals?" "Are our supervisors behaving in ways that reflect our values and allow us to attain our goals?"

The division's recently published organizational chart (Figure 6.4) is the result of attention focused on the first question. At first glance, the chart could be simply dismissed as a traditional organizational chart turned upside down. Lines of authority and traditional programs are clearly represented, and work units are clearly segregated. Closer inspection and comparison with the division's value-based decision structure reveals significant meaning. Alabama's children and adults with disabilities are represented at the top of the chart in keeping with value I. In descending order are service delivery staff, first-line supervisors, middle management, and central office staff, including administrators. The symbolism of the chart is clear: The division serves persons with disabilities, and management and administrative staff serve and support those who serve. The chart also depicts the larger political context in which the organization operates.

Conceptually, Figure 6.4 is an indication that staff are willing to think outside the "lines and boxes" and could very well indicate a willingness to consider even greater departures from tradition.

Supervision. First-line supervision may well be the key to the achievement of significant change in the division. The division's successful implementation of specific process and outcome standards depends on service delivery personnel using greater levels of judgment in decision making while at the same time maintaining consistency in the decision-making process. In order to be most successful, supervisors in the division will necessarily have to become more developmental; they will be required to be more consultative, provide more support and information, and use skills more closely associated with coaching as they relate to service delivery personnel.

The division's supervisors have begun to take a systematic look at their job roles and develop functional statements of supervisory tasks. By asking the question, "What would I be doing if I were helping the division achieve its stated goals?" supervisors are generating a list of functions and behaviors that are more congruent with the prevailing management philosophy exemplified by the value-based decision structure.

The shift to developmental supervision has required another major change in the division. Coaching and consultation styles require spending time with subordinates and large spans of control obviously limit the amount of time supervisors can spend in face-to-face contact with staff. The division has expanded its first-line supervisory staff from nine to nineteen, reducing the average number of persons supervised to eight to ten per supervisor. This was accomplished by restructuring the job duties of former assistant supervisors, and no additional personnel were added. Evaluation of supervisory performance will be linked directly to the performance of service delivery staff on the new standards.

Project Teams. The division's value III, which supports greater staff participation in decision making, has spawned a greater awareness of the need to

FIGURE 6.4 Division of Rehabilitation and Crippled Children Service Client Support

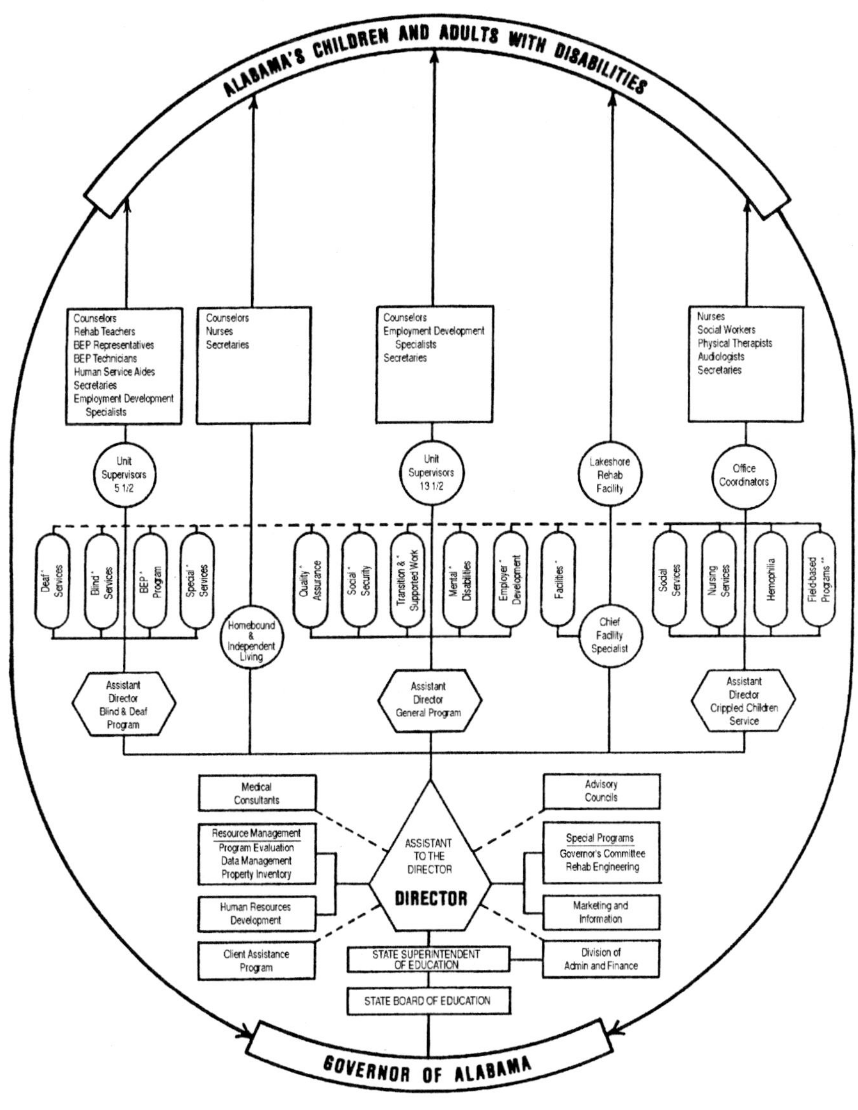

allow those most affected by decisions to participate in the process. Teams have been formed to examine and revise the division's policy, devise a marketing and employer development program, and develop the division's new performance appraisal system. The teams consist of service delivery staff, management, and others ultimately affected by proposed changes and help to enhance ownership of what is developed and ensure less surprise when change takes place. The decisions made and actions taken seem of higher quality, more thorough, and thoughtful. The additional time required to organize and staff each team is more than offset by what is being produced.

Leadership: Symbols and Patterns

It is certain that the process of transformation described above, although still in its formative stages, could not have occurred without the leadership provided by Lucas and the effect her leadership has had on other key staff members. The overall effect in the division gives meaning to a popular word, *empowerment,* a word in danger of becoming trivialized. By establishing the parameters for leadership through modeling the desired behavior, Lucas has been able to energize a significant number of staff members in the division and overcome a sense of inertia that existed prior to her arrival. The following anecdotes serve to illustrate the point.

Over the years, the division staff had developed a time-clock mentality. Staff members usually arrived a few minutes before starting time, socialized, worked until the first break, took the standard morning break, took the standard lunch break, and so on. At 5:00 P.M. each day, offices were typically empty, and people were on their way home. Lucas immediately passed the word and modeled through her own behavior that task accomplishment was the top priority. If that meant working through breaks and lunch or staying late, so be it. People in the organization have now begun to focus on their work and not the clock.

It has been said that what the members of an organization focus on and spend the most time doing is dictated by what "catches a leader's attention consistently, especially that which arouses the leader emotionally" (Schein, 1985, p. 319). Lucas is a case in point. During the formulation of the value-based decision structure, she attended and spoke to staff at each session (six workshops over two months), stressing expectancies for the future. In addition, during the training and implementation phase for performance standards (a total of nine weeks for managers, six weeks for service delivery personnel), Lucas made an appearance at every session and attended several in their entirety. Staff members were convinced that it was an important endeavor.

Framed copies of the Blueprint for the Future hang on Lucas's office wall and the walls of other top managers. Formal and informal discussions about future programming and current decisions usually prompt the question: "Is it congruent with our values and goals?" Attempts to allocate decision making to the top of the organization, routine practice in the past, are now met with the message that most decisions should be made at the level closest to where the work takes place.

Attention to promotional policy has also sent a strong message to staff. When the supervisory ranks were expanded to accommodate the need for a more developmental approach to supervision, the promotions to supervisory rank were based more on competence and less on tenure. Some supervisors were promoted who had spent little time in the ranks compared with those with long histories with the division.

Leadership practices in the division are evolving toward a consultative style with an emphasis on provided support and assistance to service delivery staff. While this shift is still seen by some managers as representing a loss of power, most see the shift as an opportunity to develop greater levels of influence based on expertise and overall competence.

Tangibles. Within twelve months, the division will have some tangible evidence of its progress. Performance at that time will be measured against the baselines established prior to the training for and implementation of the performance standards. Service delivery personnel performance will be evaluated against negotiated standards on an individual basis. Supervisory performance will be evaluated based on the cumulative achievements of their respective work units and their ability to reliably assess service delivery personnel performance. It is also expected that the overall quantity of services delivered and outcomes achieved will rise over the next thirty-six months.

Intangibles. Intangible factors are already in evidence in the organization. There is a greater spirit of movement and innovation. Greater levels of staff participation have brought about both more creativity and a greater sense of expectancy that more is to come. People are having more fun and getting more attention for the work they do.

The division has an expanding state and national reputation as an organization that is operating on the leading edge of rehabilitation. Lucas has assumed a prominent position of leadership in the state-federal program, and the division's efforts are being noticed and modeled by other state programs, both within and outside the state of Alabama.

Conclusions

That fundamental change has occurred in the Alabama Division of Rehabilitation and Crippled Children Services cannot be denied. The more telling questions concern whether the desired change can be sustained, whether the change process can become institutionalized, and whether the same results would have been achieved regardless of the intervention.

Change Versus Planned Change. Three years after launching a formal change process, the division has an identified decision structure anchored by a common set of values with accompanying long-range goals. Proven systems for evaluating individual and program performance have been implemented and appear to be working with minimal slippage. Policy and procedure guidelines are more congruent with actual practice and are geared toward focusing professional behavior on critical service delivery issues. Greater numbers of people in the organization are participating in making decisions that directly affect their work. A focus on leadership and supervisory behavior has helped create a shift to a more supportive, facilitative style of management that is more in line with current theory. There is a realistic expectation that productivity will improve, including both the quality of the work performed and the quantity of outcomes achieved.

There is little doubt that, with or without structured intervention, change would have occurred in the division. Timing and good fortune are important, if not measurable, variables in achieving significant organizational change. The division exists in the context of a larger environment that is currently focusing on the need to more systematically examine the effectiveness of traditional methods and practices. A change in top leadership certainly helped trigger the division's focus on self-examination. Key retirements provided an opportunity to restructure the top leadership team and make key promotions within the division's line management ranks.

Although significant change in the division appear to have been inevitable, the use of a formal change process has increased the speed, intensity, and focus of the effort. The early teamwork of identifying issues, values, and goals helped focus staff attention and energy on a few critically important areas. Intensity was achieved by increasing the numbers of people and amount of activity focused on any given issue. And finally, the intervention process itself served to provide the structure required to keep the change occurring and better manage the speed at which change has occurred. In some ways, the intervention process itself legitimized the seeking of a broader range of alternatives for accomplishing long-range goals and the coming together of groups of people who in times past would have had little reason to do so.

It should be obvious that the Blueprint for the Future developed by the division breaks little new ground in its content. The written values express a belief system that is at the heart of most human service organizations. The goals describe ideal conditions and end states that most staff in human services organizations would agree are important. However, the uniqueness of the effort lies in the division's willingness to bring these values and goals to the surface of the organization's consciousness and hold them up for scrutiny by those in and outside the organization. Doing this allows for not only the organization to better evaluate itself but also provides a basis for those outside the formal organization to make judgments about the congruence between what the division says and what it does.

It is likely that much of the change occurring in the division will be long lasting. Changes in technical systems, for example policy, procedure, and performance standards, tend to become quickly routinized. Of greater concern is maintenance of individual and group behavior change that occurs more slowly and is easily negated unless attention and reinforcement are focused on the desired behavior. Failure on the part of the division to realign its reward systems with desired change will result in some regression to old habits.

Lessons Learned. The truism that fundamental organizational change occurs slowly has been demonstrated by the division's effort. Although significant amounts of time and energy have been spent in the formative stages of the process, three years have elapsed with much effort remaining. Some goals have proven elusive, and others have receded into the background. Management of the change process has required constant attention to the routine, often mundane daily activities of the organization.

Single-strategy interventions such as training, used often in the past by the division, would have had little effect on overall organizational movement. The intervention process used took into account the interrelationships among the many systems, both formal and informal, comprising the division. Any contemplated change in one system usually brought about the need to look at the effect on other systems. For example, development and implementation of new performance standards had an immediate effect on supervisory behavior and also brought about a need to analyze and revise policy and procedure.

Consensus and Conflict. Much of the conflict and debate in organizations is the result of individuals and groups "owning" the one best means to achieve some end. The intervention process used in the division reinforces debate and ultimate consensus building over ends rather than means and seeks to minimize conflict over how to achieve those same ends. For example, if staff in the division can agree that achieving quality outcomes constitutes a primary goal and if that goal can be quantified, then alternatives for goal achievement can be allowed to vary somewhat, thus preserving ownership for individuals while maximizing goal achievement.

Moving Toward the Future. The Alabama Division of Rehabilitation and Crippled Children Service is reshaping its culture to meet the demands of a new and more complex environment. It has done so by launching a change program that has as its basic tenet that an organization can change for the better by systematically painting a picture of its future and then moving toward it. Many members of the division have acted on faith, believing both in their own leadership abilities and the leadership abilities of top management.

One must conclude that a competent staff has always existed in the division and that the change process has simply energized people to move forward. We might also conclude that, while organizational change is a complex and sometimes mysterious process, it cannot occur in full force without a top leader who can, in the words of Burns (1978, p. 443), "transform followers into leaders."

At present, it is too early to predict the continued effects of the change occurring in the division. It took sixty-three years for the division to become what it was in 1984, and the last thirty years of the first sixty-three were under the leadership of only three people. Three years' investment in a new direction is only a beginning. Every sign, however, indicates that the course being charted will continue to result in greater levels of accomplishment for the division.

References

Alabama Division of Rehabilitation and Crippled Children Service. *1986 Annual Report.* Montgomery: Alabama Division of Rehabilitation, 1986.

Burns, J. M. *Leadership.* New York: Harper & Row, 1978.

Division of Rehabilitation and Crippled Children Service, State of Alabama, 1987.

Schein, E. H. *Organizational Culture and Learning: A Dynamic View.* San Francisco: Jossey-Bass, 1985.

Smith, P. C., Kendall, L. M., and Hulin, C. L. *Job Descriptive Index.* Bowling Green, Ohio: Bowling Green State University, 1975.

Stephens, J. E. *Report: Survey of Job Placement Practices in Alabama.* Atlanta: Institute of Public Administration. Georgia State University, 1982.

Stephens, J. E., and Latta, J. A. *Report: Alabama Leadership and Job Satisfaction Survey.* Atlanta: Institute of Public Administration, Georgia State University, 1983.

Stodgill, R. N. *Leader Behavior Description Questionnaire.* Columbus: Ohio State University, 1962.

7

Common Barriers to Productivity Improvement in Local Government

David N. Ammons

Various writers have identified assorted sets of barriers that they consider to be most menacing to public sector productivity, often basing their choices on obstacles encountered in the particular productivity improvement efforts they are reporting. Individually, such lists are impressive; collectively, they are imposing.

In this article, productivity barriers noted in a wide variety of public sector sources are compiled for purposes of reviewing the significance of each and considering their collective ability to thwart productivity gains. Although most barriers are applicable to all levels of government, some, such as those involving intergovernmental relations, have effects differing from one level to another. All are presented here from the perspective of local governments.

Productivity Barriers

Although individual sources typically identify only a few obstacles found to hinder productivity efforts in the particular instance being reported, a cataloging of productivity barriers found in numerous cases quickly runs to dozens. In all, 37 separate, though related, barriers common in local governments and considered significant impediments to productivity improvement are identified in this article (Table 7.1).[1]

"Common Barriers to Productivity Improvement in Local Government," *Public Productivity Review* 9 (Winter, 1985): 187–202.

TABLE 7.1 Thirty-seven Common Barriers to Productivity Improvement in Local Government

- political factors that influence decision making
- productivity improvement's lack of political appeal
- short time horizon of politicians and top executives
- policy rather than performance emphasis in local affairs
- public perceptions regarding changes and benefits
- fragmentation of local government
- inadequate research, development, and experimentation
- antiproductivity effect of federal grant provisions
- intergovernmental mandating of local expenditures
- civil service restrictions
- legal restrictions to motivational programs
- barriers to monetary incentive plans
- dominant preference for the status quo
- absence of market pressures
- perceived threat to job security
- union resistance
- bureaucratic socialization processes
- primary emphasis on effectiveness rather than efficiency
- lack of accountability
- risk avoidance
- perverse reward systems
- absence of personal rewards for innovation and productivity
- conceptual confusion
- managerial alibis
- inadequate management commitment to productivity
- reluctance to abandon
- ambiguous objectives and lack of performance measurement
- absence of cost accounting systems
- inadequate information on intracity and intercity performance
- inadequate information dissemination and reluctance to use what is known
- inadequate performance evaluation
- insufficient analytic skills or analytic staffing
- performance myths
- requirement of large initial investment for productivity efforts
- overselling productivity improvement programs
- bureaucratic rigidities and fragmented authority
- supervisory resistance

Political Factors That Influence Decision Making. Political factors often outweigh management rationale in local government decision making. Administrative recommendations to demolish ramshackle city-owned buildings that cost more to maintain than they produce in rentals and represent serious safety hazards are rejected by the city council because community groups and agencies enjoy the inexpensive, tax-subsidized space. Low-bid purchasing procedures are distorted by political decisions that favor local suppliers. Or a tax system based upon engineered work standards that would allow meter readers to leave the job upon completion of a "fair day's work" is rejected by a city council fearful of adverse public reaction. In each instance, seemingly rational recommendations offering potential productivity gains succumb to political decisions.

Lack of Political Appeal. Although political candidates frequently bemoan the growing bureaucracy and promise to cut red tape and taxes while improving services, once in office they typically find the tedious, time-consuming, and often frustrating task of productivity improvement to be less glamorous or appealing than addressing other local government problems or opportunities. Most office holders, it seems, find greater advantage in compiling records of securing federal funds for their jurisdiction than in committing their time to overseeing the management of the programs those and other funds support.[2] In a recent survey of mayors in 221 council-manager cities, productivity improvement ranked only seventh in priority among ten selected issues facing local governments.[3]

Short Time Horizon. Politicians, as well as administrators serving at their pleasure, tend to weigh decisions according to a time horizon only as distant as the date of the next election. Not surprisingly, they generally resist dealing with controversial issues when an election nears and are reluctant to favor programs with high short-term costs and the promise of major gains only in the long run—characteristics common to many productivity improvement projects." Faced with the decision to make a capital investment projected to reap benefits in four years or, with the same available resources, to put policemen on the street to fight a rising crime rate today, an elected official who must fight for reelection in two years, not surprisingly, chooses the latter."[4]

Policy Rather Than Performance Emphasis. Front-page space in the local newspaper is rarely devoted to stories dealing with the management of day-to-day municipal operations, as long as they remain within the wide band of acceptability. Matters of local policy garner high public exposure in comparison. Consequently, reputations and rewards tend to be earned in the policy arena, sending an unmistakable signal to managers struggling to allocate precious time among competing internal and external demands.[5]

Public Perceptions Regarding Changes and Benefits. First-year savings from individual productivity improvement projects—even highly successful projects—rarely represent more than a minor percentage of the municipal budget. The cumulative impact of multiple productivity improvement efforts may be substantial, but their relatively modest individual impact renders their benefits virtually invisible to the general public. As a result, productivity improvement efforts tend to foster little public appreciation. A much more likely consequence of efforts to modify services or service delivery methods for greater efficiency is the vocal and often highly emotional opposition of employees and clientele.[6]

Fragmentation of Local Government. The fragmentation of local government has long been cited as an impediment to coordination, accountability, equitable financing, and economies of scale.[7] The concentration of numerous municipal governments within a small geographic area, overlapped by a county government and numerous special districts for, perhaps, schools, fire protection, water and sewer services, and other specific functions, is criticized by proponents of a centralized approach to management as a major impediment to productivity improvement.

Inadequate Research, Development, and Experimentation. In 1984, state and local government expenditures equaled 12 percent of the gross national product. Yet the amount of research and development directed toward meeting the needs of that market remains quite small, despite the efforts of entities such as Public Technology Incorporated to bring modern technology to bear on local government problems. The disjointed nature of individual governmental units and a history of only gradual adoption of the latest technology make private investors leery.

Anti-Productivity Effect of Federal Grant Provisions. Funds from the federal government constituted 11 percent of city government general revenues in fiscal year 1982–83, making such revenues an important component in most cities' resource mix—a component most local officials would like to increase. Countering the obvious positive aspects of intergovernmental revenues, however, is a set of less desirable characteristics.

Regulations governing grant-supported programs tend to be written with an eye toward controlling the behavior of the least responsible local governments,[8] often resulting in tightly prescribed and cumbersome operating procedures that lead to red tape and delays, while eliminating flexibility in the development of improved methods. Few grant programs provide rewards for the productive, or penalize the unproductive, use of federal funds; many include maintenance-of-effort provisions, prohibiting any reductions in local expenditures; and some formula-based grants reward local governments for increased expenditures in a given program.[9] These factors, coupled with the tendency of many local officials to spend grant dollars less carefully than own-source revenues, have the unintended effect of undermining productivity.

According to Elmer Staats, former Comptroller General of the United States, federal grants have tended to increase local government expenditure pressures, to distort budget priorities, and to thwart budget-cutting efforts, and they may have contributed to fiscal instability.[10] A similar verdict by the International City Management Association's Committee on Future Horizons of the profession led that group to recommend that local governments consider the value of federal funds more critically, taking into account the strings attached and loss of local discretion, and that they even consider "buying back" at least a portion of their independence by rejecting some grants and relying more on locally raised revenues.[11]

Intergovernmental Mandating of Local Expenditures. Federal and state-imposed requirements that local governments provide specified services or benefits are rarely, if ever, established with operational productivity as a major consideration. Frequently the product of successful lobbying efforts at the national or state capital following unsuccessful attempts at city halls, such mandates divert expenditures from local priorities and restrict officials' ability to tailor service offerings to local preference or to minimize certain costs. Only 10 percent of the respondents to a recent survey of local government officials in Pennsylvania thought that mandates had led to the efficient delivery of local services and programs.[12] In a recent study, the U.S. Advisory Commission on Intergovernmental Relations characterized several mandates—including some governing operating hours of libraries and mandating wage levels for local government employees—as questionable or clearly inappropriate.[13]

Civil Service Restrictions. Civil service systems were developed as means of remedying the problems of the spoils era. In their present form, however, civil service rules and regulations have become barriers restricting managerial ability to achieve maximum return for local tax dollars. Rules restricting flexibility in staff assignments and reassignments, preventing differential treatment and rewards for varying levels of employee performance, and elongating the hiring process to the point that, when finally contacted for appointment, top candidates have already been hired by other employers, are serious productivity barriers.[14]

Somewhere along the way, the concept of merit has become overgrown with practices and procedures that have relegated employee performance to secondary status in matters of personnel management. Over time, "incompetence, inflexibility, invalidity, inaccuracy, and unreasonableness" have been shrouded inappropriately "in the cloak of merit," according to

Mushkin and Sandifer, distorting the objective of ensuring that job performance is "the basis of personnel actions taken."[15] Under current conditions, public sector employees tend to dismiss the likelihood that superior performance will lead to financial rewards. Only 30 percent of the public sector respondents in an aggregation of surveys reported in 1978 thought that better performance would improve their chances for promotion.[16]

Legal Restrictions. Motivational programs intended to enhance productivity have in some instances faced legal restrictions in addition to civil service and union contract impediments. For example, federal wage and hour laws, equal employment opportunity (EEO) requirements, and intergovernmental grant provisions have limited local managerial flexibility in areas such as working-hour variations, modified performance-appraisal techniques, shared-savings plans, and other employee incentive programs.[17]

Barriers to Monetary Incentive Plans. Monetary incentive plans often are confronted not only by restrictive civil service regulations and other legal barriers, but also by resistant employees, supervisors, and local legislators. Employee opposition often is based on fear that the award system will be administered inequitably if the plan calls for individual awards or, among high-achieving employees and supervisors, that poor performers will ride the coattails of top performers if group incentives are prescribed. Some supervisors and managers furthermore raise objections to monetary incentives, in the belief that such programs induce a factory mentality inappropriate to public service. Opposition from local government legislators often stems from a desire to maintain tight control over wages, to avoid cost increases, to avoid adverse citizen reaction, and to protect scarce resources not only by avoiding additional expenses but also by returning all productivity savings to the legislature for reappropriation rather than committing to a plan for distributing a portion of such savings to employees.[18]

Dominant Preference for the Status Quo. One point of view suggests that public bureaucracies are slow to innovate because the dominant social classes prefer the status quo.[19] Under that view, the dominant classes' satisfaction with services provided to their members works against experimentation and innovation.

Absence of Market Pressures. Operating as "unregulated monopolies,"[20] local governments function without the market pressures common to most private sector companies. Unlike the private sector, where innovative, cost-conscious businesses that produce goods or services desired by their clientele are rewarded and noninnovative, wasteful, unresponsive businesses are punished with declining market shares and perhaps bankruptcy, the public sector offers no truly analogous set of rewards and penalties for performance or nonperformance, innovation or failure to innovate.

Perceived Threat to Job Security. Productivity improvement efforts are often perceived by employees to be motivated primarily by management's desire to reduce employment. Such a perception minimizes the likelihood of gaining the cooperation and commitment normally required for program success. To reduce employee anxieties, employers often guarantee that no layoffs will occur as a result of the productivity improvement efforts, promising to handle any resulting employee reductions through attrition or reassignment.

Union Resistance. Organized labor's opposition to various management efforts to cut labor costs is well documented in the popular media, as are union efforts on behalf of the seniority principle and the establishment of work rules limiting management discretion in dealing with employees. Unions have tended to oppose differential treatment based upon productivity,[21] employee reductions, civilianization, contracting out government functions,[22] and innovations in personnel deployment or technology when the result is considered disruptive or threatening to employees.[23]

Despite the evidence of union opposition to management's efforts to improve productivity, it is possible that the impact of unions and the formidability of unions as a productivity barrier may be commonly overstated. Hayes notes that major conflicts between management and organized labor have occurred in relatively few cities and suggests that most municipal employees view productivity improvement with "equanimity, if not indifference."[24] Based on a review of 20 studies on the impact of collective bargaining, Methe and Perry conclude that although collective bargaining has driven municipal expenditures upward, in at least some large cities unionization's impact on pay levels may have been offset by a negative impact on employment.[25] In some instances, in fact, major productivity gains have been achieved through the cooperative efforts of management and organized labor.[26]

Clearly, where the opposition of organized labor occurs, it cannot be ignored. Its principal threat to productivity, however, may be less in the form of escalating wage scales than in restrictive work rules and, as noted by Morgan, in an increasingly unresponsive work force protected by growing bureaucratic autonomy.[27]

Bureaucratic Socialization Processes. "The socialization of new recruits by socializing agents with little interest in change" creates a cadre of bureaucrats resistant to innovation.[28] Opposition to a proposed productivity-enhancing program modification in such an environment may be based less on a thoughtful determination that the proposal is meritless than upon a predisposition to oppose change, meritless or not.

Effectiveness, Not Efficiency. Productivity involves effectiveness and efficiency—a concern for quality *and* a sensitivity to cost. Often, public sector practitioners emphasize the former to the virtual exclusion of the latter. Many, in fact, may become indignant at the suggestion that their performance, or that of their department, be measured, contending that their service is not measurable or that how much they do is far less important than how well they do it.[29] Encouraged by professional associations, concern for organization-wide problems is often secondary to pursuit of service quality or resource-commitment standards.

Lack of Accountability. Few local governments demand that their managers, particularly lower-level supervisors, be accountable for operational productivity.[30] Most are expected to keep their operations running essentially in the fashion that they have run in the past, to minimize complaints, and to avoid controversy.

Risk Avoidance. Szanton notes: "It is a familiar truth in local government that if you do the job the old way and something goes wrong, that's an act of God; but if you do it a new way and something goes wrong, it's your neck."[31] Risk taking offers the public sector manager few tangible rewards for success, but substantial public criticism and penalties for failure. Some suggest that this factor produces the "relatively low risk threshold of most public officials"[32] and explains their reluctance to experiment or even to pioneer in the early implementation of innovations developed elsewhere. Others perceive a barrier more serious than the existence of a system that fails to encourage risk taking, suggesting that "innovation is seemingly discouraged by the recruitment into civil service jobs of people with high risk avoidance."[33]

Perverse Rewards System. Not only do local governments normally fail to provide adequate rewards and recognition for superior performance, they typically reward managers who have expanded their budgets and increased the number of persons they supervise. Unfortunately, the local government department head who finds ways to minimize the resources necessary to continue operating effectively can expect, instead of accolades and a substantial pay increase, the reassignment of current funds to cover the overruns of a less efficient department and a reduction in the upcoming budget.

Absence of Personal Rewards for Innovation and Productivity. The absence of substantial material incentives for managerial innovation and productivity improvement is seen by many as a fundamental impediment to productivity improvement—one that contributes to many other barriers. While city managers may conceivably be rewarded for productivity improvement, they are more frequently rewarded for other types of achievement. City charter provisions for mayoral salaries typically offer little flexibility, and ordinances governing salary administration for managers below the chief executive normally provide few options beyond standard step increases—and even those step increases are more often granted for time in service than as rewards for productivity improvement.

Conceptual Confusion. Balk lists "conceptual confusion" as the first link in a chain of factors limiting enthusiasm for productivity improvement.[34] Such confusion was evidenced in a 1981 survey of city managers in which one out of every six (17 percent) identified productivity rather vaguely as "the use of any of a wide assortment of progressive techniques or improvements that seem to work better in [a given] case," 5.8 percent identified it unidimensionally as "improvements in quality of service," and smaller percentages considered it to be defined by a variety of other phrases—most far less adequate than Nancy Hayward's definition of productivity as "the efficiency with which resources are consumed in the effective delivery of services," selected by barely more than one half of the city managers (53.9 percent).[35]

Managerial Alibis. Local government managers facing difficult circumstances often excuse their failure to deal with a problem in the optimum fashion by complaining about political problems, the complexity of government, the inherent difficulties in public sector personnel management, or similar obstacles. A survey of 100 federal managers conducted for the National Center for Productivity and Quality of Working Life revealed "that the barriers so frequently cited as productivity inhibitors, such as civil service regulations and measurement, are, in many cases, excuses. Government managers do not shoulder responsibilities and authority that are allowed by the system, presumably because these are unpleasant to exercise."[36] Local government managers are vulnerable to the same criticism. With sufficient effort by a responsible manager, incompetent employees may in most instances be removed, restrictive work rules modified, and new modes of operation adopted.[37]

Inadequate Management Commitment to Productivity. Without a strong commitment by upper-level managers to productivity, the prospects for substantial performance gains are modest. But productivity issues must compete with other pressing matters for the time and attention of local government executives. In a recent poll incorporating ten such issues, productivity improvement ranked as fourth most pressing according to 298 city and county managers.[38]

Reluctance to Abandon. Drucker calls the inability to abandon the most damning of public administration's deadly sins. Every program will eventually outlive its usefulness. At some point, its original form, objectives, and policies will become inappropriate, if not irrelevant. "In its original guise it cannot produce results any longer; the objectives have either ceased to matter, have proven unattainable, or have been attained. Indeed, the more successful a public service agency is, the sooner will it work itself out of the job; then it can only become an impediment to performance, if not an embarrassment."[39] Reluctance to acknowledge that a program or agency has outlived its usefulness and to act upon that realization drains public resources while producing little in return.

Ambiguous Objectives and Lack of Performance Measurement. Also on Drucker's list of sins is the establishment of lofty objectives. "To have a chance at performance, a program needs clear targets, the attainment of which can be measured, appraised, or at least judged."[40] Too often, local government objectives, if stated at all, are presented in ambiguous terms—"to ensure public safety," "to enhance recreational opportunities," or the like. In the absence of precise, quantifiable objectives, local government performance measurement tends to be a tabulation of workload indicators—the number of calls answered, the number of cases processed, the number of applications received.

Absence of Cost Accounting Systems. Few local governments are able to specify the resources consumed by particular activities, projects, or programs. Cost accounting systems are generally either nonexistent among local government departments or restricted to only a few functions. Budget documents and financial statements provide general approximations which typically fail to assign full costs to a program, often omitting significant expenses such as fringe benefits and capital costs, and leading, according to a study of 68 cities, to a 30 percent understatement of program expenses.[41] The absence of accurate program cost information is a significant impediment to valid comparison of current operations to alternatives—either public sector options in operation elsewhere or the alternative of private sector contracting.[42]

Inadequate Information on Intracity and Intercity Performance. Few mayors or city managers have more than a subjective basis on which to judge the performance of their municipality or individual departments within it. Only rarely are sophisticated performance measures maintained in any department—much less in the two or more departments or two or more cities required for comparison, with measures of sufficient similarity to make comparison meaningful. More commonly, judgments regarding performance adequacy are based upon subjective assessments more dependent upon anecdotes than upon comparison of hard data for roughly equivalent operations.

Inadequate Information Dissemination and Reluctance to Use What Is Known. Many observers suggest that productivity would be improved if only local officials had greater access to information regarding productivity gains effected elsewhere. This argument assumes an enthusiasm for productivity literature that may not be held universally.[43] Furthermore, as Hayes points out, "knowing or, more commonly, suspecting the truth creates no mandate to use it, gives it no protective political authority or credibility, and provides no help in implementing it through an administrative cadre than may be hostile or inept."[44] Nevertheless, inadequate information regarding methods employed and degree of success enjoyed elsewhere increases uncertainty and reduces the likelihood of organizational experimentation and change.

Inadequate Program Evaluation. Many local government managers distrust or fear program evaluation. A thorough review of their operation and evaluation of its degree of effectiveness may reveal embarrassing weaknesses; a sloppily conducted evaluation may misrepresent program effectiveness. Furthermore, the time and financial resources devoted to program evaluation reduce what would otherwise be available for program operation. By allowing these and other considerations to minimize the use of program evaluation, local governments deprive themselves of useful information for defending worthy programs and modifying or abandoning those that are not.

Insufficient Analytic Skills or Analytic Staffing. A factor retarding the application of sophisticated management analysis techniques and the development of innovative approaches to the improvement of operational performance is a lack of sufficient analytic skills in most local governments. The shortage of such skills has long been recognized as a significant barrier to a local government's ability to identify performance strengths and weaknesses and to sift operational options with a high probability for success from those more likely to fail.[45] In what he terms a "management science paradox," Levine notes that those organizations that do have strong analytic capacity are unlikely to take advantage of it, since they typically are the ones with abundant resources and desire primarily to build and maintain political constituencies. Paradoxically, those most in need of analytic capacity because of severe resource problems tend to sacrifice analytic staff first in order to avoid cutting employees with service delivery functions.[46]

Performance Myths. Local government managers committed to productivity improvement are often constrained by myths revered by other managers, employees, legislators, and the citizenry. For example, one popular myth suggests that most local government programs and services, by their very nature, would not lend themselves to satisfactory performance by the private sector. Evidence to the contrary is mounting. Local government services from air pollution abatement to zoning and subdivision control have been successfully contracted out. In fact, the most studied of contracted services, refuse collection, has been found to be 29 to 37 percent more costly, though no more effective or equitable, when handled by municipal departments.[47]

Other apparent myths pertain to the manner in which specific functions are carried out. For example, in police work considerable value is placed on routine preventive patrol, rapid response, exhaustive detective work, the development of massive police data-collection systems, and two-officer patrol cars. Poole, however, cites studies by respected research organizations that challenge conventional wisdom regarding the assumed advantages of these expensive approaches to police service.[48]

Requirement of Large Initial Investment for Productivity Efforts. Ambitious productivity improvement efforts are rarely inexpensive. Most require extensive analysis and careful nurturing—both of which may be performed by current staff, but which often require recruitment of additional talent: Special equipment needs, such as automated meter reading devices, one-person garbage trucks, or additional computer terminals, also push program expenses upward, often with little hope of reaching the break-even point in the short term. Local government legislators, anxious over declining revenues and the disagreeable prospect of raising taxes before the next election, are unsurprisingly reluctant to accept short-term expenses for the prospects of possible long-term gains.

Overselling Productivity. Overenthusiastic advocates of productivity improvement programs risk raising expectations to the point that even moderately successful programs appear to be failures. Few programs amass major gains in their first year, but most quickly manage to acquire a line of detractors. If expectations of local government legislators and upper-management officials are set unreasonably high, those detractors are all too willing to document any gaps between expectation and reality. Ironically, overenthusiastic proponents may unintentionally threaten the survival of the productivity improvement efforts they promote.[49]

Bureaucratic Rigidities and Fragmented Authority. Local government structures of today reflect in large measure the concerns of turn-of-the-

BOX 7.1 A Legislative Perspective

Walter L. Balk

How can Federal, state and other local government legislatures take action in order to develop productivity policy and help provide continuity to improvement action? A philosophy of parsimonious oversight and action seems to be in order. While it is evident that legislators do not want to intrude upon the function nor replicate the detail of executive offices, they should know what the overall agency improvement targets are as well as the progress being made. Legislators need to develop short- and long-term action priorities of their own, which will help support agency and executive management change.

A Few Specifics. Even though the technical problems of gauging agency productivity present difficulties, agency administrators still have a professional responsibility to provide proof that they are running cost efficient and quality effective operations. This involves demonstrating that pockets of chronic subemployment and underemployment do not exist. Also associated is the need to show that modern managerial techniques are being employed. Basically, such proof is the responsibility of executive officers. Agency administrators will occasionally claim that it is impossible to set understandable goals for productivity increases and report upon progress. To make such a claim is to admit that one cannot administer an organization. Agency managers, in some cases, cannot provide productivity information because they are not up-to-date regarding measurement techniques. But, more commonly, the hesitancy exists because they recognize the inherent limitations of the data and the need for careful interpretation. They fear that precipitous decisions may be made by legislators and that information will be taken out of context in order to make political hay. These are realistic fears that put a sizable burden of knowledge and restraint upon legislators. They, too, must understand the pitfalls as well as the power of measurement data. Latitude for administrators to interpret data for legislative bodies is essential. Productivity programs oversight is an exchange. Administrators take the risk of providing information with the expectation that legislators will use it mainly to determine where and how they can best support their agencies over the long run in making management improvements.

(Source: Walter L. Balk: "A Legislative Perspective," in: Productivity In Government: A Legislative Focus," *Public Productivity Review* 8 (Summer 1984): 148–161.)

century reformers. Those reformers were less concerned with managerial innovation than with equity in service delivery, merit in employment practices, elimination of corruption, and performance in compliance with then prevailing standards of efficiency and effectiveness. The local government model that they designed is one that relies heavily on rules, regulations, detailed procedures, and a traditional bureaucratic hierarchy. As noted by Hayes, the various provisions "designed to maintain effective central control, to prevent unauthorized deviations in program, to preclude political decisions in employment and contracting, and to erect safeguards against fraud and embezzlement," lock in place the priorities and procedures of an earlier era. "all in all, our state and local governments are superbly equipped to do tomorrow what they did yesterday. But these governments are not designed to be highly efficient, responsive, flexible, or innovative."[50]

Bureaucratic rigidity is coupled in this traditional structure with fragmented authority that often requires an innovator to pass through several rounds of approval. Again quoting Hayes:

> The multiple clearances and approvals required and the known or suspected opposition to the changes all give advance notice that the proposed change will demand considerable effort and that it may not survive the process. Within state and local bureaucracies, the most striking characteristic, in this respect, is not resistance to change but the low credibility in the possibility of change.[51]

Supervisory Resistance. Some studies have shown department heads and supervisors potentially to be among the most formidable barriers to productivity improvement—more formidable than employee unions.[52] Supervisors, ideally situated to thwart the successful implementation of productivity-inspired changes, may oppose change for several reasons. They may resent the intrusion of outside analysts; they may fear that ideas from others will suggest to supervisors that they are weak innovators themselves; they may fear that productivity analysis will result in loss of subordinate employees or other resources; they may be concerned that new procedures will expose their own technical weaknesses or those of longtime subordinates whose friendship they value; or they may worry that organizational change will bring loss of status.[53]

Conclusions

Reciting such a lengthy list of barriers to productivity, some technical and some political,[54] carries the danger of discouragement. Rosenthal contends, however, that effective public managers overcome this discouragement and learn "which constraints to respect and which to modify to improve program operations."[55]

A barrier encountered unexpectedly is more likely to severely damage a productivity improvement effort than one examined first at a distance and approached with a suitable strategy. Most barriers are singularly incapable of counteracting even a somewhat clumsy but truly determined management effort. When encountered in combination, however, greater managerial perceptiveness and skill become necessary. Early recognition of relevant barriers, their magnitude, and options for circumventing or overcoming their potential potency is an important ingredient for managerial success.

The struggle is likely to be frustrating. McGowan, in fact, has likened it to the torment of Sisyphus, the legendary king of Corinth who was condemned to roll a heavy stone up a steep hill in Hades only to have it roll back down each time he neared the top.[56] McGowan contends that at least part of the reason for frustration "is that we fail to recognize the uniqueness of public sector service provision and all of the constraints associated with it. Simply adopting an approach or technique wholesale from another discipline or field will not always work; the patient may indeed reject the transplant."[57] Hence the need for an understanding of the special barriers to public sector productivity improvement.

Despite all of the obstacles, many local government managers have improved productivity in their organizations. They have been innovative, not because the path was easy but because they were determined to overcome the barriers to change.

Notes

1. Much of the discussion that follows is based upon the 34 barriers to productivity improvement identified in David N. Ammons, *Municipal Productivity: A Comparison of Fourteen High-Quality-Service Cities* (New York: Praeger, 1984), Chapter 6.

2. David Rogers, *Can Business Management Save the Cities? The Case of New York* (New York: Free Press, 1978), 4.

3. David N. Ammons and David J. Molta, "Productivity Emphasis in Local Government: An Assessment of the Impact of Selected Policy Environment Factors," in R. M. Kelly, ed., *Productivity, Public Policy, and Societal Well-Being* (New York: Macmillan, forthcoming).

4. Nancy Hayward and George Kuper "The National Economy and Productivity in Government" *Public Administration Review* XXXVII (January/February 1978), 3.

5. Ibid., 3–4.

6. See, for example, General Accounting Office, *State and Local Government Productivity Improvement: What Is the Federal Role?* (Washington, D.C.: U.S. Government Printing Office, 1978), 22–23.

7. For a more descriptive listing of such criticisms, see David R. Morgan, *Managing Urban America* (Monterey, CA: Brooks/Cole, 1984), 26–27.

8. Wayne F. Anderson, Chester A. Newland, and Richard J. Stillman, II. *The Effective Local Government Manager* (Washington, D.C.: International City Management Association, 1983), 182.

9. See, for example, GAO, *State and Local Government Productivity Improvement*, 43–44, 49; Hayward and Kuper, "The National Economy and Productivity in Government," 4; and Multi-Agency Study Team, "Report to the National

Productivity Council, November 1979," reprinted in *Public Productivity Review*, IV (June 1980), 170.

10. Elmer B. Staats, "An Era of Enduring Scarcity: Challenges and Opportunities," *National Civil Review*, LXIX (January 1980), 13–21, 32.

11. Laurence Rutter, *The Essential Community: Local Government in the Year 2000* (Washington, D.C.: ICMA, 1980), 25, 104–108.

12. Robert P. McGowan and John M. Stevens, "Local Government Initiatives in a Climate of Uncertainty," *Public Administration Review*, XLIII (March/April 1983), 127–136. Also see Catherine Lovell and Charles Tobin, "The Mandate Issue," *Public Administration Review*, XLI (May/June 1981), 318–331.

13. U.S. Advisory Commission on Intergovernmental Relations, *State Mandating of Local Expenditures* (A–67) (Washington, D.C.: U.S. Government Printing Office, July 1978), 3.

14. For a description of the adverse effects of delays produced by civil service hiring practices, see E. S. Savas and Sigmund G. Ginsburg, "The Civil Service: A Meritless System?" *The Public Interest*, XXXII (Summer 1973), 70–85.

15. Selma J. Mushkin and Frank H. Sandifer, *Personnel Management and Productivity in City Government* (Lexington, MA: D.C. Heath, Lexington Books, 1979), 96.

16. National Center for Productivity and Quality of Working Life, *Employee Attitudes and Productivity Differences Between the Public and Private Sector* (Washington, D.C.: U.S. Government Printing Office, 1978), 17–18.

17. John M. Greiner, Harry P. Hatry, Margo P. Koss, Annie P. Millar, and Jane P. Woodward, *Productivity and Motivation: A Review of State and Local Government Initiatives* (Washington, D.C.: Urban Institute, 1981), 385.

18. Ibid., 95–104.

19. Peter Marris and Martin Rein, *Dilemmas of Social Reform* (Chicago: Aldine, 1973), 45.

20. LeRoy F. Harlow, *Without Fear or Favor* (Provo, Utah: Brigham Young University Press, 1977), 334; and E. S. Savas, *Privatizing the Public Sector: How to Shrink Government* (Chatham, NJ: Chatham House, 1982), 81.

21. Walter L. Balk, "Organizational and Human Behavior," in G. J. Washnis, ed., *Productivity Improvement Handbook for State and Local Government* (New York: John Wiley & Sons, 1980), 497–498.

22. David T. Stanley, *Managing Local Government Under Union Pressure: Studies of Unionism in Government* (Washington, D.C.: Brookings Institution, 1972), 90–93.

23. Consider, for example, union resistance to the Public Safety officer (PSO) concept, whereby police and fire personnel are cross-trained for both functions, and the use of computer-aided fire station siting techniques when they lead to station closings and fire company reductions. See Greiner et al., *Productivity and Motivation*, 307, 354; Jan M. Chaiken and William Bruns, *Improving Station Locations and Dispatching Practices in Fire Departments: A Guide for Fire Chiefs and Local Government Executives* (Washington, D.C.: U.S. Department of Housing and Urban Development, 1978); and Warren E. Walker, *Changing Fire Company Locations: Five Implementation Case Studies* (Washington D.C.: U.S. Department of Housing and Urban Development, 1978).

24. Frederick O'R. Hayes, *Productivity in Local Government* (Lexington, MA: D.C. Heath, Lexington Books, 1977), 215, 251–252.

25. David T. Methe and James L. Perry, "The Imparts of Collective Bargaining on Local Government Services: A Review of Research," *Public Administration Review,* XL (July/August 1980), 367–368.

26. See, for example, Norman Steisel, "Productivity in the New York City Department of Sanitation: The Role of the Public Sector Manager," *Public Productivity Review,* VIII (Summer 1984), 103–126.

27. Morgan, *Managing Urban America,* 269–278.

28. Norman L. Fainstein and Susan S. Fainstein, "Innovation in Urban Bureaucracies," *American Behavioral Scientist,* XV (March/April 1972), 517.

29. See, for example, Thomas A. Mills, "Courts," in Washnis, ed., *Productivity Improvement Handbook,* 973.

30. Price Waterhouse, *Productivity Improvement Manual for Local Government Officials* (New York: Price Waterhouse, 1977), 27.

31. Peter Szanton, *Not Well Advised* (New York: Russell Sage Foundation and The Ford Foundation, 1981), 63.

32. Alan Walter Steiss and Gregory A. Daneke, *Performance Administration: Improved Responsiveness and Effectiveness in Public Service* (Lexington, MA: D.C. Heath, Lexington Books, 1980), 170.

33. Fainstein and Fainstein, "Innovation in Urban Bureaucracies," 517.

34. Walter L. Balk, "Productivity in Government: A Legislative Focus," *Public Productivity Review,* VIII (Summer 1984), 148–161.

35. David N. Ammons and Joseph C. King, "Productivity Improvement in Local Government: Its Place Among Competing Priorities," *Public Administration Review,* XLIII (March/April 1983), 113–120; Nancy S. Hayward, "The Productivity Challenge," *Public Administration Review,* XXXVI (September/October 1976), 544.

36. Hayward and Kuper, "The National Economy and Productivity in Government," 4.

37. For example, restrictive civil service regulations were eased in a successful New York City productivity effort through the "broadbanding" of several civil service titles into a single title, thereby effectively expanding the candidate pool for key management positions in the Sanitation Department from 15 to 130. See Steisel, "Productivity in the Department of Sanitation," 107.

38. Ammons and King, "Productivity Improvement," 113–120.

39. Peter F. Drucker, "The Deadly Sins in Public Administration," *Public Administration Review,* XL (March/April 1980), 105.

40. Ibid., 103.

41. E. S. Savas, "How Much Do Government Services Really Cost?" *Urban Affairs Quarterly,* XV (September 1979), 23–42.

42. Savas, *Privatizing the Public Sector,* 94, 147–148.

43. See Ammons and King, "Productivity Improvement."

44. Hayes, *Productivity in Local Government,* 287.

45. In 1943, Clarence Ridley and Herbert Simon lamented the absence of statistical skills in most city halls in Ridley and Simon, *Measuring Municipal Activities: A Survey of Suggested Criteria for Appraising Administration* (Chicago: International

City Managers-Association, 1943). More recent proponents of greater analytic talent in local government include Harry P. Hatry and Donald M. Fisk, *Improving Productivity and Productivity Measurement in Local Governments* (Washington, D.C.: Urban Institute, 1971), 8–9; Marc Holzer, ed., *Productivity in Public Organizations* (Fort Washington, NY: Kennikat Press, 1976), 20; and Multi-Agency Study Team, "Report to the National Productivity Council," 176–177.

46. Charles H. Levine, "More on Cutback Management: Hard Questions for Hard Times," *Public Administration Review,* XXXIX (March/April 1979), 180.

47. Savas, *Privatizing the Public Sector,* 62–64, 93.

48. Robert W. Poole, Jr. *Cutting Back City Hall* (New York: Universe Books, 1980), 37–38, 45–46.

49. George P. Barbour, Jr., "Law Enforcement," in Washnis, ed., *Productivity Improvement Handbook,* 962.

50. Frederick O'R. Hayes, "Innovation in State and Local Government," in Hayes and John E. Rasmussen, eds., *Centers for Innovation in the Cities and States* (San Francisco: San Francisco Press, Inc., 1972), 7–8.

51. Ibid., 8.

52. See for example, Hayes, *Productivity in Local Government,* 252.

53. Ibid.; John R. Hall, Jr., *Factors Related to Local Government Use of Performance Measurement* (Washington, D.C.: Urban Institute, 1978), 15–16; Price Waterhouse, *Productivity Improvement Manual,* 11; Clair F. Vough, *Productivity: A Practical Program for Improvement Efficiency* (New York: Amacom, 1979), 191; and Melville Dalton, "Conflicts Between Staff and Line Managerial Officers," *American Sociological Review,* XV (June 1950), 349.

54. A General Accounting Office report found the political problems to be more formidable than the technical barriers. GAO, *State and Local Government Productivity Improvement,* 23.

55. Stephen R. Rosenthal, *Managing Government Operations* (Glenview, IL: Scott, Foresman and Co., 1982), 292.

56. Robert P. McGowan, "Improving Efficiency in Public Management: The Torment of Sisyphus," *Public Productivity Review,* VIII (Summer 1984), 177.

57. Ibid., 177–178.

8

Recognizing Management Technique Dysfunctions

How Management Tools Often Create More Problems Than They Solve

Gerald T. Gabris

The purpose of this article is to question whether current management techniques used by public administrators often create more problems than they solve. Do rational management techniques, designed to increase organizational effectiveness, actually work? Or do they simply create new burdens?

This is an important issue. All too often, agencies at the federal, state, and local levels adopt rational management tools that look good in theory but become dysfunctional or problematic in practice. Public administrators often assume that new techniques will automatically increase organizational effectiveness, without first thinking through the unanticipated consequences. While management techniques can improve organizational productivity, they also contain the potential for decreasing organizational performance through faulty application and implementation. This dysfunctional potential represents a major paradox in the use of management techniques as tools for increasing organizational effectiveness.

A conceptual framework that identifies, describes, and explains the origins and general characteristics of management technique dysfunctions

---

"Recognizing Management Technique Dysfunctions: How Management Tools Often Create More Problems Than They Solve," *Public Productivity Review* 19 (Winter, 1986): 3–19.

may be of value to managers. Through such a framework, public managers may acquire better insight into how to recognize and cope with the negative consequences associated with management tools before such consequences begin to affect general organizational performance.

Why Are Management Techniques Used So Frequently?

The widespread acceptance and use of rational management techniques can be explained from a variety of perspectives. In the first place, more and more public sector managers are products of professional academic public administration programs. These programs tend to expose and socialize students to what is considered a well-rounded, state-of-the-art curriculum of public sector skills, theories, ethics, and management techniques.[1] Graduates of these programs tend to believe in techniques and become their advocates, even though very few have actual experience in implementing or evaluating them. Second, the fact that modern management techniques are grounded in scientific authority further facilitates their acceptance and legitimacy. A third factor is that public managers are under almost constant pressure by interest groups, citizens, and politicians to improve organizational effectiveness. Rational management tools that can be manipulated to give the appearance of greater efficiency and effectiveness are therefore especially attractive to managers and politicians alike. This may be true even though the application of a technique is likely to have only a marginal bearing on organizational effectiveness and to represent nothing more than a quick fix.[2] Finally, because rational management techniques are more empirically grounded and often require the use of specialized language symbols, computers, and skills, they tend to increase the importance and power of public managers; they tend to justify why the public manager is so vitally needed. For these reasons, rational management techniques have become in some ways the accepted instruments of modern public administration, even though they may generate more net losses than net gains in efficiency for the organizations that use them. What, then, are the management techniques under consideration, and what are their dysfunctions?

Modern Management Techniques

Risking oversimplification, Figure 8.1[3] identifies several commonly used modern management techniques that often lend themselves to dysfunctional application. These techniques are identified only in general terms. There are many hybrids of each technique, but the purpose of this article is neither to critically analyze each technique in its variety of forms nor to suggest that these techniques have never increased organizational effectiveness or been empirically tested. This article should also not be construed as

FIGURE 8.1 Commonly Used Management Techniques

1. Management by objectives with results
2. Organization development (OD)
3. Merit-based performance appraisal
4. Management information systems
5. Program evaluation
6. Performance budgeting
7. System IV—Participating group management

a cost-benefit analysis of management tools. The purpose of this article is to criticize the general application and implementation of these techniques and to describe the general dysfunctions that often accompany their application, rather than to analyze the techniques themselves. Thus, whether a public agency should or should not utilize a management technique is not at issue here. This article considers what happens once a public organization does decide to utilize one or more management tools.

Management Technique Dysfunction

A management technique dysfunction can be defined as a characteristic or condition associated with the implementation and maintenance that diminishes or reduces the capacity of that technique to achieve its intended objective or purpose.[4] The critical analysis of management techniques is not new; a case in point is Aaron Wildavsky's classic description of why budgetary reforms will not work well at the federal level.[5] Wildavsky contends that the attempt to transfer Planned Program Budgeting (PPB) from the Department of Defense to other federal agencies was principally a failure, in large part because PPB was based on economic rather than political rationality. Another early critic of management techniques is Wallace Sayre, who described how the rationalization of public personnel administration has led to the "triumph of technique over purpose."[6] Many discussions on why management techniques do not work in public organizations focus rather exclusively on the political environment of an agency.[7] Political rationality is often described as a hindrance to the objective application of a technique. While politics often dilutes the pure application of a technique, techniques often falter in the public sector not only for political reasons but also because of inherent technical flaws in the management tools themselves.

By focusing on management technique implementation in general, this article develops a framework for classifying different kinds of dysfunctions that may emerge but are only peripherally related to politics. For empirical verification, I shall cite examples from my own experience and research and, when appropriate provide examples from the literature on management and

FIGURE 8.2 Management Technique Dysfunctions

1. Process Burdens
2. The Georgia Giant Syndrome
3. Internal Incapacity
4. Credibility Anxiety
5. False Result Expectations

organizational behavior. This presentation should provoke a healthy skepticism toward management tool utilization. Figure 8.2[8] outlines the management technique dysfunctions to be addressed. These dysfunctions are not mutually exclusive; indeed, most are highly interdependent. At this juncture, each dysfunction will be considered in detail, and we shall see how it can arise even when a technique is applied with the sincere intent of using it to increase organizational effectiveness.

Process Burdens

The first technique dysfunction to be addressed, process burdens, is probably more bothersome than any other specific dysfunction to public managers. Process burdens can be defined as the procedural and control requirements associated with the implementation and maintenance of a technique (the paperwork requirements, forms, red tape, training sessions, and data collection processes) that take employees away from their actual responsibilities. Because management technique applications require so many nonroutine procedures, they can become extremely burdensome to employees expected to carry them out. At times, process burdens are so pervasive that they can outweigh any real gains derived from the techniques themselves. Moreover, process burdens tend to be monotonous and time consuming. As process burdens increase, employees begin to question the utility of a technique. Process burdens dampen the initial enthusiasm for a technique and may lead to a technique's not being taken seriously. If this happens, the technique's failure to produce expected results can become a self-fulfilling prophecy for those who perceive the technique as creating too many burdens in the first place.

One example of process burdens is the State of Mississippi's Variable Compensation Plan (VCP). In 1980, Mississippi inaugurated a personnel reform designed to establish a merit pay system for all state-agency personnel. In some respects, the VCP is similar to the merit pay plan at the federal level, mandated by the Civil Service Reform Act of 1978. The basic assumption underlying the VCP is that stated employees should be financially rewarded on the basis of productivity, rather than being given standard across-the-board raises. In order for the VCP to work, it was necessary for each state agency to develop and implement a valid performance appraisal instrument.

The first step in creating a valid performance appraisal instrument is to conduct a thorough job-content analysis.[9] The State of Mississippi used a standard job-content questionnaire, which was distributed to all state agencies, and each employee was required to complete it. This was done in order to identify performance dimensions or job elements associated with each agency position. One of the first problems to arise in conjunction with this task was the agencies' lack of in-house expertise in performance appraisal and behavioral science. Most agency personnel officers did complete a performance-appraisal training program, but a large number came away still uncertain of how to identify performance dimensions and, more important, of how to develop performance indicators for these job elements. Because agency personnel officers were uncertain of how the process was supposed to work, many agency employees were misguided in their efforts to develop job-related performance dimensions. This problem was compounded when agencies attempted to develop indicators measuring objective job performance. Instead of using incidents of effective and ineffective behavior, agency employees tended to define effective behavior in "results only" terms.[10]

Some agency personnel also recognized that the development of valid behavioral criteria would cost a tremendous amount of time and effort. If we assume that a typical staff employee identifies fifteen job elements and that each job element generates five critical incidents of effective or ineffective behavior, then seventy-five behavioral indicators would be necessary for just one employee.[11]

If an agency manager is responsible for evaluating ten employees, who may be performing dissimilar functions, then the manager must account for 750 bits of behavioral information. For such a system to be valid (this does not speak to the issue of reliability, which would require additional information and tests), evidence of effective and ineffective behavior must be documented and systematically recorded. Assuming that the manager is expected to document employee performance on a monthly basis for feedback and evaluation, then we are talking about documenting 9,000 bits of behavioral information per year. To most agency managers, the mere thought of such a monumental task is staggering. Indeed, very few individuals in any organization possess the intellectual, cognitive, and rational capacities to make such a system work. This documentation effort takes managers and employees away from other forms of expected work and excludes parallel techniques, such as management by objectives (MBO), which usually accompany merit pay plans and involve additional process burdens in and of themselves.

To many managers, a valid performance-appraisal system simply requires too many process burdens to make it worth the effort. In one study of a Mississippi state agency, 70 percent of all managerial employees thought the VCP would actually decrease rather than increase employee performance,[12] a finding echoed in recent reports, which suggests that federal employees are also disenchanted with and uncertain about the merit pay plan in their agencies.[13] Given the innumerable process burdens associated with the VCP, it is not being implemented successfully in most Mississippi agencies. As a consequence, the technique stands to lose its credibility and is unlikely to produce the hoped-for increases in employee output.

The Georgia Giant Syndrome

Although related to process burdens, the Georgia Giant Syndrome gets at a qualitatively different idea. According to a recent article in an outdoor magazine, a Georgia entrepreneur claimed to have developed a new hybrid fish named the Georgia Giant.[14] This fish is supposed to grow faster and larger and fight more vigorously than normal bream or sunfish. Needless to say, many farmers purchased these fish, thinking these hybrids would provide fantastic angling in their farm ponds. It so happened that an Alabama fisheries biologist decided to verify these claims. Using a classic experimental design, the biologist took some hybrids and put them in an untreated control pond. He then put another batch of bass and catfish fingerlings in an experimental pond. The experimental pond was unique in that all the existing fish were killed before the Georgia Giants were inserted in ratio to bass and catfish fingerlings. The biologist found that the hybrids placed in the control pond grew neither feistier nor larger than the existing control-pond fish. In the experimental pond, however, the Georgia Giants lived up to expectations. The point is that the hybrid worked only under closely supervised control conditions. If these conditions were not met or not monitored, the hybrid did no better than ordinary fish in the pond. The biologist also discovered that over time, if not replenished, the hybrid was subject to loss of "hybrid vigor."[15] In other words, the succeeding generations of hybrids eventually came to reflect the generic and behavioral characteristics of ordinary fish. Several lessons can be learned from the Georgia Giant experiments in relation to modern management techniques.

In the first place, management techniques may work only under rigorous and closely supervised control conditions. If control conditions are not met, the technique may not live up to expectations and potential. Rigorous diagnostic analysis prior to implementation of a management technique is frequently downplayed in the public sector, because political pressures often emphasize the adoption of a technique immediately, to make it appear as though productivity improvements are being made, even if the technique has few real effects. Too often, once a management technique is installed, monitoring and controls tend to diminish over time, assuming that controls were even set in place. Thus, succeeding generations of the technique, if control conditions become lax, show a reduction in the original impact and efficacy; the technique loses its "technique vigor." After a time, employees treat the technique as just another burdensome routine, which has no bearing on their real work.

The importance of this illustration is that management techniques cannot simply be thrust upon an agency and be expected to produce their intended results. Given pressure to increase efficiency and effectiveness, public managers like to assume that a particular technique will be a panacea. At the same time, public managers are often unwilling to accept the process burdens, monitoring requirements, control conditions, and diagnostic research necessary for a technique to produce its intended impact. Just because a particular technique increases effectiveness in one organization does not mean that it will produce similar results in other agencies.

One illustration of the Georgia Giant Syndrome is the application of organization development (OD) to the public sector. In fairness to OD practitioners, almost all of them advocate diagnostic research before any OD intervention strategy is recommended for a particular organization.[16] If proper diagnostic research is not conducted, then intervention strategies may be substantially off target and may not produce the expected results, and the OD intervention may exacerbate rather than lessen organizational problems. In one symposium on OD, featured in a public administration journal, three of the seven articles focused more on why OD does not work than on why it does work in the public sector. The remaining four articles dealt more with OD theory and concepts than with actual OD implementation experiences. In the three articles that did specifically address OD experiences, the Georgia Giant Syndrome was clearly evident. According to one of the articles, "A clear minus in the organization improvement program in the City of Tacoma was the absence of careful research designed to test the impact of the various interventions and activities. We discussed the desirability of conducting research numerous times among ourselves and the clients, but whenever it came to choosing between improvement and research, we selected the former."[17] Although this example deals specifically with OD, similar control and research problems plague other management technique applications. These problems can be illustrated by the current effort in Biloxi, Mississippi, to implement management by objectives (MBO) and merit-based performance appraisal in each of its five municipal departments.

Since the summer of 1982, I have been serving the City of Biloxi as an outside management consultant. One of the things brought up with the mayor and the department directors, before any technique application was initiated, was the necessity of conducting diagnostic research relating to each specific department's unique organizational behavior. The reason for this suggestion was clear: A department of public safety may have role expectations, group norms, reporting systems, and outputs quite different from those of a department of public works; research into these areas would facilitate the development of the MBO and performance-appraisal systems best suited to the unique needs of the various departments. Simply applying a standard MBO or canned performance-appraisal model to all departments may be expedient but will not address the unique control, monitoring, and output characteristics in a way that will produce the expected results of the technique application.

Although the mayor and the department directors were aware of these research necessities, they decided to forego all preliminary research and to begin immediately with implementation. This omission eventually led to several problems. First of all, during the MBO application in one department, it became clear that objectives were misstated and misunderstood and that the role expectations of employees and managers developing the indicators, action plans, and controls were unclear. This resulted in considerable slowdown. Second, because preliminary research was not conducted, a "shotgun" strategy of MBO implementation was employed to determine unique departmental needs, constraints, outputs, teamwork expectations, and suitable controls. As this process unfolded, it was discovered that many of the objectives designated by higher management were outside the control of the employees responsible for carrying them out. This oversight called for substantial restatement of unit objectives (and more process burdens) to recognize the importance of employees' efforts as an integral component of successful MBO implementation. Finally, since no baseline data were collected, systems actually have an improved organizational performance.

Exactly how extensive the Georgia Giant Syndrome is in the application of management tools is open to speculation, yet journal reports and personal experience suggest that this dysfunction is rather prevalent. At this point, let us turn our attention to internal incapacity, a dysfunction generically related to process burdens and to the Georgia Giant Syndrome.

Internal Incapacity

Internal incapacity can be described as the outcome of superimposing a management technique on an organization that lacks the in-house capacity to implement and monitor the technique beyond its initial phases. (It should not be confused with "trained incapacity.")[18] Internal incapacity is analogous to placing the chassis of a Cadillac over the engine and frame of a Volkswagen: It may look like a nice automobile, but it cannot get out of low gear. Too often, management techniques are recommended and adopted by public organizations that lack implementation capacity. This may be one reason why the Georgia Giant Syndrome is so prevalent. Internal incapacity is observable in a number of technique applications, but it is probably most noticeable in small municipal governments and small agencies.

One example of internal incapacity concerns the attempt of a small city, with a population of 10,000, to implement performance budgeting within its municipal departments. In this case, the municipal officials conceived performance budgeting both as a means of identifying departmental outputs and as a means of relating outputs to costs. This particular city had a "weak mayor" form of government, although it did employ a professional chief administrative officer (CAO). Part of the initial enthusiasm for performance budgeting stemmed from the CAO's involvement as a student in a nearby public administration program.

The city's performance budgeting model was developed by an outside expert in conjunction with a government technology bureau. Virtually no prior research was conducted to dovetail the city's unique needs and implementation capacity with the technique. All flow charts, forms, and systems concepts contained in the model were based on academic assumptions about what performance budgeting should look like, rather than on how it would work in this specific setting, Further, the outside experts who were developing the model were also expected to train municipal department managers on how to transform the city's line-item budget into a performance budget. Several problems began to surface with training and implementation.

The first set of problems was related directly to process burdens. In order to document and record output levels, departmental managers had to learn how to conceptualize programmatic output, as opposed to line-item output. Many of these managers had very little background in finance or budgeting, and many had difficulty understanding the system's concepts. As a consequence, the training sessions began to take much longer than initially anticipated and were having only a marginal effect on the budgetary sophistication of the city's managerial personnel. The managers began to perceive the training sessions as taking too much time away from more important responsibilities, and they did not see how the new system was going to improve effectiveness.

This city also exhibited internal incapacity in its ability to store, document, and reprocess information. The outside experts suggested a number of documentation and monitoring procedures, all of which required the use of a computer. Only after building their budgeting model did the outside consultants realize that the city's in-house computer could not handle the information load for the system they were recommending. If the system were put in place, the city would have to contract out for additional computer time from another state agency, and costs would increase greatly over original estimates. With the departure of the outside experts, city officials decided to abandon performance budgeting, not because they did not like the idea, but because they realized that the city did not have the internal capacity to make it work.

Credibility Anxiety

Because technique application so often generates process burdens and control problems and cannot address internal incapacity, it also precipitates credibility anxiety. This particular dysfunction is psychological and should be avoided at all costs. Once technique credibility is lost, it is very difficult to recover. Understanding this dysfunction, therefore, is of considerable importance to public managers.

Credibility anxiety involves the neurosis and uncertainty that surround the changes and expectations associated with the implementation of a new management technique. As James D. Thompson points out, employees at the technical level of an organization seek certainty and determinateness.[19] Often, the individuals responsible for the actual output of an organization are suspicious of changes that affect their routines and habitual ways of doing things. Indeed, many public employees perceive management techniques as just adding to process burdens, without providing worthwhile payoffs. When employees perceive a particular technique as not working well, this observation tends to reinforce the idea that techniques in general do not work well. Thus, the failure of one technique may produce a ripple effect for the credibility of other implementation efforts that may come later. Like the young man who cried "wolf" once too often, management techniques have a limited reservoir of credibility. If employees do not take a technique seriously, it often fails to develop the credibility and resilience that encourage employees to accept the process burdens and controls necessary for it to work. Without credibility, many technique applications are doomed to failure or, at best, only marginal bearing on organizational effectiveness.

The attempt by the Mississippi Department of Public Welfare to implement participative group management (Likert's System 4) among agency managers is a good example of how credibility anxiety can develop.[20] In this agency, the basic assumption was that if managers at the middle and first-line levels could be retrained in participative management techniques, the employee morale and employee performance would increase. These assumptions are similar to those held by public managers in a variety of agencies.

In order to implement participative group management, the agency contracted with management consultants and established a series of training seminars, required for all agency line managers. I had the opportunity to interview these line managers after they had completed their training.

The majority of the managers stated that they had enjoyed the training sessions and thought the sessions had served a therapeutic function. However, the same managers stated that the training sessions did not alter their own approaches to management. In the first place, middle and first-line managers did not perceive top management as practicing what it preached. Many middle and first-line managers perceived top management as authoritarian and did not see why top management should expect others to conduct superior/subordinate relationships on a more participative basis. Second, many managers believed that their subordinates sometimes did not work hard and "needed their toes stepped on" in order to carry out their prescribed responsibilities. They did not think a democratic approach to management would be credible.[21] The majority of the managers simply perceived their own current management behavior as sufficient for carrying out the agency's objectives and tasks. Most of the managers also perceived the whole training program as a cosmetic device to make the agency look better, rather than as a substantive attempt on the part of top managers to improve employee morale. For these reasons, agency managers paid lip-service to participative management but did not perceive the technique as credible.

Another illustration of credibility anxiety can be derived from the application of management by objectives to the administrative arm (0 area) of the U.S. State Department. During the 1960s, the deputy undersecretary for administration began implementation of management of programs (MOP) as a vehicle for increasing subunit autonomy and for achieving greater program decentralization.[22] The problem was whether federal employees would accept these changes as credible. The author investigating these 0 area reforms and technique applications relates: "The introduction of change in a federal agency is complicated by its sheer frequency. The life of the Washington bureaucrat is punctuated by a perpetual reshuffling of positions. . . . Political appointees come and go. . . . Though his term may be short, each new director tries to assert control over an agency by changing it. The new broom sweeps clean for a few months. Another follows who repeats the process. Consequently, the word 'reorganization' often connotes a personally inspired, impetuous, dubious, and probably ephemeral reform that is best disregarded."[23] To put the matter squarely, most technique applications lack credibility, and most attempts to implement them generate credibility anxiety. As might be expected, two years after the implementation of MOP at the State Department, the new deputy undersecretary for administration abolished the procedure.[24]

The fact that many management techniques may be piled on top of one other in a public organization, even though they do not work well, probably contributes to credibility anxiety. New management systems are expected to produce dramatic and quick results. When results do not materialize after a short time, top-level appointed and elected officials often deem a technique application a failure. The common response is then simply to try a different technique to see if its works. This is the shotgun approach. As this repetitive cycle continues, no single technique usually has enough time to develop credibility.[25] One reason why management technique applications are so frequent in the public sector may have to do with false result expectations.

False Result Expectations

I remember the frustrations voiced by Alan Kiepper during a panel presentation some years ago at a regional public administration conference. Kiepper, the director of the Metropolitan Atlanta Rapid Transit Authority (MARTA), related how Atlanta citizens assumed the new MARTA subway system would be operational after just one year. The citizens had approved the project and funded it, and now they expected quick and dramatic results. These were false result expectations on a grand scale. Part of Kiepper's job was simply to serve as a public relations advocate and explain that the construction of underground subway systems takes between six and eight years. On a smaller scale, false result expectations also abound in the application of management techniques.

False result expectations can be described as the dramatic results anticipated by policy makers and citizens from the application of management techniques in public agencies. Such expectations exert pressure on those responsible for implementing new management tools. On the one hand, this pressure may encourage the people responsible for implementation to ignore important control and monitoring requirements in order to achieve short-term application results. Technique applications done in haste create innumerable process burdens, fall victim to the Georgia Giant Syndrome, and generate considerable credibility anxiety. As a consequence, they usually fail to work after a relatively short time. On the other hand, false result expectations can also create too much work for managers implementing a technique. Thus, false result expectations can eventually lead to high organizational turnover and burnout.

The dysfunctional implications of false result expectations can be illustrated by a brief example. As indicated earlier, the City of Biloxi has undertaken a number of management technique applications. Even though the mayor and the department directors were involved in discussions specifying the limitations of these techniques, they still expected quick results. At one point, a six-month implementation phase was suggested as sufficient for installing merit-based performance appraisal in all city departments. In addition to performance appraisal, a new management-by-objectives system was also to be set in place during the same period, as a means of assessing subunit productivity. On paper, and all things being equal, these technique applications could have been implemented in six months, but in most public agencies, all things are never equal. Elected officials must respond to a variety of political and environmental demands; they cannot devote all their efforts to technique implementation. As a consequence, there is generally a large gap between anticipated results and the time required or allotted to produce them. Management technique implementation takes time, sometimes years, and the unwillingness or inability to provide a career administrator with the flexibility and time necessary to properly install a technique can eventually lead to the technique's abolition or disuse.

All too often, public officials have unrealistic expectations about the time it will take to implement a technique properly. This is not solely a problem of elected officials; career managers, too, may encourage the use of a particular technique, only to become bogged down in the process burdens, control factors, and credibility problems. Implementation is slowed down, the overall efficiency of the technique in improving organizational performance is reduced. Management techniques simply are not panaceas, even though they are often perceived as such by public managers who advocate them.

Conclusion: Strategies for Controlling Management Technique Dysfunctions

The chief purpose of this article has been to shed some light on a number of potential dysfunctions associated with commonly utilized management tools. It has not been suggested that these techniques have never worked or have not been empirically grounded. Instead, the thrust of the argument has been to suggest that the application of modern management techniques generally ignores the dysfunctional consequences these applications may bring about. The techniques are frequently perceived as quick fixes for organization inefficiency and productivity problems. Sometimes the techniques work; at other times, they may result in a variety of dysfunctions that outweigh any possible advantage to an organization. The very techniques employed for increasing organizational effectiveness contain the potential for decreasing it.

This is the paradox of modern management techniques, a riddle yet to be resolved. If these techniques are to have real value to the public sector, serious consideration should be given to developing strategies for controlling the dysfunctions associated with them.

It is beyond the scope of this article to set forth a comprehensive theory or model specifying how management technique dysfunctions can be eliminated. Nevertheless, here are some practical suggestions for countering their more serious consequences.

Share, Distribute, and Decentralize the Process Burdens. In any management technique application, process burdens cannot be completely eliminated. They are part of the ballgame. The important thing is to ensure that no employee or managerial group gets stuck with the bulk of the process burdens. Quality circles and task forces that distribute and share these responsibilities are one option. Also, top management should decentralize responsibilities throughout the organization and take part itself in technique application.

Provide Incentives for Reducing Process Burdens. The number and quantity of process burdens may not be avoided, but they can be reduced. Employees and managers who can devise ways of eliminating unnecessary process burdens should be rewarded. Rewards could take the form of pay bonuses, recognitions, high evaluations, or perhaps just the psychological knowledge that certain procedural requirements associated with a technique have been reduced.

Engage in Substantial Diagnostic Research. This may sound obvious, and in many ways it is, yet it is very expensive for many public organizations, and quality of diagnostic research varies considerably. In any event, substantial diagnostic research into values, culture, and current employee perceptions of management style and organizational needs will enable consultants to dovetail management techniques with the unique characteristics of the organization. This will help avoid the Georgia Giant Syndrome, establish controls, predict reasonable result expectations, and probably lower credibility anxiety.

Pretest and Experiment. Even if diagnostic research is conducted, it is prudent to pretest a technique on several agency divisions or on a single division in a pilot context before a technique is implemented agencywide. This will show where the bugs and kinks are in the system before they crop up everywhere at once. Also, experimentation in different variants of the technique, and the allowance of flexibility, will also probably facilitate employee acceptance and hence improve credibility.

Provide Follow-Through in Technique Implementation. Too often, management techniques are implemented but not subsequently utilized to any substantial degree by the organization. Techniques should not be used as window dressing. If an organization does not intend to use a technique once it is implemented, then it should avoid the technique application in the first place. For example, organizations establish merit performance appraisal but then do not use the instruments to award merit bonuses. Technique credibility depends a lot on the willingness of the organization to follow through in the utilization of its techniques.

Establish the Policy of Acceptance Time.[26] This is a concept derived from the literature on Japanese management, which makes a great deal of sense for American organizations. New ideas and techniques will take time for employees to accept and integrate into their schemes of work. People need time to gradually let go of the old before they accept the new. Employees cannot be forced to accept new techniques. This implies that initially techniques may face employee resistance and even sabotage. These short-run costs must be absorbed. It may take several years for a technique to become accepted before it will begin producing substantive results.

Institutionalize Periodic Technique Review. Many techniques are not utilized by organizations once they are implemented, and so technique review is usually a low priority of management. Thus, internal incapacity, senseless process burdens, and the Georgia Giant Syndrome are usually not confronted and dealt with by agency managers. These dysfunctions are simply accepted as part of the headache associated with management techniques. If public agencies would review management techniques more often and more seriously and dovetail this effort with quality diagnostic research, then many severe dysfunctions could be mitigated and avoided. Periodic review could ensure that techniques do not lose their "technique vigor" after only a short period of time.

Work to Achieve Small Successes. In implementing a management technique, work with that portion or division of the organization where the technique is most likely to be successful in the short term. This will enhance technique credibility. The communication grapevine will rapidly increase the probability that the technique will be more readily acceptable in those parts of the organization where technique application will be most difficult. Success breeds success, even if it is small and incremental.

Implement Only One Technique at a Time. Employees can become very confused and resentful when multiple management techniques are all applied at the same time. Obviously, this multiplies the number of process burdens they must deal with and taxes the capacity of the organization to absorb such efforts. Simultaneous technique implementation increases the probability that techniques will not be accepted by employees, will overtax organizational capacity, and will probably not work. Moreover, by focusing on only one major technique at a time, management will find it easier to locate the bugs and kinks in a new system and correct them before they become extremely problematic. This is more difficult when several techniques are being implemented at the same time.

Define Results Qualitatively as Well as Quantitatively. Both public and private organizations in the United States seek to quantify everything, and techniques are seen as the means to this end. While quantitative performance is a primary objective of any technique, techniques also precipitate many secondary and indirect results of a qualitative nature, some of which are as valuable as, if not more valuable than, quantitative output. For example, performance appraisal may compel supervisors to be more open with their subordinates and provide better feedback. MBO may enhance communication between otherwise isolated organizational units. Too often, this qualitative aspect of management techniques is not counted as a payoff. More organizations should broadly define results to include qualitative impact. This may buy more time for a technique to produce better quantitative results.

These are mainly suggestions concerning how management technique dysfunctions can be more effectively controlled and dealt with by public managers. In all probability, managers could add to the list of dysfunctions outlined in this article and probably provide more insightful strategies on how to control for them. This is all well and good. At the same time, students of public administration should recognize that many of the rational management techniques we advocate as tools for improving organizational effectiveness do not often work. This problem will not go away simply because we do not wish to recognize it. It must be dealt with and confronted with vigor. Unless public administration can address these technique dysfunctions and learn to control them more effectively, perhaps the skepticism the public holds toward government—as a producer more of processes than of products—is justified.

Notes

1. For example, *NASPAA Self Study Report Form 1980,* "Curriculum Analysis Matrix," p. 13.

2. For a text that attempts to avoid the quick-fix trap, see Ralph Kilmann, *Beyond the Quick Fix* (San Francisco: Jossey-Bass, 1984).

3. For example: George Morrisey, *Management by Objectives and Results in the Public Sector* (Reading, Mass.: Addison-Wesley, 1976); Robert T. Golembiewski and William Eddy, *Organization Development in Public Administration* (New York: Marcel Dekker, 1978); Gary Latham and Kenneth Wexley, *Increasing Productivity Through Performance Appraisal* (Reading, Mass.: Addison-Wesley, 1981); Peter Sarant, *Zero Based Budgeting in the Public Sector: A Pragmatic Approach* (Reading, Mass.: Addison-Wesley, 1978); and Renis Likert, *The Human Organization* (New York: McGraw-Hill, 1967).

4. This concept of dysfunction is related to that described by Peter Blau, *The Dynamics of Bureaucracy* (Chicago: University of Chicago Press, 1972), pp. 8–9.

5. Aaron Wildavsky, *The Politics of the Budgetary Process* (Boston: Little, Brown, 1979).

6. Wallace Sayre, "The Triumph of Techniques over Purpose," in *Classics of Public Personnel Policy,* ed. Frank Thompson (Oak Park, Ill.: Moore, 1979), p. 32.

7. Wildavsky, *The Politics of the Budgetary Process,* pp. 188–202.
8. The term *process burdens* was mentioned during a lecture at Mississippi State University by Sylvester Murray, City Manager of Cincinnati, Ohio, in 1982.
9. Latham and Wexley, *Increasing Productivity Through Performance Appraisal,* pp. 48–64.
10. Wayne Cascio, "Types of Performance Measures," *The Performance Appraisal Sourcebook,* eds. Lloyd Baird, Richard Beatty, and Craig Schneier (Amherst, Mass.: Human Resource Development Press, 1982), pp. 42–43.
11. This assumes one uses the "critical incident method." See Latham and Wexley, *Increasing Productivity Through Performance Appraisal,* pp. 55–76.
12. Gerald T. Gabris and William A. Giles, "Level of Management, Performance Appraisal, and Productivity Reform in Complex Public Organizations," *Review of Public Personnel Administration* 3 (1983): 45–63.
13. Lloyd Nigro, "CSRA Performance Appraisals and Merit Pay: Growing Uncertainty in the Federal Workforce," *Public Administration Review* 42 (1982): 371–375; Jone L. Pearce and James L. Perry, "Federal Merit Pay: A Longitudinal Analysis," *Public Administration Review* 43 (1983): 315–326.
14. John E. Philips, "Georgia Giant—Hoax or Super Bream?" *Outdoor Life,* February 1983, p. 89.
15. Philips, "Georgia Giant—Hoax or Super Bream?" p. 89.
16. Robert T. Golembiewski, as one OD practitioner, clearly makes this case in his lectures and books.
17. Cecil H. Bell and James Rosenzweig, "OD in the City: A Potpourri of Pluses and Minuses," *Southern Review of Public Administration* (1978): 443–444.
18. Robert K. Merton, "Bureaucratic Structure and Personality," in *The National Administrative System,* ed. Dean Yarwood (New York: Wiley, 1971), p. 380.
19. James D. Thompson, *Organizations in Action* (New York: McGraw-Hill, 1967), p. 10.
20. See Likert, *The Human Organization.*
21. This was a finding in a management study of the Mississippi Department of Public Welfare. It is not in published form. The interesting thing is that top managers generally were satisfied with their peers. It was middle and first-line managers who generally thought "toes needed stepping on" and who also thought management generally ignored the nonperformer.
22. Donald P. Warwick, *The Theory of Public Bureaucracy* (Cambridge, Mass.: Harvard University Press, 1975), pp. 37–40.
23. Warwick, *A Theory of Public Bureaucracy,* pp. 43–44.
24. Warwick, p. 55.
25. The notion of "acceptance time" can be found in the literature on Japanese management. See Richard Pascale and Anthony Athos, *The Art of Japanese Management* (New York: Warner Books, 1981), pp. 70–71.
26. Pascale and Athos, *The Art of Japanese Management,* pp. 70–71.

Part Two

Performance Strategies

The articles in the second section examine performance management strategies. Poister and Streib (1994) provide empirical evidence about the use of performance management strategies in local government. They find that program evaluation, forecasting, performance monitoring, employee involvement efforts, and strategic planning are among the most frequently used approaches. More recent tools, which are still being adopted, are of course less often used. Eadie (1983) discusses the application of strategic planning in government. Through strategic planning, organizations and communities develop new goals, update their missions, and create a shared commitment among leaders and stakeholders for current and future endeavors. Bryson and Roering (1988) lay out some lessons that public agencies have learned in applying strategic planning, including a schematic roadmap. Halachmi (1991) observes that while strategic planning often adopts a comprehensive and agency-wide perspective, many improvements are incremental and made by subunits.

Vogelsang and Cummins (1982) discuss reorganizations and reforms, which they view as a form of bureaucratic politics. Well-intended efforts to rationalize bureaucracies often come to naught when reformers fail to address the politics of reform. They examine the case of the U.S. Senior Executive Service. Odiorne (1976) considers the use of Management by Objectives in state governments. MBO aims to boost productivity by increasing responsibility, autonomy, and accountability. The object lesson is that MBO requires the "power of commitment" by employees and supervisors.

Odiorne makes many suggestions for increasing the acceptance of MBO, including the importance of being upfront and sincere. These attributes are echoed by Lukens (1947) in describing the management culture of a public organization. Griener (1986) examines other motivational strategies such as monetary incentives and training. He, too, finds that such programs require meaningful employee involvement.

Although the management of quality has increased in importance since the mid-1980s, the origins of this performance management strategy can be traced back to W.W.II. During that period, the U.S. military developed new strategies to improve the quality of war-related machines and equipment, some of which were later adapted to post-War civilian uses. Divine and Sherman (1948) discuss how statistical process control techniques can be used in government agencies to reduce costs and errors. Blair, Cohen and Hurwitz (1982) describes the use of Quality Circles, a forerunner of Total Quality Management. Swiss (1992) explains the tenets of Total Quality Management and how it can be adapted to public sector use. These tenets include client-orientation, performance tracking, worker participation, and continuous improvement. Berman and West (1995) raise the problem of token TQM adoption in the context of municipal government.

Information technology has had a profound impact on public performance. Worthley (1980) considers the implications of information technology for performance and management, including concerns for privacy, adequate resources, the need for staff training, and client unrest. Many of these problems continue today. Milward and Snyder (1996) provide examples of current information technology applications in government.

Levine (1978) examines cutback management strategies. He sets forth a framework for considering retrenchment scenarios and tactics, and builds on concepts of capacity-building, strategic planning, and motivation. Holzer (1986) considers the usefulness of reduction in force efforts as a performance management strategy for downsizing. Finally, Savas (1977) makes the case for privatization through competition and contracting of public services with private providers. His case study shows that contracting out, now widely used in many governmental settings, can result in significant savings.

9

Municipal Management Tools from 1976 to 1993

An Overview and Update

Theodore H. Poister and Gregory Streib

Throughout this century, municipal governments have pursued a variety of strategies to enhance their ability to deliver services effectively and efficiently. Some might argue that the road to improved management capacity has been filled with potholes, but the desire to find better ways to do things has never stopped gaining momentum. Local officials have been pressed forward by the academic writings of authors such as Woodrow Wilson and Luther Gulick, the shrewd exhortations of reformers such as Richard Childs, the formative influence of the International City Management Association (ICMA) and other professional groups, the early Housing and Urban Development (HUD) capacity-sharing efforts of the federal government, taxpayer revolts, and current societal demands for improved quality and customer service. Indeed, a whole profession has developed that hinges on its ability to apply the "expertise and knowledge of local government and management to urban service delivery" (Nalbandian, 1990, p. 659).

Perhaps the clearest expression of this commitment to management excellence can be found in the growing inventory of management tools that have spread throughout municipal government (Hatry, 1981). Although most of these tools have been transplanted from either the private sector or

"Municipal Management Tools from 1976 to 1993: An Overview and Update," *Public Productivity and Management Review* 18 (Winter, 1994): 115–125.

other levels of the federal system, municipal governments have in many ways become a kind of laboratory, constantly experimenting with new management tools, adapting them to fit their own needs, and often improving them in the process. They have adopted such tools as management by objectives (MBO), zero-based budgeting, and planning, programming, and budgeting systems, which were once intended to revolutionize the administration of the federal government, and they have long used other critical tools such as performance monitoring, productivity improvement programs, and program evaluation. In recent years, local governments have moved quickly to adopt more contemporary approaches, such as strategic planning and total quality management (TQM).

It should be noted, however, that not everyone favors the professionalization of municipal government or the contributions of these management innovations. From the outset, some saw municipal reform efforts as thinly veiled attempts to usurp the growing power of our nation's ethnic minorities. After all, what was inefficiency and corruption to some was a toehold on the American dream to others. Beyond the political implications, it has also been charged that these management approaches simply don't work. Many have argued that the rational model, the very foundation of most contemporary management tools, is hopelessly flawed, and that the tools derived from it are far removed from practical realities. As Downs and Larkey (1986) state, "implementation of such strategies requires analytical and personnel resources far in excess of what usually is available" (p. 4). They contend that management tools are often oversold; although they promise increased efficiency, they often produce only failure in a continuous cycle of grand promises and disappointment that has contributed to widespread cynicism about government.

Admittedly, even under the best circumstances, efforts to combine professional management skills with the give and take of politics are apt to present some difficulties. Despite the challenges, however, a wholesale rejection of systematic management improvement efforts in the near future is highly unlikely. In fact, if recent books and articles are an accurate gauge, interest in a wide variety of management innovations is stronger than ever. One way in which academic researchers can help inform further developments in this era of management tools is to continue to monitor their use in municipal government. Are new tools assuming important roles in managing local government? Has the use of traditional tools remained constant, grown, or declined rapidly? Are some tools more effective than others?

In this article, we examine data from a series of four surveys designed to track the use of management tools by municipal governments over the past eighteen years. The findings provide a long-term overview that is rare in the study of public administration. Many studies focus on individual tools of rising importance, but follow-up is rare. In addition to examining a number of traditional management tools, we also look at a couple of tools that have become much more prominent over the last five years. Although we have limited information on the tools included in this study, our findings provide data that are essential for examining long-term trends and provide a useful context for more intensive investigations of management systems and strategies.

Overview and Approach

The data reported here extend a loose time series on municipal management trends based on the findings of three earlier surveys of municipal managers conducted by Fukuhara (1977), Poister and McGowan (1984), and Poister and Streib (1989). Taken together, these studies showed that a number of traditional management tools were implemented by growing numbers of jurisdictions during the 1970s and early 1980s and were quite prevalent in local government by the late 1980s. Municipal managers were also experimenting enthusiastically with a number of newer approaches, such as financial trend monitoring, strategic planning, and quality circles during the late 1980s. Although many of these tools were adopted in the public sector first by the federal government, where they were subsequently discarded as broad-based holistic management systems, the pattern these municipal management surveys revealed was for the most part one of continued diffusion and stability rather than boom-and-bust cycles.

Since the last of these surveys, public administration literature has reflected substantial continuing interest in more established management systems as well as newer tools and techniques. For example, Swiss (1992) provided the first public management text focusing explicitly on particular management systems including MBO, performance monitoring, productivity improvement programs, and incentive systems as well as cost-accounting and performance-budgeting systems. Rodgers and Hunter (1992) characterize MBO as a "foundation of good management practice in government" based on a meta-analysis of thirty studies evaluating the impact of MBO in terms of productivity, employee performance, and other criteria. Wholey and Hatry (1992) reiterate the case for performance monitoring as a critical tool for tracking and improving the performance of programs at all levels of government in an era of decentralization, privatization, quality improvement, and customer service. Others continue to refine the role of program evaluation in government (Davis, 1990; Wholey, 1991; Newcomer, 1994).

Regarding newer techniques, a much deeper literature on strategic planning has developed to assist public managers in adapting corporate-style approaches to the needs of governmental agencies, managing the strategic planning process in the public sector, and moving from strategic planning to ongoing strategic management (Bryson, 1988; Rabin, Miller, and Hildreth,

1989; Koteen, 1989; Nutt and Backoff, 1992). More recently, a tremendous wave of interest has developed in total quality management processes, as reflected in public administration literature that both promotes TQM (Carr and Littman, 1990) and expresses caution about its feasibility or usefulness in the public sector (Swiss, 1992). Other authors examine the challenges inherent in integrating TQM with other management functions and provide examples of TQM processes in a wide array of government agencies (Hyde, 1992; Bowman and French, 1992; Gilbert, 1992; Cohen and Brand, 1993).

The continuing salience of management tools is reflected in an article by Hatry (1992–1993) that reminds public managers of the value of a variety of approaches including program budgeting, MBO, productivity improvement efforts, performance monitoring, program evaluation, and TQM. All these tools entail considerable implementation problems, but Hatry points out that in recent years some of the technical problems related to information processing have been overcome, making these techniques more feasible and useful. Acknowledging uneven development patterns, disappointments, and failures over time, Hatry contends that "while most of these approaches have ended up being castigated and even ridiculed, these efforts have provided an ever-improving series of public management/administration techniques that can, and indeed are, improving government performance" (p. 8).

Survey Methodology

Given this continued interest in many traditional management tools along with the emergence of high-visibility approaches over the past five or six years, further tracking of these tools in municipal management into the 1990s is needed. Thus, we surveyed a national sample of municipal managers in the fall of 1993 in order to examine their current use of these tools. A survey instrument that replicated portions of the earlier municipal management surveys was mailed to municipal officials in all 1,126 U.S. cities with populations between 25,000 and one million and a mayor-council or council-manager form of government. The addressees were city managers, mayors, or other senior officials identified as the ICMA's principal contacts in each of these cities. This is the same population that was surveyed in the earlier studies.

A total of 520 usable surveys were returned from two mailings, for a response rate of 46 percent. The resulting sample closely resembles the entire population on relevant parameters such as population region, and form of government, although the response rate tended to be slightly higher for municipalities in the South and the West and for those with the council-manager form of government. The survey asked respondents to indicate whether they use any of a number of management techniques in their jurisdiction and how they rate the effectiveness of these tools.

Current Use of Tools by Municipal Managers

Figure 9.1 shows the management tools included in the 1993 survey, arranged by their current level of use. Five of these tools were used by 70–75 percent of the responding jurisdictions. These include two finance-oriented tools (revenue and expense forecasting and financial trend monitoring), two evaluation-oriented tools (program evaluation and performance monitoring), and employee involvement efforts. It is not surprising that the financial management techniques are used in so many municipal jurisdictions because they were heavily promoted by HUD's capacity-sharing program in the late 1970s and early 1980s. Similarly, program evaluation and performance monitoring are fairly noncontroversial approaches that have been supported by academics and professionals for years and are often used in conjunction with other management systems such as program budgeting and management by objectives. Employee involvement programs have become popular as a result of the wave of enthusiasm for decentralization and empowerment as a means of building employee commitment and improving organizational effectiveness.

The second group of tools includes strategic planning (63 percent), program budgeting (60 percent), incentive programs (58 percent), productivity improvement programs (53 percent), and MBO (47 percent). Strategic planning is a widely heralded approach adapted from the private sector and promoted heavily by public administration professional associations in the 1980s; program budgeting—often remembered for its demise in the federal government in the late 1960s—has had sustained credibility with finance directors and budget officers at the state and local level for decades. Employee incentive systems, both individual- and group-based, appear to be popular with public managers as a means of motivating employees and work groups in civil service systems, where it is otherwise difficult to reward star performers. Formal productivity improvement programs are maintained by many municipal jurisdictions even though national attention has shifted to other performance-enhancing strategies such as quality improvement, customer service techniques, and continuous improvement processes. MBO; which is often thought of as a discard of the federal government, is also quite popular at the local level as an effective approach to performance management.

Near the bottom of Figure 9.1 are TQM, used in 39 percent of the responding jurisdictions, and quality circles, used by 33 percent of these cities. Quality circles are a somewhat shallow intervention for strengthening organizational capacity, and to a degree they have been incorporated or superseded by the newer and more comprehensive TQM movement, which has developed a widespread following in public management circles over the past few years. There is probably some overlap between quality circles and

FIGURE 9.1 Use of Management Tools in 1993

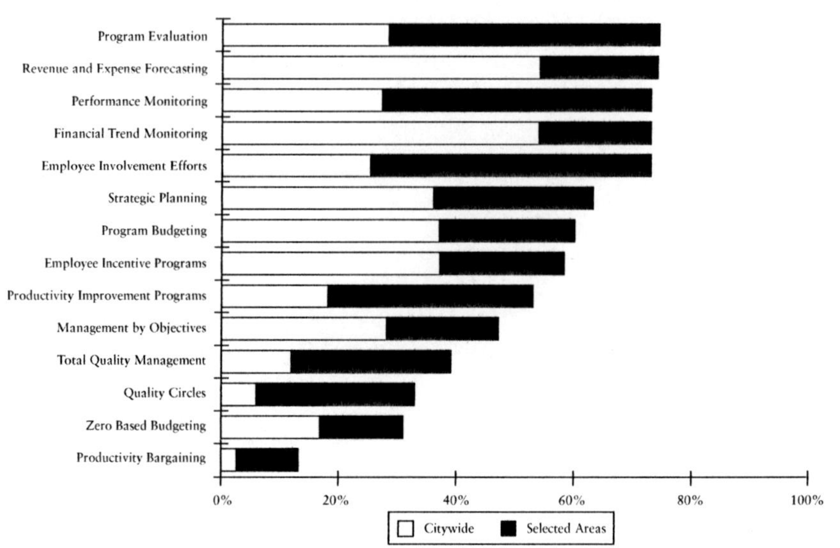

TQM in these survey responses, as well as between these two approaches and other employee involvement programs. These findings suggest that TQM has begun to penetrate local government rapidly. Zero-based budgeting, which is not often addressed in recent literature, is still used in nearly one-third of these municipal jurisdictions, and productivity bargaining—which requires both the presence and cooperation of unions—is used in only 13 percent of these jurisdictions.

Some of these tools tend to be used principally on a citywide basis, whereas others are more commonly used in selected departments or program areas. It is not surprising that system-oriented approaches such as strategic planning, program budgeting, MBO, and zero-based budgeting are more likely to be found in citywide applications. The same is true of revenue and expense forecasting and financial trend monitoring, tools that are usually used to track and assess financial conditions for the jurisdiction as a whole. The finding that employee incentive systems also tend to be used on a citywide basis is somewhat surprising. Because some municipal operations involve routinized production processes that lend themselves more to setting work standards and measuring actual outputs against targets, it would seem reasonable for incentive systems to be implemented in selected areas rather than across-the-board applications.

Conversely, both program evaluation and performance monitoring, which are often considered particularly appropriate for citywide implementation, are used significantly more often in selected departments or program areas. Although some cities have comprehensive systems for monitoring and evaluating all municipal operations, these techniques may be more beneficial in some program areas than others. In addition, employee involvement programs, TQM, and especially quality circles are used predominantly in selected departments, suggesting that many cities are interested in allowing or encouraging experimentation with these employee-centered approaches in pilot projects on a piecemeal basis rather than committing the entire city to them.

Consistent with the earlier surveys, these management tools are generally more likely to be used in larger jurisdictions, especially in cities with 100,000 people or more, and are used less in the northeast than in other regions of the country. Generally speaking, many of these tools, including financial trend monitoring, strategic planning, MBO, program budgeting, performance monitoring, program evaluation, productivity improvement programs, incentive systems, and employee involvement programs, are more closely associated with the council-manager form of government. In city-manager cities, financial trend monitoring, revenue and expense forecasting, strategic planning, MBO, program budgeting, and incentive systems are even more likely to be implemented on a citywide basis, whereas performance monitoring, program evaluation, productivity improvement programs, TQM, and employee involvement programs are found more often in selected areas.

Trends over Time

The overall pattern of use of these tools by municipal governments currently is quite similar to that found in the 1987 survey, which seemed to mark the end of a period of rapid expansion in the use of many of these tools. This plateau effect is still evident today, as can be readily seen in Figure 9.2. Reported use of most of the traditional management tools increased substantially between the 1976 and 1982 surveys, then leveled off or decreased in the 1987 survey, and decreased a little more in the 1993 survey. Recent declines are most notable for program or zero-based budgeting, MBO, incentive systems, productivity bargaining, and program evaluation. Among the traditional tools, only performance monitoring is an exception to this trend. Strategic planning and quality circles showed substantial initial reported use in 1987, with small increases at best in 1993.

The breakdown between citywide versus selected applications of these tools in 1993 is very similar to that in 1987, with three exceptions. Whereas strategic planning, then a fairly new technique, was reportedly used more in selected departments than in citywide applications in the 1987 survey, the 1993 survey shows that now it is used more on a citywide basis. The same

FIGURE 9.2 Use of Traditional Tools over Time

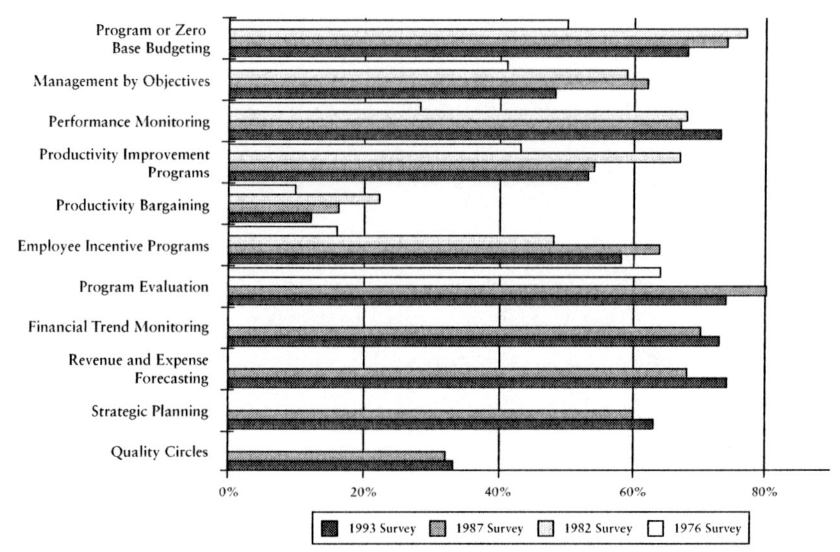

is true of incentive systems. In 1987, almost three times as many cities used incentive systems on a selective basis, whereas in 1993 more than 58 percent of the jurisdictions with incentive systems used them on a citywide basis. On the other hand, almost twice as many cities use productivity improvement programs on a selective rather than citywide basis, whereas in 1987 they were used slightly more in citywide applications.

The perceived effectiveness of these tools in 1993 is also highly consistent with the results of the previous survey. Table 9.1 shows the percentage of the respondents who reported using each tool who rate it as very effective as an aid to management and decision making. Overall, the tools rated the highest were revenue and expense forecasting, rated as very effective by 58 percent of all the managers whose jurisdictions use it, and strategic planning (42 percent); at the low end of the scale, only 20 percent of those using productivity bargaining rated it as very effective. These ratings decreased noticeably over the past six years for two of these tools: the number of managers rating their zero-based or target-based budgeting systems as very effective dropped from 45 percent in 1987 to 41 percent in 1993, and the percent rating their MBO systems as very effective dropped from 41 percent to 30 percent over the same period.

Consistent with the 1987 survey, these tools tend to be rated more favorably when they are implemented on a citywide basis. For example, only 23 percent of the managers whose cities use strategic planning in selected departments or program areas rated this tool as very effective, compared with

TABLE 9.1 Effectiveness Ratings of Management Tools in 1987 and 1993 (percentage rating as very effective)

Tools	*Year*	*Number of Cities Using Technique*	*All Users*	*Citywide*	*Selected Areas*
Program budgeting	1987	284	43%	58%	21%
	1993	312	41	57	14
Zero-based or target-based budgeting	1987	142	45	66	24
	1993	246	30	41	12
Management by objectives	1987	268	41	57	18
	1993	246	30	41	12
Performance monitoring	1987	283	30	48	16
	1993	376	29	42	21
Productivity improvement programs	1987	219	24	45	15
	1993	274	27	44	18
Productivity bargaining	1987	65	12	33	7
	1993	63	20	50	13
Employee incentive programs	1987	277	23	27	14
	1993	305	22	26	14
Program evaluation	1987	333	34	49	26
	1993	384	36	53	25
Financial trend monitoring	1987	305	39	51	22
	1993	382	52	59	33
Revenue and expense forecasting	1987	298	49	62	26
	1993	382	58	64	41
Strategic planning	1987	249	38	59	23
	1993	328	42	55	23
Quality circles	1987	136	25	61	18
	1993	170	32	58	27
Total quality management	1993	203	26	48	17
Other employee involvement efforts	1993	380	30	44	22

55 percent of the managers from jurisdictions where strategic planning is used on a citywide basis. This pattern holds up to some degree for every management tool included in the survey. In addition, beyond the breadth of coverage, most of these management tools tend to be rated as more effective in cities with the council-manager plan than in mayor-council cities.

Conclusions

The results of this research are self-evident: a number of traditional management tools continue to be used by high percentages of municipal governments in the United States, and these jurisdictions are also quick to experiment with newer approaches that come along. One important benefit of the longitudinal data provided by this series of surveys is a confirmation of the relevance of management tools in municipal government over time. Just about every tool included in this study, including the newer ones, has been denigrated as oversold, impractical, or a passing fad at one time or another, suggesting that they are likely to be short-lived in actual practice. However, the data reported here indicate that municipal managers have maintained a strong commitment to many of these approaches over the long run, and not only in council-manager jurisdictions.

In 1976, program evaluation was the only tool included in the original survey that was used by more than 50 percent of the responding municipalities with populations between 25,000 and one million. The explosive growth and subsequent leveling off in the use of many of these tools over the past two decades, along with the emergence of newer approaches, has been remarkable. The 1993 survey documents a wide variety of tools that are used by more than half of the responding jurisdictions, although a few of these techniques, such as MBO, have declined in popularity somewhat over the past few years.

Does the fact that none of the tools included in the survey are used in every jurisdiction in the population of interest suggest that they are less attractive or less useful than they should be? Probably not. There seems to be a ceiling effect under which the use of any one of these individual tools is capped at about 75 percent, and this makes sense. As Hatry (1992–1993) notes, all of these techniques are based on sound principles, and it is difficult to argue against the desirability of allocating budgets based on systematic assessment of alternatives, setting targets and tracking performance, focusing on productivity and quality improvement, and involving employees in improving work processes, and logically it seems beneficial for all municipalities to use the management strategies. However, we must also recognize that all these approaches require investment in people, time, development, training, and equipment, which might well be prohibitively expensive to many of these jurisdictions, especially the smaller ones. The fact that some jurisdictions' benefit-cost calculus does not favor these techniques does not detract from their demonstrated utility in many other cities.

On the other hand, there is clearly room for improvement in the use of these approaches. The overall effectiveness ratings of these tools by high-level municipal managers is favorable, but certainly not enthusiastic. With the exception of revenue and expense forecasting and financial trend monitoring systems, both of which are highly technical functions that involve few managers or employees directly, most of these tools were rated very effective by 40 percent or fewer of the managers who use them. These ratings probably reflect realistic assessments based on suboptimal use of these tools in many cities in terms of breadth of coverage and thoroughness of design and implementation. Using most of these techniques effectively requires resources, technology, management capability, leadership, and sustained commitment, and in the absence of these necessary conditions, approaches such as MBO, performance monitoring, productivity improvement, employee incentive systems, and TQM are unlikely to be effective.

Nevertheless, municipal managers continue to show considerable interest in a wide variety of management tools, even though in some cases they are implemented in less-than-ideal circumstances. The pattern of use over time has been both stable and dynamic, with managers continuing to use approaches that are now considered traditional while they experiment with newly emerging tools. Thus, we have seen a changing variety of tools over time that is likely to change further in the future. For example, to the extent that TQM is adopted by municipal jurisdictions as an overarching management philosophy, we may expect to see MBO and individual-based incentive systems deemphasized while more compatible approaches such as performance monitoring and employee involvement programs continue to grow. Municipal governments in the United States have substantial long-term experience using management tools to improve their performance, and as the toolkit continues to evolve, tracking this experience will continue to provide knowledge and insight into effective public management.

References

Bowman, J. S., and French, B. J. "Quality Improvement in a State Agency Revisited." *Public Productivity & Management Review,* 1992, *16* (1), 53–64.

Bryson, J. M. *Strategic Planning for Public and Nonprofit Organizations: A Guide to Strengthening and Sustaining Organizational Achievement.* San Francisco: Jossey-Bass, 1988.

Carr, D. K., and Littman, I. D. *Excellence in Government: Total Quality Management in the 1990s.* Arlington, Va.: Coopers & Lybrand, 1990.

Cohen, S., and Brand, R. *Total Quality Management in Government: A Practical Guide for the Real World.* San Francisco: Jossey-Bass, 1993.

Davis, D. F. "Do You Want a Performance Audit or a Program Evaluation?" *Public Administration Review,* 1990, *50* (1), 35–41.

Downs, G. W., and Larkey, P. D. *The Search for Government Efficiency: From Hubris to Helplessness.* Philadelphia: Temple University Press, 1986.

Fukuhara, R. S. "Productivity Improvement in Cities." In *The Municipal Yearbook—1977.* Washington, D.C.: The International City Management Association. 1977.

Gilbert, R. G. "Quality Improvement in a Federal Defense Organization." *Public Productivity & Management Review,* 1992, *16* (1), 65–75.

Hatry, H. P. "The Boom in Management Tools—The U.S. Experience." *Local Government Studies,* 1981, *7* (6), 59–70.

______. "The Alphabet Soup Approach: You'll Love It!" *Public Manager,* 1992–1993, *21* (4), 8–12.

Hyde, A. C. "The Proverbs of Total Quality Management: Recharting the Path to Quality Improvement in the Public Sector." *Public Productivity & Management Review,* 1992, *16* (1), 25–37.

Koteen, J. *Strategic Management in Public and Nonprofit Organizations.* New York: Praeger, 1989.

Nalbandian, J. "Tenets of Contemporary Professionalism in Local Government." *Public Administration Review,* 1990, *50* (6), 654–662.

Newcomer, K. E. "Opportunities and Incentives for Improving Program Quality: Auditing and Evaluating." *Public Administration Review,* 1994, *54* (2), 147–154.

Nutt, P. C., and Backoff, R. W. *Strategic Management of Public and Third Sector Organizations: A Handbook for Leaders.* San Francisco: Jossey-Bass, 1992.

Poister, T. H., and McGowan, R. P. "The Use of Management Tools in Municipal Government: A National Survey." *Public Administration Review,* 1984, *44* (3), 215–223.

Poister, T. H., and Streib, G. "Management Tools in Municipal Government: Trends Over the Past Decade." *Public Administration Review,* 1989, *49* (3), 240–248.

Rabin, J., Miller, G. J., and Hildreth, W. B. *Handbook of Strategic Management.* New York: Marcel Dekker, 1989.

Rodgers, R., and Hunter, J. E. "A Foundation of Good Management Practice in Government: Management by Objectives." *Public Administration Review.* 1992, *52,* 27–39.

Swiss, J. E. *Public Management Systems: Monitoring and Managing Government Performance.* Englewood Cliffs, N.J.: Prentice-Hall, 1992.

Wholey, J. S. "Using Evaluation to Improve Program Performance." *The Bureaucrat,* 1991, *20* (2), 55–59.

Wholey, J. S., and Hatry, H. P. "The Case for Performance Monitoring." *Public Administration Review,* 1992, *52* (6), 604–610.

10

Putting a Powerful Tool to Practical Use

The Application of Strategic Planning in the Public Sector

Douglas C. Eadie

Introduction

During the last quarter-century, strategic planning has gained wide acceptance in the American corporate community as a powerful management tool. Corporate strategies receive frequent, close attention in such widely read publications as *Fortune* and *Business Week*. American graduate schools of business increasingly offer courses in strategic planning, and there is rapidly growing serious literature on the theory and practice of this relative newcomer to the planning scene in the private sector. Although at this point we have little hard evidence on the specifics of application in particular firms, especially regarding the return on the corporate investment in the planning techniques, there is ample evidence that strategic planning of some kind is widely practiced by large business. And it is certainly commonly considered a primary avenue to business growth.

Strategic planning has barely penetrated the collective consciousness of the public sector, at least to judge from the paucity of articles addressing either the theory or practice of these techniques in the public arena.[1] The

---

"Putting a Powerful Tool to Practical Use: The Application of Strategic Planing in the Public Sector," *Public Administration Review* 33 (September/October 1983): 447–566.

territory will not long be virgin, however. Resource scarcity and service demands place public organizations under great pressure to apply better planning techniques. In addition, there will be no dearth of salesmen anxious to capture a potentially lucrative market.

Dangers lurk along this yet-to-be-traveled road for those public organizations choosing to pioneer strategic planning in the coming months. Those venturing in the near future into this largely unknown territory will make the mistakes from which their followers will learn. The history of public planning is replete with tales of overexpectation, underestimation of costs, and disillusionment; the siren song of simple, inexpensive solutions to highly complex problems has certainly claimed its share of victims. In light of the largely private sector experience with strategic planning, and the sophistication of the techniques, the danger of costly failure in public sector application is clear and present.

The primary purpose of this article is to provide public sector executives and managers with practical guidance in the application of strategic planning in their organizations. This is not a survey of the public sector literature, such as it is, but an examination of practical approaches which appear likely to provide substantial benefit at an affordable cost. Examples are drawn from my experience as both an executive and a strategic management consultant in the public sector. If there is a message, it is that successful application is a matter of careful tailoring to the unique circumstances of a particular public organization. While there are themes, to be sure, tying all public sector organizations together, the variations are often crucial to success in planning process design. A boilerplate approach, in short, is likely to prove inadequate, if not fatal, and the organization that knows itself well and adapts its planning approaches accordingly is far more likely to experience success in planning.

To Glimpse a Passing Train

The field of strategic planning is developing so rapidly that a snapshot is quickly outdated. Another difficulty lying in the path of public practitioner understanding is the volume of writing on the subject as its popularity grows by leaps and bounds. The observer is in danger of being overwhelmed by the trees. Rather than attempting to summarize all facets of this complex topic, I have attempted to pin down the essence of the techniques and to suggest where the developing field is headed.

Traditional long-range planning, with its extrapolation of clear trends five and even ten years into the future, has proved increasingly less useful as, in the years since World War II, environmental change has escalated. The "Age of Discontinuity," as Peter Drucker has called it, demands planning that is at the same time more flexible and responsive to the environment surrounding the planning organization. The focus on understanding and interpreting an organization's environment is a basic characteristic of strategic planning. Another is change as a product of the planning effort. By contrast, traditional operational planning—short and long-range—is basically concerned with the refinement of existing "businesses" or programs and with productivity improvement.[2]

There are strategies, and there are strategies—big and little, broad and narrow—and a precise, universally acceptable definition is not available. For example, Richard F. Vancil has called strategies the "primary source of cohesiveness" in an organization,[3] and George A. Steiner has written that they deal with "anything that is highly important to the success of the company."[4] Alfred Chandler has observed that a strategy is the determination of the basic long-term goals and objectives of an enterprise, and the adoption of courses of action and the allocation of resources necessary for carrying out these goals."[5]

In my work in the public sector, I have found it useful to treat strategies as courses of action at differing levels of specificity:

- At the more global end of the strategy spectrum, an organization's overall strategy describes its basic "businesses" or areas of service and the broad ends to be achieved in each area. This is often set forth in a mission/goals statement. Slightly narrower, but still quite broad, is the blueprint which describes an organization's overall goals and technical approach in a particular program area, say, economic development in city government.
- Strategies may also be much narrower, serving as implementation plans to achieve specific change targets or objectives within a program area. In this instance, the target and strategy, taken together, might best be described as a strategic project.

Each of these approaches to the strategy question will be discussed in more detail later in this article. At this point, suffice it to say that the latter, narrower application of strategic planning may for many public organizations be the most utilitarian. While overall blueprints are certainly desirable, if not essential, it is through the narrower approach that near-term payoff is possible. Such immediate benefits may be an important way of building strong support for the planning effort. Narrower project-like applications are also more manageable, enabling a public organization to take chewable bites of a highly complex and demanding process.

The strategic planning process consists of the following basic activities:

- The organization must have a firm grasp of those aspects of its environment identified as pertinent to its mission and goals. Often called environmental scanning, this activity involves identifying the scope of the scan (international, national, regional, state, and local), the demographic, economic, technological, cultural, political, and other factors to be scanned, and their implications for the organization. A variety of other activities are involved, including the determination of how much time and other resources to invest in this ongoing intelligence gathering and what technologies to employ.

- The organization must also have a good sense of itself, financially, operationally, and in the human resource dimension. The point of this resource audit or analysis is to assess the organization's strengths and weaknesses vis-a-vis particular potential courses of action (strategies).
- The environmental scanning activity will surface opportunities for new services or new approaches to service delivery within a given service area. Potential strategic targets are compared to the organization's resource base in order to determine as fully as feasible the costs of implementing a particular strategic target. Strategic objectives are selected on the basis of rough cost/benefit analysis.
- Strategies are formulated to achieve the selected targets. In practice, they may be thought of as implementation plans, setting forth the major steps, accountabilities, deadlines, and resource requirements involved in achieving the target.
- No matter how well-conceived a particular strategy, implementation depends on the allocation of resources to cover the essential costs. What this basically means is that the chief executive officer, and perhaps the legislative body, specifically budget the first year costs in the current or upcoming budget of the organization.

Of Special Interest in Application

The experience of the past quarter-century in applying strategic planning has resulted in the accumulation of considerable practical wisdom, which, while it falls short of a scientific body of knowledge, is important to the practitioner. Two of the more important "golden rules" merit brief mention here before turning to the public planning environment.

First, experience indicates that successful application depends on giving at least as much, if not more, attention to the practical problems of implementing strategies as to the analytical approaches to strategy formulation. Indeed, overreliance on such sophisticated techniques as portfolio analysis may actually have impeded successful implementation.[6] And the human factor looms large in strategy implementation, as well as in formulation and selection of strategies. People perceive the environment and make judgments about the significance of events; people choose among alternative courses of action; and people supply the most precious resource in strategy implementation: their understanding, commitment, and time. Although the human factor in strategic planning has long been recognized, serious attempts to build an integrated (people with systems) approach are fairly recent.[7]

Another useful rule is to apply strategic planning as a continuous, rather than cyclical, process, and to limit the generation of formal planning documentation. In a time of constant, rapid environmental change, environmental scanning and strategy formulation must be ongoing activities if an organization is to respond effectively to both threats and opportunities. And if the documentation involved is too elaborate, essential flexibility and responsiveness will be lost as an organization concentrates on paper management.

H. Igor Ansoff and Michael Kami, among others, have commented on the importance of maintaining a continuous environmental intelligence gathering function.[8] Often, they suggest, if an organization is to respond effectively to an environmental event, it must have the capability to spot weak "signals"—isolated happenings that are not clearly a trend and whose implications for the organization are not clear—and to crack those signals until determining whether they are, indeed, significant enough to be treated as strategic issues.

Public Sector Planning

Generalizations are obviously dangerous when the empirical base is slim. Although there is substantial literature on public planning, we do not know much about the actual application of planning techniques, in terms of the seriousness of particular applications or the actual outcomes for the planning organization (beyond merely documentation). So, while we can say that considerable planning has been, and is being, done by public sector organizations, hazarding generalizations about the effectiveness of one approach or another is a risky business. It is useful, however, to attempt a rough and hardly scientific assessment of the status of planning in the public sector as a very important step in determining how best to approach the application of strategic planning. But the practitioner should always keep in mind that most golden of all maxims: tailor the application to thine own organization, with its own unique conditions and needs.

Looming largest on the public (and probably private) sector planning landscape is the annual (and sometimes biennial) operational planning and budget preparation process. Much of the history of public sector planning reform appears to be a story—sometimes inspiring, often not—of attempts to upgrade the planning content of the annual operational budget. This is a sensible course since the familiar object-of-expenditure budget remains the preeminent vehicle for the allocation of organizational resources and perhaps the most basic tool for day-to-day management. Certainly the language of planning has attached itself to the operational budget, which is no longer merely a statement of fiscal targets; but the extent to which planning influences resource allocation decisions is impossible to pin down. I would regretfully guess that traditional incremental decision making—often of the gross, across-the-board percentage type—still holds general sway.

The more grandiose reforms, most notably PPB, have slipped beneath the waves after the initial hoopla has died down, victims of overexpectation and under-investment in human and other resources.[9] There is some evidence that policy analysis has enhanced the rationality of budget decision making in several public organizations, but we do not really know how widespread its use is, or, more important, how much influence it has had on budget decisions.[10]

Formal long-range planning in the public sector has little in common with strategic planning. Rather than looking outward and focusing on organizational change, long-range planning has tended to be an extension of the annual operational planning process. This is to say that it starts on the inside and focuses on the projection of current activities into the future, usually for some arbitrary period, say, five years.

A limited amount of strategic planning is being done in the public sector, and the reports are beginning to come in. Several state and city governments in recent years have used strategic planning techniques to fashion broad gameplans or blueprints, often in particular issue areas. Examples are California in natural resources; Colorado, Memphis, and Eugene, Oregon in economic development; and Utah in capital investment.[11] However, as a recent *PAR* article points out, such applications are only a small beginning.

> ... (O)ne can say that current efforts to manage fall short of what is necessary in today's climate of uncertainty and resource decline. Granted, there are exemplary cases in which public managers and organizations have adopted innovative approaches and practices in systematically dealing with change, and those efforts are beginning to surface. However, most government managers, particularly those at the local level, continue to respond in a decremental fashion—making marginal adjustments while hoping that resources and services can somehow be restored.[12]

Guidelines for Application

My basic advice to the public executive considering the application of strategic planning is:

- First, to view application as a multi-year process, starting on a limited basis and gradually widening application as the organization gains experience and expands its capability to use the techniques.

- Second, to incorporate the strategic planning initiative into a broader framework of planning improvements—an overall planning strategy for the organization.
- Third, to ensure that the strategic planning application is very carefully planned, that there is, in essence, a strategic planning game plan clearly setting forth the desired outcomes, methodology, schedule, and responsibilities.

I would like to examine briefly the concept of an overall planning strategy within which strategic planning must fit. The basic idea behind this approach is that any organization needs a variety of different *outcomes* of its planning activities. Some are externally required, say, by the federal government or the public-at-large. Some are the result of an internal assessment of management need. At any given time, the need for one outcome or another will vary, as will the cost of achieving one outcome or another. No single planning technique will achieve all the desired or required planning outcomes. Nor can all the different kinds of planning be neatly encompassed in a unitary planning "system."

The basic methodology for coming up with an overall planning strategy is to compare desired and required outcomes with actual outcomes of current planning. The gap will indicate where improvements in planning must be made, and the relative priorities will determine the schedule for improvements. The costs of planning (basically time and technology) should also be factored into the analysis because, obviously, an organization may not have the means to achieve an outcome as quickly or as fully as desired. As Daniel R. Jensen points out in a recent *PAR* article, an organization's planning budget should be based on relating the "scope of the planning effort . . . directly . . . to the potential value of the planning results."[13]

One obvious match between a planning outcome and planning process is that of productivity improvement with annual operational planning and budget preparation. Overall organizational cohesion and common commitment is frequently cited as an important planning outcome. It is not likely to result from annual operational planning, but from mission and broad goals formulation, an activity in which the techniques of strategic planning are pertinent. Often important issues cannot be dealt with through operational planning because they cross too many intra-organizational lines, or are heavily influenced by a complex, changing environment—or, frequently, both. In this instance, the need is for innovation and creativity, which calls for applying the techniques of strategic planning. A common example would be a city's formulation of an economic development strategy.

A public organization's overall planning strategy for, say, the next two years might consist of the following basic elements:

- During the first year, an interdepartmental task force will engage in strategic planning in a particular issue area, the result of which will be the formulation of recommended strategies in the area. The annual operational planning process will be upgraded by requiring additional performance data to be collected for use in monitoring the plan. In addition, the planning department staff will be trained in-depth on the techniques of strategic planning as a first step in building an ongoing capability.
- During year two, continuous environmental scanning will be undertaken by the planning department, and a standing interdepartmental strategy committee will be established to review environmental data, to identify strategic issues meriting closer attention, and to oversee specific strategic planning initiatives to be carried out by ad hoc task forces. In addition, in a two-day retreat, the chief executive officer and legislative body will review environmental trends and conditions, with the assistance of the planning department, and will formulate a set of priorities to be addressed in the preparation of the annual budget.

All of the foregoing planning activities have associated costs, and must, therefore, be scheduled so as to remain within the resource limits of the organization. It is clear that no one-fell-swoop approach is being employed. Rather, incremental—though very important—improvements in planning are being made to achieve carefully defined outcomes. All of this is to say that our organization is planning according to its own, consciously adopted planning agenda, which reflects its rank-ordering of planning outcomes.

Examples of Application

Over the past three years, I have had the opportunity to assist several public organizations in the application of strategic planning techniques in a variety of ways. These tests of strategic planning would be found aesthetically wanting by the planning purist, in that for the most part they utilize the techniques on a relatively small scale. Their beauty lies in their practicality and manageability. They demonstrate that a powerful and sophisticated set of planning techniques can be used selectively, within reasonable resource limits, and can enable a public organization to effect significant change and to formulate creative solutions to complex issues in the near-term. Brief descriptions of certain of these tests should prove helpful to the practitioner contemplating the use of strategic planning.

A Two-Year College System. Over the past three years, a large urban two-year college system has experimented with strategic planning in two major ways.[14] The institution, it should be noted, has, over a ten-year period, invested heavily in the development of a sophisticated and effective operational planning process, characterized by a strong long-range financial planning capability and substantial productivity improvement. In recognition of the need for additions to its planning portfolio in order to capitalize on a changing environment, the institution first formally applied strategic planning in an important issue area, urban community development. A panel of community service professionals from outside the college was charged by the president to formulate recommendations as to the mission, strategic goals, and organizational structure in the area. After several meetings over six months, at which panelists reviewed the environment and the college's resources and considered strategic alternatives, the panel presented its recommendations to the president. They were reviewed and accepted by the president and board of trustees, and a new organizational unit was established to handle the community development functions. The original panel effort was so successful that a second panel recently completed a searching review of the environmental changes since the original effort, and recommended major changes in the strategies of the community development unit (basically that it concentrate on training for local business and phase out of community service activities).

Shortly after the original strategic panel submitted its report, the college launched another test of strategic planning on a somewhat broader front. The Strategic Educational Planning Process (SEPP), as it is called, is designed to generate innovative pilot projects which appear to have high growth potential. A reserve of up to $500,000 is set aside each budget year for investment in the innovation projects generated by the SEPP. A Strategic Educational Planning Advisory Committee, representing the four major operating units, meets in lengthy sessions in order to review detailed environmental data, resource analyses, and potential investment opportunities. Task forces are employed to explore in greater detail particular investment possibilities, which are assessed along four lines:[15] the fit with college mission; the newness of the venture; the prospects for success; and the institution's implementation capability. An example of a strategic target which has been funded is the creation of a comprehensive career assessment program to serve students, staff, and community workers seeking to improve or change their careers.

This experiment in strategic planning has been quite successful in several important respects. Participation on the advisory committee has been enthusiastic. Significant innovations have actually been funded and fully tested. And new "business" has been generated for the college. There is no question that setting aside a large fund for innovation has been a strong

BOX 10.1 Lessons from Strategic Planning

John M. Bryson and William D. Roering

The efforts of eight governmental units to initiate strategic planning are analyzed and discussed. All eight units are in the Twin Cities area of Minnesota.

Each used the same basic strategic planning process (see Figure). The process consists of eight steps: an initial agreement or "plan for planning"; identification and clarification of mandates; mission formulation; external environmental assessment; internal environmental assessment; strategic issue identification; strategy development; and development of a description of the organization in the future—its "vision of success."

Strategic Planning Process

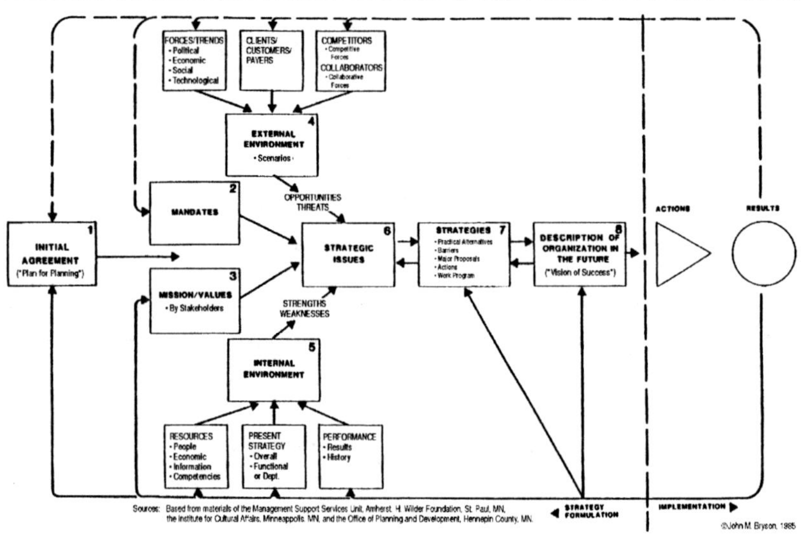

Sources: Based from materials of the Management Support Services Unit, Amherst. H. Wilder Foundation, St. Paul, MN, the Institute for Cultural Affairs, Minneapolis, MN, and the Office of Planning and Development, Hennepin County, MN.

©John M. Bryson, 1985

It appears that the following elements must be in place for the initiation of strategic planning by a government to succeed: (1) a powerful process sponsor. (2) an effective process champion, (3) a strategic planning team, (4) an expectation of some disruptions and delays, (5) a willingness to be flexible concerning what constitutes a strategic plan, (6) an ability to think of junctures as a key temporal metric, and (7) a willingness to construct and consider arguments geared to many different evaluative criteria.

(Source: John M. Bryson and William D. Roering, "Lessons from Strategic Planning," in: "Initiation of Strategic Planning by Governments," *Public Administration Review 48* (November/December 1988): 995–1004.)

incentive for active involvement in the process and has enhanced its credibility. By way of contrast, the college's traditional long-range planning process, while it definitely strengthened knowledge of and control over current programming, provided no incentive for unconventional thinking, much less systematic innovation.

A State Employment and Training Agency. A large state department traditionally responsible for operating the state's employment service and unemployment insurance programs was asked by the governor to oversee all training and retraining activities of the state, regardless of funding source and administrative accountability. In light of the several funding mechanisms involved, the many different programs handled by six different departments, and the significant federal and local government roles in this area, the department executive staff recognized that a new kind of planning going beyond the departmentalized operational planning process was required. After their introduction to the techniques of strategic planning, a decision was made to utilize them in responding to the governor's charge.

A steering committee, consisting of the directors of the six departments involved in training programs was created to provide oversight and to approve strategic initiatives, and a working group of deputy directors representing the departments was assembled to do the detailed planning and to recommend directions to the steering committee. Over the first four months of its life, the working group has devoted a half-day weekly to reviewing and fleshing out a detailed environmental scan and resource analysis prepared by senior research staff assigned to the project, and to identifying managerial and programmatic innovations intended to make training programs a more effective promoter of economic development. Two subcommittees of the working group are now in the process of applying cost/benefit analysis to each of the potential innovations and mapping out implementation details.

Even though this state government application has far to go before it is completed, the consensus of members of the working group is that it has already yielded considerable benefit, in terms of far better understanding of the dynamics at work in the training arena and the resources available to tackle training issues. The executive staff members of the lead department have stayed in close contact with the planning process, and, in their opinion, the preliminary strategic initiatives appear important, manageable, and affordable—going beyond the obvious answers while not soaring off into the clouds. Partly as a result of the strategic planning application thus far, it has been decided to proceed, over the coming year, with the development of an ongoing strategic planning capability within the department.

A City Government. The government of a middle-sized city has adopted a formal planning improvement program consisting of three major elements:

city council direction and priority setting; annual operational planning/budget preparation process enhancement; and strategic planning in selected issue areas.

At a two-day planning retreat, the council agreed to the three-pronged program and to the major outcomes of each element. With regard to the council directions component, the basic intent is to ensure that priority issues are addressed in the preparation of the annual plan and budget. Accordingly, the city manager assisted by senior staff held a trends and conditions briefing for the council as a first step in the annual issue identification/priority setting process. On the budgeting front, a staff task force will soon begin to identify weaknesses in the current process and to formulate improvements intended to enhance the planning content of the process and to extend the council's role beyond merely review and approval of a basically finished document.

City executive staff in consultation with council members identified two issues on which to test strategic planning on the initial go-around: economic development of the city; and maintenance of an integrated community. The following criteria were most influential in their choice:

- The importance of the issues in terms of the perceived cost of not dealing with them effectively, and the perceptions of council members and the general public about their priority.
- The complexity of the issues in two respects, making the operational planning process an inadequate vehicle for addressing them: (1) several actors not being within the control of the city government, including federal and state agencies and the private sector; and (2) the involvement of several city departments in each issue.

An interdepartmental task force has been assembled to deal with each of the strategic issues. The charge is to formulate strategic objectives and implementation strategies which make the fullest feasible use of city resources in addressing each issue. The planning department is responsible for staffing each task force, and a strategic planning manager has been hired to provide detailed assistance. Meeting weekly for two months, the task forces have developed detailed scans of the environment and are at this time engaged in analyzing the resources available to the city government in each area. In light of strong council and executive staff interest and support and the obvious commitment and enthusiasm of task force members, it appears almost certain that the process will yield short-term as well as longer-range return on the city's investment in strategic planning.

An important element of the strategic planning effort of this city has been an intensive educational program to prepare city employees for active participation in the planning process. All executive staff and other participants

BOX 10.2 Suboptimization and Incrementalism

Arie Halachmi

Students of system analysis know that maximizing the performance of a subunit may be counterproductive and may lead to suboptimization of the whole organization. For example, a very effective educational campaign to promote the use of family planning services may generate an unexpected demand for the service. This, in turn, may force the organization to reduce the level of service, *e.g.*, the time counselors spend with each patient, in order not to refuse the service to some of the people responding to the campaign. An educational campaign that uses less than the full reach-out capabilities of the agency may not reach all those who need the service but would allow the agency to maintain its service level for those it does reach.

On the surface, the suggestion to concentrate the efforts to improve productivity of human services on subunits and subprocesses may be counterproductive to overall optimization of the system. Indeed, it might be counterproductive, but then again it might not. Some of this author's younger students fall into the trap of equating "may be" with "always" when they are exposed to systems theory for the first time. However, the experience of this author suggests that they are not the only ones. The reluctance of administrators to make an attempt to improve the productivity of one or two subunits as an isolated effort which is not a part of an overall reorganization was explained to him as a fear that such actions would interfere with the smooth operation of the whole organization.

Yet, the author suggests, incrementalism may be a preferred tactic for implementing a proactive strategy. In other words, the public manager may assume a successful proactive posture by progressive use of incremental steps to improve the organizational structure of individual subunits or the individual components of the process. Such steps may take place as part of an effort to preempt expected problems or as part of an ongoing search for ways to enhance productivity. By using an incremental approach, the public manager may be able to avoid some of the difficulties as well as the economic and political costs that ensue when major or comprehensive attempts to make changes for any reason are involved.

(Source: Arie Halachmi, "Suboptimization and Incrementalism," in: "Strategic Planning and Productivity in Human Social Service," *Journal of Health and Human Service Administration* 14 (Summer 1991):6–26.)

attended full-day workshops which introduced the theory and practice of strategic planning generally and the specifics of the city's approach. In addition, a workshop for planning department staff focused on their work in support of the planning effort.

Although the results are not fully in, there is good reason to believe that these focused applications of strategic planning will prove successful and provide a firm foundation for expansion of strategic planning and management capability in coming years. If the expectations are modest, they are at least doable, and this is no mean feat in a world filled with examples of grandiose planning failures. Public sector strategic planning is in its infancy, and only a foolish parent would expect the child to run a 100-yard dash before mastering the basic walk.

Notes

1. Two recent publications that focus on the public sector application of strategic planning are: John B. Olsen and Douglas C. Eadie, *The Game Plan: Governance With Foresight* (Washington, D.C.: Council of State Planning Agencies, 1982) and William R. Dodge and Douglas C. Eadie, "Strategic Planning: An Approach to Launching New Initiatives in an Era of Retrenchment" (published in September, 1982, by the International City Management Association as an *MIS Report*).

2. William R. King and David I. Cleland. *Strategic Planning and Policy* (New York: Van Nostrand Reinhold, 1978).

3. Richard F. Vancil, "Strategy Formulation in Complex Organizations," *Sloan Management Review* 17 (Winter, 1976): 1–2.

4. George A. Steiner, *Top Management Planning* (London: The Macmillan Company, 1969), p. 238.

5. Alfred D. Chandler, Jr., *Strategy and Structure: Chapters in the History of the Industrial Enterprise* (Cambridge: The MIT Press, 1962), p. 13.

6. Walter Kiechel, III, "Corporate Strategists Under Fire," *Fortune* 106 (December 27, 1982).

7. Two powerful looks at human learning and perception as the essence of strategic planning are: Nathan D. Grundstein, *The Managerial Kant: The Kant Critiques and the Managerial Order* (Cleveland: Weatherhead School of Management, Case Western Reserve University, 1981) and Sir Geoffrey Vickers, *The Art of Judgment: A Study of Policy Making* (New York: Basic Books, Inc., 1965).

8. See H. Igor Ansoff, "Managing Strategic Surprise by Response to Weak Signals," *California Management Review* 18 (Winter, 1975) and Michael J. Kami, "Planning and Planners in the Age of Discontinuity" (address delivered at the conference "Planning for the Fourth Quarter Century," San Francisco: May 21–24, 1975).

9. For an excellent detailed account of the PPB failure, see Allen Schick, "A Death in the Bureaucracy: The Demise of Federal PPB," *Public Administration Review* 33 (March/April, 1973). See also Schick's *Budget Innovation in the States* (Washington, D.C.: The Brookings Institution, 1971).

10. Selma J. Mushkin, "Policy Analysis in State and Community," *Public Administration Review* (May/June, 1977), pp. 245–246.

11. Olsen and Eadie, pp. 88–92. See also, Nancy Ferris, "Developing a Strategic Advantage for Your Community," *Public Management* 65 (July, 1983), p. 17.

12. Robert P. McGowan and John M. Stevens, "Local Governments Initiatives in a Climate of Uncertainty," *Public Administration Review* (March/April, 1983), p. 135.

13. Daniel J. Jensen, "Unifying Planning and Management in Public Organizations," *Public Administration Review* (March/April, 1982), p. 157.

14. For a close look at the college's application of strategic planning, see Douglas C. Eadie, Nolen M. Ellison, and Grace C. Brown, "Incremental Strategic Planning: A Creative Adaptation," *Planning Review,* May, 1982. See also, Douglas C. Eadie, "Strategic Planning: Rhyme and Reason in a Nutshell," *Community and Junior College Journal* (Washington, D.C.: American Association of Community and Junior Colleges), December–January, 1982–83.

15. Eadie, Ellison, and Brown, *Incremental Planning,* p. 5.

11

Reorganizations and Reforms

Promises, Promises

Vera Vogelsang-Coombs and Marvin Cummins

Reorganization abounds in American governments. The faith in reorganization seems to be nurtured on eternal promises. Bureaucracy is but the tool of the political government, and in political governance, as in many other difficult tasks, a great deal of energy can be displaced in preparing the tools. Preparation is, after all, the promise of performance yet to come. In fact, the frequency of executive reorganization is astounding. Seidman (1980: 3) calls reorganizations "almost a religion in Washington." Between 1949 and 1978, 100 reorganization plans were submitted to the Congress.[1] The standard rationale for reorganization is the President wants to influence the career bureaucracy by structural changes which alter the distribution of power in favor of the President. Reorganization proposals tend to be "president-enhancing" (Arnold, 1979). Heclo (1977: 7) describes the relationship as follows:

> Government performance (in the sense of both negative constraints and the positive use of the bureaucracy) can be thought of as the product of political leadership times bureaucratic power. A product rather than merely a sum is at

"Reorganizations and Reforms: Promises, Promises," *Review of Public Personnel Administration* 2 (Spring 1982): 21–34.

stake because, depending upon how politicians and bureaucrats are linked, either one can diminish or magnify the impact of the other on total performance.

Anthony Downs (1967) argues that reorganizations are equated with "progress and reform." They are responses to the perceived ossification in the bureaucracy. Yet as Seidman (1980), Kaufman (1978), Long (1979b), Downs (1967) and Heclo (1977) argue, reorganization measures are costly, both economically and politically, and they produce little change. Why, then, do reorganizations seem to be inexorable? Why are they perpetuated over and over again by Presidents?

We begin examining these questions by relaxing the assumption which underlies much executive reorganization and much of the scholarly analysis of reorganization. We assert that the problem "government isn't working" is an allegation; it is not self-evident that government isn't working. In the absence of a clear set of general goals for government or any agreed upon yardsticks to measure government performance, it is impossible to know whether or not government is or is not working on the broad level. Thus, while the diagnosis that government is not working may or may not be accurate, our concern is not with the *accuracy* of the diagnosis. What does concern us is *why* the diagnosis reappears in one form or another. The diagnosis that government is not working is a specific example of the "criteria problem," wherein the President is in a position to impose the preferred criteria for measuring government's performance. In the real world of politics, reorganization might be an attempt to apply principles of organizational analysis in public bureaucracies. It might also be political disagreement over the criteria of what constitutes effective governmental performance. Or, it might be a willingness to substitute the symbols of preparation for the consequences of performance. Reorganizations can be understood as more than solutions to the problems of maximizing some abstract measures of bureaucratic efficiencies. Reorganizations are solutions to political diagnoses as much or more than they are solutions to organizational inefficiencies.

Building upon the works of Murray Edelman (1964) and Herbert Kaufman, we analyze reorganization as a part of an executive symbolization process. It is a powerful political symbol shared by the political and career governments, reflecting their different values, perceptions, interests, and ultimately their different behaviors. The symbol of reorganization is used by the short-term President to assert influence over the long-term work force and simultaneously by the bureaucracy to re-assert its dominance over the President. The thesis of this paper is that executive reorganizations are pervasive rites of presidential polities and that civil service reform is a myth based on this rite. The thesis itself is not new. What is new is the application of Edelman's symbolic reassurance thesis to executive reorganizations. Reorganizations have expressive and symbolic political uses, irrespective of whether or not they produce long-term changes in government performance. Given our perspective, we think an apt way to describe the reorganization relationship between the political and career governments is in terms of a dialogue. In fact, it is the literal dialogue of reorganization which is to be examined here. In this study of the Senior Executive Service (SES), the most recent example of executive reorganization, we will examine the process from the perspective of those doing the reorganizing, the President, the elected government, and from the perspective of those being reorganized, the career officials of the federal bureaucracy, and from the perspective of Congress. Overall our intent is to examine the symbolisms of executive reorganization.

The data for our dialogue of reorganization are drawn from the public statements of the President and political officials who proposed the SES reorganization, and from the private statements of career bureaucrats who are the targets of the SES reorganization. The bureaucrats were randomly surveyed through a blind mailing of 1000 SES-eligible senior executives in the spring of 1979, several months before they actually entered the SES. The names of the executives were drawn by OPM staff from their computerized inventory of supergrade civil servants. The survey yielded a response of 440 questionnaires, a 44% response rate. We asked the senior executives about their initial attitudes toward the Senior Executive Service. A majority of the respondents supplemented the basic questionnaire with highly revealing personal comments concerning the SES and civil service reform in general. These data form the empirical component of our dialogue.

The plan of the paper is as follows. We first describe the dialogue between the President and the bureaucrats as they discuss whether or not government is working. Next, we examine the bureaucrats' response to the President's proposal for reorganization. Then we describe how the dialogue of reorganization is transferred to the Congress, where it is terminated. In the final section we identify the implications which arise from the dialogue of reorganization.

The Dialogue: The President

All modern presidents seem to ask two sets of questions which suggest reorganization is perceived as a solution (Weinberger, 1978). The first question is "Given that government's not working, why can't we get things done?" The second question is: "Why can't we get things done that elected officials who speak for the people want?" The first question focuses on an effectiveness dimension, i.e., on the limitations of bureaucratic effectiveness as structurally determined. The second question focuses on a responsiveness dimension. Presidents believe that government will work when there is correspondence between their policy priorities (which ostensibly reflect the wishes of the "people") and the decisions of the bureaucrats. In fact one can argue that there is a sequence to these questions. What is originally perceived to be purely an organizational problem is soon transformed into a political problem.

The first factor contributing to the dialogue is what we call the *ancien regime* factor. As each new presidential administration is sworn in, the chief executive finds himself stuck with an old regime. This bureaucratic regime is old from a policy perspective and sometimes from a partisan perspective. Even if there is no partisan change in the presidency, the new incumbent identifies a set of failures which are symbolized by his predecessor's bureaucracy. According to Carter in 1976, the problem of government is its failure to achieve the goals of the welfare state. In a *National Journal* "Forum," Carter (1976: 1448) stated:

> There are millions of people in this country who believe that the federal government simply cannot be made to work. Their belief is based not merely on a lack of confidence in politicians but on an even more serious loss of faith in the very processes of government. The word 'bureaucrat' has become a purely pejorative term, connoting in the public mind, inefficiency, ineptitude, and even callous disregard for the rights and feelings of ordinary people . . . It shouldn't be that way.

Every new president is optimistic about what he can do and he subscribes to the theories that each new administration can and should set new directions and new emphases for public policy and that the bureaucracy will automatically implement them. But after an initial honeymoon period, the president recognizes his limited ability to control the very people who are supposed to help him execute faithfully the laws of the U. S. The constraints are considerable: constraints of time, size and diversity of the bureaucracy, scope and complexity of his tasks, and the need to perform the duties associated with his other presidential roles. The president soon learns that although he might set policy priorities, he must delegate implementation to the bureaucrats who have been in government before him and who will remain after him.

The first way chief executives seek to gain control over the bureaucracy is through structural reshuffling of the boxes of the executive organization chart. To the president, the problem of government is a problem of misorganization. Government is not working because there are violations of some standard organizational principle, such as unity of command, the scalar principle, limited span of control, etc. The belief is that the political government, because of its position at the top of the hierarchy, is the appropriate place for policy to be formulated. According to orthodox organizational principles, consolidation is a primary way of achieving a coordinated policy.

Finding that sound organization principles do not automatically produce the desired outcomes, the reorganizers attempt to find another reason for the inability of the president to get things done. The bureaucracy is perceived to be out of control because it is unresponsive to the president and his priorities. In the view of the members of the political government, the bureaucracies are seen as having their own agenda, constituencies, policies and programs to protect. They are seen as placing their own survival interests, the interests of their congressional sponsors, and the interests of state and local administrators ahead of those of the president (Seidman, 1980). What was originally conceived of as an organizational issue shifts to the issue of who has proper authority. Finding that a model of a politically neutral bureaucracy does not exist, the President says that the bureaucracy thwarts the wishes of elected leaders and acts out of line with its authority.

In the Carter administration's view, government was not responsive because the personnel system was "too complicated," "excessively centralized" and "very restrictive." Flexibility in the eyes of the Carter Administration required the adoption of the methods used in the private sector. Speaking to the National Press Club, President Carter said, "We must encourage better performance in ways that are used widely and effectively in private industry. Top federal workers are ready and willing to respond to the risks and rewards of competitive life, and public service will be healthier when they have that chance."[2] The Civil Service Reform Act (CSRA) was a "reform" designed to create an energetic, politically neutral career service that responds to the President. The Senior Executive Service, the centerpiece of the Act, cut across all policy areas to break up those cozy little policy triangles that operate outside the President's authority.

The President's Solution

Having identified the problem of government as a "people" problem, Carter enlisted the help of the bureaucrats. He established Presidential Reorganization Project teams as part of his "fresh," "bottom-up," people oriented approach. This reorganization was different, said Richard Pettigrew (1978: 103), Carter's aide for reorganization, because:

> Past reorganizations have failed simply because, grand as they may have been, they were designed in an ivory tower without the benefit of public input and debate. A small group would develop the reorganization in secret, and the President would then spring it on the Congress, the agencies, the interest groups and the public at large.

The process might be new; the solution is not. CSRA, like its predecessor the Pendleton Act, changed the way government services itself. It is based on the assumption that the impediments to effective and responsive government are old career employees. First, Carter sought to establish a centralized personnel agency with a government-wide perspective. Carter charged that the old Civil Service Commission (CSC) had ceased to function because its mandates were muddled and it was too political. It would be replaced by two agencies, U. S. Office of Personnel Management (OPM) and the Merit Systems Protection Board (MSPB). The purpose of OPM would be to serve as the "president's arm" for personnel matters. The multiple heads of the CSC were to be replaced by a hierarchical arrangement involving a Presidentially appointed Director and Deputy Director of OPM. They would serve at the President's discretion. MSPB serves as the protector of the merit system, adjudicating federal employees' complaints. MSPB was set up as a separate entity from OPM to insure its neutrality. Further, although the President would appoint the three bipartisan members of MSPB (with Senate approval), he could not dismiss them except for special reasons. OPM and MSPB, together, were to be partners overseeing the implementation of SES.

The Senior Executive Service (Title IV of CSRA) addressed the *ancien regime* factor. The SES proposal sought to purify the bureaucratic blood of the most entrenched part of the *ancien regime*—the group of 9000 top federal employees in super-grade positions. The SES created a new personnel system for career executives drawn from positions of GS 16–18 and Executive Levels IV and V (which do not require Senate confirmation). Our data show that these groups of officials at the top of the general schedule have been in government service on average approximately 25 years. Because of their longevity and expertise, they have ties to the Congress, interest groups, as well as state and local administrators, and, accordingly, the loyalty of these career officials is the most suspect to the President. To penetrate this group of officials the President in his plan created an administrative cadre that operates in a gradeless, "market-place" personnel system. By converting to the SES, old employees would demonstrate their loyalty to the President and their willingness to increase their efficiency.

Second, the way the Carter Administration decided to remotivate the new members of the president's Administration would be by changing the job incentives of the merit system to those that ostensibly worked so well in the private sector. To do so, the SES system would eliminate the position classification system. Government managers were given authority to transfer and remove executives whose performance is judged to be unsatisfactory, based on annual performance reviews. Salary flexibility would be the hallmark of the SES. Longevity pay was replaced by a merit pay and performance bonus system. The SES program was supposed to provide opportunities to recognize different levels of individual achievement. The president's plan streamlined "adverse action" procedures. In this way mediocre executives could be weeded out.

Third, under the SES the issue of proper authority was converted into a procedural matter. By increasing assignment flexibility (and thereby interagency mobility), the SES supposedly created a corps that is not tied to any particular constituency. This corps should have broad perspectives rather than narrow, agency perspectives. To complement this approach the SES was supposed to facilitate the hiring and advancement of women and minorities into executive level positions. Prior to SES, an aspiring female or minority civil servant would have to start at the bottom and wait at least ten years before he or she could move to the top. The SES was supposed to correct this problem by instituting training programs to prepare "promising" women and minorities for assignments of increasing complexity and responsibility. Candidates who successfully completed these training programs could apply for entry into the SES. In addition, the Carter Administration sought to curtail preferences given to all non-disabled veterans on civil service exams and reduction-in-force situations. Thus, Carter sought to broaden recruitment and to create a more responsive bureaucracy.

The Dialogue: The Bureaucrats Respond

The bureaucrats responded to President Carter's initiative with skepticism. They did not share his interpretation of the problem of government. Although the bureaucrats said that the civil service system needs improvement, a sizable proportion of the respondents in our survey did not feel that the SES would produce a better system. Instead, there was a great deal of disenchantment with the SES and fear that the SES would politicize the federal service. For example, one senior executive said,

> It has the potential for improving executive management of government and is career attractive from that perspective. However, it is doubtful that any real or meaningful movement will actually take place between the agencies of government. The "P" factor could dominate the SES before too long.

And another said,

> The SES as outlined to me incorporates some very good ideas and some fresh very welcome approaches. I have strong reservations that SES can be implemented as intended. My feelings are that it will in the beginning be paternalistic and in the long run be politically dominated.

From their perspective the president was not a paper tiger. They felt that he could do whatever he wants to do even if it means destroying their agency through reorganization or destroying *their* federal service. One senior executive summed up the feelings of the SES as follows: "Boon doggle. My 17 GS's came hard. Any bum can be an SE (Senior Executive)." A great deal of anger surfaced in the comments of our respondents that the SES facilitates the invasion of political amateurs into their turf. Their response to the President's initiative is laden with symbols of politicization.

The anger of the bureaucrats stemmed from their disagreement with the President's characterization of them as unmotivated, incompetent and disloyal. They argued that the things that the President identified as their weaknesses were, in fact, their best strengths. For example, the fact that they are old employees does not make them *a priori* "bad,"—i.e., unmotivated and incompetent. Said one careerist:

> I am not enthusiastic nor are any of my associates. We will probably all join because the alternative is not very attractive. My experience is confined to *X Agency*, and my view is that it is a well run organization in which top executives are competent and hard working. Most of them would have little trouble obtaining an attractive position in [the private sector].

Many senior executives reported that they do not need an SES to do a good job. Another career official who felt positively about the SES said,

> Give me the tools to work with and I'll do the job—but if they don't, I'll do it anyway because I'm a professional, and if it doesn't mean anything to the federal service, it means something to me.

The bureaucrats responded that their concern is with the quality of policy, and the top does not have the information to formulate policy. Their superiors are political "dilettantes." One representative comment is:

> The basic problem in government is the lack of professional capability and experience of political appointees . . . who are appointed to positions they cannot handle. They proliferate decisions which are marginally and professionally unsound and then they depart. These are the very people who will be carrying out the performance bonuses under SES for themselves and their cronies. SES will not solve one thing in this particular (area), and this is its basic flaw.

Another stated:

> Do the executives believe that the SES will lead to a better bureaucracy. I do not know many who believe it will. . . . The fear of some bureaucrats is not being politicized; rather it is that they will be judged by bosses who did not receive appointments because of their competence. While we are often compared to business, there are two significant differences; our bosses have not risen through the business and the absence of any measuring stick, such as profits.

What these comments suggest is that the bureaucrats were asking, "Who are the right people?" Their fear is that SES members will become conformist, and partisan, and unwilling to anger the boss who controls their rewards.

Overall, the bureaucrats respond that they do not need an SES to perform their jobs. They argue that the President's characterizations of them as unresponsive and ineffective are myths. The differences in perceptions are structurally determined. The short-term politicians have different time frames, different interests and different conceptions of who should initiate policy and who has power. The president attempts to garner the loyalty of his career administrators by appealing to their self-interest. The bureaucrats respond that their loyalty is not an issue; they are in government to perform as experienced, professional policy makers. The President says the SES will establish a chain of command to enable agency heads to make coordinated decisions concerning personnel. The bureaucrats respond that the SES does not change organizational arrangements much; it just shakes things up a bit. From their perspective no chain of command exists when the politically inexperienced and transient superiors carve out SES performance bonuses. The President argues that government employees should be treated like corporate employees. The bureaucrats respond that not all of them are motivated by monetary rewards. The President says he has the exclusive right to command. The bureaucrats respond that while a reservoir of support exists for the President because he is president, they must respond to many other political actors in this fragmented political system. The President is pre-eminent contender for power, but he is not the only one (Aberback and Rockman, 1976). The debate moves to the Congress.

The End of Reorganization: The Congress Joins the Dialogue

The shift of the conflict to the Congress is crucial. The move to Congress adds new contestants to the battle, contestants who side with the bureaucrats. According to Seidman (1980: 161–162), "Hostility to political executives is shared and encouraged by committees and subcommittees of the Congress and State legislatures which are as preoccupied as the administrators with protecting and promoting the purposes of individual programs under their respective jurisdictions." Because the bureaucrats help legislators with their re-election goals, legislators are reluctant to offend the bureaucrats. Similarly, bureaucrats are dependent upon Congressmen for various types of assistance, most notably budgetary appropriations. Bureaucrats who work closely with legislative staffs know that the Congress is weak on oversight. Thus, because Congress and the bureaucrats are often allies, it is often costly and time-consuming to enact laws which are unpopular among civil servants.

Because Nigro (1979) describes the "Politics of Civil Service Reform" in the Congress, we do not need to repeat the series of events here. We will list the ways in which the Congress changed the Administration's bill to reflect its own concerns, changes which in the end favored the bureaucrats. The Congress worked to make the heads of OPM and MSPB more independent of the president. First, the OPM director was given a four year term. The OPM director was empowered to delegate any of his functions to the agencies, except for overseeing competitive exams. MSPB was set up as a bipartisan agency. Its heads were given seven year terms, and Congress strengthened the powers of MSPB to serve as a check on OPM. MSPB was empowered to review OPM rules and regulations and to veto rules it believed constituted prohibited employee practices.

Congress included in the Act the power to discontinue the SES by concurrent resolution in 1984, making the SES program an experiment rather than a permanent part of the career personnel system. Congress also strengthened the neutrality of career personnel system. Congress also strengthened the neutrality of career government by establishing two types of positions in the SES. These positions are called "Career-reserved" and "General positions." "Career-reserved" jobs are ones that are believed to be so sensitive that public confidence would be undermined if the functions were performed by political appointees. Overall, 40 percent of all government jobs would be designated as career reserved. The remaining government jobs would be classified as general positions—which can be filled by either careerists or political appointees. By *law,* only 10 percent of the total number of SES executives could be non-careerists, but the number of non-career appointments may vary from agency to agency, up to a maximum of 25 percent non-career appointees in any single agency.

The Congress also strengthened protections of career officials in the performance appraisal system. Agency heads were given the power to evaluate subordinates in a new way. Supervisors and employees annually establish performance standards which are used to evaluate whether or not employees should be rewarded, removed or re-trained. Performance boards were set up in each agency. Career officials must be evaluated by a board composed of a majority of career officials. Further, no performance appraisal can be conducted during the first 120 days of a new administration or during the first 120 days after a new agency head is appointed, preventing career officials from being summarily dismissed at the beginning of a new political administration. GAO and OPM are supposed to monitor agency performance. An executive who claims his or her evaluation is discriminatory, politically motivated or punitive can appeal to MSPB, where the burden of proof is on the agency officials.

Congress also gave the agencies *more flexibility* in personnel matters. Agencies are empowered to designate which positions they want included in the SES. Employees in these designated positions had 90 days to decide whether or not to convert into the SES or to remain in their present positions. Congress also changed the five basic pay rates in the SES, giving agency heads authority to determine the pay for each executive. Congress further re-established the rule of three and rejected the president's curtailment of veterans preferences. While the law eliminated veterans preferences for non-disabled military veterans at or above the rank of major or lieutenant commander, those veterans who have a disability of 30 percent or more can still receive non-competitive appointments which can be converted into career positions.

As the result of the legislative skills of Alan Campbell and of Morris Udall's management of the Administration's bill in the House, Carter obtained the symbol of what he wanted—a law. The President declared a victory, withdrew from the field, and turned his interests to foreign crises. In like fashion, the bureaucrats got what they wanted. The Congressional formulation legitimizes bureaucratic norms. As implementation of CSRA falls into their hands, the bureaucrats turned their attention away from the issue of intrusion of politicians and back to the matter of running the government. The dialogue allowed the President and the bureaucracy to "battle" their criterion problem and then to abide by the "results." This was a victory for both. The alleged problem disappeared although whether or not government performance will change is debatable. This is the subject of our next section.

Implications

Inherent in the structure of American government and politics is the tension between the political and permanent governments which produces the dialogue of reorganization. We have described the dialogue which took place between the president, the bureaucracy, and the Congress in the case of SES. But there are many policy arenas in which this dialogue can be played out. The President can take the dialogue to the Congress, to the Court, or directly to the people as Carter did in the summer of 1979. Wherever the dialogue is played out, the dynamics of the process suggest that the result will be similar—few major changes in government performance and the perpetuation of reorganization at some future date.

The difference between our work and that of Mosher, Heclo, Seidman, *et al.,* is that they provide ameliorative solutions on how to reform the civil service. The implications of their arguments are that the bureaucracy problem can be solved, that an objective bureaucracy is possible. The bureaucratic segment of American government has advanced the view of public bureaucracies as technically neutral instruments which administer political decisions. Much of the analysis of reorganization has followed that assumption. Our analysis has deviated from that assumption.

In the case of the SES, the reorganizers claimed to attack the isolated nature of the bureaucracy *per se.* They attempted to deal with a no-growth, tenured public personnel system by using methods based on an idealized notion of the private sector. The underlying assumptions of the reorganization are: (1) that the private sector is highly productive, and (2) that market place remedies are automatic and easily applicable. These assumptions are questionable.

But the issue that we have raised goes beyond the accuracy of the assumptions of any particular reorganization. Our analysis of the dialogue of reorganization produces a set of implications that is very different from those generated by other analysts. By suspending the assumption of the objective nature and context of governmental bureaucracies *per se,* we raise a different set of questions from those raised by other scholars on executive reorganization. We are not asking, "Is SES working?" or "Is the use of the business model successful?" or "What kind of reorganization is most likely to be successful?" Our perspective is that the problem of government is largely perceptual; it does not have an independent, real-world solution. Reorganization cannot be conceived simply as an independent variable that directly affects government performance, the dependent variable, as Heclo suggests. Reorganization is not simply a sign of objective needs and concrete solutions. It is exactly because bureaucracies essentially involve the implementation of political choices that they will never be reduced to permanent, optimum solutions. Shifts in the criteria of performance, in the preferences among performances, and even in the desirability of performance over nonperformance are inherent in the political processes. And the fundamental tools of performance for the president *are* the public bureaucracies. Reorganizations change organizational form but not necessarily the underlying political reality. Thus, we examine how the manipulation of the symbols of reorganization reflect the interests of political actions, in which institutional context are the symbols likely to be invoked; and, in what sequence are the symbols manipulated. In brief, we analyze reorganization first and foremost as a component of political expressions.

In effect what we are saying is that reorganizations tend to be bureaucratic activities. While presidents propose reorganizations, they become bureaucratic activities. Politics and bureaucracy intermingle. What we find here is an example of the bureaucracy being a "permanent machine," to use Weber's terms. Once the machine gets into operation, it takes over the implementation of reorganization. When the bureaucracy takes over, presidents lose "leadership." Moreover, the reorganizational arrangements are copied. OPM was designed along the lines of OMB in order to give the OPM Director and Deputy Director more influence as the President's chief management arms. It is arguable whether or not the new structure of OPM will automatically increase its influence.

While the rhetoric of the SES reorganization contends that at root the reform is a unidirectional realignment of authority, the reality is that it is not. Underlying the SES reform is the premise that authority is perceived to flow downward; that if the top of the hierarchy is remotivated, one can remotivate the rest. But, as Norton Long (1979: 144) said thirty years ago, "A picture of the Presidency as a reservoir of authority from which the lower echelons of administration draw life and vigor is an idealized distortion of reality." Authority flows upwards, downwards and sideways in an organization. Long's observations suggest that even if the SES is 100 percent successful in recruiting the "right" managers, it does not deal with the basic fact of politics. Bureaucrats can not rely on the formal chain of command to give them enough power to achieve their missions. The career bureaucrats need to acquire and supplement political power from both within and outside the bureaucracy in order to do their jobs.

To conclude, the reorganization phenomenon is in part a symbolic process of putting new frills on old skirts. Politicians rarely have the opportunity to begin from scratch, so redecorating old arrangements is not a trivial political activity. The SES reform will not automatically produce a government that "promises what is needed and delivers what is promised."[3] Instead it produces an SES that "promises, promises." The prospect of the SES, like other reorganizations, is that it will be costly both politically and economically. Similar to death, taxes, and red tape, reorganizations like the SES are an inevitable part of life in presidential politics. *Plus ca change, plus c'est la meme chose.*

Notes

1. Seidman cites that between 1949 and 1972, 92 reorganization plans were submitted to the Congress. For the years. 1973–1978. *CQ Almanac* reports that 8 plans were submitted by President's Nixon and Carter.

2. This excerpt from President Carter's speech appears in OPM's booklet on the SES.

3. This expression is Heclo's.

References

Aberbach, J. D. and B. A. Rockman (1976). "Clashing Beliefs Within the Executive Branch: The Nixon Administration Bureaucracy." *American Political Science Review* 70: 456–468.

Arnold, P. E. (1979). "The Presidency and Reorganization: A comparative Study of Six Cases, 1905–1955." Paper delivered at 1979 APSA Meeting, August 31-September 3, 1979, Washington, D.C.

Carter. J. (1976). "Making Government Work Better: People, Programs, and Process." Policy Forum Section of *National Journal* 41: 1448–1449.

______ (1975). *Why Not the Best?* Nashville: Broadman Press.

Cole, R. and D. Caputo (1979). "Presidential Control of the Senior Civil Service: Assessing the Strategies of the Nixon Years." *American Political Science Review* 73: 399–413.

Downs, A. (1967). *Inside Bureaucracy.* Boston: Little. Brown and Co.

Edelman, M. (1964). *The Symbolic Uses of Politics.* Urbana: University of Illinois Press.

Fiorina, M. (1977). *Congress, the Keystone of the Washington Establishment.* New Haven: Yale University Press.

Freeman, M. E. (1979). "Good Bureaucrats and Bad Ones." Point of View column in *Washington Star* (October 10).

Heclo, H. (1977). *A Government of Strangers.* Washington. D.C.: The Brookings Institution.

Kaufman, H. (1978a). *Fear of Bureaucracy: A Raging Pandemic,* The Edmund James Lecture. Urbana, Illinois: Department of Political Science, University of Illinois.

Kaufman, H. (1978b). "Reflections on Administrative Reorganization," in *Current Issues in Public Administration,* ed. Frederick Lane. New York: St. Martin's Press.

Landau, M. (1978). "Redundancy, Rationality, and the Problem of Duplication and Overlap," in *Current Issues in Public Administration,* ed. Frederick Lane. New York: St. Martin's Press.

Lane, F. ed. (1978). *Current Issues in Public Administration.* New York: St. Martin's Press.

Long, N. (1979a). "Bureaucracy, Pluralism and the Public Interest," Paper delivered at the 1979 APSA Meetings. August 31-September 3, 1979, Washington, D.C.

______. (1979b). "Power and Administration," in *Classics of Organization Theory,* ed. Jay Shafritz and Philip Whitbeck. Oak Park, Illinois: Moore Publishing Company.

Lynn. N. and R. E. Vaden. (1979). "Bureaucratic Response to Civil Service Reform." *Public Administration Review* 39: 333–345.

Meier, K. J. (1979). *Politics and Bureaucracy.* North Scituate, Massachusetts: Duxbury Press.

Miller, S. (1978). "Bureaucracy Baiting." *The American Scholar.* 47: 205–222.

Mosher, F. C. (1968). *Democracy and the Public Service.* New York: Oxford University Press.

Nelson, R. R. (1977). *The Moon and The Ghetto.* New York: W. W. Norton and Company, Inc.

Neustadt, R. (1964). *Presidential Power.* New York: Mentor.

Nigro, F. A. (1979). "The Politics of Civil Service Reform." Paper delivered at the 1979 APSA Meetings. August 31-September 3, 1979. Washington, D.C.

Pettigrew, R. A. (1978). "Improving Government Competence." *Publius,* 8: 99–103.

Reimer, E. (1956). "The Case Against the Senior Civil Service," *Personnel Administration,* 19:31–41.

Ripley, R. and G. Franklin. (1980). *Congress, the Bureaucracy and Public Policy.* Homewood, Illinois: Dorsey Press.

Rourke, F. (1976). *Bureaucracy, Politics, and Public Policy,* 2nd ed., Boston: Little, Brown and Company.
Schattschneider, E. E. (1960). *The Semi-Sovereign People.* New York: Holt, Rinehart and Winston.
Seidman, H. (1980). *Politics, Position and Power,* 3rd ed. New York: Oxford University Press.
Sylvia, R. (1979). "A Heuristic Typology of Presidential Organization." Paper delivered at 1979 APSA Meetings, August 31-September 3, 1979, Washington, D.C.
U. S. Civil Service Commission (1977). *Executive Personnel in the Federal Service.* Washington, D. C.: Government Printing Office.
U. S. Office of Personnel Management (1979). *Senior Executive Service: Conversion Information for Federal Executives.* Washington. D. C.: Office of Personnel Management.
Watson, J. (1978). "Making the Government Work Better." *Publius* 8: 105–109.
Weinberger, C. W. (1978). "Government Reorganization and Public Purpose." *Publius* 8: 39–48.

12

MBO IN STATE GOVERNMENT

George S. Odiorne

A constructed case study probably provides the best object lessons on managing public affairs by objectives. This is a composite of experience with MBO in three different states compiled into a single illustrative case example.

Recently the State of Old West opted in the direction of MBO and decentralized management of the state tied to MBO. It broke itself into a half dozen or more "mini-states." Each area was headed by a professional public administrator, quite similar in education and experience. Most had MPA degrees: most were old enough to have had some solid experience, but young enough to be energetic and ambitious. All were males. All were informed that they would be in charge of their own area of the state in all respects except higher education and one or two other areas. All were solemnly informed that they would be managed "by objectives" and that they were admonished to do likewise with their own responsibilities. Extensive training in MBO accompanied the program. The basic pattern of MBO as it was defined consisted of a five-part program:

1. Goal Setting. Each administrator would strike agreements with his or her superior about what was expected in terms of results, and such statements would be made in advance of the period.

2. Budgeting. The objectives would be related to resources which would be released to achieve the job. That is, the budgets would be forthcoming for the tasks to be achieved, or the results would be amended if resources were for some reason not forthcoming.

"MBO in State Government," *Public Administration Review* 36 (January/February, 1976): 28–33.

3. Autonomy. Each person would be left alone to make decisions affecting his or her territory or responsibility, except that reporting periods and forms were agreed upon in advance. It was also agreed that each would obey the law and the policies affecting the various responsibility areas.

4. Feedback. Since the managers would know how well they were doing in their work while it was going on, they were expected to know when their results were faulty, to initiate corrective action upon learning of such shortcomings, and to *notify or ask for help* if things went clearly beyond permitted exceptions in a serious fashion.

5. Payoffs. There would be rewards in proportion to achievement. For one thing, the merit system would reflect achievements rather than personality or political affiliation. Furthermore, performance reviews would be related to achievements against goals. A proposed incentive plan for managers was not strong enough to survive the political buffeting encountered, and was abandoned before birth.

As a theoretical example Old West's MBO had much to commend it. Yet it was not without its troubles, most of which comprise a cautionary tale to those in public administration wishing to use this most useful and stimulating method of management. In each of the five basic precepts which comprised the system, problems, and lessons, emerged.

I. "Tell Me What's Expected in Advance"

From the beginning when the area managers sat down with their boss to discuss objectives, it was apparent that the superiors and cabinet ranks didn't really have a clear fix on what they expected from such line managers. "When I find out what we are here for, I'll try to let you know" was one kind of response. This of course was not a defect in MBO, but in the existing state of management, for it described what had been going on for some time. In areas like conservation the results sought were clearer than in the prison system, where nobody could agree on what prisons were supposed to produce. In environment the law was reasonably clear, but the development of strategies for getting to compliance wasn't all that lucidly defined. A major corporation and large employer in one region stated baldly that to live within the state air quality laws would put the organization out of business. It was agreed that more thought would have to be given to this case, since unemployment in that sector was already over the national average. The state unemployment service, the welfare chief, and the director of economic development of the state broke into a rather noisy argument over what the environmental objectives should be.

This led to the conclusion that each mini-state must have a person responsible for shaping and recommending objectives in each functional area for its own geographical area. The bureaucracy in the state office building resisted this flowing away of their power and personnel out to the field. This battle came to a head when the state chief of mental health services went to the press over an unfortunate death of a mentally retarded child in a program initiated at the mini-state level. MBO had killed this child, he charged. The governor backed the decentralization system in this case, and the MBO program survived.

> Object lesson: Decentralization, or the moving of important decisions to lower levels in the organization is not a natural phenomenon in political organizations, and when it occurs will meet resistance from those in the bureaucracy whose power flows away from them.

There are other important lessons which were learned about goal setting in this case. First, while operational objectives must be measurable, many of the best strategic goals were not reduced to measurement, but to verbal statements of conditions which would exist if the goal were attained. Strategic objectives require criteria, but not all criteria will be measurable. . . . This distinction between strategic and operational goals is an important one in government.

The patent and staple argument against MBO in public administration that "my most important responsibilities can't be measured" is of course true, not only in government but in business. The similarities between strategic staff work in corporations and government are startling. Neither relates to the production of things. Neither in fact directly and immediately relates to profits. Neither is free of unexpected changes in the world. Both work in multi-year time frames. Both produce software rather than hardware. Both entail judgments of small groups of experts and professionals rather than short-term leadership of large corps of workers.

Yet all of these conditions have not prevented the best-run organizations from using staff MBO superbly well. Service organizations, it was discovered in the mini-state's case at hand, can state their goals if they abide with some guidelines which have evolved in practice.

1. Anticipate strategic missions as much as is possible, in defining objectives, but adjust as often as necessary.
2. Developing indicators to be watched is a means to improving output and should not become an end in itself. The indicators themselves should be changed if needed, and no manager should have more than a dozen key indicators to be watching, and probably less than that. If there are more, there should be somebody helping watch and respond to them.

3. It is important to answer the question "are we doing the right things" prior to answering the more explicit questions of measurement, and "doing things right."
4. Timing is of the essence in goal setting. Those objectives which are multi-year in character (to clean up the pollution in the Cupcake River to federal standards by June 1978) need to be stated before the budget allocations are decided, not after. Those of an operational character can be stated at the beginning of an operating period after the budget allocation and not before (to buy a new patrol boat for the Cupcake River by June 1, 1976).

The best MBO programs in government will probably have two sets of objectives, one long-range set stated prior to budgeting or resource movement, and the second or short-range set after the budget is decided.

5. Any operational indicators should be related to some kind of important output and should contain some element of time (such as park visitors per month).
6. It is a mistake to expect too much precision in operating objectives. The most exact science consists of approximations, and goal setting is far from an exact science. This need for reasonableness in goals can be achieved by stating them in *ranges* ("between 22,000 and 23,000 violations processed during the coming six months"). If some precision-obsessed soul insists upon a single number, pick the middle of the range and state it as the target.
7. Despite the special character of government objectives which often makes them difficult to measure, a *rule of rigor* can be applied: "measure that which is measurable, describe that which is describable, and eliminate that which is neither."
8. There is a division of labor in goal setting and management. A final lesson is that higher-level people who constantly are interfering in operational management will cause the MBO program to abort. The proper function of cabinet or policy-level positions is to define strategic goals. The function of operating heads is to be responsible for operations and commit to short-term (one year) goals. The case of the cabinet person who insists upon knowing every operational detail is commonplace in government. In addition to being a serious handicap to management by objectives, it is also easily recognized as bad management in general.

II. Give Me the Resources to Do the Job

Precept two of the case study at hand was the provision of resources to do the job. This meant that the manager at the lower level was given budgetary resources. But it meant more than simply getting *more* resources, it also meant some latitude in moving resources. Many state and local governmental accounting systems are labyrinths of regulations which prevent such movement ("01 funds can be spent for 01 purposes only, but 03 funds may be spent for personnel or for any other purpose exclusive of travel and entertainment").

A strategic planning system within the MBO system provided much flexibility in moving resources, for it required that for each program four questions be answered:

1. Where is this program now? Statistically, factually, and in judgments about strengths and weaknesses?
2. What trends are apparent? If we didn't do anything differently where would we be in five years?
3. What mission statements could be shaped for this program?
4. What would be the financial consequences of each mission?

These budgetary-mission statements were prepared about January of each year and forwarded upward to the state level where they comprised working papers for the compilation of the immediate budget requests and for multi-year budget planning.

The most successful application of this plan was executed by one mini-state area manager who moved personally and individually with each of the key subordinates through an interview using these four questions as an agenda. Each manager prepared some notes, but the process was operated basically on a face-to-face basis. The superior then dictated the results of the interview with the subordinate and the resulting memorandum became the strategic goals position paper for the two to make their budgetary-allocation decisions upon. The questions are not simple. For example, in one discussion these kinds of questions came about:

Superior: "Let's look at the first topic: Where is your program now? What statistics are generated for your program? Who creates them? Are we well enough informed about the present situation? Do you have enough information to know what your strengths, weaknesses, and problems are? Do there seem to be any impending threats? What risks are we exposed to in your area? What are some opportunities which you see that might be pursued in the coming year or five years?"

Note that these are probing questions which force the subordinate to dig deeply into his or her own business before sitting down with the superior.

It requires judgments about threats, risks, and opportunities. It also requires that people begin to think about new and original things as well as thinking about unthinkable possibilities.

Among the more interesting questions over-heard in one such discussion were the following:

- Imagine that your budget were suddenly cut 20 per cent. What would you be forced to stop doing? Then imagine after that move were completed that budget was restored again. What would you then add? Is it the same as the thing you dropped? If not, why not? Why can't you just do the new things within the existing resources?
- Are there skills in your organization, or even that you yourself possess, that aren't being fully used? Is there any way you could use them more fully, given the existing resources?
- What resources could be used well in your job that you don't now have? For example, what could I do, do differently, or stop doing to help you succeed?

The most important single reason for failure of MBO in government is the tendency to treat it as a paperwork system, rather than a face-to-face management system.

Memoranda are essential to verity and follow up on agreement made face-to-face. When used in the absence of such face-to-face dialog, they can be poisonous. The MBO system becomes bogged down in a morass of forms, memoranda, and unintelligible evasions. The logic of MBO alone won't carry it off if the system is depersonalized and mechanistic. This is especially true in the movement of resources, for such shifts often require human ingenuity, managerial support, and some confidence which comes with personal assurances that risks are worth taking.

This is even more valid when the manager in state government must interface with local and county officials. For them, there is no compulsion which requires that they cooperate, and only personalized and face-to-face discussions have any hope for getting mutual information, cooperation, and commitment. A random sample of the relationships which system people call "interfaces" shows that in most government agencies they are not interfaces at all, but a crossing of memorandum.

Object lesson: The allocation of resources and their movement should always be done on a face-to-face basis.

III. Leave Me Alone As Much As Possible To Do My Job

Because steps one and two are necessary, step three is not possible until one and two have been completed. If subordinate managers know what is expected, and what resources and help are available. they can then be relied upon to show self-control, and govern their actions to achieve the commitments they have made. People who make commitments to somebody else whose opinion is important to them are practically obliged to do something about those commitments. This is especially true if those commitments have been made in face-to-face discussion, and have been confirmed in writing.

The power of commitment is what makes MBO work, and the absence of such commitment can cause it to fail.

The objectives and constraints are known in advance. Thus the subordinate knows that he is to "achieve my commitments, and stay within my constraints." and thus can operate freely within these boundaries. This is significantly different from "doing what you are told to do." Under such a constraining rule, innovation and variations in methods require lengthy requests for permission, funneled through the hierarchy, and producing three effects:

1. Decision making is slowed down.
2. Innovation is dampened and ultimately dies.
3. There can be no excellence at lower levels.

The problem of managerial control remains, however. The higher level official is always responsible for the actions of subordinates, and it would be unrealistic not to expect that higher level persons will be concerned about lower level performance. Yet. through the completion of explicit goals, stated in far more detail than ever was thought necessary or possible, managerial control through subordinate self-control is possible. The tightest form of control is self-control.

The exception principle requires four major rules for subordinates if it is to function as a tool of managerial control in an MBO system:

1. The subordinate must be clear on the goals and know when they are not being met, and know earlier than anybody else.
2. The subordinate should know the reasons those goals are not being achieved.
3. The subordinate should be able to initiate corrective action as soon as a deviation appears and he or she knows its reason, even before the boss learns of the problem.

4. The subordinate should be able to call for help, and thereby notify the superior early enough. Most bosses do not favor unpleasant surprises, and should be protected against them.

In the case study at Old West State, one manager described his rules for deciding whether to call the boss for help for notification purposes: "If the boss could hear about it from some third party, I make sure I get there first. That third party could be a peer, a higher up, or simply an indignant client." In one instance a highway patrol team ran into a dispute with the Air Police from an Air Force base in the area. On the supposition that the commanding colonel might call the state capital, the regional manager called his boss and explained the situation. When the complaint arrived in due course, no adrenaline flowed at the higher levels.

The boss, on the other hand, must show some restraint when receiving a single isolated report from a citizen. Such letters to the governor or a legislator should be bucked down through the channels for more grass-roots information, and not become a basis for tearing down the management system and recentralizing all decision making.

In one highly publicized incident the entire decentralization MBO process was nearly scuttled because a state truck ran over a cow. The owner wrote an indignant letter to the legislature, and the state office bureaucracy attempted to use the incident as proof that MBO produced reckless and irresponsible behavior at lower levels, implying that every cow in the state was endangered by MBO. Fortunately the director of administration for the state was able to resolve the question quickly. One of the major influences was the fact that a speedy response was forthcoming. Within an hour of the report's reaching the state capital, a responsible official from the region was on the scene, viewing the bovine's remains, and making specific arrangements with the farmer for fair reimbursement from local funds. Under a more centralized system the payment would have been years in coming, for the state capital was more than a hundred miles from the cow.

MBO should produce a more personalized responsive system of government for citizens, by placing decision making over small matters affecting citizens in the hands of lower level organizations.

Delegation, and leaving lower level subordinates alone once their objectives are established clearly and resources defined accordingly, produces a more localized decision system to allow for local variances.

IV. Let Me Know How Well I Am Doing in My Work

Objectives, properly defined, should comprise an instrument panel of vital signs of the organization. These vital signs are analogous to the pulse, body temperature, blood pressure, and other vital signs of the human organism. Such a vital sign as body temperature could be "normal" within a range as follows:

normal at rest	98.6
after exercise	99.9
in cool climate	98.0

The physician doesn't demand that every temperature be identical with the at-rest norm. Nor should managers expect precision in measuring their own performance, nor should their superiors demand such uniformity. Take the case of the park system in Old West. Records of parks use by summer months for the past four years showed the following:

1968	7,601
1969	7,950
1970	8,310
1971	8,734

For planning purposes it was noted that a secular trend upward in excess of 300 to 400 a year was observed. Thus it could be anticipated, "other things being equal," that a rise of another 400 to 500 could be expected in 1972. This became the *normal* objective. This meant that the preparation of staff assignments, preparation of park sites, tons of refuse disposal planned, and similar demands upon the park management and staff could be anticipated.

Yet, the purpose is *not to forecast nor to predict.* The prediction is that park use in 1972 will be at a rate of about 9,200 persons per month, and the *prediction itself is a means to better management.* It affords the management a vital sign. If it goes above 9,500, then some kind of response is indicated. If it goes below 8,700, then some kind of investigation and possible response should be made by management.

> The idea of measurement is not to punish the people for being poor forecasters. The forecast is created to provide vital signs for management to make managerial responses.

Thus, when the energy crisis came along and cut sharply into the park use, for motorists could not obtain gasoline, the use of the park went down to 3,165 per month. The park manager used this opportunity to move personnel from planned services to other approved projects within the park, and to other projects which had not been thought feasible outside the park.

BOX 12.1 Practicing Management Theory at the Port Authority

Matthias E. Lukens

One of the Port Authority's most unusual attributes is our vigorous management philosophy—and the extraordinary extent we are able to live by it. Simply stated, our aim is to be the best—the best management, the best results, the best place to work. Within the framework of this policy we have utilized the best practices we can find in both business and government and have developed some on our own which others, in turn, have borrowed.

Fulfilling an organizational philosophy demands that most persons in the organization understand and believe in it. And so from the first day of his orientation course, an employee is urged to develop a questioning attitude. Similarly, every supervisor, passing as he must through a supervisory and management training course, is encouraged to train his people to develop a questioning attitude and to contribute ideas on how to do things better. As an additional stimulus, we have an effective suggestion system that has the same goal.

Toward the same end, participative management is extensively practiced, mainly resting on good staff work—all levels of the staff participating in the generation of ideas and recommendations. This has gone beyond mere requirement; it is a practice that has become a habit throughout the organization. Thus, the normal decision made in the organization has been preceded by a complete identification of facts, full consideration of alternatives, and a discussion of the problem and solutions by all persons whose responsibilities would in any way relate them to the subject matter.

It is in the same spirit that we have built a management based upon teamwork. This is a somewhat overworked term, yet it describes the way, as a matter of management policy, that we function. Probably the best way to bring this subject home is to state categorically that among the key members of our management group there are no internal politics, no favoritism, no front office cliques, no discrimination, and no power playing. The fact that such practices are not tolerated is not the only explanation; it is the spirit and attitude of staff, which springs more than anything else from inspiring top leadership.

Along with stress on striving to be the best, the questioning attitude, participative management, and management teamwork, flexibility and informality are emphasized. Abhorrence of red tape and the evils of bureaucracy amounts to a party line. Although we have the normal and necessary rules of conduct and administration, there are practically none that are inflexible or which cannot be waived for good and sufficient reason. Although the integrity of lines of authority is jealously guarded, ease and informality of communication are encouraged and fostered throughout the organization without regard for lines of authority.

The plain fact is that orderly administration requires formalization of policies, practices, and procedures. The problem is not to let orderliness become rigidity and inflexibility.

(Source: Matthias E. Lukens, "Practicing Management Theory at the Port Authority," in: "Practicing Management Theory," *Public Administration Review* 18 (1958): 223–230.)

V. Reward My Accomplishments

Perhaps the major distinction between government and business applications of MBO is not in the profit motive for the firm, but in the willingness of industry to relate achievement to pay. This is achieved in several ways, and the experience of those municipalities who have developed and installed performance payment systems has been sufficiently good that it proves such incentive compensation is viable for government.

Clearly managerial or professional compensation in government cannot be related to *profit*. But it can be related to *performance* if these performance objectives exist.

1. There must be a norm or standard of performance which is related to the public purposes of the organization and the specific performance objectives of the job.
2. Such standards must be related to *output* for a period of time, usually a year.
3. The standard should be written as a form of performance contract for that year, which require objectives to be carefully negotiated.
4. There should be statements of special conditions under which the incentive pay will not apply. If the job holder is penalized for hard luck, or rewarded for windfalls not of his own doing, the system can fail.
5. Provision for review at the highest levels must be made, both of the goals used as standards, and of the results actually achieved. This assures uniformity of treatment among equals, and prudent use of public funds.
6. Selective application of incentive payments is possible without destroying the system. For example, in one city the incentive pay principle was applied to revenue producing positions. Where the revenues went beyond historic normal standards, an ascending scale of compensation was awarded, provided certain other kinds of objectives were also met.
7. Incentives for innovative objectives can be managed through suggestion award plans. Under current systems, it would seem to be more prudent to reiate the award to the achievement by rewarding only proved savings, or demonstrated innovations which increase yield from resources.
8. Relating rewards to achievement requires a change in many performance reviews or appraisal forms and procedures. The old form of adjective-rating of performance against a list of personality traits, if related to pay increases or merit ratings,

will compete and perhaps extinguish achievement-centered behavior.

In an MBO management system. performance review and merit rating must be directly related to goals and results statements. and adjective rating systems abandoned.

Summary

MBO in government is confronted with the same kinds of bureaucratic and political traps which every new program runs into. Strong administrative overtures are met with equal and opposite countermoves. When power flows from one place to another, people from whom it is flowing will resist that flow away from themselves. The political leader tends to seek ever-increasing amounts of power, in contrast with the economic sector where leaders operate on a principle of acquisition. It is difficult to say which is loftier. Procedures which were once important, perhaps even noble, persist long after their useful life has ended. Activity for its own sake becomes a false goal, becomes firmly embedded, and ultimately becomes a religion. Changing behavior of bureaucrats is not done easily, for their security lies in doing what has worked in the past. There is a general reluctance to invest heavily in training which is innovative in character, for it promises to produce an unwanted change, and perhaps new centers of power. Finally the culture of government, especially state government, is more *affiliation centered* than achievement centered. Ideology seldom dominates state government, nor is there a strong culture of performance on behalf of the constituency, with some notable exceptions.

These are the lessons of MBO in Old West state's program of applying MBO. It does not prove that MBO has procedural nor logical flaws, nor that government is evil. It does demonstrate, however, that some special efforts are required to make it work. Turning a government into an achieving organization is never easy.

13

Motivational Programs and Productivity Improvement in Times of Limited Resources

John M. Greiner

For many state and local governments, these are times of shrinking resources and rising demands. The litany of conflicting pressures is all too familiar by now. On the one hand, the public continues to demand more and better services—more help for the increasing numbers of homeless and hungry, better police and fire protection, greater excellence in education. On the other hand, the cost of providing these services continues to rise steeply; state and local governments have faced an average annual inflation rate of 7.5 percent over the past four years, a total increase of nearly 34 percent since 1980 in the cost of doing business.[1] Meanwhile, intergovernmental transfer payments—especially Federal aid—have decreased sharply while taxpayer resistance to higher levies has continued. The upshot, as Levine has observed, is that problems of perennial resource *scarcity* have been converted into problems of resource *shrinkage* for many state and local governments.[2]

Productivity improvement—the production of more and/or better services for each tax dollar and staff hour invested—has been an especially attractive strategy for many governments facing tight or shrinking resources. A 1983 survey of local governments found that 67 percent of the 460 responding cities had undertaken formal productivity efforts,[3] and a recent

---

"Motivational Programs and Productivity Improvement in Times of Limited Resources," *Public Productivity Review* 10 (Fall 1986): 81–101.

telephone survey revealed that productivity improvement activities were under way in virtually all state governments.[4] Productivity improvement has been particularly attractive to local governments under serious financial stress. In a recent study of responses by seventeen Massachusetts local governments to the funding cuts that accompanied Proposition 2½ (a property tax initiative similar to California's Proposition 13), productivity improvement was found to be the second most common response (after cost cutting and reductions in service levels) for police and fire departments; it was also popular among libraries and public works departments.[5]

A variety of productivity improvement strategies are available to state and local governments. Most of them fall into five broad categories: (1) introduction of new or improved technology, (2) improvement of operational procedures, (3) revision of organizational structures, (4) enhancement of the skills of management and line employees, and (5) improvement of employee motivation. Each of these strategies requires the acquiescence and cooperation of government employees—management as well as labor—to succeed. From accepting new technologies to responding to employee incentives, public employees represent a critical element in the productivity improvement equation.

Of all the major approaches to productivity improvement, motivational strategies are probably affected the most by employee concerns and values. For purposes of this article, a motivational strategy is any effort to induce employees to initiate and sustain activities that can directly or indirectly improve service productivity. This definition is quite broad, encompassing everything from monetary incentives to quality circles, suggestion awards to career ladders.[6]

The potential productivity benefits from the introduction of motivational programs are considerable: 42 percent of the operating expenditures of state governments in fiscal year 1983 and 56 percent of those for local governments that year involved salaries and wages.[7] For some services, for example, police and fire), personnel costs account for 70 to 80 percent of operating expenditures. Thus, there are likely to be opportunities for significant savings through better utilization of human resources in state and local governments.

The need for incentives and other programs to improve employee motivation appears to be especially strong in an environment of tight resources and cutback management. During such periods, governments tend to reduce and/or delay the investments needed to maintain their human capital.[8] The subsequent erosion of the government's human capital is manifested in numerous ways—less training; deterioration of salary levels and other reward systems; fewer opportunities for career growth, and so forth. This often triggers what Levine terms employee "disinvestment": Employees attempt to cut their losses by reducing their contributions to the organization.

The result is all too often "a decrease in the skill levels of public workforces, a decline in their energy and responsiveness, a concomitant decline in their performance, and worst of all, a further decline in the confidence and support of the public for government in general."[9]

In the wake of Proposition 2½, many of these symptoms were evident in Massachusetts cities and towns, including increased employee stress, poor morale, loss of skilled staff, curtailment of prior employee incentives, and concern that increasing numbers of employees would suffer occupational burnout.[10] These symptoms often persisted well after the initial shock of Proposition 2½ had begun to abate and funding levels had once again begun to rise.[11] By not turning their attention to renewal of their human resources through the use of motivational and other such strategies, these governments risk future personnel problems that can seriously damage long-range service delivery and productivity.

Three Important Motivational Approaches

To provide an indication of the scope and variety of the motivational programs available to governments, as well as of the potential trade-offs and conflicts that must be faced in implementing such programs, the remainder of this chapter will focus on three popular motivational approaches: performance targeting (in particular, the use of management by objectives); monetary incentives; and job enrichment (specifically, the use of quality circles).

Performance Targeting

Performance targeting is the process of (1) making explicit to employees, either individually or as a group, the level and type of work performance expected and (2) providing subsequent feedback on and discussions of performance achievements. While several types of performance targeting can be found in state and local governments, probably the most important variant is management by objectives (MBO). According to the MBO paradigm, superior and subordinate managers jointly identify common goals and objectives, areas of responsibility, and expected results for the coming performance period. In some cases, these expectations and targets are formalized as a performance contract between a manager and his or her superior. Such contracts typically include a work plan for achieving the given objectives and indicate mutual responsibilities in support of that work plan. After the objectives and the corresponding performance targets have been agreed upon, there are periodic assessments and reviews of the manager's performance in meeting the specified targets.

Performance targeting in the form of MBO is common in state and local governments. In a 1976 ICMA survey, 42 percent of the 377 responding local governments reported using MBO.[12] A 1983 survey of municipal police departments found that 47 percent of the 300 respondents utilized MBO.[13]

Information on the effectiveness of such programs in improving productivity is, however, much more difficult to come by. A review of the (limited) "hard" evidence available on the impacts of state and local MBO efforts suggests that target setting per se, for example, exclusive of any linkage to monetary rewards has led to documentable but modest improvements in service productivity.[14] There have sometimes been other benefits as well, including improved communication, better understanding by employees of what is expected of them, more effective management, and better documentation for the public of agency achievements.

Nevertheless, a review of public sector MBO (findings suggest that the effectiveness of state and local government MBO efforts is greatly influenced by the manner in which programs are designed, implemented, and administered. The achievement of productivity improvements appears to depend in large part on the use of performance targets that either are clearly focused on service outcomes (rather than processes) or emphasize the identification and completion of productivity improvements projects, for example, "Identify at least one project per quarter that will reduce costs or improve services without sacrificing service quality, and implement at least half of them"). Other factors that appear necessary for an effective MBO effort include the specification of work plans for target achievement; provision of interim targets; central review and oversight of all performance objectives and targets to ensure that they are fair, challenging, and realistic; regular, timely feedback to employees on their performance; and one-to-one meetings between managers and their superiors to review overall target achievements.[15]

There are indications that the motivational potential of MBO efforts is often overlooked.[16] To take advantage of this potential, governments need to fully utilize the participative features of MBO, (for example, by involving line employees in the specification and review of performance targets).[17] Governments also need to ensure that the MBO program is taken seriously—for example, by stressing regular, one-to-one (and perhaps group) reviews of target achievements; by not making it too easy to revise (loosen) targets if they are not met; and by establishing individual accountability for target achievement, through sanctions and counseling when targets are not met and through praise and (nonmonetary) rewards when targets are exceeded.

Monetary Incentives

Monetary incentives are cash awards used to induce desired behavior or results. The awards can be contingent on the performance of an individual or of a group. In the public sector, such incentives can take many forms—performance bonuses, merit and other performance-based wage increases, shared savings plans, suggestion awards, safety and attendance incentives, and so forth.[18]

While it may seem at first inappropriate to consider the introduction of monetary incentives in periods of tight or shrinking resources, such programs should not be dismissed out of hand. When properly designed, such incentives appear to be among the most effective of the various motivational approaches available. Moreover, some types of monetary incentives—in particular, shared savings plans—may not require additional financial resources.[19] Furthermore, it has been suggested that the introduction of monetary incentives and other special employee rewards may be especially important during a period of tight resources, when such recognition can serve as a means for combatting employee disinvestment.[20]

Except for merit increases, monetary incentives have not been especially common in the public sector. Of the respondents to a 1978 member survey by the International Personnel Management Association, 42 percent reported the use of merit increases based on performance.[21] Suggestion awards and performance bonuses were reported by only 16 percent and 12 percent, respectively, of the responding jurisdictions, and shared savings plans were even less common.

While "hard" information on the effectiveness of public sector monetary incentives plans is scarce, a few useful findings have emerged.[22] Merit pay, as usually handled in the public sector, is not generally very effective at stimulating improved productivity, but performance bonuses, shared savings plans, and performance-based wage increases for line personnel have given evidence of significantly improving service productivity if they are based on clearly defined, objective, outcome-oriented performance criteria. While group incentives (with monetary awards contingent upon the performance of an entire group) are motivationally less effective than individual incentives (which focus on the performance of individual employees), group plans appear to be considerably more acceptable (and, therefore, feasible) for public employees.

Still, public sector pay-for-performance plans have not given consistent evidence of being effective in stimulating professional and management personnel. In particular, linking target achievement to monetary rewards for managers within the context of an MBO system led to no additional improvements in performance in three cities where such systems were studied.[23] Similarly, in a recent test of incentive bonuses for local offices of the Employment Service in the states of Kansas and New Jersey, cash awards did not serve as a major productivity stimulus for management and professional personnel, although lower-level, nonprofessional staff were often motivated by such awards.[24] Indeed, in many of the foregoing examples, the establishment of a linkage between pay and performance provoked considerable dissension and job dissatisfaction among management personnel.

As in performance targeting, the effectiveness of a monetary incentive plan depends critically on careful, sensitive design and implementation of the program. Great care must be taken to ensure that the performance assessment procedure is objective and equitable and that the linkage between rewards and performance is direct, timely, and understandable. The awards themselves should be large enough to serve as meaningful stimuli (preferably at least $1,000 and, ideally, 10 percent of an employee's salary)[25] and abundant enough for all deserving individuals or groups to receive them (artificial limits on the number of persons who can receive awards in any given incentive period should be avoided). Finally, there should be plenty of timely feedback on employee (or group) performance during the incentive period, and again when the awards are announced. It is important to ensure that all persons clearly understand just how the winners earned their rewards.

Overall, successful implementation of monetary incentives in the public sector is usually very difficult, requiring the investment of considerable time, effort, and patience while demanding exceptional care and sensitivity on the part of those responsible for implementation. Governments contemplating the introduction of monetary incentives must be willing to assume the risks, tolerate the criticisms, and provide significant top management and staff support over the long haul. Indeed, private sector monetary incentive plans often require four to five years before the "bugs" are worked out; it would be unrealistic to expect the process to proceed much faster in the public sector.

Quality Circles and Increased Participation. Quality circles are small groups of mostly nonsupervisory personnel who meet voluntarily on a regular basis to identify, analyze, and solve problems they experience in their own work.[26] Quality circles represent a form of increased participation, a class of formal programs designed to give nonsupervisory personnel greater opportunities to contribute to decision making and problem solving concerning their own work units. Other public sector examples of increased participation include joint labor-management committees, councils composed of elected employee representatives, and various forms of participative management (for example, the inclusion of a line employee on a city's management team). Increased participation, in turn, is one aspect of job enrichment, a large class of motivational programs that includes the use of teams, task forces, job rotation, and job redesign.[27]

Quality circles are attracting increasing interest among state and local governments. Such programs have recently been reported in nineteen states, and in a 1984 ICMA survey, 8 percent of the 1,238 responding municipalities reported the use of quality circles.[28] In a similar survey of municipal police departments, 16 percent of the 300 respondents indicated that they were using quality circles.[29]

Systematic assessments of public sector quality circles have been quite rare, although some evaluative information is now available on programs in Orlando, Florida; Dallas, Texas; and Los Angeles and Hayward, California.[30] To date, however, there appears to be little evidence that quality circles involving government employees produce major improvements in service delivery or productivity.[31] Such circles have usually focused on improving working conditions and in solving relatively small-scale operating problems. Only infrequently has any attention been directed to significant issues of service delivery with the potential for major production improvements.

As with performance targets and monetary incentives, quality circles effectiveness appears to depend critically on proper design and implementation. Inadequate attention to fundamentals—ensuring that participation is voluntary; alleviating potential attendance problems due to shift conflicts; providing the circle with direct access to top management in presenting recommendations; giving adequate recognition to participants—has apparently limited the effectiveness of a number of quality circles in the public sector.[32] However, public sector use of quality circles is currently at an embryonic stage. With more experience, the above problems can be alleviated, and perhaps productivity impacts can be increased.

Tradeoffs and Conflicts in Implementing Motivational Programs

In selecting and implementing motivational strategies for government employees, administrators must overcome a number of potentially serious obstacles. In a 1978 ICMA survey of municipal use of employee incentives, 38 percent of the 1,661 responding municipalities reported encountering one or more obstacles in trying to implement such programs.[33] Fiscal constraints constituted the most common barrier (they were reported by 69 percent of the 546 cities reporting at least some implementation obstacles). Other common problems included political obstacles (36 percent), restrictive labor agreements (29 percent), management opposition (21 percent), employee opposition (20 percent), legal barriers (20 percent), and civil service rules and policies (18 percent).[34]

In the following paragraphs, we will review some of the major tradeoffs and conflicts that must be faced in using motivational techniques to improve productivity. For the purpose of this discussion, attention will be focused on the three types of motivational programs already described.

Effectiveness. Many have expressed concern regarding the effectiveness of motivational techniques for improving the productivity of public employees. For instance, Klingner recently reported that many local public managers were "quite unenthusiastic about the potential of improved human resource management for increasing productivity."[35] Given the scarcity of objective, systematic information on the impacts of such programs, these views are not suprising.

As a group, motivational approaches have not given much evidence of being able to produce major, across-the-board improvements in public sector productivity. To be sure, a few highly successful programs have been undertaken in such cities as Flint (Michigan) and Philadelphia,[36] but, in general, savings have been modest.

In a synthesis of private sector and academic research on the effectiveness of various types of motivational programs, the median change in performance after the introduction of monetary incentives was +30 percent; the median change after implementation of target setting was +16 percent; and the median performance change for programs to increase participation was +0.5 percent.[37] Combined approaches—for example, target setting combined with monetary incentives—were even more effective, with a median performance change of +40 percent. Private sector research has also shown that the effectiveness of a monetary incentive program in stimulating improved performance decreases with the size of the incentive group.[38] Thus, individual incentives are the most effective variant, followed by group incentives and, in last place, organizationwide incentives (for example, a Scanlong plan, whose group of interest is the entire organization). While the above findings are based on private sector and laboratory results, the data available from the public sector seem to support these relationships and orderings.

The foregoing results pose some dilemmas for state and local use of motivational techniques. The most effective programs—monetary incentives—are the most difficult to implement and have been of questionable value for management and professional employees, at least for the magnitudes of incentive awards likely to be feasible in most governments. In addition, the most effective type of monetary incentive program—individual incentives—has been especially controversial (and often ineffective) in the public sector. Therefore, it is likely that public administrators will often have to compromise on effectiveness in order to facilitate implementation—for example, by focusing on target setting and monetary incentive plans involving group rather than individual bonuses.

The effectiveness of public sector motivational plans is also, however, strongly affected by design and implementation considerations. Inadequate attention to such factors can compromise the effectiveness of even the most carefully selected incentive approach.

Resource Needs

Implementation and operation of motivational programs for public employees can generate a requirement for several different kinds of resources, including dollars, time, expertise and support from management and the general public. Of course, any such resource needs must be viewed within the contexts of (1) the fiscal stress and scarcity that characterize many of the governments most in need of motivational initiatives and (2) the uncertainty concerning the magnitude of the savings and productivity improvements expected from the use of a given motivational technique.

Costs. Out-of-pocket expenditures are generally highest for monetary incentive programs, although well-designed shared savings plans and suggestion awards have frequently recovered their costs from the savings they generate. A major expenditure in connection with monetary incentives is the cost of the awards. Indeed, some of the guidelines noted previously for designing effective monetary incentives tend to drive the cost of the awards even higher (for example, rewards that are at least $1,000 and, ideally, 10 percent of salary, and no limits or quotas on the number of persons who can earn awards in any given performance period). Other likely expenses in connection with monetary incentives include the extensive amount of staff time needed to develop and properly implement such a program; expenses for training, recordkeeping, data collection, and data processing; and, in some cases, the cost of auditing the performance data.[39] Expenditures of these magnitudes (often in the tens and hundreds of thousands of dollars) may be hard to sell to employees at a time when wages are being frozen and staff are being laid off.

Out-of-pocket costs for quality circles and MBO programs are usually much more modest, typically several thousand dollars. The primary expenses will be for consultants to help with program initiation and training and—in the case of quality circles—training materials for use by the jurisdiction after the consultants are gone. Another important cost in connection with these two programs is the time spent by program participants in training activities, quality circle meetings, negotiation, documentation, review of MBO targets, and so forth. In the case of MBO, however, such costs are often viewed as a necessary element of agency management, rather than as special program expenses.

Training. Adequate training is a vital input for each of the three types of motivational programs. Too often, training in connection with public sector motivational efforts has been inadequate. When training materials from private sector programs are available (for example, for MBO and quality circles), such materials should be carefully adapted to the needs of public sector employees and environments. (For instance, police officers in Orlando, Florida, complained that their training materials, which came from the private sector, seemed almost childish; they moved too slowly for police tastes, oversimplified analytic procedures most officers already knew or were capable of grasping quickly, and utilized industrial examples that were far removed from the kinds of problems typically addressed by a police department.)

Adequate training is essential in connection with monetary incentives. Employees must clearly understand how a program works—the precise connection between pay and performance—if such incentives are to be effective. Unfortunately, these connections are sometimes rather complex (for instance, regression techniques may be used to establish performance standards or to adjust for external factors). Such sophisticated features are likely to be useless and perhaps even counterproductive if there is not adequate training to explain how they work, so that employees can accept them as valid.

Monetary incentive groups, newly appointed managers coming under MBO programs, new members of quality circles—are also important, especially in view of high turnover in some government agencies. Periodic "refresher" training for all employees involved with motivational programs is also needed; without it, one is likely to find that employee enthusiasm is waning, program procedures are increasingly being misapplied, and the overall effort is being taken for granted.

Specialized Expertise and Advice. Governments are unlikely to have all the in-house expertise necessary for implementing motivational plans. Outside consultants are usually necessary in connection with MBO and quality circle efforts to help with program design and startup, provide training and advice to the initial program participants, and train the trainers—a process necessary for institutionalization of the program. Although the design and implementation of monetary incentives can often be completed without outside help, external expertise may be needed in connection with the more complex incentive efforts (for example, when sophisticated analytic techniques are employed to adjust for potential inequities and changing external factors).

Time and Energy Needed to Implement and Operate the Program. All three types of motivational programs require considerable expenditures of energy, time, and patience if they are to be implemented properly. This is especially true for monetary incentives, which are usually the most difficult programs to implement. Program administrators must take the time to ensure that the necessary groundwork is done and done properly. This groundwork includes meaningful, early involvement of employees; careful and thorough design and testing of program mechanisms and procedures (monetary incentive formulas, centralized review and oversight mechanisms for MBO, overtime or comp time for employees participating in quality circles, and so forth); establishment of data collection and performance feedback mechanisms that are accurate, valid, and timely enough to support the intended motivational effort; and adequate training of supervisory and nonsupervisory personnel. Hurriedly implemented motivational programs have rarely succeeded in the public sector. A government must be ready to move slowly but deliberately, perhaps using a phased approach that includes pilot efforts, and it must be ready to invest its energies and commitment over a long enough period (at least several years) for the inevitable "bugs" to be identified and worked out.

Management Time and Support. One of the most critical resources needed for a successful motivational program is a commitment of top management's support and involvement. If a monetary incentive plan, MBO system, or quality circle is to be taken seriously by government employees, top management must demonstrate the seriousness of its own commitment to the long-range success of the effort. This means investing management time and prestige in the program. Anything less will be a signal to employees that "this too shall pass."

Public and Political Support. Political and public opposition has rarely been a problem in connection with public sector MBO and quality circle efforts. Indeed, the implementation of such programs has often stimulated support from these quarters. Thus, introduction of these techniques is often perceived as indicative of effective, innovative public administrators who are ready to adopt the latest methods. Several public officials have noted that an important side benefit of MBO programs is the ability to clearly demonstrate the accomplishments of an agency, using target achievement data.

Public and political support for monetary incentives has, however, been less consistent. While some have praised such approaches for bringing business techniques to the public sector, others have been quick to complain about "paying public employees a bonus to do what they are already being paid to do." Administrators must plan carefully and avoid giving critics any basis for such concerns—for example, by actively involving line employees in the design of incentive plans, by relying on objective performance data and precisely specified formulas for making any rewards, by establishing challenging performance targets, and by providing for audits of performance data and other checks that may be needed to ensure the accuracy and credibility of the information.[40]

In summary, although motivational programs place demands on the availability of a variety of critical resources, most of these resources are internal and likely to be available to a committed government, even in a time of fiscal stress. When resources—for instance, financial resources and specialized expertise—must come from outside, the needs of MBO and quality circles are likely to be modest. Only monetary incentives are likely to require costly external resources that may be difficult for an agency to afford. In such instances, outside "seed" money may be needed, although in the case of shared savings programs, such investments may ultimately be repaid from savings generated by the program.

Personnel and Organizational Structures and Policies

Motivational programs are frequently constrained by a variety of structures and policies that have their roots in the organization. These include legal barriers, civil service rules and policies, and contractual stipulations.[41]

Legal Constraints. There appear to be few if any legal barriers to the use of MBO or quality circles. However, some state and local governments have laws or ordinances that specifically prohibit giving employees any monetary rewards except in the form of regular wages and salaries (including merit increases). Other legal constraints affecting monetary incentives may include restrictions on the use of certain types of appropriations for employee rewards. In such cases, special action by the city council or state legislature is likely to be needed to authorize monetary incentives.

Civil Service Rules and Regulations. Civil service requirements do not generally serve as an obstacle to the introduction of quality circles. MBO efforts may, however, be constrained by civil service regulations that prescribe other procedures for assessing employee performance. The existence of competing techniques for judging management performance is likely to weaken the effectiveness of both procedures. A better approach would be to modify civil service rules to make them compatible with the MBO effort—for example, by including a review of MBO target achievements as part of the existing performance appraisal process.

Monetary incentives, in contrast, are likely to be greatly hampered by existing civil service rules and regulations. Among the possible constraints are limitations on procedures for granting wage increases (for example, limits on the frequency or amount of any increases; prohibitions against awards to persons at the top step of the pay scale) and requirements demanding jurisdictionwide uniformity on the availability of any form of compensation, including incentive awards (under such policies, a monetary incentive plan must be made available either to all employees or to none). Levine has suggested a number of other modifications of personnel rules and regulations to help combat human resource erosion during a period of fiscal stress.[42]

Contract Stipulations. Collective bargaining agreements can also limit a government's freedom to implement various types of motivational programs. For instance, contractual stipulation of performance appraisal procedures (or levels of compensation) can make the introduction of MBO (or monetary incentives) a negotiable change.

Public employees associations can also facilitate the introduction of certain types of motivational programs. In several instances, such organizations have gone on record in support of particular approaches, such as shared savings plans, joint labor-management committees, and quality-of-worklife efforts.[43]

Organizational Constraints. Organizational structures and constraints sometimes play a role in the design and implementation of motivational programs for public employees. For instance, the specification of the groups in a group incentive plan will often depend largely on organizational considerations. In New Jersey's recent trial of productivity incentives for local offices of the Employment Service, the organizational structure of the Division of Employment Services (which contained two major units, the Employment Service and the Office of Special Programs) made it necessary (for reasons of equity and labor peace) for the state to develop and implement a parallel incentive plan for employees in the Office of Special Programs.

Organizational constraints have sometimes created difficulties in the operation of police department quality circles. In departments with strong traditions of adhering to the chain of command, police quality circles have sometimes been hampered in their efforts to attack problems that involve units outside their own direct chains of command, since there exist strong compulsions not to bypass chains of command by dealing directly with such units. In such cases, central coordination, perhaps through a steering committee, seems needed to get around such organizational constraints.

In summary, personnel policies and organizational structures can impede the implementation and effective functioning of motivational programs. Such constraints appear to be most serious for monetary incentives, and a few of them potentially affect quality circles. Nevertheless, they appear to pose few obstacles for MBO and other target-setting efforts. The obstacles in the case of monetary incentives and quality circles are not insurmountable, but they are likely to require cooperation from (and negotiations with) a number of parties—civil service boards, labor unions, and possible legislatures or city councils. Thus, the presence of personnel and organizational barriers is likely to delay the development and implementation of motivational programs while testing the resolve of those interested in achieving implementation.

Compatibility with Employee Needs, Values, and Attitudes

As noted previously, employees constitute a critical element in the productivity improvement equation, especially when it comes to motivational strategies. Three concerns are particularly important in connection with the match between employees and the motivational approaches applied to them: program compatibility with employees concerns and needs, program effects on job satisfaction, and program compatibility with management's goals and interests.

Compatibility with Employees' Concerns and Needs. To the degree that a motivational program is incompatible with the needs and concerns of the employees it addresses, the motivational effectiveness of the plan is likely to be compromised. Gross incompatibilities can lead to resistance toward or rejection of the plan. The term *productivity improvement* is itself enough to threaten some employees (for instance, they may fear the loss of their jobs if such improvements are successful). Thus, some states are currently trying to avoid use of the term *productivity* in characterizing their improvement efforts.[44]

The various motivational approaches already described will not be appropriate for everyone, since they focus on different motivational factors. The issue, then, is this: What motivates public employees?

In principle, performance targets and MBO should be compatible with the needs, drives, and motivational structures of most employees. Performance targeting is based on goal-setting theory, which postulates that human actions are instigated by conscious intentions expressed as specific goals.[45] A goal, therefore, is what an individual or a group is consciously trying to achieve; it constitutes the most immediate determinant of performance. Motivational techniques based on goal-setting theory should therefore be applicable to all employees. (However, personal characteristics may still influence the motivational effectiveness of such efforts, to some extent.)[46] Although strong employee resistance to target setting and MBO has not been reported very often, some cases have been recorded (for example, resistance to performance targets on the part of mental health center professionals).[47] Such resistance frequently centers on the alleged unfairness or inconsistency of the targets for different employees or on whether specification of such targets is compatible with professionalism.

Monetary incentives, however, seem somewhat less likely to be generally compatible with the needs of public employees. To be sure, numerous studies have indicated that public employees view pay as an important job factor and, when questioned about possible incentives, public employees often rate bonuses and other cash awards very highly.[48] However, as noted previously, monetary incentives focusing on management and professional personnel in the public sector have been much less successful than those focusing on line employees.[49] Similar issues underlie much of the controversy concerning the likely value of merit pay for teachers.[50] To some extent, the restraint that management and professional employees in the public sector have exhibited toward monetary incentives may reflect the limited sizes of the awards typically available. However, in many cases in the public sector, it appears that, for professional and managerial personnel, factors other than money—for example, the work itself, professional goals and pride, promotional recognition—constitute a stronger motivational force than pay. Thus, efforts to develop motivational plans for such employees should probably consider the use of rewards other than cash—for instance, choice of rewards (including additional training, attendance at professional conferences, additional amenities for the office, and so forth) or a mix on nonmonetary incentives (for instance, performance targets coupled with job enrichment).

Even nonmanagement employees, however, are quick to react against monetary incentives that are poorly designed or implemented. Group incentives usually generate much less resistance among public employees than individual incentives do, and they appear to be an especially promising direction for governments interested in trying monetary incentives. In general, public employees appear to be concerned most about the equity (fairness) and objectivity of monetary incentive plans.[51] Design efforts should therefore place top priority on ensuring that the incentive plan developed is as fair and objective as possible.

Quality circles have not yet sparked the kinds of resistance often found in connection with monetary incentives. Nevertheless, quality circles are not for everyone. Many management and employee styles are incompatible with the participative approach needed to make quality circles effective. At a minimum, top-level management and the circle members should be comfortable with a participative style in agencies where quality circles are being used. (However, one should not prejudge managers; quality circles and related participative approaches have been found to flourish even in the authoritarian, paramilitary environment of a police department.[52] To avoid possible incompatibilities, at least with regard to line employees, participation in quality circles should always be entirely voluntary; coerced participation can quickly undermine the effectiveness of such circles.

Mid-level managers, however, often feel threatened by quality circles. While some mid-level management dissatisfaction with quality circles can be tolerated, efforts should be made to minimize such resistance by keeping mid-level managers fully informed of quality circles' proceedings and soliciting mid-level managers' comments.

The issues just outlined underscore the importance of seeking early and meaningful involvement from the employees affected by motivational plans, as well as from their associations or unions. A cooperative effort to address the potential points of friction noted above can go a long way toward alleviating conflicts and ensuring employee acceptance of the effort.

Compatibility with Management Goals and Actions. In general, motivational programs are interventions initiated and sustained by management.

How do such programs fit with other management responsibilities and desires? A number of potential conflicts are apparent.

An important concern is the degree to which management is willing to divert scarce resources to the implementation of motivational initiatives during a time of fiscal stress. One must invest money to save money, and for programs like monetary incentives, such investments can be substantial. However, the payoffs from monetary incentives in terms of productivity improvement can also be significant. MBO efforts have also been moderately successful. Given the need of governments to maximize productivity improvements while limiting program expenditures, it would appear that shared saving plans and/or MBO efforts (not linked to pay) offer the best promise.

A related concern is the degree to which management believes that improvement of job satisfaction is as important as (or more important than) productivity improvement. To the extent that improved job satisfaction is an important goal in and of itself (as may be the case in a turnaround period following a time of fiscal stress), other motivational techniques become attractive—job enrichment approaches, highly participative MBO efforts, nonmonetary rewards and recognition, and so forth. If management is primarily concerned with improving job satisfaction, quality circles can be allowed to follow their natural inclinations to focus on alleviating immediate work problems and improving working conditions. However, if management's primary concern is with productivity improvement, some form of management intervention and guidance may be needed to get circles to focus on major service delivery and productivity issues (in contrast to the usual way of handling quality circles).

Another potential concern is conflict between management's stated intentions in fostering a motivational program and management's later actions and decisions. There should be a high degree of consistency between motivational programs and management actions; inconsistency in this regard will signal a certain cynicism on the part of management and can undermine motivational effectiveness. For instance, the presence of multiple procedures for appraising and rewarding employee performance (for example, a performance bonus plan and a separate performance appraisal system) can send conflicting signals to employees concerning the relative importance of each. Thus, if major promotions continue to depend on a traditional checklist appraisal, the performance bonus plan is likely to be disregarded. Similarly, management should not introduce monetary incentives as a way to compensate for inadequate salary levels or try to make small monetary rewards appear too significant. If significant monetary rewards are impossible, it would be better to downplay the size of the awards and stress the role of such awards, as token of recognition rather than as measures of excellence.

MBO can also be the victim of inconsistent management actions that undermine its effectiveness. In particular, if management ignores information on performance and target achievements that is produced in connection with the MBO effort and makes decisions on resource allocations, promotions, or staff cuts on the basis of other considerations, it will be difficult to get employees to take the MBO effort seriously, as several governments have found out.

In the case of job enrichment programs, management must be sincere in its reasons for initiating such efforts. If the goal is primarily to improve job satisfaction, that should be made the basis for evaluating and continuing the program. If, however, productivity improvement is the primary reason behind the introduction of such programs, that should be made explicit, and the programs should be oriented and evaluated accordingly. Employees will quickly see through the hypocrisy of programs designed primarily to get them to assume more responsibilities at the same pay or to solve difficult management problems under the guise of "job enrichment"!

The survival and success of a motivational program will depend finally on management's ability to provide strong, continuing support in a changing political context and to institutionalize the program so that it can survive inevitable management turnover. Motivational programs are ultimately management creations. As such, they are quite fragile and depend critically on continuing, strong management support. Many programs have been short-lived, suffering from declining (or diverted) management interest and attention. However, to take full advantage of the potential of motivational programs often requires several years of experience and continued learning and adjustment on the basis of those experiences. This can occur only if there is sustained management interest and support, coupled with an early (and successful) effort to institutionalize the program.

Conclusion

This chapter has examined two interrelated issues: (1) the need for and use of motivational strategies for improving productivity, especially in a period of tight or shrinking resources; and (2) the tradeoffs, concerns, and conflicts that must be addressed in implementing such efforts. The following important points have emerged:

1. Motivational approaches constitute a potentially attractive means of improving productivity, especially during (or immediately after) a period of fiscal stress.
2. Although management by objectives (MBO) is relatively common, state and local governments rarely take full advantage of the *motivational* potential of MBO systems.

3. "Hard" information on the effectiveness of public sector motivational efforts is scarce. However, as a group, motivational approaches generally have provided modest improvements in productivity, at most.
4. Monetary incentives are potentially the most effective motivational approach from the standpoint of improving productivity (although group monetary incentives tend to be more practical than individual incentives in the public sector). MBO and other target-setting approaches have also given evidence of modest productivity improvements. Quality circles, while promising, have not yet demonstrated a capacity to generate major productivity increases in the public sector.
5. Shared savings plans and MBO systems seem to be among the most attractive motivational approaches from the standpoints of cost, effectiveness, and ease of implementation.
6. In general, effectiveness depends critically on the manner in which the motivational plans are designed and implemented. Careful, sensitive design and implementation of such programs is imperative (and very difficult, especially in the case of monetary incentives).
7. Important elements of any effort to introduce employee motivational programs should be the use of a carefully planned and unhurried design and implementation period, as well as early meaningful involvement of employees at all levels (and of their unions) in designing and planning the motivational effort.
8. Other important issues and concerns that must be addressed include acquisition of adequate resources; alleviation of constraints imposed by existing laws, personnel rules, organizational structures, and contractual agreements; and resolution of potential incompatibilities between the motivational program selected and the employees' (as well as management's) needs and values.
9. The key to effective, satisfying motivational programs is sustained, visible commitment and support from top management, and early institutionalization of the effort to ensure that it will survive long enough (four to five years) for the inevitable "bugs" to be worked out.

Motivational programs represent a fragile, management initiative. Without adequate nurturing and support from management, such efforts will die, but with care in their selection, design, and execution, many such programs offer considerable promise for improving productivity and renewing a government's human capital.

Notes

1. The average annual inflation rate was computed from quarterly data on the implicit price deflator for state and local government purchases of goods and services. *Survey of Current Business,* 63 (July 1983): 87, and 64 (July 1984): 87.

2. Charles H. Levine, "Retrenchment, Human Resource Erosion, and the Role of the Personnel Manager," *Public Personnel Management Journal,* 13 (Fall 1984): 249–263.

3. Theodore H. Poister and Robert P. McGowan, "The Contribution of Local Productivity Improvement Efforts in a Period of Fiscal Stress," *Public Productivity Review,* in press.

4. Theodore H. Poister, Harry P. Hatry, Donald M. Fisk, and John M. Greiner, *Centralized Productivity Improvement Efforts in State Government* (Washington, D.C.: The Urban Institute, 1984).

5. John M. Greiner and Harry P. Hatry, *Coping with Cutbacks: Initial Agency-Level Responses in 17 Local Governments to Massachusetts' Proposition 2½* (Washington, D.C.: The Urban Institute, 1982); reprinted in Lawrence E. Susskind and Jane F. Serio, eds., *Proposition 2½ : Its Impact on Massachusetts* (Cambridge, Mass.: Oelgeschlager, Gunn, and Hain, 1983).

6. For reviews of state and local government usage of various types of motivational programs, see John M. Greiner, Harry P. Hatry, Margo P. Koss, Annie P. Millar, and James P. Woodward, *Productivity and Motivation: A Review of State and Local Government Initiatives* (Washington, D.C.: The Urban Institute, 1981); John M. Greiner, Lynn Bell, and Harry P. Hatry, *Employee Incentives to Improve State and Local Government Productivity* (Washington, D.C.: National Commission on Productivity and Work Quality. 1975): and John M. Greiner. "Incentives for Municipal Employees: An Update," *Urban Data Service Reports,* 11, 8 (August 1979).

7. *Government Finances in 1982–83,* Series GF83 no. 5, U.S. Department of Commerce, Bureau of the Census (Washington, D.C.: U.S. Government Printing Office, 1984), p. 17.

8. Levine, "Retrenchment," pp. 252–253.

9. Levine, "Retrenchment," p. 255.

10. Greiner and Hatry, *Coping with Cutbacks,* pp. 130–131.

11. John M. Greiner, *The Impacts of Massachusetts' Proposition 2½ on the Delivery and Quality of Municipal Services* (Washington, D.C.: The Urban Institute, 1984), pp. 55–56.

12. *The Status of Local Government Productivity* (Washington, D.C.: International City Management Association, 1977).

13. Harry P. Hatry and John M. Greiner, *How Can Police Departments Better Apply Management-by-Objectives and Quality Circle Programs?* (Washington, D.C.: The Urban Institute, 1984), p. 7.

14. See, for instance, Greiner and others, *Productivity and Motivation,* chapter 10; Harry P. Hatry, John M. Greiner, and Richard J. Gollub, *An Assessment of Local Government Management Motivational Programs: Performance Targeting With and Without Monetary Incentives* (Washington, D.C.: The Urban Institute, 1984); and Hatry and Greiner, *How Can Police Departments Better Apply Management-by-Objectives. . . ?*

15. See the references cited above.

16. See, for instance, Harry P. Hatry and John M. Greiner, *Issues and Case Studies in Teacher Incentive Plans* (Washington, D.C.: The Urban Institute, forthcoming), chapter 7; and Hatry and Greiner, *How Can Police Departments Better Apply Management-by-Objectives. . . ?*

17. See, for instance, John P. Mohr, "MBO: The Horse to Pull Your Quality Circle Cart," *The Quality Circle Journal,* 5 (November 1982): 4.

18. For a review of these and other monetary incentives used in the public sector, see Greiner and others, *Productivity and Motivation,* part one (especially chapter 3).

19. Shared savings plans involve monetary rewards for groups of workers. Under such plans, a specific portion of the cost savings achieved by a group within a given period is distributed—often as a bonus—among the employees in the group.

20. Levine, "Retrenchment," p. 257.

21. Greiner, "Incentives for Municipal Employees," p. 3.

22. See, for instance, Greiner and others, *Productivity and Motivation,* chapters 4 and 5.

23. Hatry, Greiner, and Gollub, *An Assessment of Local Government Management Motivational Programs.*

24. John M. Greiner and Annie P. Millar, *Employee Productivity Incentives for Local Offices of the Employment Service: The Experiences of Kansas and New Jersey,* vols. 1 and 2 (Washington, D.C.: The Urban Institute, 1984).

25. Charles Peck, *Pay and Performance: The Interaction of Compensation and Performance Appraisal* (New York: The Conference Board, 1984), p. 16.

26. For more details on quality circles, see James L. Mercer, "Quality Circles: Productivity Improvement Processes," *Management Information Service Report,* 14, 3 (March 1982); Joyce L. Roll and David L. Roll, "The Potential for Application of Quality Circles in the American Public Sector," *Public Productivity Review,* VII (June 1983): 122–142; Robert Wood, Frank Hall, and Koya Azumi, "Evaluating Quality Circles: The American Application," *California Management Review,* XXVI (Fall 1983): 37–53; and *The Police Chief,* 51 (November 1984): 46–56 (a series of four articles on police applications of quality circles).

27. These approaches are described in Greiner and others, *Productivity and Motivation,* chapters 20, 22, and 23.

28. Poister and others, *Centralized Productivity Improvement Efforts,* p. 13; and unpublished data from ICMA's survey, "Employee Incentives—1984."

29. Hatry and Greiner, "How Can Police Departments Better Apply Management-by-Objectives. . . ?", p. 7.

30. Hatry and Greiner, above. See also Quality Circle Steering Committee, *Pilot Quality Circle Program Evaluation* (City of Hayward, California, 1983); and Susan Page Hocevar and Susan A. Mohrman, *Quality Circles in a Metropolitan Police Department,* Report G84–12(60) (University of Southern California, Center for Effective Organizations, 1984).

31. Hatry and Grenier, "How Can Police Departments Better Apply Management-by-Objectives. . . ?, p. 122.

32. Hatry and Grenier, above.

33. Grenier, "Incentives for Municipal Employees," p. 17.

34. Grenier, "Incentives for Municipal Employees," p. 16.

35. Donald E. Klingner, "Personnel, Politics and Productivity," *Public Personnel Management Journal,* 11 (Fall 1982): 277–281.

36. John M. Greiner, Roger E. Dahl, Harry P. Hatry, and Annie P. Millar, *Monetary Incentives and Work Standards in Five Cities: Impacts and Implications for Management and Labor* (Washington, D.C.: The Urban Institute, 1977), chapters 4 and 5.

37. Edwin A. Locke, Dena B. Feren, Vickie McCaleb, Karyll N. Shaw, and Anne T. Denny, "The Relative Effectiveness of Four Methods of Motivating Employee Performance," paper presented to the American Psychological Association. (New York, September 1979).

38. Raymond A. Katzell and Daniel Yankelovich, *Work, Productivity, and Job Satisfaction: Are Evaluation of Policy-Related Research* (New York: The Psychological Corporation, 1975), pp. 318–321.

39. For instance, the need to follow up and verify a sample of reported job placements in connection with productivity incentives for local offices of the Employment Service in Kansas and New Jersey added $72,000–$80,000 to the cost of each plan over the eighteen-month trial period. See Greiner and Millar, *Employee Productivity Incentives for Local Offices of the Employment Service,* vol. 2, p. 147.

40. For instance, to ensure that data on reported placements were above reproach in connection with a trial of productivity incentives for local offices of the Employment Service in Kansas and New Jersey, a monthly sample of the placements reported by *each* office was followed up with employers to check the validity of those placements. On one occasion, the presence of the follow-up effort convinced an investigative reporter that it would not be worth his time to look for possible irregularities in the distribution of the incentive rewards. See Greiner and Millar, *Employee Productivity Incentives for Local Offices of the Employment Service,* vol. 2, p. 231.

41. For a more extensive review of some of these issues, see Greiner and others, *Productivity and Motivation,* part five.

42. Levine, "Retrenchment," p. 258.

43. Greiner and others, *Productivity and Motivation,* pp. 109n, 354.

44. Poister and others, *Centralized Productivity Improvement Efforts.*

45. See, for instance, Gary P. Latham and Gary A. Yukl, "A Review of Research on the Application of Goal Setting in Organizations," *Academy of Management Journal,* 18 (December 1975): 824–845; and E. A. Locke, N. Cartledge, and C. S. Knerr, "Studies of the Relationship Between Satisfaction, Goal-Setting, and Performance," *Organizational Behavior and Human Performance,* 5 (1970): 135–158.

46. See Greiner and others, *Productivity, and Motivation,* chapter 11.

47. Mardell Buckner and Stephen W. Larcen, "Strategies for Increasing Productivity and Revenues in Community Mental Health Centers," *Journal of Community Mental Health,* in press.

48. For three such studies, see William A. Nowlin, "Factors That Motivate Public and Private Sector Managers: A Comparison," *Public Personnel Management Journal,* 11 (Fall 1982): 224–227; *Establishment of an Improved Employee Incentive Plan: Report of Committee No. 7, Employee Task Force on Morale, Productivity, and Involvement* (Trenton: State of New Jersey, Department of Labor and Industry, 1975); and *Attitudes Towards Work in County Government: A Workforce*

Survey of Westchester County, New York (Albany: Center for the Study of Public Policy, 1978), p. 28.

49. Hatry, Greiner, and Gollub, *An Assessment of Local Government Management Motivational Programs;* and Greiner and Millar, *Employee Productivity Incentives for Local Offices of the Employment Service.*

50. Hatry and Greiner, *Issues and Case Studies in Teacher Incentive Plans.*

51. Greiner and others, *Productivity and Motivation,* p. 350.

52. Hatry and Greiner, "How Can Police Departments Better Apply Management-by-Objectives. . . ?", p. 106.

14

A Technique for Controlling Quality

William R. Divine and Harvey Sherman

Pressures to improve management in government have long been couched in terms of efficiency and economy. As a result, considerable progress has been made in the direction of increasing production and reducing costs. Comparatively little use has been made, however, of effective methods for controlling the equally important element of the quality of work.

Reduced costs and increased production are illusory gains if they are achieved at the expense of serious deterioration in quality. In any activity it is imperative to determine standards of quality as well as standards of quantity and cost. Although the relative importance of these three factors may vary in different situations, each of them must be considered in every case. The purpose of this article is to stress the importance of defining the degree of quality wanted in government operations and to point out that once these quality goals are set, management can use the relatively new technique of statistical quality control to see that these goals are met.

Quality cannot be controlled until a decision is reached upon the desired quality standards or goals. In most cases it is possible to design a procedure to attain almost any degree of accuracy. But the higher the degree of accuracy desired, the greater will be the cost. It is possible to approach perfection, but only at the expense of excessive checks to correct the errors, which inevitably appear in any process. The taxpaper will get the most for his dollar if quality goals are realistic enough so that expenditures to prevent errors are not greater than the costs resulting from the errors.

"A Technique for Controlling Quality," *Public Administration Review* 8 (Spring, 1948): 110–113.

Once quality goals have been set and operations stabilized, statistical quality control enters the picture. Statistical quality control is simply a method for determining the extent to which quality goals are being met without examining every item produced, and for telling management whether or not the errors or variations which occur are exceeding normal expectations. It was introduced into large-scale manufacture in the United States in the 1930's. During the war the technique spread rapidly in British and American war factories and resulted in tremendous savings. The Western Electric Company, for example, cut its rejects on some items up to 50 percent and saved millions of dollars in overhead.[1] In another case, armor-plate rejection percentages were reduced from 33 to 3.[2]

In industry, especially when dealing with manufactured items, quality goals are usually stated in terms of such characteristics as dimensions, weight, or durability; in terms of fraction defective (e.g., the ratio of broken panes of glass to the total number inspected); or in terms of defects per unit (e.g., the number of imperfections in a bolt of cloth, or the number of missing parts in an assembled item). These types of goals are not appropriate, however, to the clerical operations so frequently found in government operations. In most government agencies, whether at the local, state, or federal level, quality goals can be set more effectively in terms of number of errors made.

In general, the quality of a given product can be determined in three ways: (1) by analyzing the complaints of those people who use or are affected by the product, (2) by surveying the opinions and attitudes of people familiar with the product, or (3) by some form of inspection, review, or test of the product itself. Although industry has made significant strides in the analysis of customer complaints and in surveying customer opinion, government has done little exploring in these areas. Government seems to have concentrated on the third method, with the result that many a citizen's complaint of government delays and red tape can be traced to excessive inspections, checks, and reviews. Despite this emphasis, government offices have made relatively little use of the most modern version of inspection—statistical quality control. This recently developed technique appears to offer the greatest possibilities for effectively and economically insuring that quality goals are met.

Statistical quality control employs two statistical techniques: the control chart and statistical sampling. Both of these techniques are based on the laws of probability.

The Control Chart

The control chart has been developed in various forms. Essentially, however, it is a device for plotting data (such as dimensions, errors, weights, or similar pertinent figures) so as immediately to reveal the frequency and extent of variation from standards or goals. Control limits based upon the established tolerance limits for the data being dealt with are placed upon the chart. Variations that fall within the control limits may be considered as due to chance or unknown causes. These causes bring about what may be called the natural variability of a process. Variations that fall outside the control limits are danger signals and indicate that there is a definite, assignable cause at work helping to bring about the variations. The control chart tells the manager at a glance whether his process is in control (i.e., within the control limits); thus he need not dissipate his energies tracking down random variations, but can begin to act the moment an assignable cause appears.

The control chart has been likened to a highway whose control limits are the shoulders on one side and the center line on the other. No car driving along the highway can maintain a perfectly straight path. Unevenness in the road, play in the steering wheel, gusts of wind, and a host of other factors cause slight variations in the path of the car. It would hardly be worth while to investigate the causes of these small irregularities. However, the moment the car swerves outside one of the limits, an assignable cause can be assumed to exist and an investigation should be begun. The cause may turn out to be a defect in the steering mechanism, a sleepy driver, a "one-armed" driver, or some similar specific correctable factor.

The primary value of control charts is that they tell the manager when assignable causes for variations are at work. They contribute an additional advantage, however, in that they publicize production results; thus they furnish a convenient way of stimulating competition, either among groups doing similar work, or within the same group by permitting comparison of present and past records.

Statistical Sampling

The second technique involved in statistical quality control is statistical sampling. Statistical sampling attempts to insure a true picture of the whole by use of a random sample (i.e., one in which every item has an equal chance of being inspected) which is at the same time thorough (i.e., all variations in the sample are discovered) and regular (i.e., recurring consistently rather than at long and irregular intervals). Statisticians have worked out tables so that once the quality goal is determined (e.g., 1 percent errors allowed) and the percentage of errors made by the inspectors is known, the size of sample to be used to insure the quality goal can be determined. In certain cases the system of sampling permits the use of a larger sample if the variations in the sample taken exceed a specified amount. This method is frequently used when testing the relative acceptability of purchased items.

Sample testing or inspection has two primary advantages. In the first place, it saves time and money. The size of the sample can be calculated so as to assure the desired degree of quality. To the extent that the sample size represents less than 100 percent review, there is a saving in inspection time and cost. In the second place, sample testing often results in improving the quality of work. A worker who knows that only a portion of his work is to be reviewed feels an increased sense of responsibility and exercises greater care. Experience has shown that the work of the inspector also will be more reliable when he concentrates his attention upon only a selected portion of the items.

Quality Control in Office Operations

The statistical quality control system described above is usually said to have originated with Walter A. Shewhart of the American Telephone Company in the early 1920's.[3] During the last war, the great need for speedy production, the enormous increase in actual production, and the shortage of qualified inspectors made it imperative that effective methods of quality control be adopted. As a result, the use of statistical quality control spread rapidly in both the United States and Great Britain in ordnance factories (including Army and Navy ordnance plants) and in industries producing such items as electrical equipment, steel, automobiles, and photographic equipment.

The application of statistical quality control to clerical operations (i.e., mass paper work activities) as opposed to manufacturing is of more recent vintage. Observers and practitioners of public administration are especially interested in this particular use of quality control, for much government work consists in the routing and processing of a huge volume of paper work. One of the best examples of the use of statistical quality control in clerical operations is found in Aldens' Mail Order House in Chicago. Statistical quality control was begun at Aldens' early in 1945 by the installation of sample inspection and the control chart in one of the order-picking departments. Within two months, the error ratio in this department fell from 3 percent to less than 1 percent while efficiency increased from 82 percent to 107 percent.[4] Since then, use of the system has been extended throughout the organization (23 departments by June, 1947) with such outstanding success that it has gained the complete support of top management. Over a two-year period, statistical quality control brought about a reduction in errors of 25.4 percent as indicated by customer adjustments.[5]

With few exceptions, statistical quality control in the federal government has been confined to engineering or construction activities (e.g., Army and Navy ordnance). The Bureau of the Census and the National Office of Vital Statistics of the Federal Security Agency have experimented with dif-

BOX 14.1 Quality Circles

John D. Blair, Stanley L. Cohen, and Jerome V. Hurwitz

Quality circles (QC) are organizational interventions that seek to increase an organization's productivity and the quality of its products through direct employee participation. The underlying assumption is that such participation will result in useful suggestions for improving work methods and quality control, and for increasing employee commitment to implement these changes. A quality circle is composed of a small group of employees, doing similar work, who volunteer to meet periodically to discuss production, quality, and related problems, to investigate causes, recommend solutions, and take corrective actions to the extent of their authority.

Normally, a company-wide steering committee of both union and management representatives decides where in the organization quality circles should be introduced and what types of problems are appropriate for the quality circles to work on. Once initiated, a quality circle (consisting of about ten employees from a work unit and their immediate supervisor) holds a weekly one-hour meeting to discuss ways of improving productivity and related issues. To aid their effectiveness, the group and its leader are trained in group dynamics, problem solving, data analysis, quality control, and the presentation of information and recommendations to management. Circle leaders usually receive about three days of training prior to the circle's first meeting. Circle members receive their training during the first eight to ten circle meetings. These meetings are held on company time and at company expense, and the decision to implement any of the group's suggestions remains ultimately with management. External facilitators, who have received about five days of training in the use of quality circle techniques and are usually company employees, guide and assist the quality circle during the meetings.

Within the federal sector, the Navy was the first to implement a quality circle program in 1979 in its Norfolk Naval Shipyard. By 1980 the shipyard claimed to have achieved a four-to-one cost-benefit ratio. The Navy has since expanded its QC program to a number of its bases and shipyards. In addition, a variety of other federal agencies (including the Air Force, the Veteran's Administration, and the Public Health Service) have all begun to experiment with their own quality circle programs. Interest in the QC process among federal agencies appears to be rapidly growing.

(Source: John D. Blair, Stanley L. Cohen and Jerome V. Hurwitz, "Quality Circles," in: "Quality Circles: Practical Considerations for Managers," *Public Productivity Review* (March/June 1982):9–18.)

ferent versions of the technique. The Bureau of the Census, for example, in processing 1940 census figures for housing and population used statistical sampling in the verification of card punching and maintained quality control charts on each individual puncher.[6] Great care was taken when setting up the sampling system to develop criteria for selecting the punchers whose work should be sample verified. Length of experience, average error rate, and fluctuations in error rate were determined to be the controlling factors. Over 90 percent of the qualified punchers stayed within the upper control limit plotted on their respective charts. Investigation of the reasons for errors in the case of those who exceeded the permitted limit revealed such assignable causes as (1) schedules poorly filled out by the enumerator, (2) a puncher who had returned to work too soon after a siege of measles, and (3) sickness in the family of a puncher. With this knowledge as to the causes of errors, management was able to take intelligent action to remedy situations. This statistical quality control system was estimated to have saved $263,000 in direct labor costs; indirect savings were estimated to have paid for the cost of the system. In addition, speedier service in the preparation of the final statistical tables was obtained.

This example of statistical quality control in the federal Bureau of the Census is one of the rare instances in which that technique has been used in government clerical operations. Yet there are a great number of similar kinds of operations performed by federal, state, and local agencies where the technique appears to be applicable. The test of applicability is whether like articles are turned out in quantity. Apparent possibilities include large-scale repetitive operations such as warehousing, purchasing, tabulating, mailing, billing, filing, publications distribution, reproduction operations, processing of personnel actions, and processing of various types of claims. Any government department handling a large volume of work—a city water department or assessor's office, a state highway or welfare department, or almost any large bureau or agency—offers fertile ground for the application of this technique.

The major obstacle to the spread of statistical quality control seems to have been the failure of government management people to promote it. The government has made commendable progress in adapting the technique to its research, engineering, and scientific activities. It remains for government management people to carry on in the vast areas of government which have been relatively untouched by the engineer, scientist, or statistician.

The increasing recognition of statistical quality control as an effective management tool is testified to by a growing body of literature on the subject, the introduction of courses dealing with it at a number of universities, and the establishment in 1946 of the American Society for Quality Control.[7] Its widespread use in government will depend in part upon further experimentation with the technique as applied to mass paper work activities; primarily it will depend, however, upon the development of an awareness of its usefulness on the part of people dealing with broad management problems whether from the line or staff point of view. Statistical quality control of itself cannot put quality into a product; its function is to inform management effectively and economically of the degree to which quality goals are being met and whether assignable causes for variation are at work.

Notes

1. "Quality Control," 28 *Fortune* 127 (October, 1943).

2. Alexander L. Berliner, "Controlling Quality of Office Production," 22 *The Office* 41 (July, 1945).

3. See W. A. Shewhart, "Finding Causes of Quality Variations," 11 *Manufacturing Industries,* 125–28 (February, 1926). See also by the same author, "Statistical Control in Applied Science," 65 *Transactions of the American Society of Mechanical Engineers,* 222–25 (1943).

4. Robert W. Jackson, "Quality Control at Aldens'," in *Conference Papers* of the First Annual Convention of the American Society for Quality Control and Second Midwest Quality Control Conference, June 5–6, 1947, p. 14.

5. *Ibid,* p. 15. For a detailed account of statistical quality control at Aldens', see James M. Ballowe, "An Adaptation of Statistical Quality Control at Aldens'," published by the Carnegie Institute of Technology as its Quality Control Report No. 7, September, 1945.

6. Information on statistical quality control in the Census Bureau is from W. Edwards Deming and Leon Geoffrey, "On Sample Inspection in the Processing of Census Returns," 36 *Journal of the American Statistical Association,* 351–60 (September, 1941).

7. The American Society for Quality Control publishes a bimonthly magazine, *Industrial Quality Control,* which is devoted to quality control applications and procedures and to news of the Society.

15

Adapting Total Quality Management (TQM) to Government

James E. Swiss

During the past ten years, total quality management (TQM) has had a major impact on business management practices, and has been adopted by such high profile corporations as General Motors, Motorola, and Xerox (Gabor, 1990). More recently, TQM has begun to spread to many government organizations.[1] TQM has even been endorsed by President Bush, who said, "Reasserting our leadership will require a firm commitment to total quality management and the principle of continuous improvement. . . . Quality improvement principles apply . . . to the public sector as well as private enterprise" (Carr and Littman, 1990, p. 2).

Such enthusiastic endorsements often suggest that TQM can be transferred from the private sector to the public sector with very little modification. These suggestions are mistaken. TQM can indeed have a useful role to play in government, but only if it is substantially modified to fit the public sector's unique characteristics. This article attempts to sketch the adaptations necessary to turn orthodox, business-oriented TQM into a reformed TQM that will succeed in the public sector.

Total Quality Management's Business Background

Total quality management requires adaptation for use in the public sector because it is very much a product of statistical quality control and industrial

---

"Adapting Total Quality Management (TQM) to Government," *Public Administration Review* 52 (July/August 1992): 356–362.

engineering, and almost all of its early applications were for assembly-line work and other routine processes. TQM was originally developed by an American statistician, W. Edwards Deming, but his approaches were adopted much more enthusiastically in post–World War II Japan than in his native country. When Japanese products such as electronics and automobiles began to outperform and outsell American products, the U.S. business sector started to reemphasize quality, in part by borrowing such Japanese techniques as TQM. There were a number of false starts; for example, many organizations broke off a relatively small piece of TQM—quality circles—and attempted to make them the primary and free-standing technique for achieving quality. However, by the mid–1980s, many U.S. corporations began to encourage quality through integrated, multifaceted systems.

The Principal Tenets of (Orthodox) Total Quality Management

Several related but distinct systems attempt to increase organizational quality. Although Deming-based TQM is not the only quality system,[2] his version, encapsulated in TQM, is by far the most influential and widespread. Because Deming is a synthesizer, TQM contains many of the concepts of other quality management systems, even those not using the term TQM. Accordingly, I will term Deming's TQM the orthodox approach and will discuss its particulars.

TQM is a complicated and demanding system that cannot be completely summarized in a few paragraphs. Nonetheless, many of its most important points can be captured in seven basic tenets.[3] Because TQM was first applied to manufacturing, its tenets sometimes refer to products. However, TQM proponents maintain that a delivered service can be viewed as a product, and, therefore, TQM principles need only minor modifications when applied to business or government services (Kennedy and Young, 1989, p. 87; Deming, 1986. p. xi).

TQM's Primary Tenets

First and foremost, the customer is the ultimate determiner of quality. A product may meet all specifications. However, if it does not provide the customers with the performance they wish—if it is too complex, or expensive, or unattractive—then the quality test has been flunked.

Second, quality should be built into the product early in the production process (upstream) rather than being added on at the end (downstream). Many products and services go through the stages of design, production, inspection, reworking (for products), and then response to consumer complaints. The early, upstream stages of design and production are the crucial ones. If the product or service is designed to be easy to produce, and if those producing it have the training and incentives to maintain consistently high quality, then downstream inspections, reworkings, and responses to consumer complaints are unnecessary. This saves money, but more importantly, it makes the customer much happier. Accordingly, TQM generally opposes mass inspections of products because such inspections provide a safety net that shifts quality responsibilities away from the initial designers and producers.

Third, preventing variability is the key to producing high quality. Slippages in quality arise from too much variation in the product or service. As products and services deviate from a desired norm, their dependability drops rapidly. Deming has said, "If I had to reduce my message for management to just a few words, I'd say it all had to do with reducing variation" (Bryce, 1991, p. 16). Because preventing variability is the most important path to quality, TQM's most important tools are process control charts. Such charts are used to track quality by charting a product's deviation from the optimum; these deviations are then categorized and analyzed.[4]

Fourth, quality results from people working within systems, not individual efforts. When quality slips, it is almost always the system that is wrong, not the people (Carr and Littman, 1990, p. 196; Walton, 1986, p. 92). Because it is the system working through committed people that produces results, it is a grave mistake to focus on individuals. Most of the time, when one individual appears to be performing better than others, the difference in performance is only random variation. Thus today's superior worker is likely to be tomorrow's average one, because a well-working system should lead *all* workers, responding to intrinsic motivators, to perform well.[5] Merit pay and other individually oriented rewards are accordingly misguided and represent a "lottery" (Deming, 1986, p. 110). Because management by objectives (MBO) is so often used for individual measures, it, too, leads the manager astray. All MBO, according to TQM, should be dropped.

One TQM article summarized this approach by saying, "It is worth noting that management by objectives and performance standards works against a quality-supportive organizational culture. Objectives and performance standards focus on individual performance when the individual can seldom control the system within which he or she must work. . . . People become victims or beneficiaries of normal variations built into the system" (Scholtes and Hacquebord, 1988b, p. 47). Another said, "In the Deming view, certain practices are always wrong. Among these are merit pay, incentive programs, the annual review of people, any system that ranks the employees, management by objectives . . . " (Aguayo, 1990, p. 131).

Fifth, quality requires continuous improvement of inputs and processes. Quality is not a static attribute; it is a constantly changing target because it represents a delighted (not just satisfied) customer. As the customer's expectations rise, so must the product's quality. What is a high-quality product today will not be one tomorrow. This tenet leads to the principle of *continuous improvement*—every month new ways of improvement must be considered and implemented.

Moreover, this continuous improvement should be directed not at outputs but at the inputs and processes that the manager can directly control. The business manager should stop focusing on the output measure of profits, because profit is a short-term measure that can lead to cutting corners. The manager should focus instead, according to TQM, on improving organizational processes and inputs in order to improve quality, because increased quality will lead to customer loyalty, and long-range profits will inexorably follow (Scholtes and Hacquebord, 1988a, p. 31).

This tenet directly contradicts the rationale of all recent government management reforms. Program budgeting, zero base budgeting (ZBB), MBO, and pay for performance all attempted to move the government manager's focus away from measuring inputs and processes and toward results. TQM urges business managers to move in the opposite direction. Deming, in fact, made elimination of MBO one of his 14 points, and later elaborated: "Focus on outcomes . . . must be abolished, leadership put in its place" (Deming, 1986, p. 54).

Sixth, quality improvement requires strong worker participation. Because quality depends upon the production workers doing it right the first time and upon constant improvement of inputs and processes, which only workers know intimately, worker participation in the ongoing improvement process is crucial. Managers and workers should work together "without fear"—without worrying that each mistake discovered will be punished. They also need to work "without barriers"—using matrix-like structures and quality circles to break down communication barriers between hierarchical levels and between functional units.

Seventh, quality requires total organizational commitment. Quality is achieved only when managers create an organizational culture that focuses on consistently producing quality products and then on improving them every period. If this total commitment flags, quality will drop off rapidly, and the organization will inevitably begin to slip behind competitors.

This requirement for total organizational commitment seems clearer when considered in light of the other TQM tenets already discussed. TQM is an extremely demanding regimen. It requires *all* members of an organization to *constantly* change in order to improve, even after achieving what seems to be a high standard of performance. It requires such high levels of performance that virtually no mistakes are made, and after-the-fact inspections to catch mistakes become unnecessary. Because TQM is so demanding, only an unusually intense and unambiguous organizational culture can keep workers so committed and focused. This organizational culture must be maintained by active and continuous intervention from the top.

Orthodox TQM in Government

In its unmodified or orthodox form, TQM is strikingly ill suited to the government environment. The use of TQM in government has several major problems: insufficient modification for services; insensitivity to the problems of defining governmental customers; inappropriate emphasis on inputs and processes; and demands for top-level intensity that can rarely be met by the governmental culture.

Services Versus Products

TQM was originally designed for routine processes such as manufacturing, yet most government agencies produce services rather than products. Although the problem of applying TQM to business services is widely discussed in the TQM literature (Deming, 1986, pp. 171ff; Ferderber, 1981; King, 1987; Plsek, 1987), solutions are elusive. TQM remains much more difficult to apply to services because services are more labor intensive, and they are often produced and consumed simultaneously. This makes uniformity of output more difficult, and it also means that the consumer will evaluate the service not only on the result but also on the behavior and even the appearance of the person delivering it. If an efficient police officer quickly locates stolen cars but seems ill-groomed or curt, many of his or her customers will not be totally satisfied, despite receiving a high quality output.

Accordingly, quality measures for services are extremely complex. Factor analyses of customer surveys have indicated that overall quality measures for services can be broken into such components as access, communication, competence, courtesy, creativity, reliability, responsiveness, security, tangibles, and understanding (Parasuraman *et al.,* 1985; Cravens *et al.,* 1988; Garvin, 1984, 1988). For many services each of these components must be measured and weighed before it can be determined that a high-quality service has been delivered.

TQM's tenet about reducing variation is also more difficult to apply to services. The quality tracking charts and the concern about the product drift away from the optimum apply much more directly to assembly-line production (e.g., measures of how well the auto door is fitted) than to government services that often have controversial or unclear norms. For example, no clear consensus exists about what processes should be tracked and standardized for a street-level bureaucrat such as a mental health professional or a classroom teacher.

The Problem of Defining the Government Customer

TQM's most important principle is to delight the customer. Accordingly, the single most important question is: Who is the customer? Most discussions of

TQM in government pay little or no attention to that question. In business, the company can usually choose its own market niche, and thus define its target customers: luxury car buyers, for example, or price-conscious food purchasers. For many public agencies, on the other hand, defining the customer is a difficult and politically controversial issue. For the Bureau of Land Management (BLM), is the main customer the grazing interests, the mining interests, or the environmentalists? If some combination, how much weight should be given to each? Whether or not BLM is delivering quality services depends entirely upon the answer. Competing clients, with directly contradictory demands, can be found in most government services, from education to health care. Although these battles may be less fierce for those few government services that have routine, uncontroversial missions, they are never totally absent. For example, James Q. Wilson (1989, pp. 122–126) has pointed out the competing clienteles that fight for the outputs of the seemingly noncontroversial postal service.

Moreover, government organizations have obligations to more than their immediate clients. Sometimes the agency's most important customers—the general public—are not only absent but totally inattentive, and yet the agency must risk offending its immediate customers in order to serve the general public. For example, a government agency that oversees banks and treats banks as its customers will greatly damage the public good by keeping banks, in TQM's phraseology, delighted. Yet if the agency puts the taxpaying general public first, it will look in vain for their delighted reaction; the general public will remain resolutely uninterested in the agency's work unless there is a crisis.

This conflict between a program's direct customers (clients) and its ultimate customers (the general public, most of whom are taxpayers) is often very acute for programs that are not universally distributed. The problem arises because any definition of quality is always constrained by cost—a high quality $15,000 car is of course not the same as a high quality $60,000 car. In business this cost constraint does not usually affect customer satisfaction because the buyer of the product is also its recipient, so he or she can choose the appropriate level of cost and quality in order to be delighted. No such balance is likely for nonuniversal government services such as health care, education, or water projects because the buyer is often not the recipient. The buying customers (general taxpayers) will often prefer to minimize costs. At the same time, the direct customers (recipients) of such programs may expect a level of quality that is found only at a very high price, because they do not pay the full cost. No balance between costs and features is likely to please both groups.

The literature on citizen surveys in government has pointed out the difficulty of measuring government performance by public reaction. Generally, public ratings of programs are only tenuously related to objective measures of program performance. Survey results are easily biased by isolated but highly publicized events or by ideological attitudes.[6] Of course, surveys remain useful if viewed as one piece of organizational information, but these survey weaknesses reflect these same inescapable problems of defining customers and of measuring services.

Because government agencies must serve a wide variety of customers who have widely divergent and even contradictory demands and because the general public remains a "hidden customer" with yet additional, often incompatible demands, government agencies often have to deliver a service or product that reflects an uneasy compromise. In such cases, the principle of delighting or even satisfying customers begs too many questions to be a clear or useful goal.[7]

Focusing on Inputs and Processes

Government has traditionally paid relatively little attention to outputs for many reasons: Outputs are politically controversial and difficult to measure; legislators are primarily concerned about inputs such as budgets; bureaucratic prestige often accrues from control of inputs, especially personnel; and legal requirements often demand constant attention to strict procedural rules (Behn, 1982; Wilson, 1989). With all the incentives in government to focus on inputs and processes, there is a constant threat of goal displacement—managers who blindly hew to the minimal legal requirements, or build empires, or put out fires, rather than help the public.

Given this unpromising environment, many public organizations are justifiably proud that over the past 15 years they have implemented results-oriented systems such as MBO performance monitoring systems, and program budgets. Recent surveys show that such systems have been widely installed, that they continue to spread, and that most governmental users rate them a success.[8] Such systems allow many public agencies to now track results, not just processes. Because it is so difficult to determine outputs in the public sector, every success should be savored and nurtured. As already noted, orthodox TQM disputes all this. According to one TQM book, "Many government agencies have difficulty developing performance indicators. This is because they focus on *results indicators* related to final output to external customers, rather than on how processes are performing in making those products and services. Remember, if processes perform as intended, output should be of high quality. You begin by moving away from the concept of results indicators to *process control indicators*" (Carr and Littman, 1990, pp. 61–62).

TQM proponents correctly point out that in business, outputs in the form of quarterly profit reports represent short-term vision and can often lead to goal displacement. They fail to recognize that in the very different world of government, it is stressing inputs and processes that represents short-term business as usual, and therefore focusing on governmental processes is likely to lead to goal displacement. In the public sector, a move toward stressing outputs is in fact usually a move toward the desired longer-range vision.[9]

The Problem of Government Culture

Orthodox TQM depends on an extremely strong organizational culture with an almost single-minded commitment to quality. In order to shape that culture, the managers must be continuously involved in improving management (Walton, 1986, pp. 66, 92; Aguayo, 1990, pp. 92, 117). However, turnover of top-level managers is rapid for many government agencies, and government culture, structured to be open to many outside forces, is almost necessarily weaker than those of business.[10] After summarizing the many disincentives to concentrating on management,[11] one analysis concludes, "What is surprising is that government executives spend any time at all on managing their departments" (Wilson, 1989, p. 217).

Orthodox TQM Summarized

In sum, orthodox TQM can easily do more harm than good because it can encourage a focus on the particularistic demands of direct clients rather than the needs of the more important (but often inattentive) customers, the general public. Orthodox TQM can also cause an organization to neglect or even—if Deming's advice is followed—dismantle such established systems as MBO, program budgets, and performance monitoring systems that set clear output goals and monitor results.[12] Finally, orthodox TQM makes a number of demands for output uniformity and strong, continuous organizational culture that government is intrinsically unable to meet.

Despite all these major problems, a great deal is worth saving in TQM. However, public managers must adapt the system drastically to gain the advantages.

Implementing Reformed TQM in Government

What would a reformed TQM look like? It would retain orthodox TQM's feedback from clients, its emphasis on tracking performance, and its principles of continuous improvement and participation of the workers.

Client Feedback

Despite the problems in making customer reaction the guiding principle in government management, it is still useful to track the reactions of an

BOX 15.1 Who's Doing TQM?

Evan M. Berman and Jonathan P. West

A common problem with the implementation of productivity improvement innovations such as TQM is that many organizations implement them at *a token level* rather than fully committing themselves to success (Downs and Mohr, 1980; Miller, 1993). Token implementation, or paying lip service, occurs because organizations and individuals receive recognition and other benefits from being, or appearing to be, in line with current thinking, while avoiding the risks of actual innovation. Such behavior is reinforced by perceptions of meager rewards for success or often severe, punitive consequences of failure. Token implementation also occurs as the result of a flawed implementation plan, inadequate commitment and follow-through by those mandating the implementation of innovation, a lack of training in applying the innovation, incongruent organizational policies, and other factors (Radin and Coffee, 1993).

This study finds that TQM is well underway in municipal government. Through a composite of multiple measures, it shows that 11 percent of cities with populations over 25,000 have a substantial commitment to TQM. In addition, an estimated 22 percent have a token commitment to TQM. Half of all efforts are less than four years old, and many interviewees stated that although they are satisfied with progress to date, there is a need to diffuse efforts throughout other departments and agencies. Cities use a wide range of transformational, transactional, and representational strategies in implementing quality initiatives, all of which are significantly associated with municipal commitment to TQM.

The data also suggest that while TQM is well underway, it is still too early to evaluate the outcomes of these efforts. An important finding is that over

(continues)

agency's immediate clients and to use them as *one* consideration in decisionmaking. TQM provides valuable advice on how to do this.

Tracking Performance

TQM strongly condemns "managing by the numbers." At the same time, one of its major components is quantitative tracking of quality through control charts and other quantitative tools. This performance tracking can make TQM a useful first system for some government agencies. After TQM is implemented, its success can lead to the addition of other quantitative but results-oriented systems, such as program budgeting, MBO, and performance monitoring systems. TQM is likely to be a particularly useful first system for those government workers and managers who have resisted other management systems because they feared such systems would "turn people into numbers." Because TQM emphasizes both intangibles (quality)

BOX 15.1 (continued)

40 percent of our respondents stated that it is "too early to tell" when evaluating the results of their efforts. Of those reporting results, respondents note only modest, albeit positive, impacts. Using a five-point scale (−2 = very negative impact to 2 = very positive impact), respondents gave the following ratings: efficiency gains (0.98), cost reductions (0.84), quality of service (1.04), and customer satisfaction (0.99). Similarly, some gains were made in improving group decision making (0.92), delegating responsibility (0.77), increasing communication in units (1.01), and coping with resource constraints (0.88). These outcomes are moderately associated with the level of municipal commitment to TQM, and cities with recent implementation efforts report significantly higher levels of commitment and impact of TQM.

It is too soon to tell whether TQM will be just another fad. Critics of TQM point to myriad challenges that this encompassing strategy poses, and they recall previous productivity-improvement efforts which floundered after initial, widespread enthusiasm. However, if lessons from past efforts are an indication, one would expect that orientations toward debureaucratization, customer focus, and cost effectiveness will continue in some shape or form. This is because customer focus is overdue, feasible, and consistent with modern notions of public administration. Indeed, only the most cynical observers might suggest reversing a charted course that aims to improve government.

(Source: Evan M. Berman and Jonathan P. West. "Who's Doing TQM?" in: "Municipal Government to Total Quality Management: A Survey of Recent Progress." *Public Administration Review* 55 (January/February 1995): 57–66.)

and people (participation), as well as tracking through numbers, it can be a nonintimidating first step for those who have been put off by the quantitative aspects of other systems.

Continuous Improvement

Each earlier public management innovation was resisted by many workers. Moreover, once the systems were implemented, they were often taken for granted and therefore atrophied over time. For both these reasons, TQM's continuous improvement principle, if internalized by workers and managers, may be its most valuable contribution. The principle suggests that receptivity to new approaches is essential for high performance. If fully accepted, this principle would lessen the resistance to future system innovations and would also decrease the likelihood that they would later stagnate. As a useful side effect, acceptance of this principle would lessen the temptation to oversell future changes, since overselling is often aimed at mitigating resistance.

Worker Participation

Worker participation, now often called empowerment, has been a important management axiom for decades, but it is difficult to put into operation. TQM's quality circles represent a valuable concrete step toward increased participation.

TQM: Relabeling Old Ideas?

In all of its forms, TQM incorporates some truly fresh ideas, particularly the new tools for tracking and improving routine government processes. However, because reformed TQM also emphasizes such long-standing managerial principles as worker participation and quantitative output tracking, a natural critique is that reformed TQM is primarily old wine in new bottles. There is a little truth to this critique, but new bottles are often very valuable. For the same reason that people change fashions, ministers change sermons, and organizations change logos, management analysts must periodically change the way they present enduring principles—listener boredom can cause even the best approaches to seem stale over time. If TQM represents a new framework that helps freshen enduring management principles, that can be an additional major advantage.

Summary

Orthodox TQM is ill suited to most government agencies and, in fact, represents a step backwards (away from results) for many of them. Reformed TQM, however, jettisons orthodox TQM's hostility to output goals and measurements, deemphasizes its demands for output uniformity and organizational culture continuity, and sensitizes managers to the dangers of satisfying just an immediate clientele. Yet at the same time, reformed TQM saves the orthodox principles of employee empowerment, continuous improvement, and quantitative tracking of product quality and of client reactions.

If introduced without overselling and with sensitivity to government's unique circumstances, reformed TQM can make a useful contribution to contemporary public management.

Notes

1. Among the public TQM systems that are discussed in the literature are the city government of Madison, Wisconsin (Sensenbrenner, 1991); the Madison police de-

partment (Couper, 1990); the Naval Publications Center (Whitten, 1989); and the Environmental Protection Agency (Cohen and Brand, 1990). The Department of Defense has a new position: Deputy Undersecretary of Defense for Total Quality Management (Keehley, 1991). For a good discussion of the federal history of TQM, see Milakovich (1991). TQM programs within such state governments as Wisconsin, California, Texas, and Florida are mentioned briefly in Carr and Littman (1990).

2. Deming's influence in Japan is reflected by the fact that Japan's most prestigious business award is the Deming Prize (Walton, 1986). Pioneering work in this area has also been done by Deming's mentors, Walter Shewhart and Armand Feigenbaum. Among the most important contemporary quality theorists are Joseph Juran (1989), Kaora Ishikawa, Genichi Taguchi, and Philip Crosby (1979). As noted, Deming is a synthesizer, and so some of the principles of all the above except Crosby are cited and incorporated in his TQM.

3. Deming has summed up his approach in "Fourteen Points" and "Seven Obstacles" (Deming, 1986, chpts. 2 and 3). Because Deming's writings are neither fluid nor tightly structured, other authors have attempted to sum up his thoughts in fewer, clearer points. Among these are Gabor (1990, pp. 18–30), Walton (1986), and Aguayo (1990). The list of tenets given here draws from each of these authors, but reflects a greater emphasis on points most relevant to government management. An overview of some of the applications for government managers is contained in Wagenheim and Reurink (1991).

4. The analysis of process charts—distinguishing common causes of variation, which fall within statistical expectations, from special causes, which do not—is central to TQM, but beyond the scope of this discussion. For the same reason. I have also omitted a discussion of the many other statistical and graphical tools of TQM, most of which are very useful. For a good explanation, see Gabor (1990, chap. 2).

5. Deming's belief in the universality and near omnipotence of intrinsic motivators is striking. He has said that in his 60 years of experience he has never met a worker who was not trying his or her hardest (Aguayo, 1990. p. 31). Reflecting his distaste for evaluations and for extrinsic motivators. Deming gives an A to all the students in his university courses (Walton, 1986, p. 91). Not all TQM theorists would endorse those exact views, but almost all (see note 9) would endorse the same practical applications: downplaying output measures, goals, rewards, and ratings.

6. Among the articles that point out the discrepancy between objective output indicators and subjective survey responses are Stipak (1979); Brown and Coulter (1983); and Houghland (1987). On the other hand, Parks (1984) has argued that there are connections, but even he concedes that they are not direct ones. See also the debate by Stipak and Parks (1984).

7. An extreme example of a misplaced focus on only direct clients was the federal Department of Housing and Urban Development (HUD) in the 1980s. Reed (1982) reported that two of the three criteria on which HUD executive bonuses were based were: (1) "Decisions rarely, if ever, questioned by client groups" and (2) "Decisions consistently praised by affected groups." Because these goals ignore the invisible customer—the general public—in retrospect, they seem to reflect the priorities that led to the massive HUD scandals.

8. These systems are most widespread at the local level. Streib and Poister (1989a) found that by 1988, 66 percent of local governments used program budgeting, 62 percent used MBO, and 67 percent used performance monitoring systems. Larger cities employed all these techniques at even higher rates, and the usage figures represented particularly substantial gains throughout the 1980s for program budgeting and MBO. Over 90 percent of the users characterize these systems as "somewhat" or "very" effective (Streib and Poister, 1989b). Quality circles (before the current TQM drive gained momentum) were used by 32 percent of cities, but only 25 percent of the users rated them as "very effective." TQM proponents would ascribe this low effectiveness rating to the fact that the circles were not part of a broader supporting quality system.

Although information about usage is not as complete at the state and federal levels, the overall pattern seems similar. A survey of state budgets indicated that they have increasingly incorporated many program budget features (Lee, 1991). At the federal level, program budgeting never died in the Defense Department (Ferrara and Dunmire, 1988), and MBO has lived on there and in a number of the largest federal departments.

9. Of the main quality approaches, that of Philip Crosby (1979) is the most unlike the Deming-based TQM discussed here, and Crosby seems to see the largest place for goal setting. Nonetheless, the arguments made here about quality systems' maladaptation for government may be strongest for Crosby. His definition of quality is very much specification-based: quality is "conformance to requirements." He espouses "zero defects," an approach with little application to such government functions as school teaching, regulation, and job training. Finally, he deemphasizes the quantitative tools that give substance to TQM's quality exhortations.

10. A praiseworthy attempt to allow each agency to adapt TQM to its particular culture may have motivated OPM's very loose guidelines in implementing federal TQM. However, OPM may have overcompensated. In a thoughtful and interesting critique. Hyde (1991) applauds the lack of rigid guidelines but argues that OPM has been so careful to avoid prescribing specific steps for implementing federal TQM that no clear system is left. He calls for a number of remedies, including much more attention to TQM's means and methodologies. The argument in this article that reformed TQM must retain the quantitative tools of TQM is, I think, in accordance with Hyde's point.

11. The lack of incentives for top political officials to focus on management is well illustrated by the mayor of Madison, Wisconsin, Joseph Sensenbrenner. He was perhaps the elected official most committed to TQM throughout the 1980s. In an article, he enumerates the many efficiency gains, the increased union support, and the national publicity engendered by TQM, but then states, "But this recognition was not enough to win me a fourth term. Other political factors were more compelling" (Sensenbrenner, 1991, p. 75). Sensenbrenner's case is an illustration that elected officials cannot put their *primary* focus on management matters: their success is usually more closely tied to their political, rather than managerial, skills.

12. Most proponents of output-oriented systems, and particularly of MBO, characterize the systems as participatory, with the subordinates joining the superiors in setting goals and with both parties adjusting the goals jointly as the situation

changes. Unilaterally set goals are treated as examples of an improperly functioning system. Within the TQM literature, however, MBO and performance monitoring system goals are usually portrayed as nonparticipatory "quotas" (i.e., Aguayo, 1990, p. 26). Accordingly, output-oriented systems are almost invariably characterized as obstacles, not complements that could potentially be incorporated within a participative TQM system. Thus two pro-TQM authors say of the output-oriented system in the Environmental Protection Agency (EPA). "The actions of one regional program manager provide an example of how to avoid numerical quotas." He placed himself as a buffer between his staff and the EPA's numerical accountability system. He told his staff, 'You keep working on improving the process, and don't worry about this quarter's quotas' (Cohen and Brand, 1990, p. 112).

References

Aguayo, Rafael, 1990. *Dr. Deming: The American Who Taught the Japanese About Quality.* New York: Lyle Stuart.

Behn, Robert D., 1982. "Policy Analysis and Policy Politics." *Policy Analysis,* vol. 7, pp. 199–226.

Brown, Karin and Phillip B. Coulter, 1983. "Subjective and Objective Measures of Public Service Delivery." *Public Administration Review,* vol. 43 (January/February), pp. 50–58.

Bryce, G. Rex, 1991. "Quality Management Theories and Their Application." *Quality,* vol. 30 (January), pp. 15–18.

Carr, David K. and Ian D. Littman, 1990. *Excellence in Government: Total Quality Management in the 1990s.* Arlington, VA: Coopers & Lybrand.

Cohen, Steven and Ronald Brand, 1990. "Total Quality Management in the U.S. Environmental Protection Agency." *Public Productivity and Management Review,* vol. 14 (Fall), pp. 99–114.

Couper, David C., 1990. "Police Department Learns Ten Hard Quality Lessons." *Quality Progress,* vol. 23 (February), pp. 37–40.

Cravens, David W. *et al.,* 1988. "Marketing's Role in Product and Service Quality." *Industrial Marketing Management,* vol. 17, pp. 285–304.

Crosby, Phillip, 1979. *Quality Is Free.* New York: New American Library.

Deming, W. Edwards, 1986. *Out of the Crisis.* Cambridge: MIT Press.

Ferderber, Charles J., 1981. "Measuring Quality and Productivity in a Service Environment." *Industrial Engineering,* vol. 13, pp. 38–48.

Ferrara, Joseph A. and Daniel J. Dunmire, 1988. "Bureaucratic Influence of Budget Preparation: A Practitioner's View of Pentagon Budgeting." *Management Science and Policy Analysis,* vol. 5 (Winter), pp. 1–13.

Gabor, Andrea. 1990. *The Man Who Discovered Quality: How W. Edwards Deming Brought the Quality Revolution to America.* New York: Times Books.

Garvin, David A. 1984. "What Does 'Product Quality' Really Mean?" *Sloan Management Review,* vol. 25, pp. 25–43.

______, 1988. *Managing Quality.* New York: Free Press.

Houghland, James, 1987. "Criteria for Client Evaluation of Public Programs." *Social Science Quarterly* (June).

Hyde, Albert C., 1991. "Rescuing Quality Measurement from TQM." *The Bureaucrat,* vol. 19 (Winter), pp. 16–20.

Juran, Joseph. 1989. *Juran on Leadership for Quality*. New York: Free Press.

Keehley, Pat, 1991. "FQI Highlights Quality Management." *Public Administration Times,* vol. 14 (July 1), p. 3.

Kennedy, David A. and Barbara J. Young, 1989. "Managing Quality in Staff Areas." *Quality Progress,* vol. 22 (October), pp. 87–91.

King, Carol A., 1987. "A Framework for a Service Quality Assurance System." *Quality Progress,* vol. 20 (September), pp. 27–32.

Lee, Robert D., Jr., 1991. "Developments in State Budgeting: Trends of Two Decades." *Public Administration Review,* vol. 51 (May/June), pp. 254–262.

Milakovich, Michael E., 1991. "Total Quality Management in the Public Sector." *National Productivity Review* (Spring), pp. 195–213.

Parasuraman, A., Valarie Zeithami, and Leonard L. Berry, 1985. "A Conceptual Model of Service Quality." *Journal of Marketing,* vol. 49 (Fall), pp. 41–50.

Parks, Roger B., 1984. "Linking Objective and Subjective Measures of Performance." *Public Administration Review,* vol. 44 (March/April), pp. 118–127.

Plsek, Paul E., 1987. "Defining Quality at the Marketing/Development Interface." *Quality Progress,* vol. 20 (June), pp. 28–36.

Reed, Leonard, 1982. "Bureaucrats 2, Presidents 0." *Harper's* (November).

Scholtes, Peter R. and Hero Hacquebord, 1988a. "Beginning the Quality Transformation." *Quality Progress,* vol. 21 (July), pp. 28–33.

______, 1988b. "Six Strategies for Beginning the Quality Transformation." *Quality Progress,* vol. 21 (August), pp. 44–48.

Sensenbrenner, Joseph, 1991. "Quality Comes to City Hall." *Harvard Business Review,* vol. 69 (March/April), pp. 64–75.

Stipak, Brian, 1979. "Citizen Satisfaction with Urban Services: Potential Misuse as a Performance Indicator." *Public Administration Review,* vol. 39 (January/February), pp. 46–52.

Stipak, Brian and Roger B. Parks, 1984. "Communications." *Public Administration Review,* vol. 44 (November/December), pp. 551–552.

Streib, Gregory and Theodore H. Poister, 1989a. "Established and Emerging Management Tools: A Twelve-Year Perspective." *The Municipal Yearbook 1989.* Washington, DC: International City Managers Association.

______, 1989b. "Management Tools in Municipal Government: Trends Over the Past Decade." *Public Administration Review,* vol. 49 (May/June), pp. 240–248.

Wagenheim, George D. and John H. Reurink. 1991. "Customer Service in Public Administration." *Public Administration Review,* vol. 51 (May/June), pp. 263–269.

Walton, Mary, 1986. *The Deming Management Method.* New York: Praeger.

Whitten, Shirley K., 1989. "Award Winning Total Quality at the Naval Publications and Forms Center." *National Productivity Review,* vol. 8 (Summer). pp. 273–286.

Wilson, James Q., 1989. *Bureaucracy.* New York: Basic Books.

16

Computer Technology and Productivity Improvement

John A. Worthley

The city manager of a major municipal government recently observed that "automated information systems are among the more significant productivity tools presently available to local government."[1] This potential of computer technology has long been recognized, and the advent of minicomputers has made the possible uses of technology in productivity improvement efforts all the more interesting. More and more we read of examples of major productivity gains in government, which stem from automation. In fact, to hear the computer vendors tell it, computer technology is the answer to a broad range of productivity needs in government.[2]

A current study of local governments throughout the United States, however, has found "a gap between what conceivably can be done with the technology and what is actually being done."[3] The authors, Kenneth L. Kraemer and John L. King, conclude that "governments generally cannot hope to improve productivity through automation of production processes and increased use of special tools alone." A major review of the use of computer technology by the state of New York documented serious productivity problems. Its headline summarized its findings: "Computer Confusion Counts Up to Wasted Millions."[4]

It seems, in brief, that while computers offer tremendous opportunities for productivity improvement, there is often a disparity between promise and performance. That phenomenon is the concern of this article. What is

"Computer Technology and Productivity Improvement," *Public Productivity Review* 4 (March, 1980): 205–213.

the promise of computer technology for productivity? What, specifically, are some of the more prevalent problems that have been encountered in employing the technology? What measures can public managers take to smooth the application of computers to productivity efforts?

The Potential

The powers and capabilities of computer technology are staggering. Computer speed and storage capacity alone provide innumerable possibilities for productivity gains. They can upgrade processing accuracy nearly 100 percent (provided the input is accurate) by eliminating human processing errors that frequently decrease productivity. They can provide needed data almost instantly to remote sites, thus reducing productivity losses that frequently result from communication and retrieval time. Their central storage capacity, if properly managed, enables elimination of redundant data collection, which, in turn, can improve productivity.

In federal, state, and local governments, we find many cases confirming the potential of computer technology for improving productivity. The New York State legislature, for example, recently automated its bill processing procedures and found that the new system "served the productivity purpose even more than the coordination purpose."[5] The Pennsylvania sales tax collection office increased collection of delinquent taxes by $19 million in the first year of use of an on-line computerized system. In Brooklyn, the fire department automated its dispatching center and reduced response time from ten minutes to twenty seconds.[6] The Saginaw, Michigan, roads department improved road crew productivity by computerizing a complaint process.[7] The list of such success stories is impressive, but there are also numerous cases of productivity problems arising from the use of computer technology.

The Problems

Last year, United Press International reported that the Byelorussia Power Engineering Construction Department put its computer up for sale, declaring that it turned out to be more trouble than it was worth. Instead of increasing productivity, automation had decreased the output of both workers and management.[8] At about the same time, the *New York Daily News* reported that "a computerized sleuthing system designed to modernize [New York City] police investigations of stolen cars has created more problems than it has solved, and the police have recovered fewer stolen cars since . . . the computers were put to work."[9] These are just two examples of the technology contributing to decreased, rather than increased, productivity. Hundreds of similar cases have been experienced. In fact, disappointments have been described as a sequence of (1) wide euphoria, (2) growing concern, (3) disillusionment, and (4) disaster.[10] These "disasters," reviewed below, include personnel difficulties, security breakdowns, privacy invasions, clientele unrest, and operational failures.

Personnel. Personnel difficulties connected with automation have been perhaps the single greatest obstacle to harnessing computer technology for productivity purposes. As Richard A. Bassler correctly notes, "the public administrator is spending an increasing amount of time on issues relating to the human element in data processing."[11] Chief among these "human elements" are recruitment, training, retention, redeployment, and resistance problems.

While acquisition of hardware and software technology is greatly aided by the availability of vendors, recruitment and retention of the technical people needed to utilize the machines have entailed considerable difficulties. Although this is less a difficulty for small systems (for which existing staff can usually be trained), larger systems require technical operators, programmers, and systems analysts, all of whom are in short supply. The problem is aggravated because the public sector is unable to match the salaries that private business can offer, thus making retention of technical people in the public sector difficult. The result of the recruitment problem has often been faulty employment of the technology. In one not untypical case, the State Department of the United States underestimated the value of weapons sales to foreign nations by $1.4 billion due to, according to officials, "an oversight involving improper computer programming."[12]

Training of personnel has proved to be an oft-occurring problem. A study of New York City's sophisticated financial computer system, for example, pointed to inadequate personnel training as the chief cause of difficulties with the system.[13] Not only have line users of systems frequently been untrained, but staff technicians have typically received inadequate training on the goals and methods of the organizations.

Insufficient training has, in turn, contributed to the most serious and pervasive problem that has been experienced: resistance of personnel to the use of computers. Forms of resistance have run the gamut from outright sabotage of equipment, to the input of inaccurate data, to simple nonuse of the system, the result of which is usually a decrease in productivity. Causes of such resistance have been analyzed elsewhere.[14]

A fifth notable personnel problem has been the need to redeploy staff when processes are automated. For example, clerks are no longer needed but key punch operators are. Redeploying clerks requires some time and effort, including advance training; and failure to treat this situation adequately has been one of staff resistance

Security. Literature on the security problem associated with automation is voluminous, ranging from scholarly books, like the work of O. E. Dial and

E. M. Goldberry, to popular magazine columns in *The New Yorker, People,* and *Newsweek,* to articles in professional journals.[15] The problem is complex, befitting the complexity of the technology, and includes loss of data, manipulation of information, unauthorized use and access, and misuse of computer systems by authorized personnel. Horror stories of incidents are numerous, and some of the most representative cases are recounted in the literature cited above. Suffice it to say that millions of dollars are lost annually due to insufficient security involving computers;[16] not surprisingly, the impact on productivity has been considerable. The technical nature of automation, the invisibility of computerized information are the major elements of the problem.

Privacy. A related problem involving computers concerns the legal requirements of privacy rights. Laws exist today that place requirements on a public agency's collection and use of personal data. In terms of productivity impact, the relevant requirements concern updating, purging, notification, and inspection of information.

Increasingly strict regulations provide that personal information must be periodically updated and purged after a set time period, that notification of data storage must be provided to citizens, and that citizens must be given, on request, copies of information for inspection, verification, and correction. Because public agencies that use computers tend to collect huge amounts of data, these requirements can entail considerable outlays of time and money that obviously can impact operations. The United States Defense Department, for example, has criticized privacy statutes as "cumbersome, time consuming, and costly."[17] This refrain has been repeated in many public agencies subject to similar inspection, notification, and verification requirements.

Clientele Unrest. The reaction of consumers or clients to the use of technology has occasionally caused disruption of automated systems. Directions not to "fold, spindle, or mutilate" have been disobeyed and processes slowed. More clever, "computer-literate" consumers have been known to manipulate offensive systems by making additional key punches. Some clients, like the residents of one nursing home known to the author, simply refused to accept computerized statements. Thus, the managers had to transcribe manually the computerized printout onto written forms. The costs to productivity in such cases can be considerable.

Operational Failures. Operational failures with computers, sometimes technical in nature, sometimes human, have resulted in productivity problems. Most public agencies have experienced "down-time" problems during which workers must sit idle because needed information is available only on the computer. Many social service agency personnel, for example, have experienced the frustration of the cathode ray tube (CRT) "going down" while the client is in the chair awaiting assistance.

A more subtle, but no less debilitating, operational problem that occurs increasingly as automation has expanded is "data pollution," a condition in which so much data is stored on the computer, in such a disorganized fashion, that needed information is obscured. This productivity-preventing phenomenon was found to be widespread by researchers who studied local government use of computers. The report from this national study observed: "Executives believe the information they need exists somewhere in their government but is not organized and stored so it can be used effectively."[18]

Because of these and related problems, organizational experience with computer technology has been, in the pithy words of Professor Joel Ross, "something of a bust." His analysis of computer use in the private sector is equally applicable to the public domain: "Despite enormous technological advances, the computer has not yet reached anything approaching maturity in business use."[19] We hasten to ask why has such a powerful and potentially useful tool for productivity proved to be so problematic. The root of the situation is not technical. Indeed, as Ross implies, the necessary hardware and software have long existed and are today highly refined. Rather, the underlying problem has been managerial. Managerial "brainware" has not been sufficiently applied to the planning, design, and implementation of computerized information systems.

Toward Harnessing the Potential

The Commission on Federal Paperwork, in reviewing the problems encountered in the use of computer technology, observed: "We are being enslaved by the tool rather than harnessing the tool to serve our needs."[20] It pointed to managerial action as the remedy for that condition, a conclusion also reached by Kraemer and King: "It is important that managers . . . understand what computers do, how they should be applied to organizational tasks, and how they should be organized and managed."[21]

What are the implications of this for public managers? What "managerial action" is needed? In broad terms, the most widely urged managerial remedies can be summarized. First, managers must be thoroughly involved in the development of computerized systems. The difficulties encountered in employing the technology are usually not technical. They are managerial and can be overcome only by managers. Second, automation requires careful planning. Application of the technology to productivity efforts requires time and attention to the problems that inevitably arise. Managers should ensure that proper planning takes place. Third, communication between the technicians and the actual users of any computerized information system must be

BOX 16.1 IT: An Update

H. Brinton Milward and Louise Ogilvie Snyder

Information technology has had many applications in public administration in recent years. In the excerpts, the authors discuss some recent uses:

For public organizations, information technology holds particular promise in the area of service delivery. Davidow and Malone (1992) discuss virtual organizations and cite as an example that it is now possible for a car buyer to sit at a car dealer's terminal and input the design features he wants in orders to the factory. Similarly, the constituent who e-mails her legislative representative about an upcoming vote or the citizen who requests tailored information from a legal information kiosk participates in the design of public policy. Moreover, programs using information technology that permit users to identify themselves according to age, sex, ethnicity, or other characteristics could help agencies shape the population segments most in need of specific bundies of services. For example, information kiosks that solicit demographic information from users can be used to compile profiles of different population groups and what information and services they seek most. The resulting statistics then can be used to enhance existing programs and develop new services for targeted groups based on their kiosk queries and requests.

Many localities and government agencies already have computerized delivery systems for legal services, social services, and medical services.

In Arizona, citizens in need of legal aid can save both time and money by consulting Victor, the cyber-lawyer (Periman 1994, 37), rather than seeing an expensive private attorney or standing in line to consult a courthouse official. Via QuickCourt computer kiosks in three cities, Victor dispenses without cost both legal advice and court-ready documents in either English or Spanish at the touch of a button. He can assist citizens with no-fault divorce filings, child support calculations, landlord-tenant disputes, and small claims—the most popular category of inquiries. Furthermore. Victor also offers bankruptcy advice and helpful information regarding liens and wage garnishing.

Taxpayers in Massachusetts can file their taxes from their home phones. Using the new TeleFile telephone system. up to 480,000 Massachusetts residents can file their 1995 state tax returns from any touch-tone phone. Before calling, taxpayers complete a special form that organizes the data needed for filing. Then when taxpayers call, a series of voice prompts guide them through the data entry process. Through a combination of touchtone and voice-recognition

(continues)

continual. Managers should ensure that interaction occurs and that technical jargon is not used to discourage or inhibit user participation. Finally, a "people" strategy needs to be developed. Because resistance by personnel to computerization has been one of the greatest obstacles encountered, managers should give particular attention to ameliorating the personnel problem.

But what, specifically, constitutes "managerial involvement"? How does a manager "plan" the application of computers? How is communication

BOX 16.1 (continued)

technology the system processes the data and generates the total tax obligation or expected refund, whichever applies. Refunds are mailed within four days, and since "taxpayers enter the data themselves, the state saves 80 percent of the original tax-processing costs" (Richter 1995, 62).

Welfare recipients in Camden, New Jersey, are also experiencing the revolution in electronic service provision. The Families First program, which began in February 1994, distributes cash subsidies and food stamp benefits to needy families via an electronic ATM-style system. Program participants each are given their own plastic ATM card with which they can withdraw cash and purchase food ". . . at stores equipped with magnetic-stripe machines. Cash and food benefits are kept in separate accounts, which are held by the state's welfare division" (McLarin 1994. 38). System administrators also benefit from reduced fraud: it is much more difficult to transfer card funds than to sell food stamps on the black market. Since subsidy checks and food stamps no longer have to be printed or mailed. New Jersey expects to save an average of S3 million per year once the program is expanded into other pilot areas.

Some Atlanta commuters may be pleased with the transportation technology recently introduced in their city. In order to alleviate rush hour congestion on the city's streets and highways, transportation officials have constructed a new toll road. Georgia 400, which circumvents central city traffic. Commuters using special computer-coded devices known as cruise cards affixed to their windshields pay their tolls electronically (Beasley 1993a): they drive through the toll plaza at the posted speed limit of 35 miles per hour. and an electronic sensor deducts the cost of the toll from a prepaid account. Cameras posted at the toll booths ". . . automatically photograph the license plate of any car bearing a stolen ID tag . . . [and are also] used to nab motorists who try to go through the toll booths without paying" (Beasley 1992. B1). Violators receive their tickets by mail and are assessed the value of the unpaid toll plus a $25 fine (Beasley 1993b. C1).

(Source: H. Brinton Milward and Louise Ogilvie Snyder, "Electronic Government," in: "Electronic Government: Linking Citizens to Public Organizations Through Technology," *Journal of Public Administration Research & Theory* 6 (April 1996): 261–275.)

between technician and user accomplished? How are people problems recognized and approached? How, in short, can a manager exercise control over the task of employing computer technology?

One practical answer is systematic analysis before, during, and after the utilization of computers. Most problems can be anticipated if the relevant questions are posed, most obstacles can be recognized if the process is systematically monitored, most difficulties can be handled if managers systematically observe and learn from their own organizational experience. Systematic analysis is one way managers can anticipate, recognize, and address the problems of employing the technology.

Systematic analysis of computerization entails attention to the process as well as to the content of planning, designing, and implementing computerized information systems. Content refers to the series of questions and tentative answers that guide the effort to develop and use computers. Process involves developing the computerization effort in systematic phases, monitoring carefully the actual experience as it evolves, and modifying the effort as important, new questions are discovered and better tentative answers learned.

Managing the Content of Computerization

In terms of content, most public agencies have, historically, employed a kind of systems analysis for computer applications. They have generally addressed the matters of problem definition, goal specification, alternatives consideration, impact analysis, and system development. The problem in the past has been that technicians and consultants, instead of managers, have been determining the questions to be raised for each of the five items. Consequently, nontechnical questions have often gone unaddressed. In particular, impact analyses have typically been limited to fiscal and technical considerations. What will the computer cost and what technical staff will be needed? Often the impact of a proposed computer system on personnel and client resistance, on security and privacy, is excluded from the planning and analysis. Clearly, systematic analysis of the possible impacts in these areas would assist managers in anticipating the kinds of problems that have, time and again, impeded an automation effort.

In terms of content, then, planning analyses must deal not only with technical questions but with numerous nontechnical matters; managers/users must be actively involved in developing these plans and analyses. Managerial as well as technical "brainware" is essential.

Managing the Process of Computerization

Even an extraordinary plan and analysis cannot anticipate all the problems that might impede a particular computerization effort. Some problems will occur unexpectedly or in a different form than initially predicted. For this reason, systematic analysis should also entail a phased process of monitoring developments and modifying the plan accordingly as a computer application is developing. In the past this monitoring process has seldom been done. Typically, a systems study has been performed by technicians or consultants, a computer capability (i.e., hardware/software has been acquired, and a system implemented—all with only marginal managerial control.

A controlled process of systematic analysis entails a phased progression of managerial monitoring and decision making. It includes, at a minimum, the following steps: (1) preliminary study, (2) system design, (3) system test, (4) system installation, and (5) audit/evaluation. At the completion of each phase, the manager can intervene, review the outcome, and provide direction to proceed to the next phase, to halt the project, or to return to the previous phase for additional work. For example, a preliminary study might be reviewed by a manager who finds that questions on privacy impact and personnel resistance were not raised. The manager could then direct the systems analysis to address these questions before a decision is made to proceed with system design. Answers to privacy questions, for example, might result in an addition to the system design that would otherwise not have been made and that, as a consequence, might have produced legal suits months after the system's implementation.

A system test is a key phase because it can uncover impacts that were not anticipated in the preliminary study and that, by being identified and addressed at a test stage, can be better controlled. At the completion of a test, for example, a manager might direct that the preliminary study be expanded to explore a problem (such as personnel resistance) discovered in the test. The manager might then direct that a second test be conducted to full implementation.

In addition to a system test phase, the most neglected step, historically, in the use of computer technology has been audit and evaluation. Seldom have computerized processes been systematically reviewed by managers to see whether the computer has produced increased productivity. Consequently, many unproductive uses of computer technology remain in operation. Systematically conducted, periodic evaluation can disclose problems that were not recognized in the preliminary study or test, and they can point to modifications in system design that might improve the effectiveness of the operation.

The important aspect of the process of systematic analysis is that it allows the manager to *manage* the use of the computer. Using this approach, problems can be identified and addressed before an inordinate amount of time, money, and output are spent; the use of the technology can be steadfastly focused on organizational realities and needs, such as increased productivity.

Conclusion

The net result of such a systematic approach to organizational use of computers is greater managerial involvement and control over the problems that have, too frequently, made the road from productivity promises to productivity performance a rocky trail. Systematic analysis can alert managers to training needs and undesired shifts in organizational relationships; it can prompt managers to stay abreast of privacy laws, policies, and developments and to ensure that the agency is in compliance; it can keep computerized information systems focused on objectives and agency needs and help minimize "data pollution."

Without doubt, computers can be of tremendous assistance in productivity improvement efforts. But harnessing the technology tool toward productivity requires rigorous managerial effort and attention to the various nontechnical obstacles that consistently confront organizations in utilizing modern computer technology.

Notes

1. John E. Dever, "Using Computers to Achieve Organizational Objectives," *Public Management,* LIX (December 1977), 10.

2. Most vendors, for example, publish periodic reports on the application of their products. One such publication is the Sperry-Univac *World-wide News,* which typically depicts new computers as, for instance, "a real winner in coping with a hefty workload for five local government organizations." (See issue no. 11, 1977.)

3. Kenneth L. Kraemer and John L. King, *Computers and Local Government* (New York: Praeger, 1977), 1, 2, 6.

4. *Albany Times Union,* March 8, 1977.

5. Frank Mauro quoted in *New York Times,* July 16, 1978.

6. Charles Kaiser, "Brooklyn Firemen Use New Computer," *New York Times,* August 30, 1977.

7. John D. Moorhead, *Christian Science Monitor,* December 7, 1977.

8. *New York Times,* March 20, 1978.

9. Cass Vanzi, "Stolen Car Computer Is a Bust," *New York Daily News,* October 25, 1977.

10. E. McLean and L. Welke, *Datamation,* June 1972, 5.

11. Richard A. Bassler, *Computer Systems and the Public Administrator* (Alexandria: College Readings, 1976), 139.

12. Long Island *Newsday,* November 12, 1977.

13. *New York Times,* December 6, 1977.

14. See, for example, Robert E. Quinn and Joseph Whorton, "Computers and Public Administration: Predicting Resistance to Change" (Paper Annual Meeting of the American Society for Public Administration, Phoenix, April 1978).

15. See O. E. Dial and E. M. Goldberry, *Privacy, Security and Computers* (New York: Pracger, 1975); Thomas Whiteside, "Dead Souls in the Computer," *The New Yorker,* August 16 and August 29, 1977; "Computer Crime Is a $100M a Year Rip-Off," *People,* November 1977; "The Computer Bandits," *Newsweek,* August 9, 1976; and Brandt Allen, "The Biggest Computer Frauds," *Journal of Accountancy,* May 1977.

16. See Allen, "The Biggest Computer Frauds," for rather astounding statistics on this matter.

17. *Navy Times,* February 1976.

18. Kenneth L. Kraemer and John King, *Computers, Power and Urban Management* (Beverly Hills: Sage Publications, 1976), 19.

19. Joel E. Ross, *Modern Management and Information Systems* (Reston, VA: Reston Publishing, 1976), 2.

20. Forest W. Horton, "Computers and Paperwork," *The Bureaucrat,* VI (Fall 1977), 99.

21. Kraemer and King, *Computers and Local Government,* 3.

17

Organizational Decline and Cutback Management

Charles H. Levine

Government organizations are neither immortal nor unshrinkable.[1] Like growth, organizational decline and death, by erosion or plan, is a form of organizational change; but all the problems of managing organizational change are compounded by a scarcity of slack resources.[2] This feature of declining organizations—the diminution of the cushion of spare resources necessary for coping with uncertainty, risking innovation, and rewarding loyalty and cooperation—presents for government a problem that simultaneously challenges the underlying premises and feasibility of both contemporary management systems and the institutions of pluralist liberal democracy.[3]

Growth and decline are issues of a grand scale usually tackled by only the most brave or foolhardy of macro social theorists. The division of scholarly labor between social theorists and students of management is now so complete that the link between the great questions of political economy and the more earthly problems of managing public organizations is rarely forged. This bifurcation is more understandable when one acknowledges that managers and organization analysts have for decades (at least since the Roosevelt Administration and the wide acceptance of Keynesian economics) been able to subsume their concern for societal level instability under broad assumptions of abundance and continuous and unlimited economic growth.[4] Indeed, almost all of our public management strategies are predicated on

---

"Organizational Decline and Cutback Management," *Public Administrative Review* 38 (July/August 1978): 316–325.

assumptions of the continuing enlargement of public revenues and expenditures. These expansionist assumptions are particularly prevalent in public financial management systems that anticipate budgeting by incremental additions to a secure base.[5] Recent events and gloomy forecasts, however, have called into question the validity and generality of these assumptions, and have created a need to reopen inquiry into the effects of resource scarcity on public organizations and their management systems. These events and forecasts, ranging from taxpayer revolts like California's successful Proposition 13 campaign and financial crises like the near collapse into bankruptcy of New York City's government and the agonizing retrenchment of its bureaucracy, to the foreboding predictions of the "limits of growth" modelers, also relink issues of political economy of the most monumental significance to practices of public management.[6]

We know very little about the decline of public organizations and the management of cutbacks. This may be because even though some federal agencies like the Works Progress Administration, Economic Recovery Administration, Department of Defense, National Aeronautics and Space Administration, the Office of Economic Opportunity, and many state and local agencies have expanded and then contracted,[7] or even died, the public sector as a whole has expanded enormously over the last four decades. In this period of expansion and optimism among proponents of an active government, isolated incidents of zero growth and decline have been considered anomalous; and the difficulties faced by the management of declining agencies coping with retrenchment have been regarded as outside the mainstream of public management concerns. It is a sign of our times—labeled by Kenneth Boulding as the "Era of Slowdown"—that we are now reappraising cases of public organization decline and death as exemplars and forerunners in order to provide strategies for the design and management of *mainstream* public administration in a future dominated by resource scarcity.[8]

The decline and death of government organizations is a symptom, a problem, and a contingency. It is a symptom of resource scarcity at a societal, even global, level that is creating the necessity for governments to terminate some programs, lower the activity level of others, and confront tradeoffs between new demands and old programs rather than to expand whenever a new public problem arises. It is a problem for managers who must maintain organizational capacity by devising new managerial arrangements within prevailing structures that were designed under assumptions of growth. It is a contingency for public employees and clients; employees who must sustain their morale and productivity in the face of increasing control from above and shrinking opportunities for creativity and promotion while clients must find alternative sources for the services governments may no longer be able to provide.

Organizational Decline and Administrative Theory

Growth is a common denominator that links contemporary management theory to its historical antecedents and management practices with public policy choices. William Scott has observed that ". . . organization growth creates organizational abundance, or surplus, which is used by management to buy off internal consensus from the potentially conflicting interest group segments that compete for resources in organizations."[9] As a common denominator, growth has provided a criterion to gauge the acceptability of government policies and has defined many of the problems to be solved by management action and organizational research. So great is our enthusiasm for growth that even when an organizational decline seems inevitable and irreversible, it is nearly impossible to get elected officials, public managers, citizens, or management theorists to confront cutback and decremental planning situations as anything more than temporary slowdowns. Nevertheless, the reality of zero growth and absolute decline, at least in some sectors, regions, communities, and organizations, means that management and public policy theory must be expanded to incorporate non-growth as an initial condition that applies in some cases. If Scott's assertions about the pervasiveness of a growth ideology in management are correct, our management and policy paradigms will have to be replaced or augmented by new frameworks to help to identify critical questions and strategies for action. Put squarely, without growth, how do we manage public organizations?

We have no ready or comprehensive answers to this question, only hunches and shards of evidence to serve as points of departure. Under conditions and assumptions of decline, the ponderables, puzzles, and paradoxes of organizational management take on new complexities. For example, organizations cannot be cut back by merely reversing the sequence of activity and resource allocation by which their parts were originally assembled. Organizations are organic social wholes with emergent qualities which allow their parts to recombine into intricately interwoven semi-lattices when they are brought together. In this study of NASA's growth and drawdown, Paul Schulman has observed that viable public programs must attain "capture points" of public goal and resource commitments, and these organizational thresholds or "critical masses" are characterized by their indivisibility.[10] Therefore, to attempt to disaggregate and cutback on one element of such an intricate and delicate political and organization arrangement may jeopardize the functioning and equilibrium of an entire organization.

Moreover, retrenchment compounds the choice of management strategies with paradoxes. When slack resources abound, money for the development of management planning, control, information systems, and the conduct of policy analysis is plentiful even though these systems are relatively irrelevant to decision making.[11] Under conditions of abundance, habit, intuition, snap judgments and other forms of informal analysis will suffice for most decisions because the costs of making mistakes can be easily absorbed without threatening the organization's survival.[12] However, in times of austerity, when these control and analytic tools are needed to help to minimize the risk of making mistakes, the money for their development and implementation is unavailable.

Similarly, without slack resources to produce "win-win" consensus-building solutions and to provide side payments to overcome resistance to change, organizations will have difficulty innovating and maintaining flexibility. Yet, these are precisely the activities needed to maintain capacity while contracting, especially when the overriding imperative is to minimize the perturbations of adjusting to new organizational equilibriums at successively lower levels of funding and activity.[13]

Lack of growth also creates a number of serious personnel problems. For example, the need to reward managers for directing organizational contraction and termination is a problem because without growth there are few promotions and rewards available to motivate and retain successful and loyal managers—particularly when compared to job opportunities for talented managers outside the declining organization.[14] Also, without expansion, public organizations that are constrained by merit and career tenure systems are unable to attract and accommodate new young talent. Without an inflow of younger employees, the average age of employees is forced up, and the organization's skill pool becomes frozen at the very time younger, more flexible, more mobile, less expensive and (some would argue) more creative employees are needed.[15]

Decline forces us to set some of our logic for rationally structuring organizations on end and upside down. For instance, under conditions of growth and abundance, one problem for managers and organizational designers is how to set up *exclusionary* mechanisms to prevent "*free riders*" (employees and clients who share in the consumption of the organization's collective benefits without sharing the burden that produced the benefit) from taking advantage of the enriched common pool of resources. In contrast, under conditions of decline and austerity, the problem for managers and organizational designers is how to set up *inclusionary* mechanisms to prevent organizational participants from avoiding the sharing of the "*public bads*" (increased burdens) that result from the depletion of the common pool of resources.[16] In other words, to maintain order and capacity when undergoing decline, organizations need mechanisms like long-term contracts with clauses that make pensions non-portable if broken at the employee's discretion. These mechanisms need to be carefully designed to penalize and constrain "*free exiters*" and cheap exits at the convenience of the employees while still allowing managers to cut and induce into retirement marginally performing and unneeded employees.

As a final example, inflation erodes steady states so that staying even actually requires extracting more resources from the organization's environment and effectuating greater internal economies. The irony of managing decline in the public sector is particularly compelling under conditions of recession or so called "stagflation." During these periods of economic hardship and uncertainty, pressure is put on the federal government to follow Keynesian dictates and spend more through deficit financing; at the same time, critical public opinion and legal mandates require some individual agencies (and many state and local governments) to balance their budgets, and in some instances to spend less.

These characteristics of declining public organizations are like pieces of a subtle jigsaw puzzle whose parameters can only be guessed at and whose abstruseness deepens with each new attempt to fit its edges together. To overcome our tendency to regard decline in public organizations as anomalous, we need to develop a catalogue of what we already know about declining public organizations. A typology of *causes* of public organizational decline and corresponding sets of *tactics* and *decision rules* available for managing cutbacks will serve as a beginning.

The Causes of Public Organization Decline

Cutting back any kind of organization is difficult, but a good deal of the problem of cutting back public organizations is compounded by their special status as authoritative, non-market extensions of the state.[17] Public organizations are used to deliver services that usually have no direct or easily measurable monetary value or when market arrangements fail to provide the necessary level of revenues to support the desired level or distribution of services. Since budgets depend on appropriations and not sales, the diminution or termination of public organizations and programs, or conversely their maintenance and survival, are political matters usually calling for the application of the most sophisticated attack or survival tactics in the arsenal of the skilled bureaucrat-politician.[18] These strategies are not universally propitious; they are conditioned by the causes for decline and the hoped-for results.

The causes of public organization decline can be categorized into a four-cell typology as shown in Figure 17.1. The causes are divided along two dimensions: (a) whether they are primarily the result of conditions located either internal or external to the organization, or (b) whether they are principally a product of political or economic/technical conditions.[19] This is admittedly a crude scheme for lumping instances of decline, but it does cover most cases and allows for some abstraction.

FIGURE 17.1 The Causes of Public Organization Decline

	Internal	External
Political	Political Vulnerability	Problem Depletion
Economic/ Technical	Organizational Atrophy	Environmental Entropy

Of the four types, *problem depletion* is the most familiar. It covers government involvement in short-term crises like natural disasters such as floods and earthquakes, medium length governmental interventions like war mobilization and countercyclical employment programs, and longer-term public programs like polio research and treatment and space exploration—all of which involve development cycles. These cycles are characterized by a political definition of a problem followed by the extensive commitment of resources to attain critical masses and then contractions after the problem has been solved, alleviated, or has evolved into a less troublesome stage or politically popular issue.[20]

Problem depletion is largely a product of forces beyond the control of the affected organization. Three special forms of problem depletion involve demographic shifts, problem redefinition, and policy termination. The impact of demographic shifts has been vividly demonstrated in the closing of schools in neighborhoods where the school age population has shrunk. While the cause for most school closings is usually neighborhood aging—a factor outside the control of the school system—the decision to close a school is largely political. The effect of problem redefinition on public organizations is most easily illustrated by movements to *de*institutionalize the mentally ill. In these cases, the core bureaucracies responsible for treating these populations in institutions has shrunk as the rising per patient cost of hospitalization has combined with pharmaceutical advances in anti-depressants and tranquilizers to cause public attitudes and professional doctrine to shift.[21]

Policy termination has both theoretical import and policy significance. Theoretically, it is the final phase of a public policy intervention cycle and can be defined as "... the deliberate conclusion or cessation of specific government functions, programs, policies, or organizations."[22] Its policy relevance is underscored by recent experiments and proposals for sunset legislation which would require some programs to undergo extensive evaluations after a period of usually five years and be reauthorized or be terminated rather than be continued indefinitely.[23]

Environmental entropy occurs when the capacity of the environment to support the public organization at prevailing levels of activity erodes.[24] This type of decline covers the now familiar phenomena of financially troubled cities and regions with declining economic bases. Included in this category are: market and technological shifts like the decline in demand for domestic textiles and steel and its effect on the economies and quality of life in places like New England textile towns and steel cities like Gary, Indiana, Bethlehem, Pennsylvania, and Youngstown, Ohio;[25] transportation changes that have turned major railroad hubs and riverports of earlier decades into stagnating and declining economies; mineral depletion which has crippled mining communities; and intrametropolitan shifts of economic activity from central cities to their suburbs.[26] In these cases, population declines often have paralleled general economic declines which erode tax bases and force cities to cut services. One of the tragic side effects of environmental entropy is that it most severely affects those who cannot move.[27] Caught in the declining city and region are the immobile and dependent: the old, the poor, and the unemployable. For these communities, the forced choice of cutting services to an ever more dependent and needy population is the cruel outcome of decline.[28]

Environmental entropy also has a political dimension. As Proposition 13 makes clear, the capacity of a government is as much a function of the willingness of taxpayers to be taxed as it is of the economic base of the taxing region. Since the demand for services and the supply of funds to support them are usually relatively independent in the public sector, taxpayer resistance can produce diminished revenues which force service reductions even though the demand and *need* for services remains high.

The *political vulnerability* of public organizations is an internal property indicating a high level of fragility and precariousness which limits their capacity to resist budget decrements and demands to contract from their environment. Of the factors which contribute to vulnerability, some seem to be more responsible for decline and death than others. Small size, internal conflict, and changes in leadership, for example, seem less telling than the lack of a base of expertise or the absence of a positive self-image and history of excellence. However, an organization's age may be the most accurate predictor of bureaucratic vulnerability. Contrary to biological reasoning, aged organizations are more flexible than young organizations and therefore rarely die or even shrink very much. Herbert Kaufman argues that one of the advantages of organizations over solitary individuals is that they do provide longer institutional memories than a human lifetime, and this means that older organizations ought to have a broader range of adaptive skills, more capacity for learning, more friends and allies, and be more innovative because they have less to fear from making a wrong decision than a younger organization.[29]

Organizational atrophy is a common phenomenon in all organizations but government organizations are particularly vulnerable because they usually lack market generated revenues to signal a malfunction and to pinpoint responsibility. Internal atrophy and declining performance which can lead to resource cutbacks or to a weakening of organizational capacity come from a host of system and management failures almost too numerous to identify. A partial list would include: inconsistent and perverse incentives, differentiation without integration, role confusion, decentralized authority with vague responsibility, too many inappropriate rules, weak oversight, stifled dissent and upward communication, rationalization of performance failure by "blaming the victim," lack of self-evaluating and self-correcting capacity, high turnover, continuous politicking for promotions and not for program resources, continuous reorganization, suspicion of outsiders, and obsolescence caused by routine adherence to past methods and technologies in the face of changing problems. No organization is immune from these problems and no organization is likely to be afflicted by them all at once, but a heavy dose of some of these breakdowns in combination can contribute to an organization's decline and even death.

Identifying and differentiating among these four types of decline situations provides a start toward cataloging and estimating the appropriateness of strategies for managing decline and cutbacks. This activity is useful because when undergoing decline, organizations face three decision tasks: first, management must decide whether it will adopt a strategy to resist decline or smooth it (i.e., reduce the impact of fluctuations in the environment that cause interruptions in the flow of work and poor performance); second, given this choice of maneuvering strategies it will have to decide what tactics are most appropriate;[30] and third, if necessary, it will have to make decisions about how and where cuts will occur. Of course, the cause of a decline will greatly affect these choices.

Strategic Choices

Public organizations behave in response to a mix of motives—some aimed at serving national (or state or local) purposes, some aimed at goals for the *organization as a whole,* and others directed toward the particularistic goals of organizational subunits. Under conditions of growth, requests for more resources by subunits usually can be easily concerted with the goals of the organization as a whole and its larger social purposes. Under decline, however, subunits usually respond to requests to make cuts in terms of their particular long-term survival needs (usually defended in terms of the injury which cutbacks would inflict on a program with lofty purposes or on a dependent clientele) irrespective of impacts on the performance of government or the organization as a whole.

The presence of powerful survival instincts in organizational subunits helps to explain why the political leadership of public organizations can be trying to respond to legislative or executive directives to cut back while at the same time the career and program leadership of subunits will be taking action to resist cuts.[31] It also helps to explain why growth can have the appearance of a rational administrative process complete with a hierarchy of objectives and broad consensus, while decline takes on the *appearance* of what James G. March has called a "garbage can problem"—arational, polycentric, fragmented, and dynamic.[32] Finally, it allows us to understand why the official rhetoric about cutbacks—whether it be to "cut the fat," "tighten our belts," "preserve future options," or "engage in a process of orderly and programmed termination"—is often at wide variance with the unofficial conduct of bureau chiefs who talk of "minimizing cutbacks to mitigate catastrophe," or "making token sacrifices until the heat's off."

Retrenchment politics dictate that organizations will respond to decrements with a mix of espoused and operative strategies that are not necessarily consistent.[33] When there is a wide divergence between the official pronouncements about the necessity for cuts and the actual occurrence of cuts, skepticism, cynicism, distrust, and noncompliance will dominate the retrenchment process and cutback management will be an adversarial process pitting top and middle management against one another. In most cases, however, conflict will not be rancorous, and strategies for dealing with decline will be a mixed bag of tactics intended either to *resist* or to *smooth* decline. The logic here is that no organization accedes to cuts with enthusiasm and will try to find a way to resist cuts; but resistance is risky. In addition to the possibility of being charged with nonfeasance, no responsible manager wants to be faced with the prospect of being unable to control where cuts will take place or confront quantum cuts with unpredictable consequences. Instead, managers will choose a less risky course and attempt to protect organizational capacity and procedures by smoothing decline and its effects on the organization.

An inventory of some of these cutback management tactics is presented in Figure 17.2. They are arrayed according to the type of decline problem which they can be employed to solve. This collection of tactics by no means exhausts the possible organizational responses to decline situations, nor are all the tactics exclusively directed toward meeting a single contingency. They are categorized in order to show that many familiar coping tactics correspond, even if only roughly, to an underlying logic. In this way a great deal of information about organizational responses to decline can be aggregated without explicating each tactic in great detail.[34]

The tactics intended to remove or alleviate the external political and economic causes of decline are reasonably straightforward means to revitalize eroded economic bases, reduce environmental uncertainty, protect niches, retain flexibility, or lessen dependence. The tactics for handling the internal causes of decline, however, tend to be more subtle means for strengthening organizations and managerial control. For instance, the management of decline *in the face of resistance* can be smoothed by changes in leadership. When hard unpopular decisions have to be made, new managers can be brought in to make the cuts, take the flak, and move on to another organization. By rotating managers into and out of the declining organization, interpersonal loyalties built up over the years will not interfere with the cutback process. This is especially useful in implementing a higher level decision to terminate an organization where managers will make the necessary cuts knowing that their next assignments will not depend on their support in the organization to be terminated.

The "exploit the exploitable" tactic also calls for further explanation. Anyone familiar with the personnel practices of universities during the 1970's will recognize this tactic. It has been brought about by the glutted market for academic positions which has made many unlueky recent Ph.D's vulnerable and exploitable. This buyers' market has coincided neatly with the need of universities facing steady states and declining enrollments to avoid long-term tenure commitments to expensive faculties. The result is a marked increase in part-time and non-tenure track positions which are renewed on a semester-to-semester basis. So while retrenchment is smoothed and organization flexibility increased, it is attained at considerable cost to the careers and job security of the exploited teachers.

Cutback management is a two-crucible problem: besides selecting tactics for either resisting or smoothing decline, if necessary, management must also select who will be let go and what programs will be curtailed or terminated. Deciding where to make cuts is a test of managerial intelligence and courage because each choice involves tradeoffs and opportunity costs that cannot be erased through the generation of new resources accrued through growth.

As with most issues of public management involving the distribution of costs, the choice of decision rules to allocate cuts usually involves the tradeoff between equity and efficiency.[35] In this case, "equity" is meant to mean the distribution of cuts across the organization with an equal probability of hurting all units and employees irrespective of impacts on the long term capacity of the organization. "Efficiency" is meant to mean the sorting, sifting, and assignment of cuts to those people and units in the organization so that for a given budget decrement, cuts are allocated to minimize the long-term loss in total benefits to the organization as a whole, irrespective of their distribution.

Making cuts on the basis of equity is easier for managers because it is socially acceptable, easier to justify, and involves few decision making costs. "Sharing the pain" is politically expedient because it appeals to common sense ideals of justice. Further, simple equity decision making avoids costs from sorting, selecting, and negotiating cuts.[36] In contrast, efficiency cuts involve costly triage analysis because the distribution of pain and inconvenience requires that the value of people and subunits to the organization have to be weighed in terms of their expected *future* contributions. In the public sector, of course, things are never quite this clear cut because a host of constraints like career status, veteran's preference, bumping rights, entitlements, and mandated programs limit managers from selecting optimal rules for making cuts. Nevertheless, the values of equity and efficiency are central to allocative decision making and provide useful criteria for judging the appropriateness of cutback rules. By applying these criteria to five of the most commonly used or proposed cutback methods—seniority, hiring freezes, even-percentage-cuts-across-the-board, productivity criteria, and zero base budgeting—we are able to make assessments of their efficacy as managerial tools.

Seniority is the most prevalent and most maligned of the five decision rules. Seniority guarantees have little to do with either equity or efficiency, *per se.* Instead, they are directed at another value of public administration; that is, the need to provide secure carcer-long employment to neutrally competent civil servants.[37] Because seniority is likely to be spread about the organization unevenly, using seniority criteria for making cuts forces managers to implicitly surrender control over the impact of cuts on services and the capacity of subunits. Furthermore, since seniority usually dictates a "last-in-first-out" retention system, personnel cuts using this decision rule tend to inflict the greatest harm to minorities and women who are recent entrants in most public agencies.

A *hiring freeze* is a convenient short-run strategy to buy time and preserve options. In the short run it hurts no one already employed by the organization because hiring freezes rely on "natural attrition" through resignations, retirements, and death to diminish the size of an organization's work force. In the long run, however, hiring freezes are hardly the most equitable or efficient way to scale down organizational size. First, even though natural and self selection relieves the stress on managers, it also takes control over the decision of whom and where to cut away from management and thereby reduces the possibility of intelligent long range cutback planning. Second, hiring freezes are more likely to harm minorities and women who are more likely to be the next hired rather than the next retired. Third, attrition will likely occur at different rates among an organization's professional and technical specialities. Since resignations will most likely come from those employees with the most opportunities for employment elsewhere, during a long hiring freeze an organization may find itself short on some critically needed skills yet unable to hire people with these skills even though they may be available.

Even-percentage-cuts-across-the-board are expedient because they transfer decision-making costs lower in the organization, but they tend to be

FIGURE 17.2 Some Cutback Management Tactics

	Tactics to Resist Decline	*Tactics to Smooth Decline*
External Political	(Problem Depletion) 1. Diversity programs, clients and constituents 2. Improve legislative liaison 3. Educate the public about the agency's mission 4. Mobilize dependent clients 5. Become "captured" by a powerful interest group or legislator 6. Threaten to cut vital or popular programs 7. Cut a visible and widespread service a little to demonstrate client dependence	1. Make peace with competing agencies 2. Cut low prestige programs 3. Cut programs to politically weak clients 4. Sell and lend expertise to other agencies 5. Share problems with other agencies
Economic/ Technical	(Environmental Entropy) 1. Find a wider and richer revenue base (e.g., metropolitan reorganization) 2. Develop incentives to prevent disinvestment 3. Seek foundation support 4. Lure new public and private sector investment 5. Adopt user charges for services where possible	1. Improve targeting on problems 2. Plan with preservative objectives 3. Cut losses by distinguishing between capital investments and sunk costs 4. Yield concessions to taxpayers and employers to retain them
Internal Political	(Political Vulnerability) 1. Issue symbolic responses like forming study commissions and task forces 2. "Circle the wagons," i.e., develop a seige mentality to retain esprit de corps 3. Strengthen expertise	1. Change leadership at each stange in the decline process 2. Reorganize at each stage 3. Cut programs run by weak subunits 4. Shift programs to another agency 5. Get temporary exemptions from personnel and budgetary regulations which limit discretion
Economic/ Technical	(Organizational Atrophy) 1. Increase hierarchical control 2. Improve productivity 3. Experiment with less costly service delivery systems 4. Automate 5. Stockpile and ration resources	1. Renegotiate long term contracts to regain flexibility 2. Install rational choice techniques like zero-base budgeting and evaluation research 3. Mortgage the future by deferring maintenance and downscaling personnel quality 4. Ask employees to make voluntary sacrifices like taking early retirements and deferring raises 5. Improve forecasting capacity to anticipate further cuts 6. Reassign surplus facilities to other users 7. Sell surplus property, lease back when needed 8. Exploit the exploitable

insensitive to the needs, production functions, and contributions of different units. The same percentage cut may call for hardly more than some mild belt tightening in some large unspecialized units but when translated into the elimination of one or two positions in a highly specialized, tightly integrated small unit, it may immobilize that unit.

Criticizing *productivity criteria* is more difficult but nevertheless appropriate, especially when the concept is applied to the practice of cutting low producing units and people based on their *marginal product* per increment of revenue. This method is insensitive to differences in clients served, unit capacity, effort, and need. A more appropriate criterion is one that cuts programs, organization units, and employees so that the *marginal utility* for a decrement of resources is equal across units, individuals, and programs thereby providing for *equal sacrifices* based on the *need* for resources. However, this criterion assumes organizations are fully rational actors, an assumption easily dismissed. More likely, cuts will be distributed by a mix of analysis and political bargaining.

Aggregating incompatible needs and preferences is a political problem and this is why *zero base budgeting* gets such high marks as a method for making decisions about resource allocation under conditions of decline. First, ZBB is future directed; instead of relying on an "inviolate-base-plus-increment" calculus, it allows for the analysis of both existing and proposed new activities. Second, ZBB allows for tradeoffs between programs or units below their present funding levels. Third, ZBB allows a ranking of decision packages by political bargaining and negotiation so that attention is concentrated on those packages or activities most likely to be affected by cuts.[38] As a result, ZBB allows both analysis and politics to enter into cutback decision making and therefore can incorporate an expression of the *intensity of need* for resources by participating managers and clients while also accommodating estimates of how cuts will affect the *activity levels* of their units. Nevertheless, ZBB is not without problems. Its analytic component is likely to be expensive—especially so under conditions of austerity—and to be subject to all the limitations and pitfalls of cost-benefit analysis, while its political component is likely to be costly in political terms as units fight with each other and with central management over rankings, tradeoffs, and the assignment of decrements.[39]

These five decision rules illustrate how strategic choices about cutback management can be made with or without expediency, analysis, courage, consideration of the organization's long-term health, or the effect of cuts on the lives of employees and clients. Unfortunately, for some employees and clients, and the public interest, the choice will usually be made by managers to "go along" quietly with across-the-board cuts and exit as soon as possible. The alternative for those who would prefer more responsible and toughminded decision making *to facilitate long run organiza-*

Box 17.1 Workforce Reduction and Productivity

Marc Holzer

Reductions-in-force or RIFs are separations, downgrades or lateral reassignments of employees. In the public sector they are usually triggered by systemic economic problems (such as recession or depression), major events (such as the end of a war) or demographic changes (such as declining enrollment in public school systems) which then cause personnel reductions to be effected, albeit reluctantly. RIFs may also be triggered by changes in priorities (such as a shift in resources from social programs to defense programs), workload decreases (such as a reduction in paperwork requirements) or reorganization (such as the consolidation of agencies).

To consider RIFs as tools for productivity is to buy into a simplistic view of the public sector and tenuous assumptions about the relationship between productivity and personnel. After all, in the private sector RIFs are typically a late and frustrating response to errors of management, errors which resulted in the not-very-profitable use of expensive human resources. Thus, RIFs may be a result of low productivity rather than a cause for high production. But even if we were to accede to the unreasonable and flawed argument that government's productivity was low in the first place, given legal constraints in the public sector which make performance-based RIFs much harder to achieve than in corporations, RIFs will only result in downturns in productivity in the short run and a narrow, damaging view of productivity in the long run.

For all their faults, RIFs are, however, very real possibilities and policies. If, in contrast to questionable assumptions, their impact on productivity is to be at least ameliorated, then the RIF alternatives suggested in the literature must be examined in detail and adopted with modifications necessary to particular jurisdictions or situations. These alternatives include (1) attrition, early retirement incentives, and hiring freezes; (2) furloughs; (3) outplacement; and (4) improvements in the RIF system.

(Source: Marc Holzer "Workforce Reductions and Productivity," *Public Administration Quarterly* 10 (Spring 1986); 86–98.)

tional survival is to develop in managers and employees strong feelings of organizational loyalty and loyalty to clients, to provide disincentives to easy exit, and to encourage participation so that dissenting views on the location of cuts could emerge from the ranks of middle management, lower level employees, and clients.[40]

Ponderables

The world of the future is uncertain, but scarcity and tradeoffs seem inevitable. Boulding has argued, "in a stationary society roughly half the society will be experiencing decline while the other half will be experiencing growth."[41] If we are entering an era of general slowdown, this means that the balance in the distribution between expanding and contracting sectors, regions, and organizations will be tipped toward decline. It means that we will need a governmental capacity for developing tradeoffs between growing and declining organizations and for intervening in regional and sectorial economies to avoid the potentially harmful effects of radical perturbations from unmanaged decline.

So far we have managed to get along without having to make conscious tradeoffs between sectors and regions. We have met declines on a "crisis-to-crisis" basis through emergency legislation and financial aid. This is a strategy that assumes declines are special cases of temporary disequilibrium, bounded in time and space, that are usually confined to a single organization, community, or region. A broad scale long-run *societal level* decline, however, is a problem of a different magnitude and to resolve it, patchwork solutions will not suffice.

There seem to be two possible directions in which to seek a way out of immobility. First is the authoritarian possibility; what Robert L. Heilbroner has called the rise of "iron governments" with civil liberties diminished and resources allocated throughout society from the central government without appeal.[42] This is a possibility abhorrent to the democratic tradition, but it comprises a possible future—if not for the United States in the near future, at least for some other less affluent nations. So far we have had little experience with cutting back on rights, entitlements, and privileges; but scarcity may dictate "decoupling" dependent and less powerful clients and overcoming resistance through violent autocratic implementation methods.

The other possible future direction involves new images and assumptions about the nature of man, the state and the ecosystem. It involves changes in values away from material consumption, a gradual withdrawal from our fascination with economic growth, and more efficient use of resources—especially raw materials. For this possibility to occur, we will have to have a confrontation with our propensity for wishful thinking that denies that some declines are permanent. Also required is a widespread acceptance of egalitarian norms and of anti-growth and no growth ideologies which are now only nascent, and the development of a political movement to promote their incorporation into policy making.[43] By backing away from our obsession with growth, we will also be able to diminish the "load" placed on central governments and allow for greater decentralization and the devolvement of functions.[44] In this way, we may be able to preserve democratic rights and processes while meeting a future of diminished resources.

However, the preferable future might not be the most probable future. This prospect should trouble us deeply.

Notes

1. The intellectual foundations of this essay are too numerous to list. Three essays in particular sparked my thinking: Herbert Kaufman's *The Limits of Organizational Change* (University, Alabama: The University of Alabama Press, 1971) and *Are Government Organizations Immortal?* (Washington, DC: The Brookings Institution, 1976) and Herbert J. Gans. "Planning for Declining and Poor Cities," *Journal of the American Institute of Planners* (September, 1975), pp. 305–307. The concept of "cutback planning" is introduced in the Gans article. My initial interest in this subject stemmed from my work with a panel of the National Academy of Public Administration on a NASA-sponsored project that produced *Report of the Ad Hoc Panel on Attracting New Staff and Retaining Capability During a Period of Declining Manpower Ceilings.*

2. For an explication of the concept of "organizational slack" see Richard M. Cyert and James G. March, *A Behavioral Theory of the Firm* (Englewood Cliffs, N.J.: Prentice-Hall, 1963), pp. 36–38. They argue that because of market imperfections between payments and demands "there is ordinarily a disparity between the resources available to the organization and the payments required to maintain the coalition. This difference between total resources and total necessary payments is what we have called *organizational slack*. Slack consists in payments to members of the coalition in excess of what is required to maintain the organization. . . . Many forms of slack typically exist: stockholders are paid dividends in excess of those required to keep stockholders (or banks) within the organization; prices are set lower than necessary to maintain adequate income from buyers; wages in excess of those required to maintain labor are paid; executives are provided with services and personal luxuries in excess of those required to keep them: subunits are permitted to grow without real concern for the relation between additional payments and additional revenue; public services are provided in excess of those required. . . . Slack operates to stabilize the system in two ways: (1) by absorbing excess resources, it retards upward adjustment of aspirations during relatively good times; (2) by providing a pool of emergency resources, it permits aspirations to be maintained (and achieved) during relatively bad times."

3. See William G. Scott, "The Management of Decline," *The Conference Board RECORD* (June, 1976), pp. 56–59 and "Organization Theory: A Reassessment," *Academy of Management Journal* (June, 1974) pp. 242–253; also Rufus E. Miles, Jr., *Awakening from the American Dream: The Social and Political Limits to Growth* (New York: Universal Books, 1976).

4. See Daniel M. Fox, *The Discovery of Abundance: Simon N. Patten and the Transformation of Social Theory* (Ithaca, N.Y.: Cornell University Press, 1967).

5. See Andrew Glassberg's contribution to this symposium, "Organizational Responses to Municipal Budget Decreases," and Edward H. Potthoff, Jr., "Pre-planning for Budget Reductions," *Public Management* (March, 1975), pp. 13–14.

6. See Donella H. Meadows, Dennis L. Meadows, Jorgen Randers, and William W. Behrens III, *The Limits to Growth* (New York: Universe Books, 1972); also Robert L. Heilbroner, *An Inquiry into the Human Prospect* (New York: W.W. Norton, 1975) and *Business Civilization in Decline* (New York: W.W. Norton, 1976).

7. See Advisory Commission on Intergovernmental Relations, *City Financial Emergencies: The Intergovernmental Dimension* (Washington, D.C.: U.S. Government Printing Office, 1973).

8. Kenneth E. Boulding, "The Management of Decline," *Change* (June, 1975), pp. 8–9 and 64. For extensive analyses of cutback management in the same field that Boulding addresses, university administration, see: Frank M. Bowen and Lyman A. Glenny, *State Budgeting for Higher Education: State Fiscal Stringency and Public Higher Education* (Berkeley, Calif.: Center for Research and Development in Higher Education, 1976); Adam Yarmolinsky, "Institutional Paralysis." *Special Report on American Higher Education: Toward an Uncertain Future* 2 Vol. *Daedalus* 104 (Winter, 1975). pp. 61–67: Frederick E. Balderston, *Varieties of Financial Crisis,* (Berkeley, Calif.: Ford Foundation, 1972); The Carnegie Foundation for the Advancement of Teaching, *More Than Survival* (San Francisco: Jossey-Bass, 1975); Earl F. Cheit, *The New Depression in Higher Education* (New York: McGraw-Hill, 1975) and *The New Depression in Higher Education—Two Years Later* (Berkeley, Calif.: The Carnegie Commission on Higher Education, 1973); Lyman A. Glenny, "The Illusions of Steady States," *Change* 6 (December/January 1974–75), pp. 24–28; and John D. Millett, "What is Economic Health?" *Change* 8 (September 1976), p. 27.

9. Scott, "Organizational Theory: A Reassessment." pp. 245.

10. Paul R. Schulman, "Nonincremental Policy Making: Notes Toward an Alternative Paradigm." *American Political Science Review* (December, 1975), pp. 1354–1370.

11. See Naomi Caiden and Aaron Wildavsky, *Planning Budgeting in Poor Countries* (New York: John Wiley & Sons, 1974).

12. See James W. Vaupel, "Muddling Through Analytically," in Willis D. Hawley and David Rogers (eds.) *Improving Urban Management* (Beverly Hills, Calif.: Sage Publications, 1976), pp. 124–146.

13. See Richard M. Cyert's contribution to this symposium, "The Management of Universities of Constant or Decreasing Size."

14. See National Academy of Public Administration *Report* and Glassberg, "Organizational Response to Municipal Budget Decreases."

15. See NAPA *Report* and *Cancelled Careers: The Impact of Reduction-In-Force Policies on Middle-Aged Federal Employees,* A Report to the Special Committee on Aging, United States Senate (Washington, D.C.: U.S. Government Printing Office, 1972).

16. See Albert O. Hirschman, *Exit, Voice and Loyalty: Responses to Decline in Firms, Organizations and States* (Cambridge. Mass.: Harvard University Press, 1970); also Mancur Olson, *The Logic of Collective Action* (Cambridge. Mass.: Harvard University Press, 1965).

17. The distinctive features of public organizations are discussed at greater length in Hal G. Rainey, Robert W. Backoff, and Charles H. Levine, "Comparing Public and Private Organization." *Public Administration Review* (March/April, 1976), pp. 223–244.

18. See Robert Behn's contribution to this symposium, "Closing a Government Facility," Barry Mitnick's "Deregulation as a Process of Organizational Reduction." and Herbert A. Simon. Donald W. Smithburg, and Victor A. Thompson, *Public Administration* (New York: Knopf, 1950) for discussions of the survival tactics of threatened bureaucrats.

19. This scheme is similar to those presented in Daniel Katz and Robert L. Kahn, *The Social Psychology of Organizations* (John Wiley & Sons, 1966), p. 166, and Gary L. Wamsley and Mayer N. Zald. *The Political Economy of Public Organizations: A Critique and Approach to the Study of Public Administration* (Lexington, Mass.: D.C. Heath, 1973), p. 20.

20. See Schulman, "Nonincremental Policy Making," and Charles O. Jones, "Speculative Augmentation in Federal Air Pollution Policy-Making," *Journal of Politics* (May, 1974), pp. 438–464.

21. See Robert Behn. "Closing the Massachusetts Public Training Schools," *Policy Sciences* (June, 1976), pp. 151–172: Valarie J. Bradley, "Policy Termination in Mental Health: The Hidden Agenda," *Policy Sciences* (June, 1976), pp. 215–224; and David J. Rothman, "Prisons, Asylums and Other Decaying Institutions," *The Public Interest* (Winter, 1972), pp. 3–17. A similar phenomena is occuring in some of the fields of regulation policy where deregulation is being made more politically feasible by a combination of technical and economic changes. See Mitnick, "Deregulation as a Process of Organizational Reduction."

22. Peter deLeon, "Public Policy Termination: An End and a Beginning," an essay prepared at the request of the Congressional Research Service as background for the Sunset Act of 1977.

23. There are many variations on the theme of Sunset. Gary Brewer's contribution to this symposium, "Termination: Hard Choices-Harder Questions" identifies a number of problems central to most sunset proposals.

24. For two treatments of this phenomena in the literature of organization theory see Barry M. Staw and Eugene Szwajkowski, "The Scarcity-Munificence Component of Organizational Environments and the Commission of Illegal Acts." *Administrative Science Quarterly* (September, 1975), pp. 345–354, and Barry Bozeman and E. Allen Slusher, "The Future of Public Organizations Under Assumptions of Environmental Stress," paper presented at the Annual Meeting of the American Society for Public Administration, Phoenix, Arizona, April 9–12, 1978.

25. See Thomas Muller, *Growing and Declining Urban Areas: A Fiscal Comparison* (Washington. DC: Urban Institute, 1975).

26. See Richard P. Nathan and Charles Adams, "Understanding Central City Hardship," *Political Science Quarterly* (Spring, 1976), pp. 47–62; Terry Nichols Clark, Irene Sharp Rubin, Lynne C. Pettler, and Erwin Zimmerman, "How Many New Yorks? The New York Fiscal Crisis in Comparative Perspective." (Report No. 72 of Comparative Study of Community Decision-Making, University of Chicago, April, 1976); and David T. Stanley, "The Most Troubled Cities," a discussion draft prepared for a meeting of the National Urban Policy Roundtable, Academy for Contemporary Problems. Summer, 1976.

27. See Richard Child Hill, "Fiscal Coliapse and Political Struggle in Decaying Central Cities in the United States," in William K. Tabb and Larry Sawers (eds.) *Marxism and The Metropolis* (New York: Oxford University Press, 1978); and H. Paul Friesema, "Black Control of Central Cities: The Hollow Prize," *Journal of the American Institute of Planners* (March, 1969), pp. 75–79.

28. See David T. Stanley, "The Most Troubled Cities" and "The Survival of Troubled Cities," a paper prepared for delivery at the 1977 Annual Meeting of the American Political Science Association. The Washington Hilton Hotel, Washington DC, September 1–4, 1977; and Martin Shefter, "New York City's Fiscal Crisis:

The Politics of Inflation and Retrenchment," *The Public Interest* (Summer, 1977), pp. 98–127.

29. See Kaufman, *Are Government Organizations Immortal?* and "The Natural History of Human Organizations," *Administration and Society* (August, 1975), pp. 131–148; I have been working on this question for some time in collaboration with Ross Clayton. Our partially completed manuscript is entitled, "Organizational Aging: Progression or Degeneration." See also Edith Tilton Penrose, "Biological Analogies in the Theory of the Firm," *American Economic Review* (December, 1952), pp. 804–819 and Mason Haire, "Biological Models and Empirical Histories of the Growth of Organizations" in Mason Haire (ed.) *Modern Organization Theory* (New York: John Wiley & Sons, 1959), pp. 272–306.

30. For a fuller explanation of "smoothing" or "leveling," see James D. Thompson, *Organizations in Action* (New York: McGraw-Hill, 1967), pp. 19–24.

31. For recent analyses of related phenomena see Joel D. Aberbach and Bert A. Rockman, "Clashing Beliefs Within the Executive Branch: The Nixon Administration Bureaucracy," *American Political Science Review* (June, 1976), pp. 456–468 and Hugh Heclo, *A Government of Strangers: Executive Politics in Washington* (Washington, D.C. The Brookings Institution, 1977).

32. See James G. March and Johan P. Olsen, *Ambiguity and Choice in Organizations* (Bergen, Norway: Universitetsforlaget, 1976); and Michael D. Cohen, James G. March, and Johan P. Olsen, "A Garbage Can Model of Organizational Choice," *Administrative Science Quarterly* (March, 1972), pp. 1–25.

33. See Charles Perrow, *Organizational Analysis: A Sociological View* (Belmont, Calif.: Wadsworth Publishing Company, 1970) and Chris Argyris and Donald A. Schon, *Theory in Practice: Increasing Professional Effectiveness* (San Francisco, Calif.: Jossey-Bass, 1974) for discussions of the distinction between espoused and operative (i.e., "theory-inuse") strategies.

34. For extensive treatments of the tactics of bureaucrats, some of which are listed here, see Frances E. Rourke, *Bureaucracy, Politics, and Public Policy* (second edition, Boston: Little, Brown and Company, 1976); Aaron Wildavsky, *The Politics of the Budgerary Process* (second edition, Boston: Little, Brown and Company, 1974); Eugene Lewis, *American Politics in a Bureaucratic Age* (Cambridge, Mass.: Winthrop Publishers, 1977); and Simon, Smithburg and Thompson, *Public Administration.*

35. See Arthur M. Oken, *Equity and Efficiency: The Big Tradeoff* (Washington, D.C.: The Brookings Institution, 1975).

36. For a discussion of the costs of interactive decision making see Charles R. Adrian and Charles Press, "Decision Costs in Coalition Formation." *American Political Science Review* (June, 1968), pp. 556–563.

37. See Herbert Kaufman, "Emerging Conflicts in the Doctrine of Public Administration," *American Political Science Review* (December, 1956), pp. 1057–1073 and Frederick C. Mosher, *Democracy and the Public Service* (New York: Oxford University Press, 1968). Seniority criteria also have roots in the widespread belief that organizations ought to recognize people who invest heavily in them by protecting long time employees when layoffs become necessary.

38. See Peter A. Pyhrr, "The Zero-Base Approach to Government Budgeting," *Public Administrative Review* (January/February. 1977), pp. 1–8; Graeme M. Taylor, "Introduction to Zero-base Budgeting," *The Bureaucrat* (Spring, 1977), pp. 33–55.

39. See Brewer, "Termination: Hard Choices—Harder Questions": Allen Schick, "Zero-base Budgeting and Sunset: Redundancy or Symbiosis?" *The Bureaucrat* (Spring, 1977), pp. 12–32 and "The Road From ZBB" *Public Administration Review* (March/April, 1978), pp. 177–180; and Aaron Wildavsky, "The Political Economy of Efficiency," *Public Administration Review* (December, 1966), pp. 292–310

40. See Hirschman, *Exit, Voice and Loyalty,* especially Ch. 7, "A Theory of Loyalty," pp. 76–105; Despite the attractiveness of "responsible and toughminded decision making" the constraints on managerial discretion in contraction decisions should not be underestimated. At the local level, for example, managers often have little influence on what federally funded programs will be cut back or terminated. They are often informed after funding cuts have been made in Washington and they are expected to make appropriate adjustments in their local work forces. These downward adjustments often are also outside of a manager's control because in many cities with merit systems, veteran's preference, and strong unions, elaborate rules dictate who will be dismissed and the timing of dismissals.

41. Boulding, "The Management of Decline," p. 8.

42. See Heilbroner, *An Inquiry into the Human Prospect;* also Michael Harrington, *The Twilight of Capitalism* (New York: Simon & Schuster, 1976

43. For a discussion of anti-growth politics see Harvey Molotch, "The City as a Growth Machine," *American Journal of Sociology* (September, 1976), pp. 309–332.

44. Richard Rose has made a penetrating argument about the potential of governments to become "overloaded" in "Comment: What Can Ungovernability Mean?" *Futures* (April 1977), pp. 92–94. For a more detailed presentation, see his "On the Priorities of Government: A Developmental Analysis of Public Policies," *European Journal of Political Research* (September 1976), pp. 247–290. This theme is also developed by Rose in collaboration with B. Guy Peters in *Can Governments Go Bankrupt?* (New York: Basic Books, forthcoming 1978).

18

An Empirical Study of Competition in Municipal Service Delivery

E. S. Savas

The notion that competition in the delivery of a public service is beneficial to the citizen-consumer, while self-evident in a common-sense sort of way, and theoretically sound for all but natural monopolies (i.e., those with ever-declining marginal-cost curves), is sometimes viewed with suspicion or hostility by practicing public servants. Impractical, administratively burdensome, wasteful, impossible to implement—are some of the explanations offered to justify the refusal to consider experimenting with or institutionalizing a competitive environment for the delivery of public services.

Nevertheless, the strong pressure to reduce, or at least stabilize, the cost of government, and to increase the productivity of public services, has brought about renewed interest in alternative means for service delivery, and growing belief that competitive market forces can sometimes be utilized to improve government services.[1,2,3]

It is useful, therefore, to seek out situations where such competition exists, and to examine them empirically. One common service is particularly suitable for such an examination: refuse collection. Every household has to take some action with respect to refuse removal every day, and refuse collection services have the virtue of being relatively easy to measure, quantify, and compare.

"An Empirical Study of Competition in Municipal Service Delivery," *Public Administration Review* 37 (November/December 1977): 717–724.

Residential refuse collection is generally carried out under one of three arrangements which differ greatly with respect to the element of competition: permanent monopoly, periodic competition (which can also be called temporary monopoly), and continuous competition. The first, permanent monopoly, describes the commonplace situation in which a local government agency or bureau provides the collection service. A recent, comprehensive survey[4] found that 37 percent of communities in metropolitan areas have such "municipal collection." (In addition to permanent public monopolies, permanent private monopolies can be said to exist in those relatively rare instances where a long-term, exclusive franchise is awarded to a private firm, or where a franchise is granted in perpetuity, for all practical intents and purposes.)

In periodic competition, or temporary monopoly, an exclusive contract or franchise of limited duration is awarded—on a competitive basis—by the community to a private firm. The aforementioned survey found that 21 percent of communities in metropolitan areas utilize such "contract collection." (In a few cities, it is believed that illegal behavior has converted the system of periodic competition into one of permanent monopolistic service by a private firm.) A large-scale, cross-sectional study[5,6] established that contract collection is less costly to the household than service by municipal agencies—at least in cities larger than 50,000 population. This finding supports the contention of Niskanen,[7] Downs,[8] Tullock,[9] Savas,[10] and others, that government bureaucracies as monopoly providers of public services are inefficient.

In addition to the many cities which employ periodic competition for residential refuse collection, an even larger number (38 percent) permit direct, continuous competition among private firms. In such cities, private firms compete for customers, and often one finds several different firms servicing a single street. (Portland, Oregon, and St. Paul, Minnesota, are two of the largest cities with this arrangement, called "private collection.") The above-cited study found that such competition results in higher costs per household than contract collection (but no higher than municipal collection). There are economies in having one truck collect refuse from every house on the block, and one would expect similar "economies of contiguity" in delivering newspapers, milk, mail, or campaign literature; in reading utility meters; or in mowing the postage-stamp lawns of suburban housing developments.

After examining (1) the relative performance of public and private refuse collection organizations, (2) the relative performance of systems of permanent monopoly (municipal collection), periodic competition (contract collection), and continuous competition (private collection), and (3) the effects of economies of the scale, the author[5],[11] concluded that for large cities the ideal system is to divide the city into districts of greater than 50,000 population and to contract with a different service provider to service each district, selecting the contractor through a process of periodic competition. The reason for using more than one service provider, of course, is to retain a competitive climate. Furthermore, in order to minimize the possibility of collusion—an ever-present fear, perhaps exaggerated, in the minds of local officials—it is desirable to have a public agency service one or more of the districts. By using both public and (several) private service providers, each could be used as a yardstick to measure and evaluate the performance of the others.

This kind of public and private competition has been recommended for various services.[12] However, there are few cities today which consciously foster such direct competition between the public and private sectors.[13] A number of communities can be said to have both municipal and contract collection of residential refuse, but in most of those cases the municipal agency services most of the city, while a private firm is engaged to service a small, recently annexed, outlying area. Because the two service areas generally differ drastically in terms of population density, per capita income (which is related to per capita refuse generation), and distance from the vehicle depot and the disposal site, proper comparisons usually cannot be made.

A city was found, however, in which service conditions are virtually identical and in which neither the public agency nor the private sector predominates, as both sectors service large fractions of the households. As a case study, this relatively unique city enables one to examine the performance of the two sectors and the effects of competition. The remainder of this article is devoted to this examination.

Background

The City of Minneapolis, with a population of 434,000 in 1970, has undergone a significant evolution in its refuse collection services. Prior to 1971, the city had separated collection. That is, the municipal Sanitation Division collected wet garbage (putrescible food wastes) from all households in the city, while the numerous private firms were available for hire by individual households to collect rubbish and trash. Other households, which did not hire private haulers to remove this material, burned it on their own premises. Due to a newly enacted state law banning on-site burning, the city decided to change to combined collection of all refuse.[14]

A major issue arose as to who should provide the service. City employees argued that their department should continue servicing all households, and that the department should be enlarged to handle the increased workload (the amount of waste would prove to be triple the amount previously collected by the city). On the other hand, the private firms argued that they should not be put out of business and the city should contract with them to provide the service. Ultimately, a committee reflecting all viewpoints was established by the city council. Its recommendation, which was accepted, was that the city department be retained at its current size to service part of the city, while a consortium of private firms under contract to the city would service the remainder. (Because of a general desire to keep the local firms in business, it was decided to award the contract by negotiation, rather than by competitive bidding, for under the latter arrangement it was thought possible that one of the nationwide agglomerates might submit a low bid and capture the business. The city charter was interpreted as permitting the award of a contract in this manner in cases involving public health. Whether the public interest was best served by this process can be debated.)

A corporation was formed, Minneapolis Refuse, Inc., comprised of the several dozen private firms that had been engaged in residential refuse collection in the city. Shares in the corporation were awarded in proportion to the number of residential customers each members had previously serviced.

City engineers divided the city into districts that were assigned essentially at random to the city agency and to the corporation. There were no significant differences between the city's territory and the corporation's territory in terms of housing types (multiple dwellings and single-family dwellings), tons per household per year, or the relative abundance of alley or street collection points. The corporation assigned compact, contiguous areas to its member firms, with the number of customers proportional to the number of shares held by the firm. Most of the member firms were small, utilizing only one truck each for residential service.

It should be noted that this arrangement does not correspond to the hypothetical ideal situation described above, in that there are only two service providers (the city and the corporation) instead of the city and several private firms. In principle, this would seem to make it relatively easy for a "live-and-let-live" accommodation to emerge gradually between the two organizations, to the possible detriment of the public interest. However, the fact that the corporation in this case consists of almost 50 private firms, which continue to compete with each other for commercial and industrial refuse-hauling accounts, minimizes this danger.

The five-year contract between the city and the corporation called for the city to pay a certain amount of money to the corporation every month for every household in its territory. The size of the payment was to be renegotiated annually. The contract carefully spelled out the terms of service, including such elements as service frequency, complaint handling procedures, and posting of a performance bond. The refuse collected by the corporation's trucks was to be delivered to selected disposal sites, where the disposal charge was to be paid by the city.

Whereas in some cities "contracting out" results in near-abdication of responsibility by the city, this was not at all the case in Minneapolis. The city devoted considerable attention to monitoring the performance of the corporation and its conformance with the contract. The city calculated its cost of monitoring to be equivalent to three percent of the cost of the contract. It assigned two people to the task of maintaining an accurate inventory of the number of households serviced by the department and by the corporation, it received all inquiries from the citizenry and kept close track of complaints, and its field foremen spot-checked the corporation's trucks to make sure that no refuse from commercial establishments was mixed in with the residential refuse. (Such mixing was prohibited, because the city was obligated to pay the disposal fee, but only for residential refuse. One errant firm was expelled by the corporation for repeated infractions of this rule.)

In retrospect, one might conclude that a better arrangement would have been to let the corporation pay the disposal fee, thereby eliminating any city concern about the admixture of commercial refuse. The contract price would have been greater, but the net cost to the city for both collection and disposal would presumably have been unchanged, and might even have been lower to the extent that more efficient truck routes could have been designed by the corporation, and the resultant savings passed on to the city. On the other hand, the way it was done—segregating the residential refuse—enabled the city to measure the number of tons collected by each of the corporation's trucks, thereby permitting a productivity comparison with the city's work crews, and a comparison of the refuse generation rate per household in both the city-serviced and the corporation-serviced territories, to assure equivalence.[15]

Analysis

The city kept excellent records on the work of both its own department and the corporation, and prepared annual reports[16] which are analyzed here. Four performance measures are calculated below: cost per ton, cost per household, tons collected per truck per shift, and telephone calls per year per household. The first two measure economic performance, the third measures performance in terms of work load, and the last is a (not very satisfactory) measure of quality.

It is important to understand the basis of the measures. For contract collection, the cost per ton was obtained by dividing the total price paid to the corporation by the total number of tons collected by the corporation (all the refuse was weighed at the disposal sites). The price paid does not include the above-cited cost of monitoring the contractor's performance. For municipal collection, the cost figure does not include any departmental overhead costs nor any overhead costs for city staff agencies (personnel, finance, legal, budget, etc.).[17]

Data on the number of households serviced by the city and by the corporation were available, thereby permitting calculation of per-household, service costs. This is a common measure of performance in this industry, although in this case the figure adds little information to the cost-per-ton measure.

Weight records at the disposal points were compiled to produce the information on tons collected per truck per (eight-hour) shift. This refers to the time period for which workers are paid, although the average number of hours actually worked per shift may be less than eight hours if there is an incentive system which permits workers to leave work when they have serviced all the stops on their route for that day (see below).

Residents telephone the city agency, but not necessarily with complaints; many calls were simple inquiries. Although the calls were not analyzed regularly, they were tabulated according to the location of the residence—in a city-serviced area or in a corporation-serviced area. City officials considered the types of calls to be similar in both territories, and estimated that the proportion of calls that were complaints was the same for both areas. Therefore, the number of such calls per year, divided by the number of households served, can be considered a measure of citizen satisfaction. More direct citizen surveys, of the type recommended by Webb and Hatry,[18] could be used and would be better for this purpose. Inadequate though this number may be, it does provide some evidence and it has the undeniable virtue of being available.

The city-provided statistics on the relative performance of municipal and contract collection since the change to combined collection appear in Table 18.1. Several important points are quickly evident:

1. Since the inception of the competitive system, the cost per ton (excluding the city's monitoring costs) has been lower for contract collection than for municipal collection.
2. Until 1975, the cost per household (again excluding the city's monitoring costs) was lower for contract collection than for municipal collection.
3. The city has been closing the gap between contract and municipal costs, as shown in Table 1, by the generally declining ratio of municipal to contract costs.
4. The rate of increase in cost per ton for municipal collection dropped sharply after competition was introduced, as is apparent from the slopes of the "before" and "after" curves in Figure 18.1. (This is not an artifact resulting from different inflation rates in the two periods. As also shown in Figure 18.1, when the cost figures

TABLE 18.1 The Relative Performance of Municipal and Contract Collection Since the Introduction of Competition Between the Public and Private Sectors

	Cost Per Ton[1]			*Annual Cost Per Household*[1]			*Tons Per Shift*		*Inquiries Per Household*	
Year	*City*	*Corp.*	*City/ Corp.*	*City*	*Corp.*	*City/ Corp.*	*City*	*Corp.*	*City*	*Corp.*
1971	$32.08	$28.91	1.110	$35.16	$30.60	1.149	5.74	6.11	N.A.	.0948
1972	32.52	32.36	1.005	33.20	32.04	1.036	5.95	5.96	.0372	.0416
1973	33.75	32.75	1.031	33.52	33.12	1.012	5.95	5.96	.0269	.0349
1974	36.38	35.96	1.012	35.22	34.80	1.012	7.12	6.20	.0263	.0236
1975	37.97	37.44	1.014	37.78	38.23	.998	7.35	6.69	.0226	.0224

N.A. = Not available.

1. Not including the city's cost of monitoring the contractor.

are deflated to constant 1967 dollars,[19] an even more dramatic difference is evidenced in the rate of cost increase before and after competition was initiated: the costs of both municipal and contract collection actually declined.) The large, sudden decline in cost that occurred in 1970–1971 is, of course, due to the change from separated to combined collection, and is not the focus of attention in Figure 18.1. The significant point to note in the figure is the marked difference in the rate of cost increase (whether inflated or deflated) before and after the introduction of competition. One would not expect the change to combined collection by itself to change the slope of the cost curve, because there was no change in technology or collection activity (see below). The only operational change was an increase in the amount of refuse collected at each stop, which led to the increase observed, sharp reduction in the cost per ton. The various factors that produced the steep cost increase before 1971 remained unchanged, except for the introduction of competition.

5. Tons collected per shift by municipal crews has been increasing since competition was introduced, while the corresponding figure for contract collection has been relatively static. (One cannot make too much of the fact that city crews appear to have surpassed contract crews in productivity, according to this measure: 7.35 tons vs. 6.69 tons per crew shift in 1975. City crews consist of three workers, whereas many of the corporation's trucks have one-man crews.)
6. Citizens are about equally satisfied with municipal and contract collection, and the number of telephone complaints has been declining for both.

FIGURE 18.1 Cost Per Ton for Collection by the City, Before and After Introduction of New, Competitive System

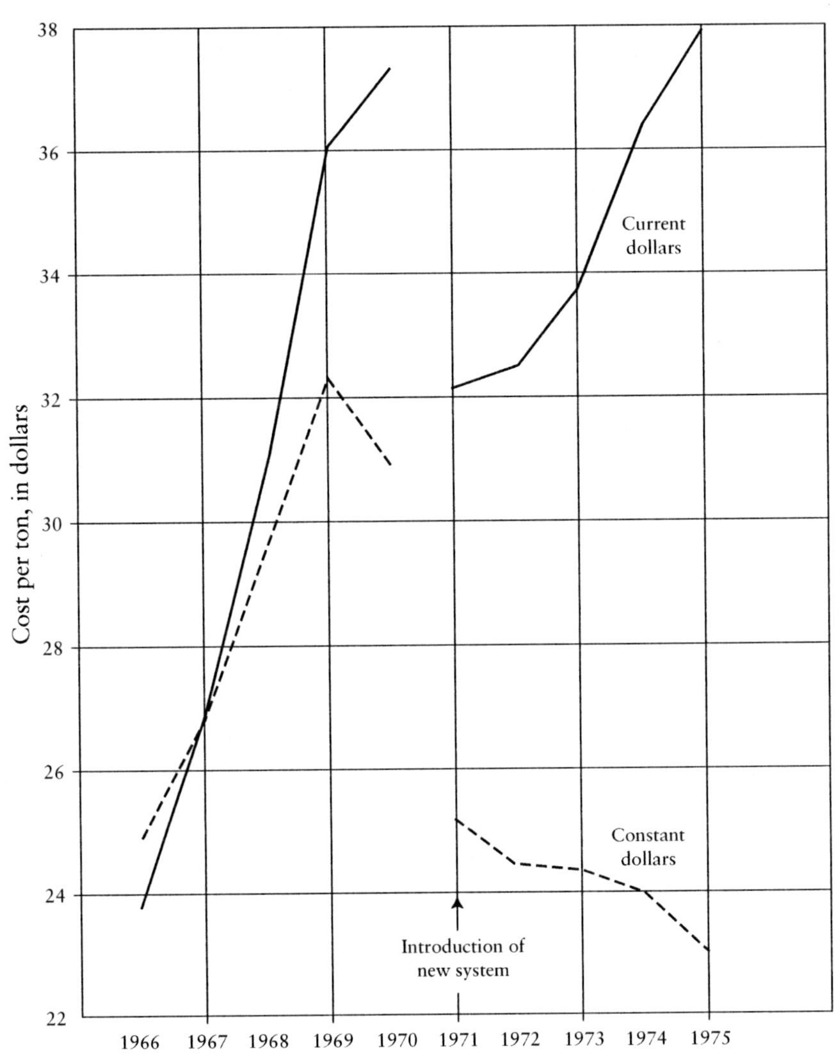

Discussion

It is clear from the foregoing that the productivity of the city agency, whether measured in cost per ton, cost per household, or tons per shift, has been increasing since the competitive system was introduced in 1971, and the perceived quality of service also appears to be improving. Although these data do not prove causality, that is, they do not prove that competition was the cause of the improvement, additional operational information provides further support for the theory that:

> competition, the presence of a yardstick systematically used for comparison of alternative delivery systems, was primarily responsible for the large observed increase in productivity.

It should be noted, first of all, that there was no change in the technology of refuse collection between 1971 and 1975; rear-loading compactor trucks were used throughout the period, and the frequency of collection, the point of collection, the crew size, and the location of disposal sites remained unchanged.

Nor could the city agency's improvement during the period of head-to-head competition, 1971–75, reasonably be attributed to the lingering effect of the prior change from separate to combined collection, in the sense of fine-tuning the routes and gradually reaping the full benefits from that change. A transition of that magnitude, like a change in frequency or a change in collection location, is generally fully "broken in" within a few months or a year at most.

However, whereas the city used 34 three-man crews each working day in 1971, it gradually reduced the number to 27 crews in 1975, although the number of households serviced increased. What happened, in essence, was that the superior productivity and lower cost of contract collection caused the city to emulate the private firms by introducing an incentive system in which workers could leave the job after completing their routes. They would be paid for eight hours of work even though they had not worked a full eight hours.

Upon introducing this incentive system in 1974, it quickly became evident that the assigned work load had been very light, and that the routes should be redesigned and lengthened. In the face of the comparative performance data, the union representing the workers agreed to these productivity improvements. In 1976, even with the number of crews reduced to 27, much spare time was still available; nevertheless, the unwritten understanding with the union was that the size of the work force will not be reduced further, according to a city official. Instead, more work will be provided to occupy fully the under-utilized crews. The plan calls for increasing the city department's share of the work to 50 percent of the households, from 39.5 percent in 1974. City officials note that this change could have been made in 1976, but to avoid undue hardship to the private firms, they decided to make the change gradually.

Table 18.2 presents additional operational measures which demonstrate the increased productivity realized to date, and the projected improvement that is considered realizable (i.e., using 27 crews to service half the house-

TABLE 18.2 Changes in Municipal Productivity Since the Introduction of Public Versus Private Competition

Year	Direct Labor Hours Per Household Per Year	Tons Per Man-hour	Households Serviced Per Paid Shift (by 3-man crew)
A. Productivity Data			
1971	4.86	.226	257
1972	4.26	.243	293
1973	4.20	.240	297
1974	3.52	.284	355
1975	3.22	.309	388
Projected	2.67	.379	467
B. Productivity Increase			
1971–1975	35%	37%	51%
1971–Projected	45%	68%	82%

holds). Direct labor hours per household per year have declined by 35 percent. Tons collected per man-hour have increased 37 percent. The number of households serviced per shift has increased by 51 percent. Projected improvements totalling 45, 68, and 82 percent respectively since competition was introduced are within the city's grasp.

Competition works both ways, of course. The corporation, acutely conscious of its work performance relative to that of the city agency, has added more services at no extra cost (e.g., free pickup of bulky objects), and agreed to a four percent price reduction in 1975. As a further indication of the strong competitive feelings that exist, the comparative performance data that are issued annually by the city are awaited expectantly and are pounced upon immediately—with glee by the city workers when their cost per household finally dropped below the contract price, and with skepticism by the corporation. The latter scrutinize the data and have questioned the omission of certain municipal costs and the generous attribution of some of the city's operating costs to the cost of monitoring the corporation's performance.

Conclusion

Regardless of the accuracy of these criticisms, it seems clear that a healthy competitive climate exists, a climate which tends to produce explicit and open reporting, increased productivity, and more cost-effective service delivery for the citizens. The city administration, and the public works director in particular, have assiduously cultivated a constructively competitive environment and have exploited the powerful tool of competition to the advantage of the citizens, with due regard to the welfare of the city's workers and its local business firms.

The City of Minneapolis eschews the role of a model, and its officials make no effort to proselytize or to claim universal applicability of their approach. Unique circumstances in that city made it possible to initiate its system of competition with *relatively* little effort. After all, the work was split roughly in half between the public and private sectors before the change, and it remained that way after the change. That is, before the change, the city collected garbage while the private sector collected trash. After the change, the city collected combined refuse from roughly half the people, while the private firm collected from the other half. Therefore, no major economic loss was levied on either sector. In other cities, however, one might expect substantially more difficulty in attempting to reduce by half the role of a monopolist, whether public or private.

In summary, Minneapolis provides pragmatic evidence that the delivery of a public service can be improved by introducing competition. The empirical findings reported here should encourage officials in local governments elsewhere to adopt competition as a conscious management policy and as a strategic weapon with which to improve their public services.

Notes

1. Committee for Economic Development, *Improving Productivity in State and Local Government* (New York: CED, 1976).

2. Charles McC. Mathias Jr., "Privatization." *Congressional Record,* Vol. 121, No. 158, October 19, 1975.

3. "City Hall Shuffle," *The New York Times.* December 30, 1975, editorial.

4. E.S. Savas and C. Niemczewski, "Who Collects Solid Waste?" *1976 Municipal Year Book,* International City Management Association (Washington, D.C.; ICMA, 1976), pp. 167–172.

5. E.S. Savas, "Policy Analysis for Local Government: The Private Delivery of a Public Service," *Policy Analysis* (1976).

6. Barbara J. Stevens, "Scale, Market Structure, and the Cost of Refuse Collection," Working Paper series, Graduate School of Business, Columbia University, 1976.

7. William A. Niskanen, Jr., *Bureaucracy and Representative Government* (Chicago, IIL: Aldine-Atherton, Inc., 1971).

8. Anthony Downs, "Why the Government Budget is Too Small in A Democracy," in E.S. Phelps, (ed.), *Private Wants and Public Needs* (New York: W.W. Norton and Company, Inc., 1965).

9. Gordon Tullock, *The Polities of Bureaucracy* (Washington, D.C.: Public Affairs Press, 1965).

10. E.S. Savas, "Municipal Monopoly," *Harper's Magazine* (December 1971), pp. 55–60.

11. E.S. Savas, "Evaluating the Organization of Service Delivery: Solid Waste Collection and Disposal," *Waste Age* (December 1975).

12. E.S. Savas, "Municipal Monopolies Versus Competition in Delivering Urban Service," in W.D.Hawley and D. Rogers (eds.), *Improving the Quality of Urban Management* (Beverly Hills, Calif.: Sage Publications, 1974).

13. In 1977 Oklahoma City was divided into five districts for residential refuse collection. After competitive bidding, two private firms were awarded contracts to service one district each, and the city agency continued to serve the other three districts

14. For a description of the background of the Minneapolis system and an assessment of its operations in late 1971, see "Case Study of the Municipal Solid Waste Management System of Minneapolis," Applied Management Sciences, prepared for the Office of Solid Waste Management Program, Environmental Protection Agency, October 19, 1973.

15. For a more detailed description of the operating practices and procedures, see *Solid Wastes Management,* Vol. 17, No. 10 (October 1974), pp. 12–14, 58, 60, 84, 86.

16. Annual Reports, Sanitation Division, Department of Public Works, Minneapolis, Minnesota, 1971, 1972, 1973, 1974, 1975.

17. These overhead costs were systematically excluded from the cost figures in the annual reports. While this affects the absolute level of reported expenditures, it does not affect the validity of the comparative analysis presented below. (If these costs are included in the cost of municipal collection, and if the uniform cost accounting scheme used for analyzing other cities is employed,[3] and if the city's three percent cost of monitoring the contract is added to the cost of contract collection, the annual per household costs of municipal and contract collection in 1975 are $42.02 and $39.38 respectively. These can be compared to figures in Table 18.1.

18. K. Webb and H.P. Hatry, *Obtaining Citizen Feedback: The Application of Citizen Surveys to Local Governments* (Washington, D.C.: Urban Institute, 1973).

19. The deflator used was the Consumer Price Index for Services, published in the *Monthly Labor Review.* It is very similar to the Average Weekly Earnings for Transportation, Communication, Electric, Gas, etc., published in the *Survey of Current Business.*

Part Three

Performance Measurement

Measurement is basic to improving organizational performance and assists in providing accountability. Stanley (1964) discusses the need for measurement in the public sector. He notes that many assessments of service performance are impressionistic, based on citizen complaints or managerial claims of excellence. In addition, public managers sometimes assume that their services are good because they have ensured that services conform to standards. But how good are they really? Stanley calls for the use of program evaluation and standards for the assessment of people.

However, performance measurement is problematic. Wildavsky (1972) asks "Why don't organizations evaluate their own activities?" He sees evaluation as primarily an organizational rather than a technical problem. Evaluation is not undertaken because it conflicts with the needs of the organization and the people within it. Organizations may learn through evaluation that they lack the authority or resources to address the problems that merit improvement. Evaluators also face the problem of being bearers of bad news. According to Wildavsky, evaluation requires a degree of trust among many different stakeholders if it is to result in any real change. Similarly, Havens (1981) believes that the process of evaluation should be informed by the concerns of program management in order to increase the relevance of evaluation: "a lot of evaluation effort is wasted answering questions which have no bearing on decisions." Evaluators need to work with program stakeholders to ensure that recommendations are relevant to program concerns.

Hatry (1980) describes principles and techniques of performance measurement, which grew out of the desire to make program evaluation more relevant and timely for program management. He discusses the measurement of resources, processes, outputs, (i.e., immediate consequences of activities) and outcomes (goals). He advocates the use of workload ratios, resource-utilization measures and productivity indices to assess program performance on an on-going basis. He also discusses how this approach requires the use of government records, trained observers, citizen and client surveys, and other data collection and analysis activities. The box by Epstein (1991) raises some additional concerns relating to performance measurement in human services.

Grizzle (1982) suggests that managers should consult many stakeholders before developing performance measures; hold programs accountable for performance, resolve goal conflicts, and eliminate distortions due to measurement itself. In addition, managers need to consider the high costs of data collection, as well as the difficulties of measuring impacts or outcomes. Indeed, the latter has proven to be a formidable challenge. Although some advocates suggest that such measures can be used to rationalize the budget process, Joyce (1993) suggest that while these data can inform the political decision-making process, they are unlikely to drive it.

Finally, Poister (1982) discusses an effort to introduce performance measurement in the Pennsylvania Department of Transportation. His case study shows how agencies can develop new data collection strategies and use these for tracking performance and increasing accountability to stakeholders.

19

Excellence in Public Service—How Do You Really Know?

David T. Stanley

An impressive number of words have been produced on the topic of excellence in the public service. Many of these words are wise, and some of them are inspired, but there is a near-fatal shortcoming that has run through all of them: *we don't really know.* We don't know enough about the quality of the people we already have in the public service, and, not knowing, we are guessing at what ought to be done about it.

This shortcoming extends into most management and personnel studies. In the course of the Brookings analysis of New York City government's problems in getting and keeping professional, technical, and managerial personnel, we found few absolute measures and few relative measures of the quality of such employees.[1] The Municipal Manpower Commission report, which enumerates an impressive array of problems in getting excellent manpower for local governments in the United States, faced the same problem. Indeed, the Commission had to face the matter presumptively and speculatively:

> "In summary, such evidences *as there are* of the quality of today's APT [administrative, professional, technical] personnel in local governments—evidences of their age, training, and experience; observation of their vitality and performance; and the judgment of their peers in the public service—raise substantial doubts as to whether this body of men and women is equal to the changing role of local governments and the new large and challenging responsibilities that are to be thrust upon them.[2] (emphasis supplied)

"Excellence in Public Service—How Do You Really Know?" *Public Administration Review* 24 (1964): 170–174.

In these and other studies systems and concepts are analyzed, and changes are recommended in institutions and procedures. It is rare, however, that we get to the bare question of quality of people and the quality of their performance. We tend to deal with a tissue of folklore, assertions, and surface logic. Lacking more real evidence, it is hard to do otherwise.

In trying to judge quality in the public service, we can identify three levels of measurement of excellence: first, one we shall call *impressionistic;* second, one that might be called *presumptive;* and the third, *proven.* They are presented in ascending order of validity.

Impressionistic

This is the level at which the quality of public employees is most commonly and most noisily judged. It consists of people's *impressions* of the quality of public service. On the positive side it may lead to statements that a public employee or a group of such employees are truly excellent. Why? Because a citizen has been efficiently treated by someone giving information about taxation; because a bookkeeper in a government agency has completed 50 years of service without ever taking an hour of sick leave or a dollar from the petty cash drawer; or because a public employee has invented something or saved somebody's life or written an excellent publication.

On the negative side, where the press, legislative investigating committees, antagonistic politicians, and perhaps the public generally are busiest, impressions of the quality of the public service consists of magnification or perhaps simply factual recording of individual errors and failures. An ambulance fails to answer a call promptly, a revenue official takes public money to the dog track, a bureau chief makes a terrible speech, or the Dallas police fail to safeguard a prisoner.

On a broader scale we can make systematic surveys of what people think of the excellence of the public service. This was done in the recent book, *The Image of the Federal Service,* by Kilpatrick, Cummings, and Jennings of the Brookings Institution.[3] Among many other things it reports the judgments of samples of the population about the abilities of federal employees.

Presumptive

We proceed upward now to the next level at which the excellence of the public service is measured, that which *presumes* that the public service is good because we have made certain arrangements to assure its being good. Or, on the contrary, that the quality of the public service is poor because we have failed to make such arrangements. Examples: the public service is good because we have a merit system, or because we pay salaries which are nearly competitive with those of private industry, or because we have a procedure to dismiss the incompetent, or because we have a training program, or because we give medals to outstanding public servants. All these are good and positive provisions and it is easy to believe that the public service is better with them than without them.

The logical inadequacy of this approach will be pretty obvious. A merit system will not assure top quality personnel in and of itself. The achievements of a training program depend on who is trained and for what and how well. The person who receives the superior service medal may simply be the best of a bad lot.

It is this presumptive level of evaluation which runs through personnel studies like those previously mentioned and which fills a fair part of the writings on this topic sponsored by the American Society for Public Administration and the American Academy of Political and Social Science.

Proven

We come now to the level of investigation of excellence which is at the top and which we may call the *proven* level. Proving or disproving excellence in the public service is difficult and indeed distasteful. If you really mean it and really plan to go ahead with it many people will not want it to be done. It may also involve the establishment of systems of fact-finding or evaluation which will replace or conflict with existing systems and will therefore encounter that well-known impediment to the improvement of public administration: resistance to change.

Now how do we go about it? Let us consider two aspects of this: first, proving how good a government *program* is and second, how good government *people* are.

Program Evaluation

The evaluation of how good a government program is as a means of judging excellence in the public service is risky and returns to the area of presumptive judgments. An excellent government program can have a few poor people in it; a beautiful barn may house some terrible turkeys. Nevertheless, one may with reasonable validity presume that an excellent program is at least partly due to excellent management and excellent individual performance. How then can we evaluate government's programs?

Measured Progress Against Stated Goals. This is familiar to any student of government. Any agency that is well managed will have clearly and specifically identified its goals, have chartered a course for reaching them, and have provided means of measurement for judging their attainment. The goal may be the laying of so many cubic yards of concrete, or a reduction in the venereal disease rate or an increase in the number of home mortgage policies handled, or whatever. It is essential that the goals be set by experts and that the means of measurement and progress be pretested and carefully validated and scrupulously observed.

The measurements, at least the statistical ones, can be quite convincing. A penal institution may be judged in part, for example, by the number of escapes; public health programs may be judged by trends in morbidity and mortality; credit programs can be judged by percentages of good loans and bad loans; rehabilitation programs may be judged by percentage of cases rehabilitated.

Accreditation. This is a familiar method of evaluation used for schools, colleges, and hospitals. If such an organization is officially accredited we know that it has attained at least a certain standard. The method is obviously deficient since many of us have had unfortunate educational experiences in accredited institutions and perhaps even unfortunate therapeutic experiences in accredited hospitals.

Productivity Analyses. This technique of evaluation is belatedly coming into recognition and use in the literature. Productivity analysis requires sophisticated and rigorous work by economists and statisticians to determine measures of productivity for a government agency. The federal Bureau of the Budget, as you may know, has been experimentally working on this with four or five federal agencies.[4] By productivity measurement one arrives at some interesting clues to possible improvement and some overall judgments. Of course it will not reveal the many individual successes and failures within the agency program which either contribute to or detract from its overall productivity and which may be matters of proper concern to anyone studying the excellence of the public service.

Ad Hoc Professional Evaluation. This method is often used, but it would benefit from more incisiveness, objectivity, and courage. It involves the use of expert commissions of inquiry to evaluate the quality of a government program. Many agencies have been "worked over" by such groups, some several times. The Social Security Administration has been reviewed by insurance experts; our aerial defense is checked by outside mathematicians; New York City's health laboratories are inspected by experts in the life sciences. Such studies too often do not make frank statements about quality of personnel. They are more likely to feel such professional kinship with the agency officials as to pull their punches on criticisms which may sound personal. They may also be reluctant to praise as warmly as they would like to for fear that this may blunt the effect of corrective recommendations.

Management Appraisal. This is a familiar technique, much used. Government agencies can be (and have been) systematically appraised on their program effectiveness by representatives of a higher echelon of management or by an independent organization. This concept includes the idea of the inspector general in the military services and the type of appraisal given (or that ought to be given) to government agencies by investigators of the United States General Accounting Office. There is a danger that such appraisals will be too often hasty and too often done by people who may have generalized investigative skills but who lack background in the program under study. Nevertheless they can provide impressive evidence of program quality.

Cost Reductions. A government agency may also be judged by the economy with which it does its work. This may be assessed partly by its ability to maintain present staffing levels or even to reduce them in the face of increasing workloads or it may be judged by its ability to turn money back to the treasury at the end of the fiscal year. The validity of such judgments tends to be a function of some of the assumptions made at the start. An overgenerous beginning may make a government agency look better than it really is.

Technological Progress. Government programs may be judged also by the extent to which they have adapted to their own use the latest techniques of management and operation such as automatic data processing, or operations research. Also, by the extent to which they are using the most advanced knowledge in science, economics, medicine or whatever their field is.

Management Control and Coordination. Finally a government program may be judged by its own provisions for planning, supervision, control, coordination, and program replanning. This is based on the thought that the bureaucrat who is too busy cutting down a tree to sharpen his axe has muscles where his brains ought to be.

All the types of program judgments here covered must be tempered both with mercy and with care. Some governments are more favorably situated as to finances, geography and political climate than others, and proper allowance must be made for these factors. Perhaps these programs should be evaluated against those of others so situated. The government programs of the state of Mississippi, for example, could not fairly be set alongside of those of the state of New York or the state of California, but there is basis for comparing them with those of Alabama, Georgia, and Arkansas.

Evaluation of People

We come now to proven evaluations of the public servants themselves. One can use several kinds of measures based largely on accepted criteria in the professions and occupations concerned and upon criteria which would be used by any thoughtful, careful, aggressive employer. These measures can be listed as follows:

Academic Degrees. The possession of a master's degree in social work presumes (there is that word again) a degree of understanding and general competence not present in those who lack it. A college graduate doing employer relations work for a department of labor may well know more than a high school graduate doing the same work.

Professional Registration or Certification. A P.E. engineer registration, or a CPA rating, or board certification in a field of medicine all are clear evidence of professional attainment. One may argue of course that many an engineer without his "PE" is better than many an engineer who has one. Nevertheless it is one indication. If the bridge and sewer department of city A has 70 percent engineers with PE licenses and that of city B has 10 percent, it may be appropriate to judge that the quality of the former is superior and for the city management of the latter to concern themselves with possible remedies. Again, there are many other factors to be taken into consideration.

Actual Performance. This may be a bold suggestion. Experts may be called in to watch the public servant performing his duties and to reach judgments accordingly. Such appraisal must of course be based upon preplanned, validated, accepted goals, the recording of facts and judgments about performance must be based on clearly understood criteria, and these data must be recorded objectively. Such evaluation must particularly provide for the evidence of creativity or of analytical skill or of skill at synthesis.

Evidence of Growth and Development. One important factor that one gathers from reading the literature on excellence and on human potentiality is that the outstanding people are the people who never stop growing, developing, advancing. This leads one to suggest that public employees may be judged by evidence of growth and progress. Do they add to their skills? Do they belong to professional societies? Do they write for publication? How do they spend their spare time? Do they take courses or do they engage in civic activity? It may not be fair to judge people this way, for a man with eight young children has no money or time for self-fulfillment—at least in other ways. This is true and perhaps it *isn't* fair. Still if a man goes to his job day after day and does the same work without giving any evidence of efforts to do it better or to develop himself into a more effective person, it may be concluded that he is a less excellent public employee than his counterpart who does those things. And in making these judgments we have to have tangible, valid evidence.

Ability to Use and Develop Others. This is a key factor in the excellence of any public official. How many people of outstanding ability has he recruited or has he developed? This, too, can be reported and judged.

The Sum of These Parts

Whoever wants to assess the quality of the public service—the citizen, the advisory commission, the investigative panel, the legislator, the professor—has all these proofs and clues available. Some will have been used already; some, not. Some will have been used for another purpose and will need to be interpreted. Some will need to be weighted heavily; others, lightly. It all depends on the situation to be evaluated.

What To Do About It?

Now that we have considered some tangible though difficult means of determining how excellent our public servants are, we consider what to do about it. It most cases the remedy will be suggested by the problem. If the agency doesn't have program goals, they must be set. If it has good goals, and they are being ignored, something can be done about it. If the hospital isn't accredited, it's generally obvious why. If the books are being kept with quill pens, get a systems analyst. If costs must be cut 10%, there are ways of doing it that are rarely apparent to the people in the agency.

As to people—qualified, excellent people—this part of the story has been told frequently, but it can be summed up in a few sentences:

- We must recruit for the public service on nearly equal terms. This means challenging work, comparable pay, rapid decisions on selections, adequate fringe benefits, and clear prospects of personal training and development.
- Training programs must be so fully developed and so generously financed that there is no question but that the public employee is being given the most advanced techniques, skills, and knowledges related to his job.
- Selection, particularly selection for promotion, must be severely competitive and must use *valid* measures of comparison.
- Discharge, reassignment or out-placement of those who do not measure up to their responsibility must be done rigorously.
- Along with all this we must do everything possible to improve the attractiveness of the public service, and the steps listed will help in doing that.
- Finally, publicity is essential—essential to participation by the citizen in improving the quality of his government. He must

> know about and feel a share in any activity which contributes to the quality of the service he is getting.

The most advanced and most objective techniques possible should be used to determine how good our public servants actually are. If we do not use them we shall continue to be handicapped by the combination of ill-developed assertions and impressions that have heretofore clouded our efforts to identify and do something about genuine excellence in the public service.

Notes

1. David T. Stanley et al., *Professional Personnel for the City of New York* (Brookings Institution, 1963).
2. Municipal Manpower Commission, *Governmental Manpower for Tomorrow's Cities* (McGraw-Hill, 1962), p. 88.
3. Franklin C. Kilpatrick, Milton C. Cummings. Jr., and M. Kent Jennings, *The Image of the Federal Service* (Brookings Institution, 1964).
4. John W. Kendrick. "Exploring Productivity Measurement in Government." 23 *Public Administration Review* 59–66 (June, 1963).

20

The Self-Evaluating Organization

Aaron Wildavsky

Why don't organizations evaluate their own activities? Why do they not appear to manifest rudimentary self-awareness? How long can people work in organizations without discovering their objectives or determining the extent to which they have been carried out? I started out thinking it was bad for organizations not to evaluate, and I ended up wondering why they ever do it. Evaluation and organization, it turns out, are to some extent contradictory terms. Failing to understand that evaluation is sometimes incompatible with organization, we are tempted to believe in absurdities much in the manner of mindless bureaucrats who never wonder whether they are doing useful work. If we asked more intelligent questions instead, we would neither look so foolish nor be so surprised.

Who will evaluate and who will administer? How will power be divided among these functionaries? Which ones will bear the costs of change? Can evaluators create sufficient stability to carry on their own work in the midst of a turbulent environment? Can authority be allocated to evaluators and blame apportioned among administrators? How to convince administrators to collect information that might help others but can only harm them? How can support be obtained on behalf of recommendations that anger sponsors? Would the political problem be solved by creating a special organization—Evaluation Incorporated—devoted wholly to performing the analytic function? Could it obtain necessary support without abandoning its analytic mission? Can knowledge and power be joined?

"The Self-Evaluating Organization," *Public Administration Review* 32 (September/October, 1972): 509–520.

Evaluation

The ideal organization would be self-evaluating. It would continuously monitor its own activities so as to determine whether it was meeting its goals or even whether these goals should continue to prevail. When evaluation suggested that a change in goals or programs to achieve them was desirable, these proposals would be taken seriously by top decision makers. They would institute the necessary changes; they would have no vested interest in continuation of current activities. Instead they would steadily pursue new alternatives to better serve the latest desired outcomes.

The ideal member of the self-evaluating organization is best conceived as a person committed to certain modes of problem solving. He believes in clarifying goals, relating them to different mechanisms of achievement, creating models (sometimes quantitative) of the relationships between inputs and outputs, seeking the best available combination. His concern is not that the organization should survive or that any specific objective be enthroned or that any particular clientele be served. Evaluative man cares that interesting problems are selected and that maximum intelligence be applied toward their solution.

To evaluative man the organization doesn't matter unless it meets social needs. Procedures don't matter unless they facilitate the accomplishment of objectives encompassing these needs. Efficiency is beside the point if the objective being achieved at lowest cost is inappropriate. Getting political support doesn't mean that the programs devised to fulfill objectives are good: it just means they had more votes than the others. Both objectives and resources, says evaluative man, must be continuously modified to achieve the optimal response to social need.

Evaluation should not only lead to the discovery of better policy programs to accomplish existing objectives but to alteration of the objectives themselves. Analysis of the effectiveness of existing policies leads to consideration of alternatives that juxtapose means and ends embodied in alternative policies. The objectives as well as the means for attaining them may be deemed inappropriate. But men who have become socialized to accept certain objectives may be reluctant to change. Resistance to innovation then takes the form of preserving social objectives. The difficulties are magnified once we realize that objectives may be attached to the clientele—the poor, outdoor men, lumbermen—with whom organizational members identify. The objectives of the organization may have attracted them precisely because they see it as a means of service to people they value. They may view changes in objectives, therefore, as proposals for "selling out" the clients they wish to serve. In their eyes evaluation becomes an enemy of the people.

Evaluative man must learn to live with contradictions. He must reduce his commitments to the organizations in which he works, the programs he carries out, and the clientele he serves. Evaluators must become agents of change acting in favor of programs as yet unborn and clienteles that are unknown. Prepared to impose change on others, evaluators must have sufficient stability to carry out their own work. They must maintain their own organization while simultaneously preparing to abandon it. They must obtain the support of existing bureaucracies while pursuing antibureaucratic policies. They must combine political feasibility with analytical purity. Only a brave man would predict that these combinations of qualities can be found in one and the same person and organization.

Evaluation and organization may be contradictory terms. Organizational structure implies stability while the process of evaluation suggests change. Organization generates commitment while evaluation inculcates skepticism. Evaluation speaks to the relationship between action and objectives while organization relates its activities to programs and clientele. No one can say for certain that self-evaluating organizations can exist, let alone become the prevailing form of administration. We can learn a good deal about the production and use of evaluation in government, nonetheless, by considering the requirements of obtaining so extraordinary a state of affairs—a self-evaluating organization.

The Policy-Administration Dichotomy Revisited

Organization requires the division of labor. Not everyone can do everything. Who, then, will carry out the evaluative activity and who will administer the programs for which the organization is responsible?

Practically every organization has a program staff, by whatever name called, that advises top officials about policy problems. They are small in numbers and conduct whatever formal evaluation goes on in the organization. They may exert considerable power in the organization through their persuasiveness and access to the top men, or they may be merely a benign growth that can be seen but has little effect on the body of the organization. Insofar as one is interested in furthering analytical activities, one must be concerned with strengthening them in regard to other elements. The idea of the self-evaluating organization, however, must mean more than this: a few men trying to force evaluation on an organization hundreds or thousands of times larger than they are. The spirit of the self-evaluating organization suggests that, in some meaningful way, the entire organization is infused with the evaluative ethic.

Immediately we are faced with the chain of command. How far down must the spirit of evaluation go in order to ensure the responsiveness of the organization as a whole? If all personnel are involved there would appear to be insuperable difficulties in finding messengers, mail clerks, and secretaries to meet the criteria. If we move up one step to those who deal with the public and carry out the more complex kind of activity, the numbers involved may still be staggering. These tens of thousands of people certainly do not have the qualifications necessary to conduct evaluative activities, and it would be idle to pretend that they would. The forest ranger and the national park officer may be splendid people, but they are not trained in evaluation and they are not likely to be. Yet evaluational activity appropriate to each level must be found if evaluation is to permeate the organization.

There has long been talk in the management circles of combining accountability with decentralization. Organizational subunits are given autonomy within circumscribed limits for which they are held strictly accountable to their hierarchical superiors. Central power is masked but it is still there. Dividing the task so that each subunit has genuine autonomy would mean giving them a share in central decisions affecting the entire organization. Decentralization is known to exist only to the extent that field units follow inconsistent and contradictory policies. One can expect the usual headquarters–field rivalries to develop—the one stressing appreciation of local problems and interests, the other fearing dissolution as the mere sum of its clashing units. Presumably the tension will be manifested in terms of rival analyses. The center should win out because of its greater expertise, but the local units will always be the specialists on their own problems. They will have to be put in their place. We are back, it seems, to hierarchy. How can the center get what it wants out of the periphery without over-formalizing their relationship?

One model, the internalized gyroscope, is recorded in Herbert Kaufman's classic on *The Forest Ranger*. By recruitment and training, the forest rangers are socialized into central values that they carry with them wherever they go and apply to specific circumstances. Central control is achieved without apparent effort or innumerable detailed instructions, because the rangers have internalized the major premises from which appropriate actions may generally be deduced. The problem of the self-evaluating organization is more difficult because it demands problem solving divorced from commitments to specific policies and organizational structures. The level of skill required is considerably higher and the locus of identification much more diffuse. The Israeli Army has had considerable success in inculcating problem-solving skills (rather than carrying out predetermined instructions) among its officers.[1] But their organizational identification is far more intense than can be expected elsewhere.

Suppose that most organizational personnel are too unskilled to permit them to engage in evaluation. Suppose it is too costly to move around hundreds of thousands of government officials who carry out most of the work of government. The next alternative is to make the entire central administration into an evaluative unit that directs the self-evaluating organization. Several real-world models are available. What used to be called the administration class in Great Britain illustrates one type of central direction. They move frequently among the great departments and seek (with the political ministers involved) to direct the activities of the vast bureaucracy around them. They are chosen for qualities of intellect that enable them to understand policy and for qualities of behavior that enable them to get along with their fellows. At the apex stands the Treasury, an organization with few operating commitments, whose task it is to monitor the activities of the bureaucracy and to introduce changes when necessary. Economic policy, which is the special preserve of the Treasury, is supposed to undergo rapid movement, and its personnel are used to changing tasks and objectives at short notice. Though divorced in a way from the organizations in which they share responsibility with the political ministers, top civil servants are also part of them by virtue of their direct administrative concerns. Complaints are increasingly heard that these men are too conservative in defense of departmental interests, too preoccupied with immediate matters, or too bound by organizational tradition to conduct serious evaluation. Hence, the Fulton Report claimed, they adapt too slowly, if at all, to changing circumstances. Tentative steps have been taken, therefore, to establish a Central Policy Review Staff to do policy analysis for the cabinet and to otherwise encourage evaluative activity.

Germany and Sweden have proceeded considerably further in the same direction. Departments in Sweden are relatively small groups of men concerned with policy questions, while administration is delegated to large public corporations set up for the purpose.[2] The state governments in Germany (the *Lander*) do over 90 percent of the administrative work, with the central government departments presumably engaged with larger questions of policy. The student of public administration in America will at once realize where he is at. The policy-administration dichotomy, so beloved of early American administrative theorists, which was thoroughly demolished, it seemed, in the decades of the '40's and '50's, has suddenly reappeared with new vitality.

The policy-administration dichotomy originated with Frank Goodnow and others in their effort to legitimate the rise of the civil service and with it the norm of neutral-competence in government. They sought to save good government from the evils of the spoils system by insulating it from partisan politics. Congress made policy, and the task of the administrative apparatus was to find the appropriate technical means to carry it out. Administrative actions were thought to be less general and more technical so that well-motivated administrators would be able to enact the will of the people as received from Congress or the President. Civil servants could then be chosen on the basis of their technical merits rather than their partisan or policy politics. An avalanche of criticism, begun in earnest by Paul Appleby's *Policy and Administration,* overwhelmed these arguments on every side. Observation of congressional statutes showed that they were often vague, amblguous, and contradictory. There simply were not clear objectives to which the administrators could subordinate themselves. Observation of administrative behavior showed that conflicts over the policy to be adopted continued unabated in the bureaus and departments. Important decisions were made by administrators that vitally affected the lives of people. Choice abounded and administrators seized on it. Indeed, they were often themselves divided on how to interpret statutes or how generally to frame policies under them. Interest groups were observed to make strenuous efforts to get favorable administrative enactments. Moreover, sufficiently precise knowledge did not exist to determine the best way to carry out a general objective in many areas. Given the large areas of uncertainty and ignorance, the values and choices of administrators counted a great deal. Taken at this level there was not too much that could be said for maintaining the distinction between policy and administration. Nevertheless, nagging doubts remained.

Were politics and administration identical? If they were, then it was difficult to understand how we were able to talk about them separately. Or was politics simply a cover term for all the things that different organs of the government did? If politics and administration could be separated in some way, then a division of labor might be based on them. No doubt the legislative will, if there was one, could be undermined by a series of administrative enactments. But were not these administrative decisions of a smaller and less encompassing kind than those usually made by Congress? Were there not ways in which the enactments of Congress were (or could be) made more authoritative than the acts of administrators? Overwhelming administrative discretion did violence to democratic theory.

As the world moves into the 1970's, we will undoubtedly see significant efforts to rehabilitate the policy-administration dichotomy. The dissatisfactions of modern industrial life are being poured on the bureaucracy. It seems to grow larger daily while human satisfaction does not increase commensurately. It has become identified with red tape and resistance to change. Yet no one can quite imagine doing away with it in view of the ever-increasing demand for services. So politicians who feel that the bureaucracy has become a liability,[3] clientele who think they might be better served under other arrangements, taxpayers who resent the sheer costs, policy analysts who regard existing organizations as barriers to the application of intelligence, will join together in seeking ways to make bureaucracy more responsive. How better do this than by isolating its innovative functions from the mass of officialdom? Instead of preventing administration from being contaminated by politics, however, the purpose of the new dichotomy will be to insulate policy from the stultifying influences of the bureaucracy.

Who Will Pay the Costs of Change?

While most organizations evaluate some of their policies periodically, the self-evaluating organization would do so continuously. These evaluative activities would be inefficient, that is, they would cost more than they are worth, unless they led to change. Indeed the self-evaluating organization is purposefully set up to encourage change.

The self-evaluating organization will have to convince its own members to live with constant change. They may think they love constant upset when they first join the organization, but experience is likely to teach them otherwise. Man's appetite for rapid change is strictly limited. People cannot bear to have their cherished beliefs challenged or their lives altered on a continuing basis. The routines of yesterday are swept away, to be replaced by new ones. Anxiety is induced because they cannot get their bearings. They have trouble knowing exactly what they should be doing. The ensuing confusion may lead to inefficiencies in the form of hesitation or random behavior designed to cover as many bases as possible. Cynicism may grow as the wisdom of the day before yesterday gives way to new truth, which is in turn replaced by a still more radiant one. The leaders of the self-evaluating organization will have to counter this criticism.

Building support for policies within an organization requires internal selling. Leaders must convince the members of the organization that what they are doing is worthwhile. Within the self-evaluating organization the task may initially be more difficult than in more traditional bureaucracies. Its personnel are accustomed to question policy proposals and to demand persuasive arguments in their support. Once the initial campaign is proven successful, however, enthusiasm can be expected to reach a high pitch after all existing policies have been evaluated, new alternatives have been analyzed, and evidence has been induced in favor of a particular alternative. The danger here is overselling. Convinced that "science" is in their favor, persuaded that their paper calculations are in tune with the world, the evaluators believe a little too much in their own ideas. They are set up for more disappointment from those who expect less. How much greater the difficulty, then, when continuous evaluation suggests the need for another change in policy. Now two internal campaigns are necessary: the first involves unselling the old policy and the second involves selling the new one. All virtues become unsuspected vices and last year's goods are now seen to be hopelessly shoddy. Perpetual change has its costs.

Maintenance of higher rates of change depend critically on the ability of those who produce it to make others pay the associated costs. If the change makers are themselves forced to bear the brunt of their actions, they will predictably seek to stabilize their environment. That is the burden of virtually the entire sociological literature on organizations from Weber to Crozier.

The needs of the members displace the goals of the organization. The public purposes that the organization was supposed to serve give way to its private acts. Its own hidden agendas dominate the organization.

Rather than succumb to the diseases of bureaucracy, the self-evaluating organization will be tempted to pass them on to others. The self-evaluating organization can split itself off into "evaluating" and "administering" parts, thus making lower levels pay the costs of change, or it can seek to impose them on other organizations in its environment. We shall deal first with difficulties encountered in trying to stabilize the evaluative top of the organization while the bottom is in a continuous state of flux.

Let us suppose that an organization separates its evaluative head from its administrative body. The people at the top do not have operating functions. They are, in administrative jargon, all staff rather than line. Their task is to appraise the consequences of existing policies, work out better alternatives, and have the new policies they recommend carried out by the administrative unit.

Who would bear the cost of change? One can imagine evaluators running around merrily suggesting changes to and fro without having to implement them. The anxiety would be absorbed by the administrators. They would have to be the ones to change gears and to smooth out the difficulties. But they will not stand still for this. Their belief about what is administratively feasible and organizationally attainable must be part of the policy that is adopted. So the administrators will bargain with the evaluators.

Administrators have significant resources to bring to this struggle. They deal with the public. They collect the basic information that is sent upward in one form or another. They can drag their feet, mobilize clientele, hold back information, or otherwise make cooperation difficult. The evaluators have their own advantages. They have greater authority to issue rules and regulations. They are experts in manipulating data and models to justify existing policies or denigrate them.

Held responsible for policy but prohibited from administering it directly, the evaluators have an incentive to seek antibureaucratic delivery systems. They will, for example, prefer an income to a service strategy.[4] The evaluators can be pretty certain that clients will receive checks mailed from the central computer, whereas they cannot be sure that the services they envisage will be delivered by hordes of bureaucrats in the manner they would like. Providing people with income to buy better living quarters has the great advantage of not requiring a corps of officials to supervise public housing. Evaluators do not have the field personnel to supervise innumerable small undertakings; they, therefore, will prefer large investment projects over smaller ones. They can also make better use of their small number of people on projects that are expensive and justify devotion of large amounts of analytical time. Contrarywise, administrators will emphasize far-flung operations providing services requiring large numbers of people that only they can perform. In a house of many mansions they will be the masters.

There are circumstances, of course, in which administrators and evaluators will reverse their normal roles. If the evaluators feel that there is not enough government employment, for example, they may seek labor-intensive operations. Should the administrators feel they are already overburdened, they may welcome policies that are easily centralized and directed by machines performing rote operations. The more likely tendency, however, is for administrators and evaluators to expand into each other's domain. Each one can reduce the bargaining powers of the other by taking unto himself some of his competitors' advantages. Thus the administrators may recruit their own policy analysts to compete with the evaluators who, in turn, will seek their own contacts within the administrative apparatus in order to ensure a steady and reliable flow of information. If this feuding goes far enough, the result will be two organizations acting in much the same way as the single one they replaced but with additional problems of coordination.

Evaluation Incorporated

It is but a short step from separating evaluation from administration to the idea of rival teams of evaluators. A rough equivalent of a competitive market can be introduced by allowing teams of evaluators to compete for direction of policy in a given area. The competition would take place in terms of price (we can accomplish a specified objective at a lower cost), quality (better policies for the same money), quantity (we can produce more at the same cost), maintenance (we can fix things when they go wrong), experience (we have a proven record), values (our policies will embody your preferences) and talent (when it comes down to it, you are buying our cleverness and we are superior). The team that won the competition would be placed in charge until it left to go elsewhere or another team challenged it. The government might raise its price to keep a talented team or it might lower it to get rid of an incompetent one. The incentives for evaluation would be enormous, restrained, of course, by ability to perform lest the evaluators go bankrupt when they run out of funds or lose business to competitors.

The first task of the new enterprise would be to establish its own form of organization. What organizational arrangements are necessary to make competition among evaluators feasible?

Evaluators must either be assured of employment somewhere or engage in other dispensible occupations from which they can be recruited at short notice. A handful of evaluators could always be recruited by ad hoc methods from wherever they are found. But teams of evaluators sufficient to direct major areas of policy would be difficult to assemble at short notice.

They would all be doing different things instead of working together, which is part of the experience they need to be successful. Nor can they form a team unless they can all promise to be on the job at a certain time if their bid is successful, yet at the same time have other jobs to fall back on if they are turned down.

In the previous model, where the evaluators generate new policies and the administrators carry them out, these bureaucrats carried the major burden of uncertainty. Under the new model this imbalance is redressed because the evaluators have to worry about security of employment. Few people like to shift jobs all the time; even fewer like the idea of periodic unemployment alternating with the anxiety of bidding to get jobs and performing to keep them. Mechanisms will be found, we can be certain, to reduce their level of uncertainty to tolerable dimensions.

Evaluators may choose to work within existing administrative organizations, accepting a lower status, learning to live with disappointment, in return for job stability. This is one pattern that already exists. Evaluators may go to private industry and universities on the understanding they will be able to make occaisonal forays into government as part of a tiny group of advisors to leading officials. This is also done now. Both alternatives do away with the idea of competition; they merely graft a small element of evaluation onto existing organizations on a catch-as-catch-can basis.

In order to preserve evaluators who are in a position to compete for the direction of policy, it will be necessary for them to form stable organizations of their own. Like the existing firms of management consultants they resemble, these evaluators would bid on numerous projects; the difference would be that they would do the actual policy work as part of the public apparatus rather than making recommendations and then disappearing. Evaluation, Incorporated, as we shall call it, would contain numerous possible teams, some of whom would be working and others who would be preparing to go to work. The firm would have to demand considerable overhead to provide services for the evaluators, to draw up proposals, and to compensate those of its members who are (hopefully) temporarily out of work. Keeping Evaluation, Incorporated, solvent by maintaining a high level of employment will become a major organizational goal.

Evaluation, Incorporated, is an organization. It has managers who are concerned with survival. It has members who must be induced to remain. It has clients who must be served. So it will constitute itself a lobby for evaluation. When the demand for its services is high, it will be able to insist on the evaluative ethic; it will take its services to those who are prepared to appreciate (by paying for) them. But when demands are low. Evaluation, Incorporated, must trim its sails. It has a payroll to meet. Rather than leave a job when nonanalytical criteria prevail, it may have to swallow its pride and stay on. Its managers can easily convince themselves that survival is not only good for them but for society, which will benefit from the good they will be able to do in better times.

If their defects stem from their insecurities, the remedy will be apparent; increase the stability of evaluators by guaranteeing them tenure of employment. Too close identification with party or policy proved, in any event, to be a mixed blessing. They feasted while they were in favor and famished when they were out. Apparently they require civil service status, a government corporation, say, devoted to evaluation.

Perhaps the General Accounting Office (GAO), which is beginning to do analytic studies, will provide a model of an independent governmental organization devoted to evaluation. Since it has a steady source of income from its auditing work, so to speak, it can afford to form, break up, and recreate teams of evaluators. Its independence from the Executive Branch (the Accountant General is responsible to Congress and serves a 15-year term) might facilitate objective analysis. But the independence of GAO has been maintained because it eschews involvement in controversial matters. If the new General Evaluation Office (GEO) were to issue reports that increased conflict, there would undoubtedly be a strong impulse to bring it under regular political control. The old auditing function might be compromised because objectivity is difficult to maintain about a program one has sponsored, or because public disputes lower confidence in its operations. Opponents of its policy positions might begin to question its impartiality in determining the legality of government expenditures. Yet protection would be difficult to arrange because the new GEO did not have a political client.

By attending to the problems of an organization that supplies evaluation to others, we hope to illuminate the dilemmas of any organization that wishes to seriously engage in continuous analyses of its own activities.

Evaluation, which criticizes certain programs and proposes to replace them with others, is manifestly a political activity. If evaluation is not political in the sense of party partisanship, it is political in the sense of policy advocacy. Without a steady source of political support, without that essential manifestation of affection from somebody out there in society, it will suffer the fate of abandoned children: the self-evaluating organization is unlikely to prosper in an orphanage.

Adjusting to the Environment

The self-evaluating organization is one that uses its own analysis of its own programs in order to alter or abolish them. Its ability to make changes when its analysis suggests they are desirable is an essential part of its capacity to make self-evaluation a living reality. Yet the ability of any single organization to make self-generated changes is limited by the necessity of receiving support from its environment.

The leaders of a self-evaluating organization cannot afford to leave the results of their labors up to the fates. If their "batting average" goes way down, they will be in trouble. Members of the organization will lose faith in evaluation because it does not lead to changes in actual policy. Those who are attracted to the organization by the prospect of being powerful as well as analytical will leave to join more promising ventures, or old clients will become dissatisfied without new ones to take their place. As the true believers depart, personnel who are least motivated by the evaluative ethic will move into higher positions. Revitalization of the organization via the promotion and recruitment of professing evaluators will become impossible.

In order to avoid the deadly cycle—failure, hopelessness, abandonment—leaders of the self-evaluating organization must seek some proportion of success. They must select the organization's activities, not only with an eye toward their analytical justification, but with a view toward receiving essential support from their environment. Hence they become selective evaluators. They must prohibit the massive use of organizational resources in areas where they see little chance of success. They must seek out problems that are easy to solve and changes that are easy to make because they do not involve radical departures from the past. They must be prepared to hold back the results of evaluation when they believe the times are not propitious: they must be ready to seize the time for change whether or not the evaluations are fully prepared or wholly justified. Little by little, it seems, the behavior of the leaders will become similar to those of other organization officials who also seek to adapt to their environment.

The growing conservatism of the self-evaluating organization is bound to cause internal strains. There are certain to be disagreements about whether the organization is being too cautious. No one can say for sure whether the leaders have correctly appraised the opportunities in a rapidly shifting environment. If they try to do too much, they risk failure in the political world. If they try to do too little, they risk abandoning their own beliefs and losing the support of their most dedicated members. Maintaining a balance between efficacy and commitment is not easy.

Now the self-evaluating organization need not be a passive bystander negotiating its environment. It can seek to mobilize interests in favor of the programs it wishes to adopt. It can attempt to neutralize opposition. It can try to persuade its present clientele that they will be better off, or instill a wish to be served on behalf of new beneficiaries. One fears that its reputation among clientele groups may not be the best, however, because, as a self-evaluating organization, it must be prepared to abandon (or drastically modify) programs and with them the clientele they serve. The clients will know that theirs is only a marriage of convenience, that the self-evaluating organization is eager to consider more advantageous alliances, and that they must always be careful to measure their affection according to the exact degree of services rendered. The self-evaluating organization cannot expect to receive more love than it gives. In fact, it must receive less.

Evaluation can never be fully rewarded. There must, in the nature of things, be other considerations that prevail over evaluation, even where the powers that be would like to follow its dictates. The policies preferred by the self-evaluating organization are never the only ones being contemplated by the government, there are always multitudes of policies in being or about to be born. Some of these are bound to be inconsistent with following the dictates of evaluation. Consider the impact of fiscal policy upon analysis. Suppose the time has come for financial stringency; the government has decided that expenditures must be reduced. Proposals for increases may not be allowed no matter how good the justification. Reductions may be made whether indicated by analysis or not. Conversely, a political decision may be made to increase expenditure. The substantive merits of various policies have clearly been subordinated to their immediate financial implications.

Evaluation may be wielded as a weapon in the political wars. It may be used by one faction or party versus another. Of particular concern to the self-evaluating organization is a one-sided approach to evaluation that creates internal problems. It is not unusual, as was recently the case in Great Britain when the Conservative Party returned to office, for a government to view evaluation as a means of putting down the bureaucracy. A two-step decision rule may be followed: the recommendations of evaluation may be accepted when they lead to reduction and rejected when they suggest increases in expenditure. Before long the members of the organization become reluctant to provide information that will only be used in a biased way. The evaluative enterprise depends on common recognition that the activity is being carried out somehow in order to secure better policies, whatever these may be, and not in support of a predetermined position. If this understanding is violated, people down the line will refuse to cooperate. They will withhold their contribution by hiding information or by simply not volunteering to find it. The morale of the self-evaluating organization will be threatened because its members are being asked to pervert the essence of their calling.

It's the same the whole world over: the analytically virtuous are not necessarily rewarded nor are the wicked (who do not evaluate) punished. The leaders of the self-evaluating organization, therefore, must redouble their effort to obtain political help.

Joining Knowledge with Power

To consider the requirements necessary for a self-evaluating organization is to understand why they are rarely met. The self-evaluating organization, it turns out, would be susceptible to much the same kinds of anti-evaluative tendencies as are existing organizations. It, too, must stabilize its environment. It, too, must secure internal loyalty and outside support. Evaluation must, at best, remain but one element in administrative organizations. Yet no one can say today that it is overemphasized. Flights of fancy should not lead anyone to believe that inordinate attention to evaluation is an imminent possibility. We have simply come back to asking how a little more rather than a little less might become part of public organizations. How might analytic integrity be combined with political efficacy?

Evaluative man seeks knowledge, but he also seeks power. His desire to do good is joined with his will to act powerfully. One is no good without the other. A critical incentive for pursuing evaluation is that the results become governmental policy. There is little point in making prescriptions for public policy for one's own private amusement. Without knowledge it would be wrong to seek power. But without power it becomes more difficult to obtain knowledge. Why should anyone supply valuable information to someone who can neither help nor harm him? Access to information may be given only on condition programmatic goals are altered. Evaluative man is well off when he can pyramid resources so that greater knowledge leads to enhanced power, which in turn increases his access to information. He is badly off when the pursuit of power leads to the sacrifice of evaluation. His own policy problem is how to do enough of both (and not too much of either) so that knowledge and power reinforce rather than undermine one another.

The political process generates a conflict of interest within the evaluative enterprise. The evaluators view analysis as a means of deciding on better policies and selling them to others. Clients (elected officials, group leaders, top administrators) view analysis as a means of better understanding the available choices so they can control them. Talk of "better policies," as if it did not matter who determined them, only clouds the issues.

The evaluative group within an organization would hope that it could show political men the worth of its activities. The politicians, in turn, hope to learn about the desirability of the programs that are being evaluated. But their idea of desirability manifestly includes the support which programs generate for them and the organizations of which they are a part. Hence evaluation must be geared to producing programs that connect the interests of political leaders to the outcomes of governmental actions, otherwise, they will reject evaluation and with it the men who do it.

A proposed policy is partly a determinant of its own success, the support it gathers or loses in clientele is fed back into its future prospects. By its impact on the future environment of the organization, the proposed policy affects the kinds of work the organization is able to do. Pure evaluative man, however single-minded his concentration on the intrinsic merits of programs, must also consider their interaction effects on his future ability to pursue his craft. Just as he would insist on including the impact of one element in a system on another in his policy analysis, so must he consider how his present recommendations affect future ones. A proper evaluation includes the impact of a policy on the organizations responsible for it.

Consider in this organizational context the much-discussed problem of diverse governmental programs that may contribute to the same ends without anyone being able to control them. There may be unnecessary redundancy, where some programs overlap, side by side with large areas of inattention to which no programs are directed. More services of one kind and less of another are provided than might be strictly warranted. Without evaluation no one can really say whether there are too many or too few programs or whether their contents are appropriate. But an evaluation that did all this would get nowhere unless it resulted in different institutional processes for handling the same set of problems.

Even on its own terms, then, evaluation should not remain apart from the organizations on which it is dependent for implementation. Organizational design and policy analysis are part of the same governmental process. If an organization wishes to reduce its identification with programs (and the clients who support them), for example, so that it can afford to examine different types of policy, it must adopt a political strategy geared to that end.

The self-evaluating organization would be well advised not to depend too much on a single type of clientele. Diversification is its strategy. The more diverse its services, the more varied its clientele, the less the self-evaluating organization has to depend on any one of them, the more able it is to shift the basis of its support. Diversity creates political flexibility.

Any organization that produces a single product, so to speak, that engages in a limited range of activities is unlikely to abandon them willingly. Its survival, after all, is bound up in its program. If the program goes, the organization dies. One implication drawn from these considerations is that the traditional wisdom concerning governmental organization badly needs revision.[5] If the basic principle of organization is that similar programs should be grouped together, as is now believed to be the case, these organizations will refuse to change. On the contrary, agencies should be encouraged to differentiate their products and diversify their outputs. If they are not faced with declining demand for all their programs, they will be more willing to abandon or modify a single one. The more varied its programs, the less dependent the organization is on a single one, the greater its willingness to change.

No matter how good its internal analysis, or how persuasively an organization justifies its programs to itself, there is something unsatisfying about allowing it to judge its own case. The ability of organizations to please themselves must ultimately (at least in a democratic society) give way to judgment by outsiders. Critics of organizations must, therefore, recognize that their role is an essential one. Opposition is part and parcel of the evaluative process. The goal would be to secure a more intelligent and analytically sophisticated level of advocacy on all sides. Diverse analyses might become, as Harry Rowen has suggested, part of the mutual partisan adjustment through which creative use is made of conflicts among organized interests.

Competition, per se, however, need not lead to fundamental change. Organizations may go on the offensive by growing bigger instead of better, that is, by doing more of the same. The change in which they are interested is a change in magnitude. We are all familiar with the salesmanship involved in moving to new technologies or larger structures where internal dynamism and grandiose conceptions are mistaken for new ideas. Motion may be a protection against change.

Competition, if it is to lead to desirable consequences, must take place under appropriate rules specifying who can make what kind of transaction. No one would advocate unrestrained competition among economic units in the absence of a market that makes it socially advantageous for participants to pursue their private interests in expectation of mutual gain. Where parties are affected who are not directly represented in the market, for instance, the rules may be changed to accommodate a wider range of interests. Competition among rival policies and their proponents also takes place in an arena that specifies rules for exercising power in respect to particular decisions. Evaluators must, therefore, consider how their preferred criteria for decision will be affected by the rules for decision in political arenas within which they must operate.

We have, it appears, returned to politics. Unless building support for policies is an integral part of designing them, their proponents are setting themselves up for disappointment. To say that one will first think of a great idea and then worry about how it might be implemented is a formula for failure.[6] A good evaluation not only specifies desirable outcomes but suggests institutional mechanisms for achieving them.

If you don't know how to make an evaluation, it may be a problem for you but not for anyone else. If you do know how to evaluate, it becomes a problem for others. Evaluation is an organizational problem. While the occasional lone rider may be able to fire off an analysis now and then, he must eventually institutionalize his efforts if he is to produce a steady output. The overwhelming bulk of evaluation takes place within organizations. The rejection of evaluation is done largely by the organizations that ask for it. To create an organization that evaluates its own activities evidently requires an organizational response. If evaluation is not done at all, if it is done but not used, if used but twisted out of shape, the place to look first is not the technical apparatus but the organization.

Organization is first but not last. Always it is part of a larger society that conditions what it can do. Evaluation is also a social problem. So long as organizational opposition to evaluation is in the foreground, we are not likely to become aware of the social background. Should this initial resistance be overcome, and individual organizations get to like evaluation, however, it would still face multiple defenses thrown up by social forces.

Evaluation as Trust

For the self-evaluating organization all knowledge must be contingent. Improvement is always possible, change for the better is always in view though not necessarily yet attained. It is the organization *par excellence* that seeks knowledge. The ways in which it seeks to obtain knowledge, therefore, uniquely defines its character.

The self-evaluating organization would be skeptical rather than committed. It would continuously be challenging its own assumptions. Not dogma but scientific doubt would be its distinguishing feature. It would seek new truth instead of defending old errors. Testing hypotheses would be its main work.

Like the model community of scholars, the self-evaluating organization would be open, truthful, and explicit. It would state its conclusions in public, show how they were determined, and give others the opportunity to refute them. The costs and benefits of alternative programs for various groups in society would be indicated as precisely as available knowledge would permit. Everything would be above board. Nothing would be hidden.

Are there ways of securing the required information? Can the necessary knowledge be created? Will the truth make men free? Attempting to answer these profound queries would take me far beyond the confines of this exploratory article. But I would like to suggest by illustration that the answers to each of them depend critically on the existence of trust among social groups and within organizations. The acceptance of evaluation requires a community of men who share values.

An advantage of formal analysis, in which the self-evaluating organization specializes, is that it does not depend entirely on learning from experience. That can be done by ordinary organizations. By creating models abstracting relationships from the areas of the universe they wish to control, evaluators seek to substitute manipulation of their models for events in the world. By rejecting alternatives their models tell them will work out badly (or not as well as others), these analysts save scarce resources and protect the public against less worthy actions. Ultimately, however, there must be an appeal to the world of experience. No one, not even the evaluators themselves, are willing to try their theoretical notions on large populations without more tangible reasons to believe that the recommended alternatives prove efficacious.[7]

Since the defect of ordinary organizations is that they do not learn well from experience, the self-evaluating organization seeks to order that experience so that knowledge will be gained from it. The proof that a policy is good is that it works when it is tried. But not everything can be tried everywhere. Hence experiments lie at the heart of evaluation. They are essential for connecting alleged causes with desired effects in the context of limited resources.

The ability of the self-evaluating organization to perform its functions depends critically upon a climate of opinion that favors experimentation. If resources are severely constrained, for example, leading to reluctance to try new ventures, the self-evaluating organization cannot function as advertised. Should there exist strong feeling that everyone must be treated alike, to choose another instance, experimentation would be ruled out. Take the case of the "More Effective Schools" movement in New York City. The idea was to run an experiment to determine whether putting more resources into schools would improve the performance of deprived children. In order to qualify as a proper experiment, More Effective Schools had to be established in some places but not in others, so that there would be control groups. The demand for equality of treatment was so intense, however, that mass picketing took place at the school sites. Favored treatment for these schools was taken as *prima facie* evidence of discrimination. It became apparent that More Effective Schools would have to be tried everywhere or nowhere. Clearly the social requisites of experimentation would have to exist for self-evaluating organizations to be effective. Unless groups trust each other, they will neither allow experiments to be conducted nor accept the results.

Although ways of learning without experimentation may be found, no evaluation is possible without adequate information. But how much is enough? Hierarchies in organizations exist in order to reduce information. If the men at the top were to consider all the bits of data available in the far-flung reaches of the organization, they would be overwhelmed.

As information is weeded and compressed on its way through the hierarchy, however, important bits may be eliminated or distorted. One of the most frequently voiced criticisms of organizations is that the men at the top do not know what is going on. Information is being withheld from them or is inaccurate so that they make decisions on the basis of mistaken impressions. The desire to pass on only good news results in the elimination of information that might place the conveyer in a bad light. Top officials may, therefore, resort to such devices as securing overlapping sources of information or planting agents at lower levels. There are limits to these efforts, however, because the men at the top have only so much time to digest what they have been told. So they vacillate between fear of information loss and being unable to struggle out from under masses of data.

How might the self-evaluating organization deal with information bias? Organization members would have to be rewarded for passing on bad news. Those who are responsible for the flow of information must, at the least, not be punished for telling the truth. If they are also the ones in charge of administering the policy, it will not be possible to remove them for bad performance because once that is done their successors will be motivated to suppress such information. The top men must themselves be willing to accept the blame though they may not feel this is their responsibility and though their standing may be compromised. The very idea of a hierarchy may have to give way to shifting roles in which superior and subordinate positions are exchanged so that each member knows he will soon be in the other's position. The self-evaluating organization clearly requires an extraordinary degree of mutual trust.

The spread of self-evaluating organizations could enhance social trust by widening the area of agreement concerning the consequences of existing policies and the likely effects of change. Calculations concerning who benefited and to what degree would presumably aid in political cost-benefit analyses. The legitimacy of public institutions would be enhanced because they resulted from a more self-consciously analytical process that was increasingly recognized as such. Evaluation would be informative, meliorative, and stabilizing in the midst of change. It sounds idyllic.

More information, per se, need not lead to greater agreement, however, if the society is wracked by fundamental cleavages. As technology makes information more widely available, the need for interpretation will grow. Deluged by data, distrustful of others, citizens may actually grow apart as group leaders collect more information about how badly off they are compared to what they ought to be. The more citizens trust group leaders rather than governmental officials, the greater the chance their differences will be magnified rather than reconciled. The clarification of objectives may make it easier to see the social conflicts implicit in the distribution of income or cultural preferences concerning the environment or the differing styles of life attached to opposing views of the ideal society. Evaluation need not create agreement; evaluation may presuppose agreement.

Notes

1. Dan Horowitz, "Flexible Responsiveness and Military Strategy: The Case of the Israeli Army," *Policy Sciences,* Vol. 1, No. 2 (Summer 1970), pp. 191–205.
2. Hans Thorelli. "Overall Planning and Management in Sweden," *International Social Science Bulletin,* Vol. VIII. No. 2 (1956).

3. The most dramatic and visible change can be found in the American presidency. Presidents have increasingly bureaucratized their operations. Within the Executive Office there now exist sizeable subunits, characterized by specialization and the division of labor, for dealing with the media of information and communication, Congress, foreign and domestic policy, and more. At the same time, Presidents seek the right to intervene at any level within the Executive Branch on a sporadic basis. The administrators are being prodded to change while the President stabilizes his environment. Thus we find President Nixon saying that he wants something done about that awful Bureau of Indian Affairs, as if it did not belong to him, or asking citizens to elect him again so he can save them from the compulsory busing fostered by his own bureaucracy. He wants to escape blame for bureaucratic errors but keep the credit for inspiring changes.

4. See Robert A. Levine, "Rethinking our Social Strategies," *The Public Interest,* No. 10 (Winter 1968).

5. William A. Niskanen, *Bureaucracy and Representative Government* (Chicago: Aldine-Atherton, 1971).

6. For further discussion along these lines see Jeffrey L. Pressman and Aaron Wildavsky, *Implementation: The Economic Development Administration in Oakland* (Berkeley and Los Angeles: University of California Press, forthcoming).

7. An exception of a kind is found in the area of defense policy where the purpose of the analytical exercises is to avoid testing critical hypotheses. Once the hypotheses concerning a nuclear war are tested, the evaluators may not be around to revise their analyses. See Aaron Wildavsky. "Practical Consequences of the Theoretical Study of Defense Policy," *Public Administration Review,* Vol. XXV, No. 1 (March 1965), pp. 90–103.

21

Program Evaluation and Program Management

Harry S. Havens

Ideally, there should be some useful relationship between the process of managing a program and the process of evaluating it. We rarely find that ideal in the real world. The purpose here is to outline what managers and evaluators must do if they are to work together and to suggest some reasons why it is essential that they do so.

It may be useful to consider, first, what is meant by the term "program evaluation." It is a much abused label and, unfortunately, conveys many different things to many different people. In addition, because of a relatively brief but checkered history that includes a substantial number of bad program evaluations, it carries a lot of excess baggage.

Because of the fuzziness which seems unavoidable in any effort to "define" program evaluation, it seems better to approach the task by describing what it does—or at least aims to do. For purposes of this discussion, let us agree that a program is a collection of activities intended to achieve a common purpose. The process of program evaluation, then, is an effort to judge the extent and efficiency of accomplishment and to find ways of improving it.

A "good" program evaluation, like a "good" program, is one which accomplishes its purposes with reasonable efficiency. The common purpose sought by any program involves making some change in the real world. That is, the intended results are external to the program. The same is true

---

"Program Evaluation as Program Management," *Public Administration Review* 41 (July/August, 1981): 480–485.

of program evaluation. An evaluation may meet all the standards of rigorous design, careful data collection and analysis, and a beautifully written report. If it does not affect the real world, if it is not used, it has failed the test which evaluators themselves apply to the programs they evaluate.

But the real world which the evaluator usually seeks to affect is the program itself. He does so by affecting the decisions which are being made about that program. It is this central purpose of most program evaluation activity which necessitates its linkage to program management. Generally speaking, program evaluation serves little purpose if it exists in a world unto itself, isolated from the process of program management.

Those processes go well beyond the individual who may be identified as the program manager. To be realistic, the concept of program management must embrace all those decisions and actions which impinge on the program, from whatever source. The Congress is engaged in program management when it enacts, amends, or repeals laws governing the program or governing the actions of people who administer or participate in the program. The president and the Office of Management and Budget (OMB) engage in program management when they recommend legislation and funding levels for a program, or promulgate rules which affect it. State and local governments engage in program management when they exercise their discretion to decide whether and how the program will function in their jurisdictions.

Given this broad concept of program management, where should the linkage with program evaluation occur? Should the evaluator seek to affect the real world of the Congress? the Executive Office of the President? the agency head? state and local government? or the person charged with administering the program? The answer is any or all of the above, depending on the issue or issues being addressed. The evaluator should seek to have the results of his work used by whoever is in the position of making a decision to which the evaluation is relevant.

If the efficiency of internal operating procedures is at issue, the evaluator must connect with the program administrator. If the adequacy of a law governing the program is at issue, the evaluator must face the fact of a multiplicity of decision makers, including the agency head, OMB, the president, and the Congress. Each of these sets of potential users has needs which differ. The evaluator who wishes his work to affect the real world of the program must be attentive to those differing needs. If those needs are in conflict, and they may well be, the evaluator must seek ways of reconciling them. Failing that, the evaluator must reach a judgment as to which needs are most important and design the evaluation to satisfy those needs.

To say the least, this need to identify the intended audience and to design the evaluation around the needs of that audience makes life rather difficult for the evaluator. It has been known to cause a mild form of schizophrenia in practitioners. Life can be even more difficult, however, if the evaluator is one who does the work first and only afterward (if ever) thinks about the intended audience. That evaluator can look forward to a career which is likely to be short and almost certain to be full of frustration.

The evaluator who takes the problem of utilization seriously, however, may be tempted to throw up his hands at the apparent impossibility of trying to identify the intended audience before he knows enough about the program to judge, even tentatively, what may be wrong (or right) with it. But the problem really is not that difficult. Rarely, if ever, does an evaluator set forth with a blank slate, attempting a "complete" evaluation of a program. (An evaluator with that concept of his role should be given a stern lecture about the evil of hubris and then required to write "pride goeth before a fall" one thousand times before leaving the room.)

When an evaluation turns out to have been useful, it can usually be traced to the fact that it succeeded in answering a specific, clearly defined question, a question someone wanted answered. Therefore, the evaluation process should start with an attempt to articulate such a question. One hopes there is someone interested in the answer to that question, and it is usually possible to find out who and why. (If it turns out that no one is interested, the evaluator can save himself and everyone else a good deal of time, energy, money, and paper by starting over again with another question or another program.)

In many cases, perhaps most, the evaluation activity is stimulated by evidence that someone is interested in the evaluation of a program, or some aspect of it. The evaluator then translates this expression of interest into the evaluative question. If the expression of interest was properly understood, one can expect the client to be interested in the answer to the question. One should double check, however, to avoid the subsequent unpleasantness attendant on having misunderstood the request or other indication of interest.

Once the interested party or parties has been found, it is important to find out why they are interested, that is, what they expect to do with the answer. If the expectation has nothing to do with making a decision, one should be rather pessimistic about the likely utility of the report. A lot of evaluation effort is wasted answering questions which have no bearing on decisions, questions asked out of idle curiosity or a desire to keep the evaluators out of mischievous activities. One hopes the results are a useful contribution to basic research, but there is not much evidence of this, either.

In some cases, however, the person who wants the answer will want it for a very practical reason. The evaluator should seize these opportunities with great enthusiasm, for they tend to be rare. But, notwithstanding his joy at finding a candidate for useful evaluation, the evaluator is well advised to probe a bit deeper. If the question relates to a specific decision, he should find out who will be making that decision. It may well not be the person seeking the answer to the evaluation question. Rather, that person will be planning to use the evaluation results to influence a third party (or parties) who will actually make the decision. The head of an agency, for example, may want the evaluation as the basis for legislative proposals which will ultimately be considered by the Congress. In this case, the evaluation must be planned around the needs of the third party, not just the needs of the requestor.

It is also essential to find out, if possible, when the decision will be made. If the evaluation results cannot be delivered in time to be used, there may be little point in producing them at all. If time is a problem, however, the evaluator is obligated to look for ways of solving it. For example, preparing a formal written report is often a time consuming activity. The evaluator may be able to save this time by presenting the results orally. Even if these results must be characterized as tentative, they are likely to be better than nothing at all.

The evaluator must also be sure that the question is answerable or find some way of refocusing it in a way which is answerable—and still useful. Answerability has several dimensions, and the evaluator must be conscious of all of them. There are some questions, important ones, which we simply do not yet know how to answer. Others we can answer only in rather imprecise terms, and the answers are about as helpful as they are precise. In other cases, we know how to answer the question, but the precision of the answer, and our confidence in it, is a function of the time and resources available. There may be a fourth category, one in which reliable, precise answers can be obtained both quickly and cheaply. If this category exists, however, it is rarely encountered and probably involves answering some rather unimportant and uninteresting questions.

When the evaluator faces an important but unanswerable question, his responsibility is rather straightforward. His first obligation is to be honest with the client. He must explain the problem to the requestor and seek agreement on some other question (or some derivative of the question) which is both important and answerable. One hopes the requestor will accept the situation with good humor, but that is not always the case. (The world is still populated by those who would prefer to behead the messenger rather than accept the bad news, a fact to which any experienced evaluator can readily attest.)

The case in which answerability is a function of time and resources can become even more difficult to handle. It requires the evaluator to enter into an often complex process of negotiation with his client. The evaluator has a professional responsibility to assure that the client understands the limits on answerability imposed by constraints on time and resources, so that the client will have reasonable expectations about the results of the evaluation. At the same time, however, the evaluator must avoid being so negative and purist as to cause the client to lose interest in what may be a very useful project.

An evaluation which is less than perfect because of limited time and resources can still yield useful results. The utility of the findings, however, is directly related to the ability of the evaluator to provide information (however qualified it must be) which is relevant to the decision which must be made. Thus, the evaluator must walk a very narrow line. He must seek to be as helpful as possible to the client without compromising his professional responsibilities.

The process of identifying a potential user, and then defining a question which is both relevant and answerable within the limits of available time and resources can be particularly difficult for an independent evaluative organization such as the General Accounting Office (GAO). With respect to about two-thirds of its work, the decision on what to review, and when, is made through GAO's internal planning system and is guided by its basic legislative requirements. This independence is clearly a vital asset. But it carries with it a risk. The matters which GAO considers relevant may or may not be seen in the same light by its primary client—the Congress.

In order to minimize this risk, GAO engages in extensive dialogue with key committees. This serves several purposes. First, it permits the adjustment of plans in recognition of congressional needs and schedules without impinging on GAO's statutory independence. Second, it provides an opportunity to gauge the likelihood that the work will be used and thus to judge whether or not the level of investment is warranted. Finally, the discussion sometimes influences the committee agenda, leading to the consideration of issues which might otherwise have been overlooked.

This might be an appropriate point at which to mention the subject of "lost causes." There are times when GAO undertakes a review knowing full well that there is little likelihood of the recommendations being implemented in the short run. This activity is not born of a masochistic desire to be unpopular or a failure to recognize the importance of relevance. Rather, it comes from a conviction that, in time, the cumulative weight of evidence can change the boundaries of political feasibility.

When GAO undertook its review of the Davis-Bacon Act, the prospect of repeal or substantial change was remote, to say the least. Today, it is a little less remote. When GAO first recommended that Treasury collect interest on money in commercial bank tax and loan accounts, the idea was rejected. It has since been accepted.

Most of the time, however, evaluators cannot afford to define relevance in this extended fashion. They must earn their keep by being useful to decision makers today. This is the basis for insisting that the first task of the evaluator is to define a question to which an answer, useful to an identified client, can be produced within available time and resources.

Once the evaluator has done this, he can proceed to do the work for which he was presumably trained. He can start trying to answer the question. This will not be easy, either, but at least he has been trained (one hopes) to solve the problems in this part of the job. He can sally forth in search of data which he can subject to various obscure forms of analysis which, in turn, will permit him to write a report which may be of immense interest to other evaluators and, all too often, to almost no one else. He may do this very well, for it is what he was trained to do.

Having done so, however, the evaluator who is still committed to effecting change in the real world faces the task of reentering that world. That task is difficult, even for those who have done the first part well. One hopes, for example, that the issues have not been overtaken by events, that the requestor is still interested, has not been replaced by someone else, still remembers the terms of agreement under which the evaluation was undertaken, and still considers the evaluation results relevant to the decision which must be made. The reentry process is more likely to be successful if the evaluator has maintained contact with his client, providing interim results and making interim adjustments to the design which are as responsive as possible to the client's evolving needs.

This effort to assure continued relevance (and to remind the client that the evaluator has not retired) serves another purpose as well. It is likely to have given the evaluator some practice at translating his results into words which someone other than an evaluator can understand. This is one of the most difficult parts of the reentry process. Communicating effectively the results of an evaluation can be just as fraught with problems as deciding what to evaluate and how. Evaluators have only begun to understand these problems and are nowhere near solving them.

Recently, there has been greater emphasis on improving the quality of written products. This has focused on such matters as improved clarity in writing (avoidance of technical jargon, etc.) and greater use of abbreviated summaries. But the focus on written products is, itself, part of the problem. The focus, instead, should be on the process of communicating, in which written reports play an important, but by no means exclusive role. Of equal—perhaps greater—importance is the evaluator's ability to convey information orally, and to do so clearly and concisely. One often encounters decision makers with whom it would be futile to attempt to communicate in writing. Some simply do not like to read or, because of confidence in their ability to judge people in a face-to-face setting, may prefer to receive information orally. For others, preference has little to do with the matter; they would not have time to read if they wanted to.

The evaluator who wants his work used must adapt to the operating style of the decision maker. If the decision maker has no time to read, there is little point in sending him a written report. If he has five minutes of reading time, send him five minutes of reading material. If he only has time for five minutes of conversation while going from one meeting to the next, use those five minutes wisely.

This does not mean that detailed, extensive written reports are unimportant, or that the evaluator can dispense with them casually. Rather, it means that they are rarely the most effective means of communicating with the decision maker. If well-prepared, a formal written report can still serve other important purposes. It permits communication with a broader audience, those concerned about the program, who may help shape attitudes about it and influence its direction over a long period of time.

A report also facilitates communication with professional peers, whose suggestions and criticisms will help one do better work in the future, and whose opinions largely determine one's individual and institutional credibility. Finally, a written report serves as a record of what was done. This makes much easier the process of judging validity and, if used properly, permits other evaluators to avoid reinventing the wheel. Useful as these functions are, however, none rivals in importance the need to find the most effective means of telling the decision maker what he needs to know, when he needs to know it.

The discussion so far has addressed the responsibilities of the evaluator toward the manager. But the manager has responsibilities too. If the process of evaluation consistently fails to yield program improvement, the tendency is to assume that the evaluator is at fault. No doubt this is sometimes the case. But it is equally clear that the fault may well lie elsewhere—with managers who do not make use of evaluations. Some do not want to do so; others just do not know how.

Managers are rarely trained in the technical aspects of evaluation and it is pointless to wish they were. Indeed, it is not at all clear that a good evaluator would necessarily make a good manager or vice versa. The skills are quite different and it is unusual to find them embodied in the same person. Incidentally, this says something about the need to be attentive to the difficulties of managing an organization whose mission is the performance of evaluations. In this case, the managers are usually drawn from the ranks of evaluators.

But, while most program managers cannot be expected to be technically expert in evaluation, they should have a basic understanding of the subject. After all, managers are rarely personnel specialists, but they must understand the system; they are rarely budgeteers, but must understand a budget; they are rarely accountants, but must use accounting data. As an ingredient in the makeup of a good manager, the ability to understand and use evaluative information is just as important as any of these other skills.

This does not require a high level of technical understanding. The manager does not need to be able to perform a regression analysis or a chi-square test, any more than he need memorize all the rules governing selection and promotion of personnel. But he does need to understand that there are techniques for the systematic analysis of quantitative data, just as he needs to know that there are rules involved in a merit personnel system.

More important than any technical understanding, however, is a conceptual understanding of evaluation as a research process applied to the answering of questions. With this conceptual understanding must come a recognition that the manager shares with the evaluator the responsibility for defining evaluation questions which are relevant to the manager and answerable by the evaluator. The matter of relevance, particularly, is one for which the manager should assume a very heavy measure of responsibility. Only the manager can know what questions are relevant to the decisions he must make. Frequently, even he cannot be sure, but he is in a much better position to judge the relevance of a question than is the evaluator.

Left to his own devices, the evaluator can only speculate on the matter of relevance. Yet all too many managers, all too frequently, leave the evaluator in the dark. Later, they demean the process of evaluation for its lack of relevance to real world problems, ignoring the fact that it was their own behavior which led to the examination of irrelevant questions.

Along with the responsibility to take part in defining a relevant and answerable question goes the responsibility to listen to the answer. Listening, of course, is an art in itself, one in which managers should be proficient. It does not mean having the time or inclination to plow through a 500-page report alternating between turgid prose and technical jargon. Even less does it mean uncritical acceptance of findings, conclusions, and recommendations.

In this context, listening means the active process of obtaining from the evaluator the key elements of information which the manager needs in order to make a decision. At a minimum, this means learning the answers to the evaluation questions. It also means, however, that the manager must learn enough about how those answers were obtained to judge for himself how much confidence he can place in them.

All of this is a lot of work. Why should managers do it? It is realistic to expect them to take on an added dimension of responsibility, particularly one which seems likely to complicate further the decision process?

In a context of steadily increasing public skepticism about the worth of government activity, it is arguably unreasonable to expect a manager to assume an additional burden out of altruism or a sense of duty and responsibility. Many will do so, but that motivation should not be necessary in this case. Given the environment in recent years, enlightened self-interest, alone, should be enough to motivate an intelligent manager to take an interest in evaluation. That environment is one of intensifying competition for increasingly scarce public resources, at all levels of government. The manager who survives and prospers in this environment, all other things being equal, will be the one whose program is demonstrably effective.

Note both words in that characterization. In the political process which controls the competition for scarce resources, it is not enough that a program be effective, it must be demonstrably effective. Evaluation is no panacea, but it can be an increasingly useful tool, both in raising a program's level of effectiveness and in convincing others of that level of effectiveness.

The manager who makes effective use of high quality evaluation work will compete more successfully than the one who does not. That conclusion does not rely on an underlying assumption of a super-rational decision process. It only requires the assumption that better information will yield (at least marginally) better decisions. If we do not believe in that degree of rationality, we can dispense with all management processes and make all decisions by rolling dice or flipping coins.

The first dimension of utility lies in the ability to make actual improvements in program effectiveness. On this dimension, the successful manager will be the one who participates actively in defining evaluation questions, the answers to which will permit him to make better informed decisions about how to eliminate barriers to the effective delivery of services. Those barriers may exist anywhere in the spectrum from program design to administrative and operational procedures.

No program is perfect, ever, and a properly focused evaluation will almost always find something which can be improved. The key to success is to view this information as an opportunity to improve, not as a threat. In the long run, the successful manager will be the one who creates those opportunities, through well-focused, internally-generated evaluations, and then makes maximum use of the opportunities when they are handed to him.

The second dimension of utility involves the role of evaluation in demonstrating effectiveness. This may involve some risk, in that it is a little difficult to demonstrate the effectiveness of a program which is patently ineffective. But this risk has been grossly exaggerated. Few, if any, programs are patently ineffective. One may not like a particular program, believing that the costs exceed the benefits or that the benefits are unwarranted. But that is quite different from saying that a program has zero value. All programs benefit someone. If someone thinks he has found a program without beneficiaries, he should try terminating it. He will soon learn that it represents an essential service to someone in some congressional district.

In trying to demonstrate the effectiveness of a program, the key to success lies in identifying the objectives sought by those who will determine the fate of the program, maximizing that effectiveness (and improvements in it) in terms which are meaningful to those who must be convinced.

This is not as cynical as it may sound. In our system, decisions about the existence and direction of programs are fundamentally—and properly—political in nature. One of the purposes of evaluation is to provide information to be used in that political process. There is nothing wrong with a program manager who does his best to achieve objectives set in the political process and who then attempts to show that he is doing so. Indeed, there is something very wrong with a program manager who behaves differently.

None of this, of course, justifies distorting evaluations in an attempt to demonstrate effectiveness which does not exist. But this sort of cheating has become a much more risky business, anyway. It is difficult to disguise blatant bias, and there is usually someone who has the skill and motivation to detect and publicize the bias.

All things considered, therefore, the manager is well-advised, in his own self-interest, to assure that evaluation is pursued aggressively, to see that it is as balanced and objective as possible, to deal effectively with the problems it brings to his attention and to take pride in the accomplishments it reveals. Doing so will increase the prospects for his survival and that of his program.

Important as these issues are, however, there is a much larger matter at stake than the fate of individual programs. In a very real sense, what is at stake is the ability of government to serve the needs of the people. It is clear that a large part of the public no longer believes in the capacity of public institutions to serve the common good. That loss of credibility feeds on itself. It leads to actions which further impair the capacity of government to act effectively. That, in turn, further reinforces the loss of credibility, and the cycle continues.

We cannot afford for the cycle to continue much longer, but neither is there an easy or painless way of breaking it. One thing seems clear. We in the public service must assume much of the responsibility for the situation and, similarly, we must take on much of the responsibility for fixing it.

For one thing, we have been much too willing to believe in our ability to solve complex social problems and much too reticent to admit that we do not know how, or that it will take much longer and cost much more than anyone has been led to believe. Our own faith in the capacity of government contributed a great deal to the unrealistic elevation of expectations which led inevitably to our present loss of credibility in the eyes of the public. We must balance our confidence in government as an institution with a sense of realism about what government can do well and what it cannot; what it is now doing well, what it can do better, and what it should stop trying to do.

If we are to behave responsibly, it means using every tool at our command—including evaluation—to reestablish this sense of realism about expectations, both in our own minds and in the public. We must be honest with the public. Government can solve some problems, sometimes, but it cannot solve all problems, everywhere, instantaneously. Government is far from useless, but neither is it omnipotent.

We must be open and articulate about the strengths of government as an agent of progress, and about its limitations. Economic problems which have been accumulating for a decade or more can—and must—be solved, but we cannot solve them in one year. Social problems which have faced us for centuries can—and must—be solved, but we cannot solve them in one decade. If we successfully convey these realities about the capacity and limits of government, the public may begin to develop more realistic expectations of government, neither assuming government can do everything nor, at the other extreme, that it is capable of doing nothing.

As the public begins to adopt more balanced and realistic expectations about the pace at which we can accomplish the properly ambitious goals we have set for our society, we must use every tool at our command—including evaluation—to meet those expectations and to show that we are doing so. Only when the demonstrable effectiveness of our performance begins to match the greater realism we seek in public expectations can we fairly ask the public again to have confidence in us as managers and in government as an institution.

22

Performance Measurement Principles and Techniques

An Overview for Local Government

Harry P. Hatry

A simple definition of performance measurement for governments is the systematic assessment of how well services are being delivered to a community—both how efficiently and how effectively. The term "efficiency" refers to the relation of the amount of input required to the amount of output produced. "Effectiveness" refers to the impacts and quality of the service delivery, whether the service achieves its purpose, and how responsive it is to community needs. The increased knowledge about a government's service delivery system can improve the decision making of its elected officials and managers, and can improve their accountability to the public. This overview of performance measurement in local government covers four topics: the criteria for selecting measures, the various types of measures that should be considered, the data collection procedures for collecting data on the individual performance measures, and how targets for individual measures might be established.

Criteria for Selecting a Set of Performance Measures

Eight criteria are useful for selecting an appropriate set of performance measures. Both individual measures and the entire set proposed for collecting performance information should be assessed against the following criteria.

"Performance Measurement Principles and Techniques: An Overview for Local Government," *Public Productivity Review* 4 (December, 1980): 312–339.

Validity/Accuracy. Is the measure valid, does it measure what it should? Both the measure itself and the specific data collection procedures should be considered. Do they measure what they are supposed to accurately enough? It is not necessary for performance measurements to be extremely precise, but they should be reasonably accurate. A measurement might be quite accurate but the data might be invalid; it might not measure anything meaningful or might measure the wrong things.

Understandability. Will the measure be reasonably understandable by government officials? Generally, esoteric measures that are overly technical or that involve complex combinations of elements have limited use, at least for higher level officials. There are, however, circumstances where the more exotic measures can become understood and so become useful to public officials. For example, air pollution indices initially developed in technical terms are often then translated into the degree of hazard to the public. Thus they are useful both to public officials and citizens.

Timeliness. Can the information be gathered in time for it to be useful to public officials? Certain impacts of some programs take years before they can be detected, such as the long-term effects of education and other human services. Thus, for performance measurement purposes, by the time such information becomes available many aspects of the original program would have changed, and the data might be of little use.

Potential for Encouraging Perverse Behavior. Will the measure result in behavior that is contrary to the objectives of the organization? A measure such as "the number of tickets per police officer year" has a large potential for encouraging harassment of citizens.

Uniqueness. Does the measure reveal some important aspect of performance that no other measure does? This criterion is needed to keep down the number of overlapping, duplicative measurements. Multiple performance measures will inevitably be needed for most government activities, but too many measures can quickly cause both data collection and information overload.

Data Collection Costs. What does it cost to collect and analyze the data for the measure? This is probably the major constraint on performance measurement. Ultimately, the cost of performance measurement has to be justified by its value in improving decision making, reducing or avoiding service costs, improving service effectiveness, or improving service management. Unfortunately, at the onset of a performance measurement system, the value of such benefits can be, at best, only very roughly estimated.

Controllability. To what extent is the measure controllable by the agency whose performance is being measured? This has been one of the most controversial topics of debate over the utility of individual performance measures, especially effectiveness measures. Other things being equal, the more control government managers have over a measure, the more the agency can be held accountable for it. However, if an agency has only partial control over a measure, this should not exclude it from being used. Partial control is the usual situation in government. Operating agencies generally prefer to focus measurement on the more immediate workload outputs of their programs because of the direct link to their resources. They are less enthusiastic about effectiveness measures. These are often affected by external factors over which an agency's influence is questionable. Street cleanliness is not just a result of the performance of the public works department, but is also affected by citizen littering. Note, however, that even in situations of partial control, local governments can often exercise enough influence to have substantial effects, especially over the long run. In this example, government officials could pass and enforce anti-littering ordinances or conduct community campaigns aimed at litter prevention. Many effectiveness measures that are not controllable in the short run can be measures of accountability of top policy officials—including elected officials and chief executives. They provide an indication of how well these officials keep government policies and priorities responsive to the changing needs of the community.

Comprehensiveness. Does the set of measures cover all or most performance aspects of the organization's functions? If not, these omissions should be made explicit, or the measures should be designed to fill the gaps identified.

Types of Performance Measures

Measures can take a variety of shapes and forms, each measuring some different aspect about a program or service. Careful thought should be given to the purpose for a performance measure, and the appropriate type selected to suit that purpose. A variety of different types of measures are described here, with a brief discussion of their uses.

Cost Measures. These measures are simply indicators of dollars spent. It is, of course, legitimate to measure actual costs against budget costs. However, cost measures are normally not included under the label "performance measurement" and, consequently, are not covered in this overview. Cost does not by itself measure efficiency or effectiveness.

Workload-Accomplished Measures. Measures of the amount of workload that has been accomplished are the most commonly found measurements collected by operating agencies. They are frequently displayed in budget documents. By themselves, these output indicators are not performance measures as defined earlier. They say little if anything about the quality or effectiveness of an activity and, until they are related to the amount of resources expended to achieve that output, they say little about the efficiency with which the activities are provided. Of course, information on the amount of workload accomplished can be used for internal management purposes. But uses of these measures should be avoided when they merely encourage increasing the workload regardless of whether it is needed and affordable. Workload measures used as standards that are to be met or exceeded without an appropriate linkage to cost and without consideration of the work accomplished has considerable potential for encouraging perverse, make-work behavior.

Effectiveness/Quality Measures. Often the most difficult type of measure from which to obtain data, effectiveness measures are used to measure the impact and quality of a service, and whether it achieves its purpose. Each service has explicit or implicit objectives directed at its service clients. These objectives can serve as the basis for identifying effectiveness measures. Service clients may be the general public, some sub-set of the public (such as target neighborhoods, the business community, or the handicapped), or operating agencies (such as a public works department) served by internal support services (such as purchasing and data processing).

Often missed in setting objectives and developing measures is the potential for unintended, negative effects, for example, the pollution effects of some transportation systems. Effectiveness measurement, then, should include likely negative impacts of services or at least those impacts that can be identified ahead of time.

There is no complete agreement as to what effectiveness is, but some examples may suggest what governments should consider. Available goal and objective statements are a major source for deriving measures of effectiveness—if they are stated in terms of ends and not means. Examples of such measures include the following:* for recreation and library services—indicators of client satisfaction and use of facilities and services; for employment, health, and social services—measures of the extent of improvement in clients' employment and earnings, health and functioning; for

---

*For a comprehensive discussion of effectiveness measurement covering nine municipal services, including lists of measures for each, see *How Effective Are Your Community Service?* published by the Urban Institute and the International City Management Association.

street cleaning—an indicator of the cleanliness of streets; for fire—amount of spread after arrival of first fire fighting vehicle; and for support services such as purchasing, data processing, and vehicle maintenance—indicators of the timeliness and quality of the service provided.

In addition to receiving a government service, there are a number of "quality" characteristics that concern service clients. These include the timeliness, accessibility, courtesy, and equity with which each service is performed. Each of these qualities is also a candidate for effectiveness measurement. Each quality measure sheds a different light on the way the service is delivered.

Response time measures in particular have become popular; Sunnyvale, Milwaukee, and others use them for a variety of services. Response times can be measured for most programs, including the times to repair traffic lights, to respond to citizen complaints, to fill purchase orders, as well as the response time of police and fire calls. Note that these measure the timeliness of the service but not the result of the response.

Efficiency/Productivity Measures. Efficiency measures are generally defined as the relation of the amount of resources applied to a service or input to the amount of output. Ratios of output to input have typically been labeled measures of "productivity." The converse, ratios of input to output, are called "efficiency" or "unit-cost" measures. Both forms are equivalent. If five employee hours result in ten units of output, the unit cost is one-half employee hour per unit of output, and productivity is two units per hour. Units of input can be the amount of any resource. Typically, inputs are expressed in terms of the amount of employee time and in terms of dollars. Hours are not affected by inflation as are dollars. Dollars should be adjusted to "constant dollars," using a price index to give a better measure of changes in productivity. Units of energy may become used as an additional unit of input.

Units of output are measures of the amount of workload accomplished. Unfortunately, the readily available workload counts often say little about the real product of the activity. For example, the number of park acres maintained says little about how they look, the number of gallons of water treated does not indicate the quality of that water. Whenever possible, defective outputs should be identified and should not be counted as output. For example, in most cities a defective street repair, reported as an open crack or pothole and repaired again, would probably result in two output units being counted where only one was completed properly. It is perverse to encourage employees to work quickly by performing work badly. Because it is often difficult to track defective outputs, effectiveness measurement becomes an important "quality control" complement to efficiency measurement. We will return to this problem with some suggestions for alleviating it.

Actual Unit-Cost to Workload Standard Ratios. These are a special form of efficiency measurement. A "work standard," or standard amount of time that the particular activity should take, is determined. Work standards have been used for many years in the private sector, usually developed by industrial engineers. Local governments have used them in some instances, and recently they have become more widespread in all levels of government.

For a particular performance period, an agency would determine the amount of output and the total actual time applied to produce that output. The average actual time per unit would then be calculated and compared to the work standard time per unit. The resulting ratio is a comparison of the actual work accomplishment to a target based on the work standard. For example, a work standard might be that a crew of three should fill one pothole in one hour. Actual performance for the period might average one per forty-five minutes, for a production of 133 percent of the standard (that is, four potholes for every three based on the work standard).

Preferably, the standard should be an engineered work standard, calculated through some version of time and motion studies that provide a standard time systematically and reliably derived. Unfortunately, in some instances state and local governments have derived "standards" merely by having personnel keep track of their own time (for a few days), and using whatever job procedures the employees happen to choose. The existing average times are then used as the work standard "should take" times. A much better approach is first to examine the procedures to identify good practices, and then to determine the times to accomplish these good practice procedures by a systematic, objective method, such as time and motion studies. Also, work standards need to be periodically reviewed to ensure they keep up to date with current methods, technology, and requirements.

Work standards are useful only for some government activities—those for which a specific procedure can be established and a standard product identified. For example, standards for welfare eligibility determinations should be possible but may not be appropriate for client counseling; standards for the fingerprinting activity can be readily developed, but standard times for crime investigations would be much more difficult to determine. Work standards have been used for such relatively repetitive tasks as data processing, key punching, clerical work, street repairs, vehicle maintenance, park and building maintenance, and various types of inspections.

Efficiency Measures and Effectiveness Quality. As discussed earlier, most ratios of the amount of workload accomplished to the amount of resources expended say little about the quality or effectiveness of the service. Performance measurement should attempt to close this gap. If the information from performance measurement is to be used for purposes of substantial concern to employees (such as changing their budgets, appraising their performance, or as a basis for monetary incentives), the absence of quality considerations can encourage employees to perverse behavior such as focusing on the immediate workload outputs at the expense of quality. There are three approaches that can be used to alleviate this problem.

First, in some cases the output units can actually be designed as an effectiveness measure, rather than just a measure of the work completed. For employment, mental health, and social services, rather than using the number of clients served, the number of clients actually helped could be used to produce the efficiency measure: "the number of clients helped per dollar." This, of course, requires the use of reliable procedures for assessing whether clients had been helped. For parks and recreation, a government could use the "cost per household that used a recreational facility during the year and also expressed overall satisfaction with their experiences." Data for this measure could be obtained through the use of client surveys, as discussed later.

The workload measure could still be used as the output units for the ratio, but formal quality controls could be built in to ensure that only outputs passing pre-specified quality control tests would be included. Defective units would not be counted. For example, street repairs that did not pass an inspector's check, or that deteriorated before some pre-specified time, would be excluded. For its services for children, New York City has begun using the measure "percent of institutionalized placements found inappropriate after documented review." This percent could be multiplied by the total number of placements to yield a better output count for efficiency measurement. Sunnyvale, California, includes in output counts only the number of acres of park vegetation "evaluated to healthy." This approach requires a more formal quality control process in local government than is often currently the case. Private industry often has formal quality control procedures; governments much less so.

Finally, if neither of these two approaches seem feasible, then data on effectiveness-quality measures should be presented along with the input-output ratios to display how effectiveness has been changing at the same time that efficiency has been changing. If, for example, it is found that unit-costs have improved but effectiveness measurements examined during the period have worsened, then perhaps efficiency has been improving at the expense of effectiveness. Officials could then question whether there was a true efficiency improvement and take appropriate action to get effectiveness and efficiency back in line.

Resource-Utilization Measures. The term efficiency measure sometimes has been used to cover another type of measure not expressed as input-output ratios: measures of "resource utilization." These measures are often expressed in terms of the proportion of the available time that equipment or personnel were actually providing, or available for, service. They include measures of the amount of downtime for equipment and personnel. For personnel, the measure sought is usually the percent of time that was spent on "productivity" activities and not, for example, spent waiting for material or equipment such as excessive court waiting time for police. Other examples include the average number of crews on duty, "unused capacity" measures such as load factors for public transit vehicles, and the amount of water pumped into a local system that is not billed because of leakage, etc. These measures can be used to highlight operating problems or poor use of resources.

Resource utilization measures primarily indicate the potential for added resource value. They do not reflect the added amount of output or output-per-unit-of-input that is lost or gained. For example, the time personnel spend waiting for material and equipment might be reduced, but that does not by itself guarantee that the freed time will be used to produce added output. Thus, these measures are not direct measures of efficiency but can be used to point out that potential for greater efficiency. They are probably best labeled as "quasi-efficiency" measures.

Productivity Indices. These can be readily calculated from any of the previous performance measures. An index shows the relative change of a measure from a base period to another time period. The actual value of whatever performance measure is used (e.g. the number of repairs made per unit of input) for the base period would be given the value of 100. In succeeding years the index would be the ratio of the performance measured for that year as compared to the base year. Thus, if a future year's performance is seven percent higher than that of the base period, then the index for that year would be 107.

Indices for individual activities can be combined to give an overall index even with quite different activities. This is done by some form of weighting by the amount of input. For example, if one activity required twenty-five percent of the total number of employee-years whereas a second activity required fifty percent of the employee years, then the index for the second activity would be weighted twice that of the first in calculating the overall productivity index.

Productivity indices are commonly used for national assessments of private sector productivity. These have rarely been used in the public sector. The federal government has begun to attempt to measure annually the productivity of federal employees. The Bureau of Labor Statistics calculates productivity indices for each federal agency and combines these to produce an overall productivity index for federal workers covered by the productivity measurements.

Pseudo-Measures. A number of measures have been used on occasion as performance measures, but are so ambiguous and so potentially misleading that they should not be considered as performance measures. Nevertheless, they are likely to be of interest to public officials—but they do not measure efficiency or effectiveness since the amount of product, the quality, or the value obtained is not indicated.

Cost per capita or cost per dollar of assessment value, that is, the total cost for a service divided by the total population in the jurisdiction or the total assessed value, is not a measure of efficiency. Cost per capita is really an indicator of the amount of resources expended. For most services the population of the jurisdiction tells little about the quantity or quality of the output. Even where a service is directed at all citizens, cost per capita says little about the product. For example, cost per capita for police protection does not indicate anything about what is obtained for those dollars. Multi-year trends of total service costs per capita (or per dollar of assessed value) may be useful indicators of the fiscal behavior of a community. Since cost per capita measures say nothing about the output of the service, however, they should not be used to represent the efficiency or effectiveness of services.

Other examples of pseudo-measures include the number of books per capita and staff-client ratios. These measures provide no information about the product being delivered. They are primarily measures of the amount of resources applied and say nothing about the efficiency of the service. If evidence was developed that the number of books per capita (or staff-client ratios) is highly related to client satisfaction (or client progress), then the measure could be used as a proxy for service quality (though not efficiency).

Cost-Benefit Ratios. These are sometimes proposed, especially by economists, as being the ultimate in performance measures. Traditionally, cost-benefit ratios are ratios in which the output side of the ratio has somehow been converted into a dollar value. A ratio of 1 to 2 indicates that for every dollar of cost, two dollars of benefits were achieved. As long as the value of the benefits exceed the value of the cost, presumably a program is worth its cost. Programs with better cost-benefit ratios would be more desirable than ones with worse ratios.

In actual practice it is usually extremely difficult to determine a meaningful dollar value for many if not most government service outputs. How does one determine the value of additional cleanliness in the neighborhood, additional recreation satisfaction, or better quality water? Methods have been developed for some valuations such as estimates of the value of travel time and of recreation, but such procedures tend to be partly arbitrary and often are based on questionable assumptions. The use of cost-benefit ratios is not likely to be a very viable procedure in the foreseeable future. Such ratios can be useful for specific selected in-depth studies, but not for routine performance measurement.

Comprehensive Performance Measurement. Thus far, we have been talking about individual types of measures. Any single government, and any single agency, is likely to find it necessary to use a variety of measures that will form a comprehensive set of measures.

One approach is called Total Performance Management (TPM). This includes a combined set of information including workload oriented unit-cost measures, quality measures (particularly client satisfaction), and employee attitude measurement. In TPM employee attitude surveys are used to identify potential obstacles or problems that need to be alleviated to accomplish improved productivity, rather than to measure employee satisfaction. A number of local governments have tried TPM, including the cities of Sunnyvale, San Diego, and Long Beach, California, and Cincinnati, Ohio. Some governments may want to include employee attitudes as part of an overall measurement package, particularly where employee problems are believed to be an important productivity problem in the jurisdiction. Employee attitude surveys, however, are not considered part of performance measurement for the purposes of this paper.

Data Collection Procedures

For convenience, we will group data collection procedures into five categories: 1) the use of data in government records; 2) trained observer ratings; 3) a special measurement approach—work standards; 4) citizen/client surveys; and 5) miscellaneous—a catchall category to cover any procedure that does not seem to fit into one of the first three categories and to provide leeway for individual jurisdictions' ingenuity. Each data source can yield meaningful information. Each, however, is subject to large errors if not done properly.

Government Records. Use of existing record data, all other things being equal, is the most attractive source of data collection for performance measures. It is already collected and thus by definition requires little added cost. Some examples of existing data routinely collected in many communities, and that are directly applicable to performance measurement include: counts of workload completed (for use in efficiency measures) such as the number of repairs, number of records processed, number of gallons of water treated, number of tons of garbage collected; cost data for efficiency measures; service quality measures such as the number of complaints received; number of traffic accidents/casualties; number of reported crimes and number of arrests; incidence of communicable diseases; and response time to fire and police calls.

In many cases, however, existing data, or the way it is collected or calculated, will have to be at least partly modified for use in performance measurement. For some information, particularly on the effectiveness and quality of services, existing records are likely to be inadequate and will need revision. Cost data in many if not most governments are not maintained in such a way as to permit cost or employee-hours breakouts by specific activities associated with specific workload measures (e.g. to distinguish commercial collection and residential collection efficiency). Some local governments do not collect the necessary workload, effectiveness, or other data required for efficiency measures (e.g. the weight of solid waste collected is needed but not always measured to determine the cost-per-ton collected.) Though incoming complaints are sometimes tabulated, data on counts of complaints that are actually resolved (one way or another) are much less frequently available.

Thus, even where government records seem an appropriate data source, often modifications to the existing data collection procedures are likely to be needed. Following are some examples where government records can be made more useful. For determining the "number of arrests per police-employee year" rather than using the number of arrests, the "number of arrests *that survive the first judicial screening*" can be substituted to provide an estimate of arrests that are "productive." This would also reduce the temptation of police employees to make excessive arrests. However, to collect this data requires obtaining information from the judicial system as to the disposition of the arrest at the first judicial screening. Tests of such procedures have been conducted in the District of Columbia, St. Petersburg, and Nashville. Secondly, client complaints can be tallied by agency and by subject. Finally, response times can be calculated for numerous activities such as responding to client complaints, making repairs of streets and signal lights, repairing automotive vehicles, and filling requests for services. Data collection procedures would have to be added for accurately recording the time of the initial request and when it was satisfied.

The accuracy of government record information varies considerably. The accuracy of counts of workload accomplished depends on the particular procedures used to make those estimates. If, for example, scales are used to measure the amount of waste collected, the data should be fairly accurate, assuming that the scales are checked periodically; if, however, estimates of weight are made without scales, then the estimates may be unreliable. Do not assume that because data is obtained from records that the data is accurate. Following are some examples of common data accuracy problems. First, the number of reported crimes, widely used as a measure of crime prevention success, is subject to errors from nonreporting by citizens, by as much as thirty to fifty percent for some crimes. There are also problems in defining crimes consistently; police officers have considerable discretion in reporting and categorizing incidents. Secondly, in various human services such as community mental health and social services programs, counts of the number of cases closed can be misleading as an output measure—whether used for measuring efficiency or effectiveness. Problems abound in defining what a "successful" case closure is and even determining when a case is closed. Thirdly, data on the amount of time and cost for employees by specific activities will be accurate to the extent accurate procedures are used, and will depend on the motivation of employees keeping track of their time. This is not a problem when a worker has only one activity during a performance period, but it is a problem when it is necessary to allocate a person's time among more than one activity. Finally, changes in record-keeping procedures can affect the accuracy of the data (e.g. complaint counts could be affected by a change in the complaint telephone number).

Trained Observer Techniques. This is a procedure in which an observer is trained to rate characteristics of some service, primarily to assess a physical characteristic of the results of the service. Some examples of trained observer uses are: to make ratings of street cleanliness (e.g. as used in New York City's "Operation Scorecard" and in Charlotte, North Carolina); to evaluate the rideability/roughness of streets in the assessment of street maintenance activities (e.g. as in Phoenix, Dallas, and Nashville); to assess park and playground maintenance results (Honolulu, New York City); to assess the level of hazard at solid waste disposal sites (Nashville); to assess exterior housing conditions (Dallas); and to develop work standards (numerous jurisdictions).

A form of trained observer rating may be the most feasible approach for providing quality tests for some efficiency measures, such as inspecting repairs to ensure that they meet basic quality standards, or reviewing eligibility decisions to determine if they were reasonable and should be included in the output counts.

The accuracy of trained observer measurements depends on a number of elements. If the procedures are too loose or too haphazard, they may be quite inaccurate. Local governments should not treat such procedures casually. Steps for making ratings reliable include the following. 1) Provide some type of anchored scale specific as to what each grade of the scale represents, so that different observers, seeing a range of conditions at different points in time, would generally provide the same ratings. For example, the rating categories might be defined by pre-selected photographs representing each grade of street cleanliness or each grade of park maintenance quality. Written rating descriptors can also be devised to describe the individual grades. The descriptions for each grade might include quantitative descriptions such as the height of grass or amount of litter. 2) Test the procedure before full use. Have different observers rate a number of different conditions to see whether their ratings are sufficiently close to be reliable. 3) Choose raters who are independent of the unit whose work is being rated to avoid the potential for, or appearance of, bias. 4) Periodically check each observer's ratings for possible deterioration in the ratings' quality. Experience shows that ratings tend to "telescope" after a time, so that they are squeezed together toward the center of the scale. 5) Train new raters in the procedures and retrain current observers when periodic checks indicate rating problems.

Trained observer procedures require time to make the ratings. Thus, they are likely to involve extra costs unless there are persons available with time to do the ratings. In some instances, they may be personnel for whom undertaking such ratings would be a reasonable activity under their current job descriptions. For example, cities that have used solid waste collection inspectors, such as the District of Columbia, expanded the inspectors' jobs to cover cleanliness ratings. Foremen and other supervisors probably are already responsible for work quality, and they could be made responsible for such ratings. However, where the ratings are to be used to assess and compare the performance of each supervisor's work crew, rather than individual workers within the crew, supervisors might not be sufficiently unbiased to make reliable ratings.

There are two ways to reduce the costs of trained observers. First, include the ratings of a sample of items rather than all (e.g. only a sample of items being repaired, or of eligibility determinations, might be reviewed to estimate the number of outputs produced that meet quality standards). Second, have inspectors do combined ratings of different activities (e.g. only a sample of city streets might be rated, and rated "simultaneously" on both cleanliness and rideability).

The size of the sample has a substantial effect on cost. The sample size needed depends on the precision desired for the estimate and on the number of different sub-groups for which comparisons are wanted. For example, if a city wants to compare eight neighborhood areas, adequate sample sizes will be needed for each of the eight. If sampling is used, the sampling procedures should be sound; some form of random sampling should be used to produce a reasonable representative sample.

Trained observer time requirements were estimated by the Urban Institute on the basis of 1975 solid waste collection ratings in Nashville and St. Petersburg. One-half employee year was estimated to be needed for twice per year samples of streets with 250,000–750,000 people—about half this for cities under 250,000. Actual out-of-pocket costs would depend on the extent to which existing personnel are used. In addition, some resources are needed before full implementation of the rating procedures to ensure that an adequately reliable procedure is designed and that the personnel involved with making the ratings are adequately trained in the procedures.

Most rating procedures are reasonably easy to learn. The trained observer role can often be undertaken by lower-skilled, inexpensive personnel, such as clerical workers or college students. For more complex processes such as eligibility determinations and quality checks of road repairs, this would not necessarily be so.

Special Measurement Approach—Work Standards. The development and use of work standards requires both agency record information and a special form of the trained observer approach. Trained observers are used to develop the work standards. They need to use such techniques as time-and-motion studies, process flow charting, and work sampling to analyze the methods used by public employees to perform an activity. The observers or analysts then determine a work standard in the form of a "should take" time (in employee hours) to produce a unit of service. The work standard should be based on the best methods feasible considering the equipment and staff available. Generally, when a community goes to the trouble of such a study, it will try to implement the improvements determined by its methods analysts.

Industrial engineers, methods analysts, or other specially trained observers are needed to develop the work standards. But once the standards are developed, the analysts generally design a routine reporting system or modify the existing one so that employees' output and work time can be regularly reported. The new or modified reporting system essentially creates new/modified government records, from which data is periodically collected to determine the level of performance or percent of standard achieved.

When work standards are used, the agency should use the specially skilled trained observers periodically to check and update the standards. This is required if, for example, new methods or technology have been introduced. For repetitive activities, those that involve standard procedures and identifiable products, the use of these approaches to set time standards can be quite accurate. A principal source of error comes from developing standards for word procedures that are not the procedures actually used by the employees doing the job. After time standards are established, the accuracy of the actual time reported per unit depends on the particular reporting procedures, especially the extent to which there is potential for misreporting, including the lack of skill or motivation of employees to report their times accurately. Problems can also occur to the extent employees have the option of allocating their time to activities covered by work standards or to activities not covered.

Developing engineered work standards can be costly, especially because of the time required of skilled personnel or consultants. But the payoff in efficiency savings after an intensive study can be high, especially for an activity that had not been examined analytically in many years. The City of San Diego, for example, reported a 9 to 1 ratio of savings to program costs in the first five years of its engineered work standards programs.

Building periodic reporting into employees' jobs is generally not very costly, as usually no new personnel are required, but it can be a source of annoyance to the employees.

Citizen/Client Surveys. Surveys of the general citizenry, or only those citizens who have been clients of a particular service or facility, can be used to obtain ratings of various aspects of service quality, and to obtain certain factual data on service effectiveness. Annual citizen surveys have been used regularly as part of performance measures by such cities as Dallas, Dayton, Kansas City, and St. Petersburg.

To obtain factual data, citizen surveys can be used for the following. They can obtain data on victimization of citizens to get better counts of crime rates than is obtainable from reported crimes. They can obtain participation rates (i.e. the percent of different persons or households using a service) for such services as parks and recreation, libraries, and public transit. Data from fare boxes and site counts tells how many trips or visits were made, but they do not indicate how many different persons made trips or visits. They can provide estimates of the number of rat sightings by respondents of various neighborhoods to obtain an estimate of the incidence of rat populations. For clients of human services programs such as employment, training, mental health, and social services, they can obtain information from clients as to their post-service employment duration, earning levels, and the extent of improvement in mental distress or social functioning (to estimate the percentage of clients helped).

Surveys can also be used to obtain citizen or client ratings of specific characteristics of the following services: satisfaction with recreational opportunities and facilities; availability and quality of library services; perception of the cleanliness of their neighborhood; feeling of security from crime (often an important performance measure for crime control activities); adequacy and quality of transportation services; and the odor, taste, appearance, and pressure of the water they receive. Among the quality attributes these ratings can obtain are the timeliness of the services received, their accessibility (location and hours of operation), and the courtesy and dignity of treatment by government employees. These qualities are also relevant to internal services such as purchasing, data processing, payroll, and personnel. The "clients" of internal services are employees in other government departments.

Citizen survey ratings are influenced by the expectations of citizens as well as by actual conditions. Changes in citizen ratings could be due to changes in either or both. In general citizen surveys, respondents not using specific services can also be asked to identify reasons for their non-use. However, caution should always be taken when interpreting these reasons, which are not always penetrating. Responses to questions for reasons of non-use can be tallied to provide data for measures as "the proportion of citizens that do not use basic municipal services for reasons that are controllable by the government (such as accessibility, hours of operations, and safety)."

In client surveys, as well as in general citizen surveys, when a respondent expresses dissatisfaction with a particular service characteristic, the respondent can and should be asked why. This will provide diagnostic information and information on the frequency of reasons controllable by the government.

Surveys for performance measurement should be distinguished from surveys for citizen opinions on various policy issues—those that ask what the government "should do" in the future. Many, if not the majority of, current citizen surveys used in the past by local governments have tended to emphasize the latter type of question. Survey procedures then are used as a quasi-referendum. There are numerous problems with these surveys, such as leading questions and the possibility of tying the hands of elected officials. The inclusion of a few questions for these other purposes can increase the willingness of local officials to undertake the survey. However, these questions are particularly subject to bias. Special care should be used in developing such questions to minimize this.

The accuracy of information obtained from citizen/user surveys depends on a number of factors. Following are some suggestions for maximizing accuracy. First, avoid sampling errors. Give considerable attention to the precision needs; don't overdo precision, but do provide adequate sample size for each subgroup (e.g. about 100 per subgroup). Second, use a random sample. Third, make sure the list from which the sample is drawn covers all groups of interest. Accuracy depends on the completeness of the population list. Fourth, proper interviewing techniques should be used and provisions made for an adequate number of call-backs. Fifth, provide for adequate training and monitoring of interviewers. Inadequately trained and monitored interviewers can lead to errors. For example, interviewers can influence the respondent to answer in some particular way. Sixth, pretest the questionnaire on at least ten to twenty persons from different educational levels and ethnic groups. Accuracy depends on the quality of the questionnaire. It is important that the wording be reasonably clear, unambiguous, and unbiased. Finally, in performance measurement surveys, clients should be asked to respond about their own personal recent experience.

Both costs and efficiency are affected by the mode of interviewing. In-person, telephone, mail surveys, and combinations thereof, are options. Mail surveys, though the least expensive, may be inadequate because of low response rates (about ten percent return rates are common). Although they can be inexpensively sent to a massive number of households, more representative (and so more accurate) results can be obtained from a small number of households, such as 500 or less, if they have been randomly chosen and a high response rate (about seventy to eighty percent) is achieved. Mail surveys also have the problem that literacy is required. And, the questionnaire has to be quite short. Mail surveys become more of a candidate if follow-up mailings are used for non-respondents and if they are supplemented by telephone or in-person interviews for those that do not respond to the mailings. These steps are needed to get response rates up to reasonable levels, about fifty to sixty percent.

In-person interviews have long been the favorite for many professional survey organizations because of the belief that these are likely to be the most accurate, provide high response rates, and permit the longest interviews. Because of the travel time and costs involved, however, these are by far the most expensive. Recently, telephone interviews have become popular, especially those that use random digit dialing to ease the problem of obtaining a representative sample. Telephone interviewing has the advantages of lower cost, permitting many more call-backs by re-dialing at different times, easier access (in some locations it is difficult to get interviewers into respondents' homes), and controllability (where interviewing is done at one central location, a supervisor can monitor the interview). In cases where the sample is not representative due to the lack of phones in enough households, telephone interviews can still be used for most of the population. These calls can be supplemented by in-person or mail interviews.

The cost for a survey depends on the total sample size and mode of interviewing. St. Petersburg, Nashville, and Dayton have used citizen surveys that have cost ten dollars or less per respondent for sample sizes from 600 to 1,000. However, costs up to twenty dollars per respondent can occur, especially for a first-time survey. This assumes an interview of about thirty minutes in duration. Heavy reliance on in-person surveying can easily double or triple the cost. Mail surveys would cost less, but would have to be considerably shorter. Telephone surveys should average no longer than about forty-five minutes and preferably less. These cost estimates also assume that the product of the survey is primarily a series of numerical tabulations without any extensive analysis of the data. The estimates do not include the start-up costs such as the time required in developing a questionnaire.

For surveys of the total population, a considerable savings in the cost per household per question can be achieved by covering several services in the same survey. Though this lengthens the interview, some questions are applicable to all surveys (e.g. demographic questions) and thus have to be asked only once. More importantly, the major expenses of locating clients and certain other costs are affected to only a small extent by the number of questions.

In some instances it may be convenient to use a much shorter interview to obtain data for performance measurements of only one service. For example, short, five to ten minute telephone surveys have been conducted about solid waste collection. Such interviews should be possible for a cost of five dollars per interview or less.

Client surveys normally cover just one service, such as surveys of users of buses, libraries, and recreation programs. They also cover complainants about any service—to determine client satisfaction with the handling of their complaints. Client surveys often can be done less expensively than general citizen surveys. The questionnaires can be shorter and often can be handed out to users as they enter the government facility and collected as they leave. They can even be given in-person interviews at the facility. This ready access means that the expensive tasks of locating persons in the sample is greatly eased. For some other services, the number of clients is likely to be smaller and their telephone numbers or addresses conveniently available, thus reducing location problems.

The use of citizen surveys has become more common in recent years. Cities such as St. Petersburg, Kansas City, Dallas, and Dayton, as well as small locations such as Randolph Township, New Jersey, have used them periodically for performance information. Many cities have done at least one survey for special studies.

At least a small amount of expert assistance will be needed by most jurisdictions to avoid major problems. Preferably, the survey work should be contracted out to an experienced survey firm to avoid administrative and quality control difficulties. This requires dollar outlays. Dayton believes that it has been able to keep costs below ten dollars per respondent by using competitive bidding procedures.

Special Data Collection Procedures. This is a catchall category to pick up miscellaneous approaches and leave room for a government's own ingenuity. There are a number of performance measures, especially measures of effectiveness, that require special measuring equipment to obtain data. Air, water, and noise pollution testing procedures fit into this category. For many jurisdictions, these tests are becoming sufficiently common that they could fall into the category of government record data.

Another example of the use of special equipment is the use of the "roughometer." It is dragged behind a vehicle and gives physical measurements of road roughness (a number of state transportation agencies are using such procedures). Since the physical measurements obtained from technical equipment are somewhat esoteric, they preferably should be converted into more understandable categories. For the roughometer, the technical readings can be translated into overall street rideability. Rideability categories can be derived, for example, by using a group of blindfolded citizens who judge the riding comfort of each street as they ride on a sample of streets. Roughometer readings for those same streets are then related to the judges' ratings to identify ranges of roughometer measurements that are associated with particular citizen personal comfort ratings. Then for subsequent roughometer measurements, these can be converted to rider-comfort categories. A similar procedure can be used for other physical measurements.

There are likely to be many ingenious ways to get at what otherwise may appear to be difficult to measure aspects of government performance.

Consideration of Workload Difficulty and Equity

Two additional topics of importance to government performance measurement are often neglected: the need to consider somehow the difficulty of the incoming workload and the measurement of the equity of services. Each of these are briefly discussed below.

Measuring Workload Difficulty. Agency performance, whether efficiency or effectiveness, is clearly affected by the difficulty of the incoming workload. This would not be a problem if the workload was homogeneous, but in most services this is not so. For example, crimes vary considerably as to the evidence presented to investigators, street or automotive repair problems will differ considerably as to the difficulty of making repairs, and purchase requests from agencies will differ considerably in complexity. These differences greatly affect the time and ability of government agencies to perform their role in providing service.

This would still not be a significant measurement problem if the mix of workload is stable overtime and, in a comparison among units, if each unit had about the same workload mix. Unfortunately, however, significant differences in workload mix are likely to be the rule rather than the exception.

Performance measurement should explicitly consider workload mix. Preferably, performance should be measured for each category of workload difficulty. For example, criminal apprehension rates could be measured for various categories of case difficulty. The categories might be based on the amount and type of evidence provided to the investigator. The number of hours required to make repairs could be tallied for each category of street or automotive repair job (based on its apparent difficulty). This requires that specific definitions be developed for the various categories of difficulty to permit reliable categorization of incoming jobs by difficulty—with subsequent tracking of the outcomes and resources expended for jobs that fell into each category.

If such procedures are too difficult to develop, at least the mix of the incoming workload with respect to degree of difficulty should be identified. This will provide public officials with information to help them interpret whether measured changes in performance were due to changes in the mix of the incoming workload. This is a measurement subject that has only recently begun to receive attention. As yet, there is not much experience in handling this issue.

Measurement of Equity. The degree of equity of service delivery and community conditions among neighborhoods, or among other types of citizen groups, should be an important part of performance measurement. Data collection procedures such as citizen surveys and trained observer ratings lend themselves readily to tabulation by client groups. Ratings for street cleanliness and rideability, for public facility cleanliness and physical condition, and for security from crime and victimization, should all be measured for each major neighborhood. The resulting comparisons can provide valuable information as to which neighborhoods or client groups have greater needs than others.

Indicators of equity can be gathered for each major type of data collection procedure. Citizen survey responses can be tabulated for each major neighborhood area (e.g. those that represent major socioeconomic groupings) or at least areas with substantial commonality of needs and problems. Survey findings should also be broken down by major respondent characteristics such as age, sex, and income class. Trained observer procedures often lend themselves to grouping by geographical area within the jurisdiction. Finally, government records in some cases permit breakouts by client group characteristics. Where the procedures lend themselves to this, such breakouts can be made and may indicate disparity in equity of services to various client groups. Savannah, Georgia, for example, has used data from all of the above sources as part of its "Responsive Public Services Program." The purpose is to make service improvements and new public facility selection more responsive to each neighborhood's differing needs.

Determining Whether Performance Is Good or Bad

A major issue in performance measurement is how to assess whether the measured level of performance is good or bad. Information is desired to permit government managers and other local officials to compare actual performance to benchmarks. Several ways to make comparisons of performance are described below.

1. Compare actual performance against performance standards. Unfortunately, few valid standards exist today against which actual performance can be compared. Ideally, and

perhaps eventually, such standards may be constructed for many performance measures. The most common standard for performance measurement are "work standards." The comparison of the actual time it takes to produce a certain amount of output can be compared against a systematically obtained "should take" time. Long Beach, California, included questions in its citizen survey to help develop standards for certain performance measures such as police response times for non-emergency calls (by asking respondents what they felt would be a reasonable wait for a police officer to arrive).

2. Compare current performance measurements to performance in previous time periods. Previous performance can generally be used, and in practice is so used, to help assess current performance.
3. Compare the performance for different units where a service is being delivered by more than one unit doing essentially the same activities. Furthermore, the performance of any one group can be compared to that of the average of all units.
4. Compare outcomes for various client groups within the jurisdiction. For some measures it is appropriate to compare the performance levels for different types of clients. For example, wherever citizen or client ratings of services are provided, these ratings could be grouped by such characteristics as neighborhood of residence, age, sex, race, and income group. Grouping performance measurements by major geographical neighborhoods in a jurisdiction seems to be particularly informative to local officials. Average performance for the whole jurisdiction, or the area or group for whom performance was highest, could be used as a benchmark for each individual group.
5. Compare performance to that of other jurisdictions. Officials often want to be able to compare their own performance with those of other, similar, jurisdictions. A major problem here is the lack of similar performance measurement by local governments. Another problem lies in the hidden assumptions that are made when saying that two jurisdictions are similar. Population and density similarities do not necessarily mean that the type and difficulty of incoming workload as well as other factors that affect measurement are the same. Also, data collection procedures are likely to differ, and special factors unique to individual jurisdictions abound. However, when local governments are using approximately the same procedures such comparisons can be made. Even now some comparisons

are possible on crime and clearance rates, and citizen ratings of certain services can be made among a few governments that have been using similar questionnaires.

6. Compare performance to that of the private sector. For some government activities, similar activities are carried out by the private sector. For example, commercial automotive repair times are likely to be comparable to government repair times when the vehicles involved are similar. Other examples include private solid waste collection, data processing, and purchasing activities. In some instances, a government may itself use both public and private delivery such as solid waste collection and thus provide an opportunity for comparison.
7. Compare performance against pre-set and planned targets. If a jurisdiction sets targets for the forthcoming year on its performance measures, then at the end of that year actual performance can be compared to those targets. Local governments already set targets that use management by objectives. The key question is how the targets should be set. Some ways are by using the comparisons already mentioned, that is, by basing the targets in part on prior years' performance, on work standards, on other areas of the community or other organizational units, or on the private sector. A more difficult approach is to undertake an in-depth analysis of the resources, program characteristics, past performance, and conditions likely to exist over the next year, and thus analytically derive a target. Even targets not analytically derived, however, when set a little ahead of previous performance, can serve to challenge service managers to improve past performance.

A caution here about benchmarks. Benchmarks should explicitly consider the incoming workload mix. As discussed earlier, the difficulty of the incoming workload may vary—between private and public sector workload, from one government to another, from one year to another, and so on. Preferably, performance benchmarks would be set for each workload-difficulty category. Comparisons would then be made of the performance in each category.

Conclusion

There are a variety of measures and data collection procedures available. Procedures that provide substantial information on effectiveness and quality of service, whether used for effectiveness measurement alone or as part of efficiency measurement, will often require additional effort and cost

BOX 22.1 Difficulties in Measuring Human Services Performance

Paul Epstein

Measuring human services provides difficult challenges. Human services, while measurable, often present "moving targets," making performance difficult to define and data difficult to interpret.

While measuring activities of many human services is not difficult, measuring results or "outcomes" of the activities is often problematic, which makes defining and measuring the performance of many human services less certain than that of "hard" services. While many activities (*e.g.*, caseworker visits to clients or client visit to a clinic) can be counted and their costs calculated, the results of the activities are often difficult to ascertain (*e.g.*, whether a client is physically or emotionally functioning better).

The difficulties of measuring human services can be used as an excuse *not* to make the effort to measure service effectiveness and efficiency. But these same difficulties point to the importance of measuring human service performance and why human service managers should commit the resources required to do it well. Precisely *because* the performance of human services is difficult to define and measure, these services run the risk of not having clear goals and objectives for managers and staff to work toward. Even if an agency has an eloquent statement of its broad human service mission, if it is not backed up by more narrowly defined measurable objectives and measurement of changing trends in client needs, there is a danger of confusion and organizational drift as different managers and staff define and apply the mission differently in their work. Measurement can help keep the staff of a human services agency focused on common objectives which are relevant to changing client needs.

Some suggestions are:

- Clearly identify all the clients (or client groups) of each service provided by the human service agency.

(continues)

over that which governments are currently taking. Furthermore, in-house undertaking of trained observer ratings, citizen or client surveys, and data analysis probably requires skills sometimes not found in local governments, thus requiring that these new skills be obtained.

Many of the procedures such as citizen surveys and trained observer ratings fortunately can be cut back in size and cost for small cities. Smaller sample sizes generally can be used in small communities; some small communities have undertaken surveys of perhaps 300 citizens. Often they have used local volunteers such as members of the League of Women Voters or local students to help with interviewing and data processing.

The data collection procedures discussed will not by themselves identify why the performance levels are as they are. Measured reductions in performance do not necessarily mean that the agency was to blame for the reduc-

BOX 22.1 (continued)

- Define service effectiveness from clients' points of view.
- Look for key aspects of human services that are easy to measure.

  Some examples are:

  Service response times and other process items;

  Error rates and administrative burdens, especially for services involving eligibility determination; and

  Revenue, such as revenue generated from special efforts (*e.g.*, efforts to qualify more clients for Medicaid or Medicare eligibility) or from "outside sources" (*e.g.*, special purpose grants) to supplement institutional or governmental funds.
- Examine efficiency and other measures in the context of effectiveness.
- Set goals and objectives which balance various aspects of performance.
- Periodically reevaluate and review performance measures, goals, and objectives.
- Always remember the primacy of the clients who need human services.

(Source: Paul Epstein, "Difficulties in Measuring Human Services Performance," in: "Difficulties in Measuring Human Services Performance: Keeping Your Eye On the Moving Targets," *Journal of Health and Human Service Administration* 14 (Summer 1991): 27–43.)

tion. The classic example is that an increase in crime may not mean a city's crime prevention effort has worsened but could be due to worsened economic conditions. Similarly, an increase in measured performance is not necessarily due to better agency performance. To determine the extent to which an agency is responsible for observed changes in performance measures, more in-depth program evaluation and analysis are needed. A major purpose of agency performance measurement is to identify which activities require closer scrutiny. This is extremely valuable information since resources required for in-depth evaluations are always limited.

Finally, a word of caution. There is a great temptation to local governments to cut corners on performance measurement procedures and not to worry about the accuracy and validity of the information. Thus far, because of the limited use made of performance information, this may have been justified. But as more important use of performance measurement is made (such as to guide major program and policy choices, provide performance incentives to employees, as well as for performance contracting), then much more care will be needed. Good information does not come for nothing. You get what you pay for. Sound data collection practices and quality control of the data will be required and should be provided.

23

Measuring State and Local Government Performance

Issues to Resolve Before Implementing a Performance Measurement System

Gloria A. Grizzle

As public-sector productivity gets increasing national attention, state and local governments seek more ways of improving their performance. Performance measurement systems may be helpful tools for improving both productivity and accountability. This paper identifies issues that governments should consider before implementing a performance measurement system.[1]

Performance is a multidimensional concept. The term can include such concepts as efficiency (cost related to direct output), cost-effectiveness (cost related to benefit or impact), service delivery quality, service delivery equity, governmental fiscal stability, and conformance with governmental policies. A comprehensive performance measurement system might give information about how well a government, or single governmental agency, is operating in terms of all these performance dimensions.

Developing and successfully implementing a comprehensive performance measurement system is not cheap, easy, or quick. A government should consider several issues before undertaking this task. How it resolves

---

"Measuring State and Local Government Performance: Issues to Resolve Before Implementing a Performance Measurement System," *State and Local Government Review* 14 (September, 1982): 132–136.

these issues will set the performance measurement system's scope and will influence interpretation of data the system generates.

Section one of this paper discusses the factors generally involved in deciding what performance dimensions the system will address. Section two focuses upon the particular problems of measuring program benefits or impacts and explores the consequences of omitting this dimension. Section three looks at the role that goals should play in setting the scope of the performance measurement system. Section four considers the fact that performance measures can themselves affect performance and asks whether such reactive measures should be excluded from the system.

Factors to Consider When Setting the Performance Measurement System's Scope

If collecting the data required to measure performance were inexpensive, a manager might want to include all the performance dimensions previously mentioned. Unfortunately, data collection is expensive. Cost may encourage restricting the system's scope to a subset of these performance dimensions. Before doing so, the manager should carefully consider who will use the performance information and who stands to gain or lose if the performance measurement system collects information on only selected performance dimensions.

Program managers may be content—or may even prefer—to include only measures for performance dimensions that they can control. They might be content with information about what the program does and costs, how it does it, and how well it does it. Measuring efficiency might seem important, but, because program managers lack total control over outcomes, they might see cost-effectiveness measures as relatively unimportant.

Legislators and chief executives might adopt the same point of view. Those dimensions they can control through their power to enact and implement laws might receive the highest priority for performance measurement. Because chief executives and legislators have more control over some decisions than do program managers, they would probably include performance dimensions different from the managers'. Allocating resources among programs is one policy decision that might make cost-effectiveness information more important to legislators and chief executives than to managers.

Various interest groups can use performance information as political ammunition to support or attack specific programs. Therefore, while managers at any level of the agency want unbiased information about the performance of programs for which they are responsible, they also want to control the information (and how that information is interpreted) once it moves to a higher level within or outside the agency. Once performance information is collected, it is hard to limit the public's access to it or to control the way that information is used in the political process. Consequently, the manager should consider who is likely to want performance data and the purposes for which they are likely to use it.

Natural constituents for performance information about state and local governments include planners, budgeters, employees, clients, public interest groups, legislators, and chief executives, as well as agency heads and program managers. Constituents will probably demand whatever data the performance measurement system produces. If the performance dimensions measured are limited to those of greatest interest to a couple of these groups—agency heads and program managers, for example—the information provided probably will not adequately answer some questions other groups ask about program performance.

What would be the consequences of not answering these other performance questions? Actors in the political process will not withdraw from the process because they do not have performance information. They will either proceed to maneuver without performance information or will use or misuse existing performance information. The manager should remember that limiting the performance dimensions included in the measurement system will probably result in some measurements answering questions other than ones they were designed to answer.

Another problem affecting dimensions included in a performance measurement system is that people's perceptions of the most important dimensions change over time. A predominant concern for efficiency may later give way to concern about effectiveness that may, in turn, give way to concerns about equity—that may later give way to a renewed concern about efficiency. Conceptually, the easy solution would be to include all these performance dimensions in the measurement system. Frequently, however, the solution easy to conceptualize may be prohibitively expensive to implement.

A third factor affecting the appropriate dimensions to include is the stage of an agency's program development. Stages included in a program's life cycle might be: developing, implementing, operating, and refining. All the performance dimensions mentioned may be appropriate to the operating and refining stages. But using them during the developing stage would be premature. The developing stage would, for example, be too early to measure cost-effectiveness. On the other hand, measuring direct output and policy conformance might be appropriate at that time.

This discussion suggests that a performance measurement system should be designed with the idea of changing from time to time. It should be flexible enough to respond to changes in a program's developmental stages and in user perceptions about the most important performance issues in corrections. Advocating flexibility is easy, but adding and dropping performance dimensions has two disadvantages. First, it costs money. Second, it truncates the time series that result from regular annual data collection. Before dropping measures from the system, the manager might well consider that a time series not perceived as useful by today's users might be perceived as useful by future users. Finally, whoever is funding the system may insist that his or her performance measurement interests be the sole basis for deciding what measures will be included.

Excluding Outcome as a Performance Dimension

Accountability can mean that those in charge of a program are responsible to someone outside the program for the way they use program resources and the goals they seek [1. p. 417]. Information from performance measurement can help move accountability from theory to practice. Before deciding how to measure a program's performance, one should consider: (1) What is the program impact? (2) Who is responsible? These questions arise because the public and their elected representatives want to know if the programs really work and if the public is benefiting. For example, is the public safer because of crime control programs: are air and water cleaner as a result of environmental programs: did program participants get and keep good jobs because of manpower training and employment programs? This pragmatic orientation suggests that accountability should focus on the program's impact upon clients or other groups indirectly affected by the program.

Yet, impacts or outcomes are the hardest performance dimension to measure and, therefore, the dimension most likely to be left out of a performance measurement system. Reasons offered for excluding this dimension include the cost of collecting impact data, an agency's lack of control over impacts, and the time required for the impacts to occur. Adverse consequences of excluding this dimension include distorting agency effort and misusing the information provided.

Control deserves special consideration when measuring program impact. Program managers are justifiably reluctant to have their programs' success judged in terms of outcomes over which they have less than total control. Is it fair, for example, to judge the effectiveness of a rehabilitation program by its clients' subsequent behavior even though other factors besides the program also influence how clients behave? If one takes the position that performance measures should be developed only for those events over which a program has total or near-total control, one will find few events that can be measured outside the program's direct outputs. Yet these direct outputs (e.g., X number of accidents investigated. Y number of students completing educational programs. Z number of polluting installations cited for non-compliance with emission standards) do not go far in answering the questions raised by a program's varied constituent groups.

A second related problem arises when examining accountability in terms of responsibility. Measuring a program's impacts is one problem but assigning responsibility for those impacts is another. Extensive management sharing among different levels of government means that there is very little for which a single actor, agency, or program in government in the United States has exclusive responsibility [9]. When responsibility is so widely dispersed that effectively no one is in charge, accountability becomes meaningless unless it recognizes joint responsibility.

Joint responsibility provides a rationale for measuring outcomes over which no actor has exclusive control or responsibility. These outcomes must be measured for two reasons: first, to answer questions about the impact programs have upon their clients (or other people affected indirectly), the relative cost-effectiveness of various programs, and the unmet needs in a given jurisdiction. And, second, because the public, legislators, chief executives, and funding agencies want the answers.

The Role of Goals in Setting the Measurement System's Scope

What effect will goals have on performance measurement system design? Goals may be defined as broad, general statements of desired conditions external to programs. Goals provide the basic purposes for which programs were authorized and funded. If performance measurement were to be based upon a rational model of decision-making, the first step in developing a performance measurement system would be identifying the goals against which performance is to be compared. Though this step seems easy, there are several questions to be considered before the performance measurement system is built around a set of goals.

First among these questions is "*Whose* goals should be recognized?" Section one suggested that potential users of performance information included public interest groups, legislators, chief executives, agency heads and administrators, program managers, planners, budgeters, employees, and clients. These groups, if asked to agree upon a single set of goals for a program, would probably be unable to do so. For example, the public might be primarily interested in a correction program's ability to incarcerate and punish offenders and make the community safer, while the offender might be primarily interested in the quality of the program's services available to him.

One may think of corrections goals in terms of broad outcomes, such as revenge or retribution, restraint, reform or rehabilitation, reintegration into society, and restitution.[2] Goals of individuals or groups interested in corrections programs, however, may be unrelated to these broad outcomes. A community might support a prison because it employs a large part of that community's work force. Private community businesses might look at the prison as a source of revenue through sales of food, medical and dental supplies, maintenance supplies, and materials for prison industries, and through providing contract services. Business groups, then, might believe that an important goal of the prison is to provide business opportunities to the community.

Within the organization one may be confronted with three types of goals. The official, stated goals in their broadest form might be stated as follows: to rehabilitate offenders: to prevent crime through incarceration and deterrence: to punish the guilty: to provide restitution to victims of crime. Second are management goals that may make attainment of the official, stated goals possible. At their broadest level, management goals might be stated as follows: to secure the resources necessary to support the organization's programs adequately; to build and maintain employee morale; and to maintain internal stability within the organization. Third, individual employees and clients may have their own goals, such as having a pleasant work place, advancing their careers, building their retirement fund or "doing easy time." All these goals may affect the organization's performance.[3]

If all these types of external and internal goals affect the performance of corrections programs, should the performance measurement system monitor progress toward all these goals?

One approach for deciding the scope of the performance measurement system might be to limit those goals used as guides in identifying what is to be measured to corrections-oriented goals (e.g., retribution, rehabilitation, restitution) and to exclude non-corrections-oriented goals (e.g., employment, business opportunities, career advancement, "doing easy time"). This approach is broad enough to include information addressing the following sorts of questions about corrections programs: What did the program spend? What did the program produce? How was the product produced? How good was the product? What was the cost per unit of product? What was the cost per unit of benefit? What needs remain unmet? The advantage is that such a broad approach to performance measurement includes the information that many of the potential users—program managers, chief executives, legislators, and the public—consider important. The program manager, if he or she so chooses, is free to concentrate upon performance measurements that indicate what the program does and costs, how it does it, and how well it does it. The legislator, on the other hand, is free to concentrate upon performance measurements comparing the results of a program relative to cost with the results and costs of other programs.

Although such a broad approach to developing a performance measurement system is conceptually appealing, implementing such a system is likely to be expensive. Designing a system that responds to the specific information needs of selected users would be more economical. In practice, the performance dimensions included in the system may depend upon who pays for its implementation and how much that person is willing to spend. Such a practical resolution of the scope problem has the disadvantage of leaving some groups of people interested in government performance with performance data that do not fit the decisions they must make. For example, performance measurements designed to answer the questions raised by the program manager may not be relevant to the decisions the legislator must make.

However the question of whose goals are to be recognized is resolved, the problem of what to do when goals are inconsistent is likely to remain. Assume, for example, that a probation program has two goals: (1) to enhance the capability of the client to function effectively in society and (2) to protect the community by minimizing criminal activity on the part of the probationer. Following the first goal might lead a probation officer to tolerate a greater level of deviant behavior in the short run to provide probationers with opportunities to learn to make alternative choices [1. p. 9]. Yet "deviant behavior" is an outcome inconsistent with the second goal.

Should a performance measurement system be based upon a set of mutually consistent goals? Many policy areas reflect inconsistent and sometimes conflicting values held by our society. It is not the task of performance measurement (or of designers of performance measurement systems) to resolve these conflicts. Such conflict resolution is a function of the political process [4. p. 44]. Performance measurement can best serve that process by identifying multiple outcomes of public-sector programs and leaving the assessment of their relative importance to those people who will use performance information.

Given that goals may be inconsistent and even conflicting, should a performance measurement system be developed around some basis other than comparing actual performance with goals? Not setting up *a priori* goals might be analogous to the goal-free evaluation proposed by Scriven [8]. This approach to evaluation compares outcomes to needs instead of to goals. As Patton [6] has argued, however, determining what constitutes a need (or what constitutes desirable accomplishments) is the same as setting goals *ex post facto*. The main difference between *a priori* goals and *ex post facto* goals may be *who* decides the goals for a program.

Where, then, does one find a program's goals? Good places to look for goals include the legislation (if any) that established the program; records of legislative committee hearings at which the program was discussed; annual, comprehensive, or master plans of the organization responsible for implementing the program; executive orders establishing the program; applications for grants to help fund the program; annual reports; brochures communicating to the public what the program does; and the narrative section of the budget request. For some programs, one may not be able to find

BOX 23.1 Using Performance Measures

Philip G. Joyce

Why review performance measurement in the federal government now? Mainly because recent events have focused attention on the measurement of performance by federal agencies and the feasibility of applying those measures to the federal budget process. These efforts have one thing in common: the reasonable notion that federal agencies should be able to develop measures of program success and that these measurements would be useful to managers and other policymakers.

The road to improving federal performance and tying its measurement to the budget process is studded with obstacles. Current practice and past experience provide insights that may be useful in understanding the prospects for performance measurement and performance budgeting in the federal government. Those who advocate improving the measurement of government performance first need to consider the complexity of the endeavor. Creating yet another set of reporting requirements without an understanding of the complexity involved in measuring government performance and in using performance measures for budgeting runs the risk of poisoning an otherwise promising effort.

With this in mind, we should proceed cautiously. In the remainder of this article, I will discuss several conclusions of the CBO study that are relevant to the design and implementation of performance measurement systems in the federal government.

- The difficulty in agreeing on objectives and priorities of agencies is an enduring obstacle to performance measurement, and this problem is perhaps particularly acute in the federal government.
- Even where objectives and priorities can be agreed upon, developing the measures themselves is challenging.
- Local and state governments have had limited successes in using performance measures beyond the individual agency level, particularly for budgeting.

(continues)

goals explicitly stated in any of these documents. One can infer a program's implicit goals by looking at what activities are included in a program and linking these activities to the purposes (or goals) that seem logically to be served by those activities. This approach can be controversial when there is no generally accepted theory about the cause-effect relationships that exist between activities and outcomes.

If there are no explicit goals and no generally accepted theory about what the program does, it may be wiser not to use goals as a guide in deciding what aspects of performance to include in the measurement system. In such a

BOX 23.1 (continued)

- Past federal efforts to link performance to budgeting were not successful, and repetition of these mistakes should be avoided.
- Since federal agencies currently use performance measures for only limited purposes, which rarely include budgeting, the task is a challenging one. In particular, responsibilities vary widely from agency to agency; therefore, it is important not to treat the federal government as a monolithic entity.
- Any performance measurement effort must confront the issue of the appropriate combination of executive and legislative branch action.
- The pace of reform may be an important factor in its potential for success. The complexity of the endeavor suggests that a deliberate approach is better than adopting a set of uniform, and immediate, requirements for all federal agencies.
- It is important to understand how performance measures might influence the budget process, which requires understanding their limitations.

Budgeting based on performance flies in the face of existing budgeting practice. A system that affords less control over individual line items in order to hold agencies solely accountable for results would be a fundamental change from the current system. Such a system could not resolve the issue of how much money goes to the defense budget and how much goes to domestic spending solely by using performance measures. Budgeting, in a democratic society, is inherently political. No set of budget techniques can substitute for political decisions about "who wins" and "who loses." In fact, the failures of past efforts, such as PPBS, are largely the result of an inability to account for this shortcoming.

(Source: Philip G. Joyce, "Using Performance Measures," in: "Using Performance Measures for Federal Budgeting: Proposals and Prospects," *Public Budgeting & Finance* 13 (Winter 1993): 3–17.)

situation, the scope of the performance measurement system could be determined simply by learning what the potential users of the system want to know about the program. Indeed, Patton's [6] utilization-focused approach to evaluation can be applied equally well to performance measurement. Under such a utilization-focused approach to performance measurement, the decision about what performance information to produce would be made on the basis of what information would be most useful to the identified users.

This utilization-focused approach could be used even when goals have been explicitly stated. Patton [7, p. 137] suggests that goals be prioritized—not by their importance but by the usefulness of information about the goal. If a user already has enough information about a program's progress toward achieving an important goal, the user may give higher priority to obtaining information on a less important goal about which he or she has less information.

Excluding Measures Affecting Performance

Should measures that affect performance be included in the performance measurement system? Performance measurement is not a neutral managerial tool. Management control systems, for example, include performance measures for the explicit purpose of detecting deviations from plans or standards so that, when program processes malfunction, managers can take action to bring operations back on course. Neither should it come as any surprise that measures designed to compare performance with goals focus an organization's effort upon those activities that foster attaining those goals.

Yet, people tend to overlook systems politics when designing performance measurement systems. When legislators and managers use performance information for such decisions as setting priorities among programs, changing program processes, allocating funds among programs, and developing workload standards, some interests stand to gain and others stand to lose. Performance information, once generated, is likely to be used as ammunition in the political process by the constituent group whose interest is best served by having that information made known.

When workers believe that performance comparisons can help them or hurt them, they may alter their performance to achieve "good" performance ratings. The act of measuring performance, then, can itself influence the performance being measured. For example, if the measure of performance for a university is simply the number of people graduated, the university might increase the number of students graduated at the expense of quality education, research, and public service. As another example, a mental retardation program serves the purposes of both custody and training, but management measures only the performance of custodial activities. In effect, then, management is giving program staff an incentive to spend more time on custodial activities and less time on training activities.

Distorted effort is most likely when "it is impossible or impractical to quantify the more central, substantive output of an organization, and when, at the same time, some exterior aspects of the product, superficially related to its substance, are readily measurable" [3. p. 10]. This conclusion suggests that performance measurement is likely to be most dysfunctional when measurement systems focus upon program activities rather than program results or impacts. Focusing upon desired program results instead of selected program activities might give staff an incentive to use their energy in a way that best achieves goal-oriented results.

One cannot design a performance measurement system that can aid policymaking without also affecting performance. One should be sensitive to the effect that performance measurement has upon staff behavior. Including measures that foster activity at the expense of program results should be avoided. If a performance measure cannot be a neutral tool, one might at least try limiting measures to ones that affect behavior positively.

Conclusion

Several conclusions emerge from this discussion. First, performance measurement should not be confined to those events over which a program manager has near-total control. Doing so would ignore the questions about program outcomes that the public and their elected officials most want answered. Instead, outcomes, though often not controllable by a single actor, should be measured and the question of accountability approached by developing the concept of joint responsibility.

Second, the distortion of effort resulting from performance measurement is likely to be most severe when measurements focus upon program activities rather than program outcomes. Measuring outcomes has the additional advantage, then, of providing the organization with an incentive rather than a disincentive to achieve stated goals.

Third, one cannot isolate performance measurement system design and development from systems politics. Neither can one keep the information that the performance measurement system generates from being used in the political process.

Finally, the manager must resolve the dilemma of developing a performance measurement system flexible enough to respond to changing ideas about what is important to measure, yet stable enough to provide the comparisons over time needed when judging whether the performance experienced in a given year is adequate.

Notes

1. Preparation of this paper was supported in part by grant 78-NI-AX-0130 from the National Institute of Law Enforcement and Criminal Justice. U.S. Department of Justice. Views and opinions are those of the author and do not necessarily reflect the official position or policies of the U.S. Department of Justice.

2. See Carter, McGee, and Nelson [2. pp. 12–13] for one such discussion of corrections goals.

3. Perrow [7] contains an excellent discussion of different goals ascribed to organizations.

References

1. Banks, J., et al. "Intensive Special Probation Projects—Phase 1 Evaluation: Frameworks." Atlanta. Ga.: Georgia Institute of Technology. 1976.
2. Carter, Robert M., McGee, Richard A., and Nelson, E. Kim. *Correction in America.* Philadelphia: J.B. Lippincott. 1975.
3. Etzioni, Amitai, *Modern Organizations.* Englewood Cliffs N.J.: Prentice-Hall. 1964.
4. Lewis, Eugene, *American Politics in a Bureaucratic Age.* Cambridge, Mass.: Winthrop. 1977.
5. McKinney, Jerome B., and Howard, Lawrence C. *Public Administration: Balancing Power and Accountability.* Oak Park, Ill.: Moore. 1979.
6. Patton, Michael Quinn. *Utilization-Focused Evaluation.* Beverly Hills. Calif.: Sage Publications. 1978.
7. Perrow, Charles, "Demystifying Organizations." *The Management of Human Services.* Rosemary C. Sarri and Yeheskel Hasenfeld (ed.). New York: Columbia. 1978. Pp. 105–120.
8. Scriven, Michael. "Pros and Cons about Goal-Free Evaluation." *Evaluation Comment: The Journal of Educational Evaluation* 3 (December 1972):1–7.
9. Stenberg, Carl. Comment made on "Implementation of the Grants and Cooperative Agreement Act" panel, 1979 National Conference of the American Society for Public Administration. Baltimore, April 4, 1979.

24

Developing Performance Indicators for the Pennsylvania Department of Transportation

Theodore H. Poister

Regent literature on state highway programs emphasizes the shifting fiscal environment that surrounds them.[1] The reduced flow of money into several states' highway programs, coupled with rising costs and tighter constraints on allocations, have required cutbacks and changes in programs and have made programming and budgeting a more critical process. In Pennsylvania, for example, a decrease in real purchasing power and the obligation to fund a growing debt service resulted in inadequate funding available for necessary maintenance activities. This temporarily curtailed new construction and shifted priorities to the maintenance program.[2]

Continued inflation and the uncertain effects of the energy crisis on liquid fuel tax revenues, along with heightened citizen awareness of transportation costs and services, have made state transportation officials more concerned with accountability and the effective use of resources. These tighter external constraints necessitate stronger management tools. Thus, systems for maintenance management, pavement management, and project management are used increasingly at the program management level.[3]

"Developing Performance Indicators for the Pennsylvania Department of Transportation." *Public Productivity Review* (March/June 1982): 51–77.

More interest is also apparent in areas such as revenue estimation and priority programming methods.[4]

An integral part of improved management direction and control is performance monitoring—that is, developing systematic information on the progress and outcomes of program activities. This information can be used to assess program effectiveness and to identify necessary improvements. One report on monitoring the effectiveness of state transportation services suggests several uses of this information.[5] It can be used to review progress and trends in the provision of transportation services, provide guidance for resource allocation decisions, assist in budget formulation and justification, facilitate in-depth program evaluation and program analysis, encourage employee motivation, assess the performance of contractors, provide quality control checks on efficiency measurements, and improve communication between citizens and government officials. From a different perspective, the Federal Highway Administration has recently introduced a system for the nationwide monitoring of highway performance across time.[6]

This paper discusses the development of performance indicators for the highway programs of the Pennsylvania Department of Transportation. It presents a conceptual base and analytical approach that can be applied by other transportation departments and in other program areas. Indicators were developed with two purposes in mind. First, much of the data will provide various levels of management with information to help them operate programs more effectively. Secondly, stemming from the "report card" concept proposed by an earlier fiscal review,[7] the system is designed to communicate selected key indicators to external audiences (e.g. the legislature, the governor's budget office, and the public) to document the department's track record. The two purposes are closely related since internal management requires sufficient information to analyze performance and recommend adjustments, and the indicators reported to external audiences will be skimmed off the top of this data base. This would not be possible if detailed data was not in place.

Analytical Approach

Performance monitoring systems consist of three basic components: a data collection component, a processing and analysis component, and an action component.[8] In order to develop the indicators, an agency will need to proceed through five steps. It must first identify the program's objectives and outline its design—how is it supposed to operate and what is it supposed to accomplish? Secondly, given the objectives and program rationale, the agency must determine what kinds of measures would be most suitable as performance indicators. It should then identify potential data sources within and outside the agency and assess their quality and appropriateness.

The next step, where feasible, is to begin data processing or reformatting to obtain initial output and assess the appropriateness and workability of those particular indicators. Finally, the agency must refine these indicators and develop the overall performance monitoring system in terms of data processing, frequency of reporting, channels of communication, and intended use.

In developing indicators for PennDOT, the primary strategy was to rely as much as possible on existing departmental data bases. State transportation departments generate vast quantities of data and maintain many large record-keeping systems. Often there are few linkages among them; separate data banks with incompatible formats are used by different organizational units, and there is little exchange or integration among them. Thus, the potential worth of existing data sources had to be evaluated and ways of utilizing them had to be improved. Where necessary, however, new data collection procedures have been devised.

In order to develop and evaluate specific measures, the department considered the following: *reliability*—how dependable and consistent are the procedures for collecting data? *validity*—how accurately and directly does the proposed measure represent that aspect of performance being examined? and *sensitivity*—how responsive is the measurement scale to what may be small but real changes in actual performance? Complementing these considerations regarding the quality and usefulness of the information is the cost of data collection.

Overview of the Program Logic

The design of a performance monitoring system stresses the importance of end results. Thus indicators of effectiveness—whether programs are achieving their objectives and producing real effects across the state—are of central concern, as are the more customary "process" measures concerned with efficiency. The most direct way of describing a program design (what goes into it, how it operates, and what is supposed to come out of it) is to outline it as a goal-seeking system. Any public program should be designed to accomplish certain specified objectives and produce real physical, economic, social, or attitudinal changes out in the environment. Thus, in order to specify a program's design, one must identify its inputs, components or activities, outputs, linking variables, and intended effects, and relate all of these to the underlying program logic of how the objectives are to be accomplished.[9]

Resources are consumed by activities that produce direct outputs, such as lane miles reconstructed, safety projects completed, and tons of packing material put down. If these activities really contribute something, it should be evident in a well-maintained or upgraded highway network. Developing indicators of road condition and highway system adequacy (e.g. lane widths, passing opportunities, rideability) helps determine whether these assumed relationships hold up. Finally, if such improvements are worthwhile, they should favorably affect the department's objectives of fast, safe, and efficient transportation.

Figure 24.1 outlines the logic of Pennsylvania's overall highway program, including the three major components: maintenance, highway construction, and safety construction. The inputs to these programs are manpower, materials, equipment, and contract services. They are represented in the figure as dollar costs. Their most direct products are termed outputs. For the maintenance program, the department has defined production units for measuring the amount of output for various activities. Examples of these measures are the number of lane miles treated or the feet of guardrail replaced—indicators that represent how much work is actually completed in a given time period. The output for the highway construction program is commonly measured by linear miles or lane miles of new construction. Because the safety construction program includes many different types of projects, it requires various indicators of output.

The combined effect of the outputs produced by the maintenance and construction programs should improve the quality of Pennsylvania's highway system. This improved quality, or system adequacy, is not really an end in its own right, but rather a necessary step toward the goal of fast, safe, and efficient highway transportation for its users. Thus, system adequacy is actually a linking variable that connects program outputs (e.g. potholes filled) with indicators of effectiveness (e.g. reduced damage to vehicles).

Road system quality has been traditionally evaluated with sufficiency ratings based on three categories of highway features: condition, safety, and service. There is not a one-to-one relationship between the three programs and their respective outputs within these three rating categories, although there is some degree of correspondence as represented by the parallel lines in Figure 24.1. Thus, road condition is primarily dependent on the maintenance program, safety features are dependent on safety construction projects, and service aspects of the road system are dependent on the highway construction program. However, there are direct relationships that cross over these lines. The maintenance program, in particular, affects all three rating categories. Changes in the ratings of safety aspects, for example, cannot automatically be attributed to the safety construction program.

Given the overall objective of fast, safe, and efficient highway transportation, the most straightforward measures of effectiveness are the costs incurred by users, accident rates, and travel times. As before, there are no unique one-to-one relationships between the three sufficiency rating categories and the three types of effectiveness measures. Safety features, for example, affect user costs and travel times as well as accident rates. Yet, user

FIGURE 24.1 Highway Program Performance Monitoring Overview

Costs	*Programs*	*Outputs*	*System Adequacy*	*Effectiveness Measures*
$	Maintenance →	Production Units	→ Condition	Reasonable costs to users
$	Safety Construction →	Projects	→ Safety	Reduced accidents
$	Highway Construction →	Linear Miles or Lane Miles	→ Service	Improved travel times

costs might be expected to depend primarily on road conditions, while accident rates would depend primarily on safety features, and travel times mainly on service levels.

In summary, Figure 24.1 shows the general underlying logic by which the effectiveness of PennDOT's highway program might be improved. If more funds were made available for the maintenance and construction programs, or if ways were found to utilize existing resources more efficiently, then program outputs should increase. If this occurs, then highway condition ratings should improve over time, or at least stabilize instead of deteriorate. Finally, if these ratings do improve substantially, then the department should be able to contain or reduce user costs and accident rates, and shorten travel times.

Process Monitoring

Tracking the implementation of programs and the activities to carry them out is called process monitoring. Although the resulting measures do not directly represent outcomes, process monitoring is important because it indicates the quantity and quality of the work completed. For example, how well maintenance managers meet output targets can be evaluated by quantity (do lane miles of surface treatment equal the amount programmed for the season?) and by quality (is this work performed in accordance with standards?).

The main criterion in process monitoring is efficiency, and this can be measured on either a time basis or a cost basis. PennDOT has established a *Management Objectives Report,* which presents, for the first time in one place and on a monthly basis, basic data on personnel complements, expenditures, and activities. This report compares actual to planned or budgeted amounts per month, and compares cumulative figures with data for the previous year. It also allows top management to track the progress of organizational divisions and programs in terms of outputs (i.e. how much work has been accomplished). Regarding the highway programs, for example, the *Report* keeps tabs on expenditures for right-of-way, construction, and maintenance; it records the number of active and completed design, right-of-way, and construction projects; and it shows the number of road miles overlayed and widened. This type of data provides a quick picture of how much activity is going on and how much is being accomplished.

Design and Construction Efficiency. Highway design and construction involves numerous activities: planning and programming approvals, final project design, right-of-way acquisition, reviews, bid solicitations and awards, construction, inspection, and the final audit. When these activities are multiplied by several projects at various stages of completion, simply tracking their status for macro-level decision making can be very difficult. To overcome the problem, PennDOT has installed a computerized Project Management System. This system tracks projects throughout all phases of planning, design and construction, and it includes activities undertaken at both district and department levels. Designed for flexibility, it can provide detailed information for monitoring physical progress and financial obligations for projects both individually and collectively.[10]

Two measures that might be used to monitor the efficiency of design and construction activities could be drawn from this project management system. The first is the average number of days required per project from approval of the final design to the project's completion. As this number is reduced, efficiency increases. This measure could also be broken down by the average number of days required for each design and construction milestone within the project to determine the causes behind lengthy projects. With this measure, bottlenecks in design or construction could be easily identified. The second measure is the average number of worker-days or actual dollar costs for each stage of each project. When analyzing variation in worker days or dollar costs among projects, evaluators must be sure to control for size by taking each project's total dollar value into account.

Monitoring Maintenance Program Efficiency. Developing indicators of maintenance program efficiency was facilitated by the good start the department already had on a monitoring system. Its Highway Maintenance Management System (HMMS) is an ongoing computerized information system for monitoring the internal operation of routine maintenance activities such as general maintenance, winter maintenance, traffic services, roadside maintenance, and maintenance administration. For each specific work activity included in these programs, HMMS reports monthly data on manpower, materials, and equipment costs, as well as production on a county-by-county basis. Close examination of HMMS output, however, indicates

FIGURE 24.2 Maintenance Program Efficiency Framework. Production Cost Data Pertain to July–September, 1980.

Resources	Cost	Selected Program Elements	Production Units	Unit Cost
	$11,299,509	Manual Patching (Flexible Base Roads)	Tons (93,298)	$ 134.22
Production Hours				
	$18,918,625	Surface Treatment (Flexible Base Roads)	Gallons (13,680,319)	$ 2.30
Support Hours				
	$ 7,343,681	Shoulder Cutting	Miles (11,970)	$ 647.78
	$ 785,971	Cleaning Pipe Inlets and Endwalls	Each Structure (48,410)	$ 18.32
Materials				
	$ 2,157,923	Cleaning Ditches	Feet (4,640,978)	$ .84
Equipment				
	$ 1,537,694	Sign Installation	Each Site (45,046)	$ 38.18

that there are considerable problems concerning data reliability, which stem mainly from reporting error and the merging of data from different sources. Editing routines and tighter control on data input have now been established to ensure the adequacy of HMMS data for aggregate comparisons.

Figure 24.2 illustrates the framework of the maintenance program efficiency analysis for a sample of program elements or cost functions. The costs of production hours, support manhours, materials, and equipment can be measured in both their natural units and dollars. Outputs, or production units, would be measured ideally in terms of quantity and quality. HMMS reports output quantities in terms such as tons of patching, tons or gallons of surface treatment, and miles of shoulder cutting; quality indicators are not presently available. The most direct measure of efficiency, disregarding quality, is the unit cost or cost per production unit.

In comparing total costs or unit costs among counties, volume of production must be taken into account since counties can be expected to achieve economies of scale and operate more efficiently at higher levels of output. Figure 24.3 shows the regression of total cost of surface treatment on a Log_{10} transformation of production units, which have been converted from gallons and tons to linear miles. This curve, which shows costs increasing with production but at a diminishing rate, fits the data better than a linear model. The figure also shows a "tolerance band" (within ±20%) of predicted cost; counties falling above the band would appear to be the least efficient on that cost function and would warrant some investigation.

This is generally the approach taken by an earlier study, which also included other operations and environmental type variables in developing

FIGURE 24.3 Surface Treatment Costs by Production Level. Each observation is a county. The upper and lower curves show ± 20 percent from average cost based on production. Production units in tons and gallons have been converted to linear miles.

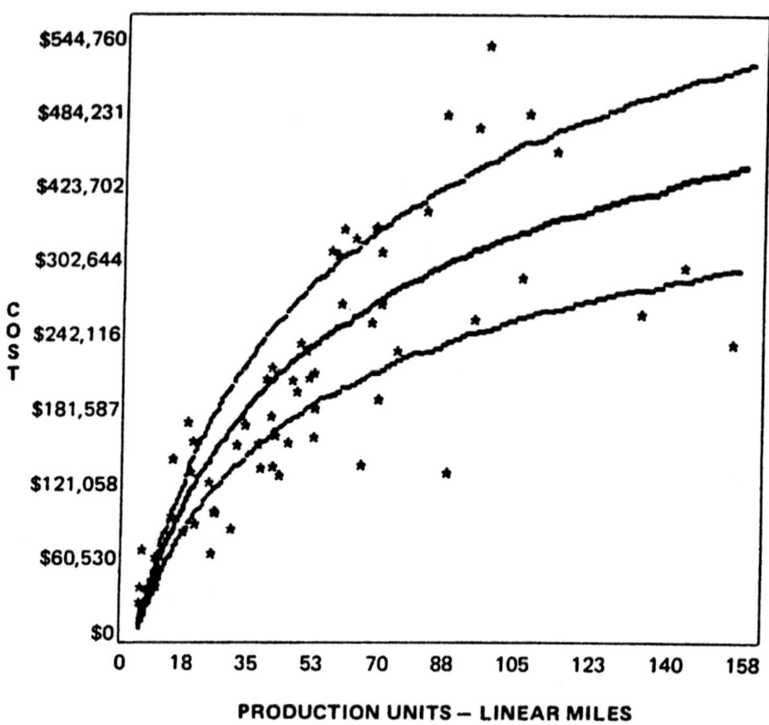

cost models for five selected cost functions.[11] When the study's results were pursued by field investigations, however, it became apparent that to some degree there was an inverse relationship between efficiency and actual quality of work (i.e. some counties looked efficient because they were doing quick but low quality work). Thus it is clear that some type of quality assurance is needed. Over the past year, top management personnel have instituted a practice of executive visits intended in part to prod maintenance managers into ensuring that work is completed according to standards. If this fails to improve the situation, it may be desirable to develop actual measures of work quality based on visits to random samples of job sites, and to incorporate the results into the kind of productivity analysis overviewed in Figure 24.2.

While HMMS tracks production units and costs on a monthly basis, use of the curvilinear regressions is probably more appropriate on the basis of the three separate four-month construction/maintenance "seasons." Additional efficiency indicators that can be looked at on either a monthly or seasonal basis include the following: completed compared to planned production; actual manhours compared to standard manhours; the ratio of support manhours to production manhours; ratios of manhours to equipment hours and cost of materials; total project costs as a percentage of total maintenance budget; and the ratio of administrative and support cost to 100 manhours of production. These measures can be used to compare the efficiency of counties or districts and to track overall efficiency in the department's maintenance program over time.

Linking Variables: System Adequacy

As indicated above, the intended linkages between outputs of the construction and maintenance programs and real effects in terms of accidents, costs, and service to users are represented by measures of system adequacy. These linking variables run the gamut of measurable changes in the physical design and condition of the roads. The usual conception of monitoring system adequacy is to use sufficiency ratings, which involve inventorying and assessing numerous highway features often grouped in the categories of condition, safety, and service. Many states have traditionally used different versions of sufficiency ratings, and in recent years there has been considerable work on developing procedures that could be applied nationwide.[12]

While it has not been recommended that the department establish a full-fledged sufficiency rating program as part of its performance monitoring system, data on many of the necessary items is readily available in any case, and the need for information on certain other key features warrants new data collection activities.

Many of the sufficiency rating items are basically design features (e.g. pavement type, lane width, shoulder width, access control, and alignment) and are fairly static over time. Although PennDOT makes improvements on these features (by widening roads, upgrading pavements, and straightening curves), these items do not fluctuate on a short-term basis. Data on most of these features is contained in PennDOT's road log, and as improvements are made they are recorded so that at six-month or yearly intervals cumulative changes in the adequacy of the network can be noted. Similarly, the data on the number of potentially hazardous locations is computerized and easily accessed as part of the accident analysis program. Information on stopping sight distance and passing opportunities is also readily available.

Trained Observer Survey. Although data on the design-related features was available, systematic feedback was not being generated on many of the more variable condition or service features. Although PennDOT's primary responsibility is to maintain the large and varied highway network, it did not have a systematic, objective basis for evaluating the condition of roads in different parts of the state or for different classes of highways. Therefore, a major effort in developing performance indicators has been to devise and test a road condition survey using trained observers. As with a similar ongoing survey in Ohio,[13] the trained observer survey entails the use of trained professionals to physically observe a number of conditions on a sample of highway stretches in each county on a periodic basis. The number of "reportable conditions" of deficiencies in surface, foundation, drainage, shoulders, and other safety features observed can be used to obtain an overall rating of the maintenance condition of the roads in each county and district.

The data generated by this system is intended to serve two purposes relating to needs assessment and performance monitoring. First, the analysis of reportable conditions and overall maintenance ratings provide a more informed basis for allocating funds for maintenance. The results should pinpoint the greatest needs for maintenance efforts, permit a better allocation of resources among counties or districts, and lead to a more efficient targeting of funds among various maintenance activities. Secondly, the trained observer system will provide Pennsylvania with a means for tracking the effectiveness of the maintenance program. Since highways in each county are sampled twice each year, time-series data will accumulate and can be examined to determine whether certain types of reportable conditions are decreasing. Such measures of change over time can be correlated with selected maintenance outputs and their associated costs to examine the impact of these activities.

Figure 24.4 lists the individual reportable conditions, grouped by the kinds of problems or deficiencies found within the four major components of roadways (surface and foundation), shoulders, drainage, and appurtenances. Many of them clearly reflect safety concerns as well as condition per se. For example, surface deterioration may be indicated by dust layering, slopes of greater than ½ inch per foot, depressions, minor cracking or "mapcracking," and gaps in traverse or longitudinal joints. Specific definitions of each type of deficiency have been established, and observers are trained and drilled in applying them before beginning actual fieldwork.

In contrast to some condition surveys,[14] which rely on general impressions of the extent of deterioration, the prevalence of any reportable condition is measured by the frequency with which the observers see specified amounts along the stretch of highway they are inspecting. The definition of each type of reportable condition specifies a minimum: how much of that condition must be observed in order to be counted. For instance, minor

FIGURE 24.4 Trained Observer Survey, Reportable Conditions

Components	*Deficiencies*	*Conditions*	*Unit Counts*
Roadways	Deterioration	Dust layering	25 LF
		Slope—½"/ft.	25 LF
		Depressions	25 LF
		Minor cracking	25 LF
		Joints	25 LF
	Obstructions	Potholes	Each
		Foreign objects	Each
		Blowups	Each
		Virginia joints	Each
	Foundation Failure	Soft spots	25 LF
		Major cracking	25 LF
		Broken up or mud	25 LF
		Bituminous patch	25 LF
Shoulders	Deterioration	Slope—½"/ft.	25 LF
		Depressions	25 LF
		Minor cracking	25 LF
		Raveling	25 LF
		Buildup	25 LF
	Obstructions	Potholes	Each
		Foreign objects	Each
		Washouts or slides	Each
		Bad drives	Each
	Failure	Major cracking	25 LF
		Rutted	25 LF
		Broken up or mud	25 LF
	Drop Off	Edge pavement 2"	100 LF
		Edge pavement 4"	100 LF
Drainage	Obstructions	Non-functional ditch	100 LF
		Non-functional inlet	Each
		Pipe ½ inlet	Each
	Failure	Bad pipe	Each
		Broken inlets	Each
		Non-functional endwalls	Each
Appurtenances	Guard Rail	Rotted posts	Each
		Non-functional elements	100 LF
		Median barrier	100 LF
	Signs and Stripes	Bad striping	500 LF
		Regular signs	Each
		Delineators	Each
		Station markers	Each
	Litter	Litter	25 LF

cracking must cover at least one square foot in order to be counted. In addition, a unit count is specified for converting the amount of the condition observed into a number of counts per section. Thus, if the observers encounter minor cracking of one square foot or more that extends twelve lineal feet, with a unit count of twenty-five lineal feet, this counts as one reportable condition. However, if the mapcracking were more extensive and found to cover sixty lineal feet, this would be counted as three reportable conditions. These unit counts, along with the precise definitions of reportable conditions, serve to enhance the objectivity of the survey and minimize problems of inter-rater reliability.[15]

In addition to recording observed reportable conditions, the crews doing the field work ride each segment in a vehicle equipped with a May's Ride Meter to obtain an indication of roughness. The resulting roughness is converted into a Present Serviceability Index (PSI). This index indicates rideability, which can then be evaluated against a Terminal Service Index, that is, the minimum acceptable value of PSI for a given type of road. Thus, this single survey provides measures for all three aspects of adequacy shown in Figure 24.1: condition, safety, and service.

The first cycle of the trained observer survey was recently completed, and sample results are shown in Table 24.1. The observers recorded counts of conditions for a sample of 2,600 highway segments across the state, or roughly three percent of the overall system. One of the main concerns of motorists in Pennsylvania is potholes. On the average it was found that there are about forty potholes per mile of state highway (actually forty 25-foot sections that are flawed by potholes). These counts vary directly by class of road—lowest for interstates and highest for local-use roads. Applying these means to the total mileage of each maintenance functional class (e.g. interstates, arterials, local-use roads) yields an estimate of total potholes in the system. The estimated total of 1,761,244 sections with potholes, if laid end-

TABLE 24.1 Selected Initial Results from Cycle 1, Trained Observer Survey

Maintenance Functional Classification	*Total Mileage*	*Potholes per Mile*	*Estimated Total Potholes*	*Terminal Serviceability (TSI)*	*Below Percent Present Serviceability Index TSI*	*Estimated Mileage Below TSI*
A. Interstate	1,139	10.5	12,012	3.3	13.3%	151
B. Principal arterial	4,301	23.1	98,758	3.2	38.8%	1,669
C. Minor arterial	8,159	26.3	214,388	3.0	37.0%	3,019
D. Collectors	18,531	37.2	688,443	2.5	46.7%	8,654
E. Local roads	12,079	61.9	747,643	2.2	70.1%	8,467
Total	44,209	39.8	1,747,643		49.7%	21,960

to-end, would constitute 8,340 miles of highway or nearly twenty percent of the overall system. Similarly, almost fifty percent of the roads are equal to or below the terminal serviceability index on rideability. In both cases, the bulk of the problems are on the lower order roads, but there is also considerable room for improvement on interstates and principal arterials. These estimates indicate maintenance needs as well as benchmarks against which to gauge the overall performance of routine maintenance and betterment projects in future years. At present, work is underway to develop a weighting scheme and an overall condition index as a basis for allocating additional maintenance funds among counties.

Effectiveness Measures

Demonstrating the highway program's impact on users is critical to the performance monitoring concept. Impact measures are usually the most difficult to interpret since they are often heavily influenced by other than program variables, and the precise nature of these linkages is generally not well known. Factors that relate to the transportation goals of fast, safe, and efficient service are essential in measuring the impact of any transportation service. In the highway area, these translate into measures of user costs, accident statistics, and level of service.[16] Table 24.2 identifies measures that might be used to quantify changes in user costs, accidents, and service levels, along with the possible sources of the data.

Cost to Users. Measuring the costs to users of transportation services is plagued by the difficulty in determining which portion of total vehicle operating costs should be ascribed to highway conditions. A partial solution is to include in a user survey a question about damage resulting from road conditions. Responses to this question, however, will be limited to motorists' general perceptions. Another solution might be information from vehicle inspection records, but such data would reflect the cost of all maintenance work done at the time of inspection, including that stemming from normal wear. It would not include work completed before inspection or at any time after inspection. In the past, information on repair costs obtained from inspection records has been unreliable in indicating the dollar amount spent on repairs. However, the department is making changes in reporting requirements and data processing, which will improve the quality of this information.

With reliable reporting and processing, this data base could be useful for a number of purposes. By collecting information on the tenth or twentieth vehicle from each inspection report, a systematic sample could estimate reliably the total number of vehicle miles driven, total repair costs at time of inspection, and the percentage of vehicles requiring alignment or suspension

TABLE 24.2 Effectiveness Measures

Cost to Users	*Measure*	*Source*
Vehicle Maintenance Costs	Average cost per respondent of vehicle repairs caused by road conditions	Citizen Survey
Vehicle Repairs	Percent vehicles requiring alignment or suspension repair	Vehicle Inspection Records
Accidents		
Number of Accidents	Total number of accidents by type, extent of damage, and contributing factors. Accidents per 10,000 vehicle miles	State Police Reports and Bureau of Accident Analysis
Accidents at potentially hazardous locations	Change in number of accidents at potentially hazardous locations after project completion (standardized by average daily travel)	Safety Improvement Program
Level of Service		
Point-to-Point Travel Time	Change in time spent commuting from residences to work	Citizen Survey
Average Speed	Average speed in m.p.h. or percent vehicles traveling 40 m.p.h.	Sample Observations
Volume-Capacity Ratio	Ration of estimated 30th hour peak traffic to design capacity	48-hour Traffic Volume HPMS Counts
Traffic Congestion	Percent responding that traffic congestion causes difficulties in getting to work or other places	Citizen Survey
Perceived Road Conditions	Percent indicating that road conditions have improved over the past year	Citizen Survey

repairs. This would serve as a surrogate measure of user costs. The estimate of total vehicle miles driven per year does not relate directly to user costs, but it would provide a reliable indicator by which other measures could be standardized, for instance, the number of accidents per 100,000 vehicle miles. It might also be combined with statewide fuel tax data to produce average vehicle miles per gallon. This direct estimate of total vehicle miles in the state would be a significant improvement, because the department presently derives an estimate indirectly by applying an average fuel consumption rate (such as 12.5 miles per gallon) to total fuel consumption based on liquid tax receipts.

Accidents. Within the department, the most readily available measures are those that relate accident statistics to the highway program. PennDOT maintains a computer-filed data base that is updated at least annually. Year-to-year change in the total number of accidents per 10,000 vehicle miles driven indicates the success of the Safety Improvement Program. More detailed analysis can be made by observing the change in yearly accident totals, broken down either by type of accident (fatality, injury, or property damage) or by contributing factor (e.g. road conditions or driving while intoxicated). Obviously, the contributing factor of greatest interest here is road condition.

The direct effect of PennDOT's activities on the number of accidents can be measured by the change in the number of accidents at potentially hazardous locations where corrective action has been undertaken. The data for this measure is provided by before and after evaluations of the number of accidents at each completed safety project site, and are aggregated for all sites over a one-year period. For each project, this Safety Improvement Program data is monitored for three years and then dropped from the report. A decrease in this measure indicates that the department is succeeding in reducing the number of accidents at locations where it has attempted to eliminate a hazard.

Level of Service. Measures of service levels should indicate whether travel times, comfort, and convenience are increasing or decreasing. Several alternatives are available for estimating point-to-point travel times. One is to select several routes in urbanized areas as representative segments and to observe changes in commuting time through the use of time and distance surveys. The difficulty here is to ensure that the segments selected are truly representative of the state system. Moreover, there is a major question as to the sensitivity of such a measure. In a period when major new construction and reconstruction is necessarily deemphasized, departmental activities may have little impact on point-to-point travel time.

Given the difficulty in collecting this data, along with the questionable significance of the measure, a more feasible approach might be to calculate the average time spent in transit between work and residence, based on responses to a survey of a random sample of highway users. A question of this type has been included in the proposed citizens' survey discussed below. A second question, asking about distance to work, would be necessary in order to control for years in which increased travel time resulted solely from increases in commuting distance.

Average speed, a corollary indicator of service level, could be calculated from speed data on a random sample of road segments similar to, or the same as, the sample used in the trained observer survey. This kind of data could be collected mechanically and could also be analyzed to monitor changes in the percentage of traffic forced to move at less than some specified "minimum desirable speed"—for instance, forty miles per hour. Technology exists for the mechanical collection of speed data, but it is not available at this time in PennDOT.

As an alternative to speed statistics, volume-capacity ratios could be used as a surrogate measure of average speed for the same random sample of road segments. Volumes would be collected by using counters, while capacity could be calculated with some additional field data, using a computer program maintained by the department. According to the Highway Capacity Manual, changes in the volume-capacity ratio are considered to be only a fair estimate of changes in average speed.[17] An Urban Institute report, however, suggests that using volume-capacity ratios (e.g. estimating the number and percentage of state road miles by class of road, with peak period volume-capacity ratios greater than .75, 1.0, and 1.25) may be a relatively inexpensive substitute for direct travel speed indicators.[18]

Citizen Survey. In addition to point-to-point travel time, statewide citizen surveys can also be used to obtain information from the user's point of view regarding both user costs and their perceptions of average speeds on the highways they travel. The Urban Institute report cited above strongly recommends using such citizen surveys on a statewide basis for obtaining feedback on the whole range of state transportation programs. While this paper is only concerned with monitoring the highway program, a citizen survey could solicit feedback on a range of DOT activities including mass transit, vehicle inspections, and driver licensing. Familiarity with citizens' assessments of conditions, needs, and performance may be as useful to transportation administrators as the professional's "inside" perspective. This is especially so given top management's orientation toward providing service that is satisfactory to the public. Survey findings can also lend weight to top decision maker's proposals for more resources for transportation programs. For instance, a recent general purpose statewide citizen survey in Pennsylvania, which found repair of state roads to be a "priority" of eighty-six percent of the respondents, is being cited now as evidence for increasing expenditures on highway maintenance.[19]

While many states use such "multi-service" citizen surveys, they are limited in the amount of information they can provide concerning transportation issues. Specific transportation-focused surveys, on the other hand, are not in use on a regular basis. Based in part on surveys conducted in North Carolina and Wisconsin, a citizen survey has been developed and tested for use by the Pennsylvania DOT.[20] The items pertain both to road condition and program effectiveness, and in general these perceptual indicators complement the hard data "factual" measures obtained from other sources. A mail-out version of this survey aimed at collecting 3,000 usable responses is being piloted in late 1981.

Two items in particular pertain to effectiveness indicators of the highway program's service levels. The percent of all respondents saying that traffic congestion causes difficulties in commuting or other regular trips, and the percent indicating that the condition of the road is better than in the past year, are two good indicators of service levels from the citizen perspective. As this survey is designed to be repeated on a periodic basis, the real value of this feedback lies in the ability to monitor whether citizen perceptions improve or worsen over time.

A Performance Monitoring System

The notion of a performance monitoring system connotes integration in processing and utilizing the wide variety of indicators discussed in this paper. This research is intended to identify, develop, and select a set of performance indicators rather than come up with a grand design for a monitoring system. However, since the development of particular indicators is keyed to specific management objectives and interests, they have been developed with some sense of likely reporting frequencies and channels as well as potential utilization. Although a "system" design has not been the objective in terms of a single computerized management information system, as existing reporting procedures around the department are modified and new data collection efforts implemented, elements are falling into place and an overall monitoring system is evolving.

The key to developing a performance monitoring system as opposed to collecting an array of data is the action component mentioned earlier in this paper. Beyond data collection and processing, the information must be utilized for the effort to be worthwhile. The indicators discussed in this paper lend themselves to analysis of trends across time, and most facilitate comparisons among organizational units. This kind of analysis serves to identify aggregate drops in performance and flag uneven performance across districts and counties. The results must then be reported to the appropriate managerial levels and relevant organization units on a timely basis, so that they can evaluate activities and take action accordingly. The action component does not refer to the corrective action itself, but to making useful information available to those in a position to take action when necessary.

Internal Management Uses. The recently developed monthly *Management Objectives Report* is the principal means of communicating much of the information the performance indicators convey, and this will be supplemented by a few special reports presenting certain types of data. Much of the "process data" fits the monthly format, especially those concerning efficiency indicators, construction and maintenance work accomplished, and dollars spent. Some of the highway status indicators, such as the number of bridges that are weight restricted, are also included in this report. With aggregate, statewide data on costs, activity levels, and efficiency measures, this report provides the primary means for top management to monitor the department's overall operations. When the report shows that the number of road miles that were surface treated in a given month falls far below the planned mileage, for example, this should prompt inquiry as to what the problem is and whether some change in policy or practice is called for. Similar data will also be reported on a disaggregated basis in the *County Management Objectives Report,* so that district and county managers can monitor their own operations in the same way.

In contrast to the routinely collected data reported in the *Management Objectives Report,* data produced by discrete and less frequent special data collection efforts should be disseminated by separate reports. While most of the process data discussed above is routinely available as a by-product of program management or operations concerns, the trained observer survey and the proposed citizen survey are intended primarily to serve a program monitoring function. The trained observer survey, to be conducted twice each year, generates data on road conditions that should interest management at a number of different levels. A summary of the aggregate data should be prepared for the department's top management, while Bureau of Maintenance staff would want very detailed data on individual deficiencies by road type for planning and programming purposes. District engineers should receive the summary reports, plus a separate and more detailed report of the same factors for the counties in their district, while county maintenance managers should be given the results for their counties compared with district and statewide averages.

The citizen survey, to be conducted annually, is designed to provide information on citizen evaluations and preferences that should have a number of uses. An executive summary of the results should be prepared for the secretary and assistant secretaries and made available to the advisory committee. It should consist of a descriptive synopsis of responses to major items, broken down by district, urban-rural location, and other classifications of respondents such as auto driver or transit user. Operating bureaus in the department should receive more detailed reports on the responses to specific items that relate to their responsibilities, and district engineers should be given complete reports on the findings from their districts.

Reporting Effectiveness Measures. The kinds of effectiveness measures discussed in this paper often seem more elusive than the process and road condition indicators; from a day-to-day operating perspective, they may appear to be less useful. Yet in the long run, these are the measures that indicate current levels and trends in the transportation characteristics of major concern. Ultimately, the department's efforts should be aimed at reducing or holding the line on user costs, accident rates, and such service characteristics as congestion and travel time. If these trends show worsening conditions, whether or not they can be traced directly to faculty programs, PennDOT should seriously consider policy changes to combat them. Most effectiveness indicators would be upgraded on an annual or semi-annual basis and could be reported in the *Management Objectives Report* when available.

The difficulty lies with the lack of clear operational response to indicators of decreasing effectiveness. Appropriate action is more readily apparent in terms of efficiency measurement, and less clear as we move to system adequacy indicators and effectiveness measures. Performance in terms of internal operating efficiency or improving road conditions is more directly under the control of PennDOT, while impacts on accidents, user costs, and service levels are less sensitive to departmental policy and subject to a whole host of external factors. Managers cannot be held responsible for these indicators or performance to anywhere near the same degree that is appropriate for internal operating efficiency, and this may make top management reluctant to use this kind of measure.

Yet it is still useful to know whether user costs and accidents are generally decreasing over time while service levels are improving. If not, the indicators should prompt investigation of whether the department can alter programs and budgets in an attempt to improve the situation. Also, by including real effectiveness measures in the system, the intended linkages can be examined over the long run. If construction and maintenance activities are becoming more efficient, and if maintenance work is being done at higher quality, is there any correspondence in road conditions as measured by the trained observer survey? If road conditions are in fact improving, is there any noticeable change in accident rates, user costs, and travel times? Monitoring real effectiveness measures will allow some analysis of these presumed relationships.

The DOT Report Card. As a means of disseminating the information developed from the performance indicators, PennDOT is establishing a "report card" aimed at audiences external to the department. This report card will be two to four pages in length and will be distributed to legislators and the public every six months to communicate progress made by the department in a number of specific areas. In large part, this is a public relations tool that complements the idea of the citizen survey in terms of soliciting citizen feedback, working toward improved programs, and then reporting accomplishments back to the public.

The report card would include a listing of perhaps twenty indicators, with a value representing the summary statewide average for the current time period compared with the same indicators for previous time periods. The indicators include measures of output, efficiency, road conditions, and effectiveness as discussed throughout this paper. Brief explanations of any adverse trends beyond the department's control would be provided along with brief interpretations of program impacts where appropriate. In general, the report card presents a quick picture of progress as well as problems facing the department, and in addition to the more independent effectiveness measures, it will provide evidence of tangible accomplishments as direct indicators of performance.

Notes

1. Heinz Heckroth, "The Changing California Highway Program," *Transportation Research Record* (No. 654, 1977), 23–27; hereafter cited as *TRR*. See also Marshall F. Reed, Jr., "Transportation Programming in Today's Rapidly Changing Fiscal Environment," *TRR* (No. 680, 1978), 20–22; R.D. Juster and W.M. Pecknold, "Improving the Process of Programming Transportation Investments," *TRR* (No. 599, 1976), 19–24; and R.R. Knox et al., "Programming Highway Improvements in the New Funding Environment," *TRR* (No. 599, 1976), 7–12.

2. See T.H Poister, T.D. Lawrence, and S. Rao, "Fiscal Planning and Highway Programming: The Pennsylvania Response to a Changing Environment," *TRR* (No. 654, 1977), 16–22; and S. Rao et al., "New Directions for PennDOT: A Fiscal Review" (University Park, PA: Pennsylvania Transportation Institute, PTI 7616, October 1976).

3. See the set of articles in "Maintenance Decision Making and Energy Use, Roadside and Pavement Management, and Preferential Bridge Icing," *TRR* (No. 674, 1978); W.R. Hudson, R. Haas, and R. Daryl Pedigo, *Pavement Management System Development* (National Cooperative Highway Research Program Report 215, 1979); and Mohamed Y. Shahin, *Components of a Pavement Maintenance Management System* (Champaign, IL: U.S. Army Construction Engineering Research Laboratory, 1980).

4. J.H. Batchelder et al., "Applications of the Highway Investment Analysis Package," *TRR* (No. 698, 1979), 1–5; C.V. Zeeger and R.L. Rizenbergs, "Priority Pro-

gramming for Highway Reconstruction," *TRR* (No. 698, 1979), 15–23; National Cooperative Highway Research Program Report No. 199, "Evaluating Options in Statewide Transportation Planning/Programming: Techniques and Applications" (Washington, DC: Transportation Research Board, March 1979); S.J. Bellomo et al., "Evaluation and Application of a Priority Programming System in Maryland," *TRR* (No. 680, 1978), 8–15.

5. *Monitoring the Effectiveness of State Transportation Services* (Washington, DC: The Urban Institute, July 1977), 3–6.

6. *Highway Performance Monitoring System: Field Implementation Manual* (Washington, DC: U.S. Department of Transportation, Federal Highway Administration, Program Management Division, January 1979).

7. *New Directions for PennDOT: A Fiscal Task Force Review* (Harrisburg, PA: Pennsylvania Department of Transportation, April 1976), 16.

8. Stan Altman, "Performance Monitoring Systems for Public Managers," *Public Administration Review,* XXXIX (January/February 1979), 32.

9. Theodore H. Poister, *Public Program Analysis: Applied Research Methods* (Baltimore: University Park Press, 1978), ch. 2.

10. Scott Kutz, "Programmed Project Management in Pennsylvania: Statewide Data Access" (Paper, 60th Annual Meeting of the Transportation Research Board, Washington, DC, January 1981). For more detail see Fiscal and Systems Management Center, *PMS Users' Manual* (Harrisburg: Pennsylvania Department of Transportation, January 1980).

11. *An Evaluation of the Production and Cost of Highway Maintenance in Pennsylvania* (Harrisburg, PA: Office of the Budget, Division of Program Planning and Evaluation, July 1978).

12. Roy Jorgenson Associates, Inc., *National System Condition Index,* Final Report Prepared for U.S. Department of Transportation, Federal Highway Administration (Gaithersburg, MD: February 1978). See also *Performance Investment Analysis Process: Technical Report* (Washington, DC: U.S. Department of Transportation, Federal Highway Administration, Office of Highway Planning, Program Management Division, September 1978).

13. See Edward L. Miller, "A Method of Measuring the Quality of Highway Maintenance." *TRR* (No. 506, 1976), 1–14; and Byrd, Tallamy, and MacDonald, *A Study of Highway Maintenance Quality Levels in Ohio* (Falls Church, VA: December 1970).

14. See, for example, the *Manual for Pavement Condition Rating Surveys* (Olympia: Washington State Highway Commission, Department of Highways, January 1977).

15. For a more detailed description of the trained observer survey, see T.H. Poister and W.R. Moyer, "The Pennsylvania DOT Trained Observer Survey: Design and Preliminary Results," *Proceedings of the Fourth Highway Maintenance Management Workshop* (Washington, DC: Transportation Research Board, forthcoming).

16. E.J. Mosback and H.S. Cohen, *Methodology for Estimating the Impacts of Changes in Highway Performance* (Washington, DC: Federal Highway Administration, August 1977); Michael J. Markow, "Incorporating Quality Standards and Impacts with Highway Maintenance Management," in *Proceedings of the Fourth Highway Maintenance Management Workshop.*

17. *Highway Capacity Manual* (Washington, DC: Highway Research Board Special Report 87, 1965).

18. *Monitoring the Effectiveness of State Transportation Services* (Washington, DC: Urban Institute, July 1977, 36–37, prepared for the U.S. Department of Transportation.

19. Dan E. Moore and Anne S. Ishler, *Pennsylvania: The Citizen's Viewpoint* (University Park, PA: Cooperative Extension Service, 1980).

20. *Transportation Issues and Answers: A Survey of Public Opinion in Wisconsin, 1979* (Madison: Wisconsin Department of Transportation, 1979); *North Carolina 1976 Transportation Effectiveness Survey* (Raleigh: North Carolina Department of Transportation, 1976). For the questionnaire proposed for Pennsylvania, see T.H. Poister, R.S. Huebner, G.I. Gittings, and K. Phillips, *Development of Performance Indicators for the Pennsylsvania Department of Transportation* (University Park, PA: Pennsylvania Transportation Institute, PTI 8012), Appendix B.

INDEX